DATE DUE

The Discovery of the Asylum

Books by David J. Rothman

The Discovery of the Asylum

Social Order and Disorder

in the New Republic

Revised Edition

David J. Rothman

Little, Brown and Company
Boston — Toronto — London

LIBRARY OF CONGRESS CATALOGING-IN-PUBLICATION DATA

ROTHMAN, DAVID J.
    THE DISCOVERY OF THE ASYLUM: SOCIAL ORDER AND DISORDER IN THE NEW
REPUBLIC / DAVID J. ROTHMAN. — REV. 2ND ED.
        P.   CM.
    INCLUDES BIBLIOGRAPHICAL REFERENCES.
    ISBN 0-316-75745-4
    1. PUBLIC INSTITUTIONS — UNITED STATES — HISTORY. 2. ASYLUMS —
UNITED STATES — HISTORY. 3. PRISONS — UNITED STATES — HISTORY.
I. TITLE.
HV91.R73 1990
361'.05 — DC20   90-5582
                                                                    CIP

              10 9 8 7 6 5 4 3 2

                          HC

            Published simultaneously in Canada
          by Little, Brown & Company (Canada) Limited

        PRINTED IN THE UNITED STATES OF AMERICA

To Oscar Handlin

Contents

List of Illustrations

Acknowledgments

I welcome the opportunity to note the generous assistance that I received in the course of completing this book. The early stages of research were supported by Harvard University's Center for the Study of the History of Liberty in America and Columbia's Council for Research in the Social Sciences; the later stages of research and writing were speeded by grants from the Social Science Research Council and the Social and Rehabilitation Service of the Department of Health, Education, and Welfare (project no. CRD-444-9). I am also grateful to Professors Yehoshua Arieli and Arthur Goren of Hebrew University for making my stay in Jerusalem not only enjoyable but productive.

Early drafts of the book were read in whole or in part by my good friends Daniel Calhoun, Blanche Coll, Charles and Susan Halpern, Beatrice and Richard Hofstadter, and Stanley Katz; their willingness to interrupt their own crowded schedules to review the manuscript greatly improved its intellectual quality and lucidity. A first statement of some of the themes treated here was presented to a 1966 meeting of the American Historical Association, and Sigmund Diamond and Bernard Bailyn raised issues that I have tried to resolve. My editor, Llewellyn Howland, carefully and patiently noted lapses of style and organization; the energetic and responsible research assistance of Richard B. Calhoun was an important asset, as was Ene Sirvet's meticulous typing of the manuscript.

As in my earlier work, it is especially pleasant to acknowledge the assistance of Oscar Handlin. The germ of the idea for this book emerged from discussions with him, and I have profited in countless ways from his continuing and painstaking review of the manuscript. The dedication to him points to my intellectual debt. And once again, my wife, Sheila Miller Rothman, shared the pleasures and burdens of research; her training in psychiatric social work was particularly important for the sections on poverty and insanity. That the book was not finished sooner is not her fault (or Matthew's). Rather, its appearance testifies to her sustained interest and participation.

Jerusalem, 1968–1969
New York City, 1969–1970

The occasion to write a new introduction to *The Discovery of the Asylum* was provided by William Phillips, editor-in-chief at Little, Brown, and I am grateful to him. I was also fortunate enough to carry out this assignment while enjoying the remarkable hospitality of the Rockefeller Foundation at its Villa Serbelloni, Bellagio, Italy.

Since the book has earned a life of its own, I have refrained from making any changes in the text. Instead, I have confined my thoughts, and second thoughts, to the new introduction.

New York City, 1990

Introduction to the 1990 Edition

Over the past two decades, a fascination with the origins and development of the asylum has grown from an idiosyncratic interest shared by a handful of researchers to a core concern for social historians. The question that this book poses — why did Americans in the Jacksonian era so energetically and confidently construct and maintain institutions to confine the deviant and dependent members of the community? — has now been asked about England in the late eighteenth century, about France in the early nineteenth century, and about various Eastern European and Latin American countries in the later nineteenth century. Before 1970, only a handful of studies explored these changes. Twenty years later, a rich and imaginative literature traces the history of American and European prisons, mental hospitals, reformatories, orphanages, and almshouses, with books and articles numbering well into the hundreds.

To understand why these institutions became central to the care and correction of the criminal, the insane, and the poor, historians (and their readers) have entered unusual places. They have gone on board sixteenth- and seventeenth-century convict ship galleys to learn who composed the hapless crew, how long was their servitude, and how many of them survived the ordeal. They have mingled with the crowds that gathered around the scaffold on execution days to gauge their receptivity to the lessons of deterrence and the extent of their horror at the torture and bodily dismemberment that often accompanied capital punishment. They have also in more traditional fashion analyzed the motives of judges, lawmakers, and philanthropists who urged the construction of asylums and have then, less traditionally, gone behind the walls of the prisons and mental hospitals to examine the conditions of confinement, the exercise of discipline, and the characteristics of the inmates. The design of the wall itself, the graffiti that prisoners scrawled in their cells, and the tattoos that they etched on their bodies all become evidence for interpreting why a system of incarceration was created and why, despite frequent scandals, it has persisted to this day.

This turn of attention to the asylum reflects, first, the new preeminence of the field of social history, its emergence as a subdiscipline of its own, distinct from the history of social thought and social movements and as vital as political and diplomatic history. The underlying concerns of social history, its preoccupation with the relationships between social classes and the institutions that promoted or subverted social order, including the family, the church, and the workplace, helped bring attention to formal institutions of control, particularly the prison and the mental hospital. At the same time, its assumption that the political and economic organization of a society could not be understood by analyzing only the ambitions and activities of the elite, that an interpretive framework had to include a full appreciation of the independent role of ordinary people (including workers, women, and racial and ethnic minorities), spurred an interest in the fate of another segment of the lower classes, namely those confined to prisons, reformatories, almshouses, and mental hospitals. That the historians' agenda was so enlarged is not surprising. Once the history of the working class became an essential element in the history of economic growth, once the process by which the workers adjusted to the discipline and routine of the factory became as important to understand as the process by which entrepreneurs accumulated the capital to build the factory, historians' constructs incorporated the experience of those who could not or would not accept this discipline. The expectation was that to investigate the fate of marginal men and women would clarify the distribution of power within the society, and this expectation has been handsomely fulfilled.

Even this brief statement of research aims points to an essential affinity with sociology. After all, it was a pioneer in sociology, Emile Durkheim, who first demonstrated that to uncover the fundamental norms of a society, so fundamental as to remain hidden and without explication, one should investigate the fate of those who frankly violated them. Durkheim's own research focused on suicide, and his analysis brought him to the concept of anomie and to a new understanding of the breakdown of social order. Durkheim's strategy crossed over into history once social history assumed its prominence, and ironically, it was the work of historians drawing on him that captured the attention of a younger generation of sociologists, thereby completing the circle and heightening the interest of both disciplines in the origins of the asylum.

The second major stimulus to the growth of the field was the work of Michel Foucault, testifying to his extraordinary influence, first through his 1965 book on the confinement of the insane (*Madness and Civilization*) and then his far more accessible book on the prison (*Discipline and Punish*). Foucault was a moral philosopher whose own construction of the historical process became the text on which he grounded a series of discourses on the nature and exercise of power and authority in western civilization. He was not by temperament, by training, or by practice a historian — that is, he not only eschewed archival research but had little respect for the nuances of time (chronology gave him little pause, and to substantiate a point he would treat as one observations made decades apart) or for nuances of place (it was as if all the world were France). Perhaps his most glaring deficiency, however, was an unwillingness to distinguish rhetoric from reality. For Foucault, motive mattered more than practice. Let public authorities formulate a program or announce a goal, and he presumed its realization. Let officials dream of a system of surveillance over the deviant classes, and he mistook fantasy for actuality. But however impatient historians may be with his methods and findings and however flawed his reconstructions, there is no minimizing the fact that he imparted a special meaning to the history of incarceration. In Foucault's analysis, the prison and the mental hospital became the most perfect representations of the modern state. More consistently and daringly than any other writer, he made asylums into the model of the industrial society. The confinement of the mad represented nothing less than the victory of reason over unreason in western culture, and the confinement of the criminal, the ultimate triumph of the bourgeois state. Foucault helped move the asylum from the wings to center stage — and researchers in a variety of disciplines, including not only history and sociology but also literature and architecture, were inspired to follow his lead.

Third, the historians' focus on the asylum followed in a very important way on the declining social legitimacy of these institutions in the 1960s and 1970s. Not that historians were in any simple sense serving or self-consciously encouraging reform movements that sought to reduce reliance on incarceration. Rather, the outbreak of prison riots in the early 1970s and the exposés of wretched institutional conditions (whether at New York's Attica prison or Alabama's Bryce State Mental Hospital), along with efforts of public interest law groups to litigate on behalf of prisoners' rights and mental patients' rights, had the effect of rendering problematic those institutions and procedures that heretofore had appeared to be natural and logical within the landscape. More, these movements drew on the work of a number of radical mental health professionals, particularly Thomas Szasz and Wolf Wolfensberger, who treated mental illness and mental retardation first and foremost as socially ascribed labels rather than inherent conditions that required assistance (and confinement).[1] In effect, these developments stripped the asylum of its cloak of inevitability, and deviancy of its biological or commonsensical reality. Historians, it is worth repeating, did not become disciples of Szasz or the hired guns for litigators. Rather, the writings and exposés bred a healthy agnosticism. They liberated the historians from conventional wisdom and prompted them to ask why asylums had been built in the first place, and why they had persisted for so long. Thus, Michael Ignatieff opened his 1978 study of the origins of the prison in England by observing that "a decade of hostage-takings, demonstrations, and full scale uprisings," first in America and then in Spain, France, Canada, Britain, and Italy, "have at least jolted prisons out of the realm of the taken-for-granted."[2] In the same way, Andrew Scull began his 1979 book on the origins of English insane asylums with a statement on the topic's "obvious contemporary relevance," observing that since the mid-1950s, "we have been moving away from . . . the primary reliance on the asylum."[3]

Indeed, asylums were only one of a number of institutions

that captured the interest of historians just as they were losing social legitimacy. The family became a central subject of inquiry when the women's movement undercut its authority and inspired the question: if the family was a cage confining women, how had it come to exercise this tyranny? Perhaps the most obvious example of this process at work is the impact of the civil rights movement on the study of slavery and the black experience in America. The dynamic is apparent: let inherited procedures or organizations become suspect, and the curiosity of historians is immediately stimulated — which is why the likes of meta-historians like Oswald Spengler correlated a flourishing historical enterprise with a society on the decline.

I emphasize this point because it helps account for the contentiousness that has marked the historical literature about incarceration. The bitterness that infused the public policy debates — especially in the confrontation between psychiatrists and civil libertarian lawyers — spilled over into history because, however unintended, there were significant policy implications to an inquiry that took as its point of departure the declining legitimacy of incarcerative institutions. Such a perspective challenged — undercut, in fact — the idea that the origins of these institutions are best understood in the single context of progressive and humane impulses. Earlier, with only one or two exceptions (Foucault the most notable), the theme of reform triumphant had dominated what little historical literature existed on the subject. Now, however, historians were making the history of the asylum something other than the history of generous philanthropy and, by implication, were raising the question of whether those who now administered and defended the asylum should be ranked among the benevolent and reform-minded. Thus, mental health professionals and their allies (more so than wardens or welfare workers) took as an affront and a personal challenge what I wrote in the original introduction to this volume:

> By describing the innovation as a reform, [historians] assume that the asylum was an inevitable and sure step in the progress of humanity. . . . It was exactly the type of device that well-meaning and wise citizens should

have supported. But such a perspective is bad logic and
bad history. . . . The subsequent history of these institutions should make historians somewhat suspicious of any
simple link between progress and the asylum. Was an
organization that would eventually turn into a snake pit
a necessary step forward for mankind?[4]

Inevitably, controversy breeds attention, and the contemporary
relevance of the analysis expanded the number of historians
ready to enter the field.

However interesting the incentives to historical investigation,
the critical concern is with the results. What have the past twenty
years of research taught us? What do we now know and appreciate about the history of the asylum?

First, a new meaning and import have been given to the social
and cultural practices of the pre-asylum era, especially the system of punishment. We understand not only the motives that
underlay the reliance on the public infliction of bodily harm but
also the crisis of legitimacy that affected it over the course of the
eighteenth century. In almost every European country as well as
in America, whether the government was monarchical, parliamentary, or republican, the traditional and accepted forms of
correction and control of the deviant became ineffective or dis-
reputable. In effect, the prison rescued punishment, replacing a
whole series of penalties that had lost usefulness and legitimacy.

At the heart of criminal sanctions in the pre-modern era was
what the historian Pieter Spierenburg has called the "spectacle
of suffering," the public execution and torture of the offender.
The death sentence was not the most common sentence —
whipping, branding, and public shaming made up the great
majority of the penalties, and some countries, like France, sentenced offenders to lifetime service as galley rowers.[5] Even so, in
the period 1700–1750, between 15 to 25 percent of all offenders
received capital punishment. For more serious crimes, particularly in urban areas, it was the punishment of choice: more than
90 percent of those who had committed homicide were executed, 50 to 60 percent of robbers, 35 to 50 percent of burglars.
Spierenburg has calculated that in Amsterdam during the eigh-

teenth century, magistrates held an average of one to four "justice days" (that is, public executions) annually, with about eight to fifteen executions at each one. "It is plain," he concludes, "that any resident of Amsterdam could have witnessed many executions during his lifetime."[6]

In fact, he was supposed to witness them, and from all available evidence, including woodcuts depicting the crowds at the execution to firsthand descriptions of the event (there was one Dutch citizen who made it his duty to attend and describe every execution in Amsterdam), the crowd was considerable. The duration of the execution itself varied with the seriousness of the crime: the more heinous, the more drawn-out the death. It was commonplace first to beat the condemned man with an iron bar and to wait before delivering the coup de grace, or hanging him. Foucault describes the execution of the regicide Damiens in 1757 and how the executioner first burned parts of his body and then with pincers tore at his flesh; to bring death, the executioner tied the victim's limbs to horses and, after several failed attempts, finally managed to dismember him. Other punishments were tailored to fit the crime in very literal ways. One burglar who killed a night watchman first had his right hand — which had delivered the fatal blow — cut off and then was hanged and had his corpse exposed; a man who murdered a neighbor by hitting him twice with an iron spade was himself struck over the head by the executioner with the very spade, garroted, and had his corpse exposed with the spade alongside it. To punish a sailor who attempted to murder a townsman with a cobblestone, the executioner strangled him and, before he was completely dead, repeatedly struck him on the head with a cobblestone.[7]

In theory, the spectacle of public torture and execution was to fulfill two goals: to confirm the majesty of the king, for crime was an offense to his authority, and punishment reasserted his prerogatives and made the kingdom whole again; and to serve as a deterrent to would-be criminals. Anyone who witnessed the terrible price exacted of the offender would take the message to heart and remain law-abiding. Did the spectacle accomplish its aims? Was the king the more revered and the criminal deterred? For the sixteenth and seventeenth centuries, the question is unanswerable; all one can say is that the form of punishment was not contested, and the right, perhaps even the need, to take such measures stirred almost no opposition or feelings of repugnance.[8] A bungled execution might pit the wrath of the crowd against the executioner, and on some occasions, albeit probably not many, the sympathy of the crowd for the victim might lead to an effort to free him from his executioners. But at least through the seventeenth century, the system appeared effective and appropriate.

Then, for reasons that are still not completely understood, over the course of the eighteenth century the spectacle fell out of favor, both with the authorities and with the audience. It seemed at once disorderly and dangerous, garish and cruel. Over the next 150 years (with the dates varying from country to country), the use of torture declined, executions moved indoors, and capital punishment itself was dramatically reduced, in some places even eliminated. What lay behind this extraordinary transformation? For one, the execution spectacle increasingly seemed to provoke disorderly behavior and riots. Although the evidence is fragmentary and impressionistic, a growing number of incidents came to mark public executions. Foucault describes several instances in which the condemned carried himself with such dignity and grace and bore his pain with such nobility that the spectators identified with him against his executioners, perceiving him as more of a martyr than a villain. Even Spierenburg, who is skeptical about the amount of disorder accompanying executions, reports numerous cases where the audience turned into a mob and even more numerous incidents in which the authorities, in anticipation of such an occurrence, called out the militia to surround the gallows and keep the spectators at a distance, thereby nullifying the very purpose of a public execution. In England, the sheriffs of London and Middlesex in 1784 canceled processions to the gallows, explaining that they had become "a mockery," the occasion for "jokes, swearing and blasphemy. . . . The final scene itself has lost its terrors and is so far from giving a lesson of morality to the beholders that it tends to the encouragement of vice."[9] The public execution was in danger of subverting the public authority.

But an even more fundamental change was taking place: audiences were perceiving the spectacle of torture and punishment as horrifying and barbaric, an affront to standards of decency. A new sensibility about the sanctity of the body and the avoidance of pain transformed cultural attitudes over the course of the eighteenth century and made the infliction of torture and capital punishment appear not edifying but corrupting. The manifestations of this new attitude were everywhere apparent. Not only was the suffering of the condemned repugnant, but so also was the suffering of animals — and here lay the roots of the humane societies dedicated to the prevention of cruelty to animals. In this same spirit, torture as an instrument in the interrogation of criminal suspects was abolished (in France in the 1780s, in the Dutch Republic in the 1790s), and so was the public display of executed corpses. We know a revolution in taste has occurred when an anonymous Amsterdam resident reacted to a public execution in 1773 by remarking:

> What a frightening spectacle! miserable man, I am indeed overwhelmed by pity for the state you are in. . . . How affected was I inside, when I saw them climb the ladder. . . . I was cold, I trembled at every step they took. I often turned away my face and distracted my eyes from the mortal spectacle to the endless number of spectators. I thought I noticed in some of them the same horror at such a terrible spectacle, the same repugnance which I felt. This raised an inner joy in me: it gave me a positive view of my fellow-creatures again.[10]

It is easier to describe the fact of change than to explain it. Undoubtedly Enlightenment ideas had their effect, although the paths by which such attitudes filtered down to ordinary citizens remain unclear. Improvements in bodily well-being (through better nutrition and a decline in the number and the devastations of plagues) may have inspired an aversion to pain. A growing secularism may also have removed a religious gloss from suffering, making it appear more pointless. A new respect for the integrity of the body may have followed on a growing appreciation of the complexity of its parts (as mapped by pioneers in physiology).[11] But even without resolving the issue, it is apparent, first, that the history of punishment is inseparable from the history of culture, and, second, that by the mid-eighteenth century the older system of punishment would not be able to survive for long.[12]

This same sensibility was also beginning to subvert the inherited system of caring for the mentally ill. Well into the eighteenth century, those disordered in mind were considered to have sunk to the level of beast, and what passed for treatment was built on the premise that the madness had to be beaten out of them, as one might beat an unruly animal. Just how pervasive this notion was — and how it permeated all social classes — is vividly demonstrated by the treatment accorded King George III in his madness. "The unhappy patient," as one contemporary described it, "was no longer treated as a human being. His body was immediately encased in a machine which left no liberty of motion. He was sometimes chained to a stake. He was frequently beaten and starved, and at best he was kept in subjection by menacing and violent language."[13] If monarchs were treated so harshly, it takes little stretch of the imagination to picture the conditions in which the poor and hopelessly insane were confined. The reports of the English philanthropists who investigated the Bedlams of the eighteenth century did not exaggerate the wretchedness they encountered: inmates chained, without clothes, sleeping on straw in cells that were unheated and covered with excrement. It was a sorry picture, but only now being brought to light and described as shameful.

The crisis that was affecting correction and care was compounded and intensified by an absence of ready alternatives. It was one thing to denigrate the traditional means, quite another to devise substitutes. None of the existing mechanisms and procedures seemed capable of bearing additional weight, of protecting the social order and at the same time satisfying social sensibilities. In the case of punishment, the whip applied too lightly would have little deterrent effect on either the offender or the audience; applied too heavily, it confronted the very sentiments that were undercutting capital punishment. Thus, it is no surprise to learn that whipping declined in England over the last decades of the eighteenth century.[14] Banishment was both too mild — leaving the offender free to conduct his crimes in another town — and too anachronistic a sentence; in an age when nations were forging a stronger identity, it made little sense to shuttle a troublemaker from one town to another. And the use of superannuated warships anchored along the Thames as floating prisons was no better a solution. As Michael Ignatieff notes, "Respectable London was kept on edge for a decade by the repeated escapes, outbreaks of typhus, and insurrections on board the hulks," to say nothing of the offensiveness of the sight of gangs of dirty, semidressed, and sickly men.[15]

Events conspired to make matters even worse for the British. To reduce reliance on corporeal punishment, they more frequently substituted a sentence of transportation to the colonies, mostly to the American colonies. In the 1770s, in particular, the mother country sent her wayward children across the ocean, that is, until the American Revolution rendered that practice obsolete. Deprived of the one safety valve they had in the realm of punishment, the English, with some desperation, sought an alternative, first experimenting with transportation to the African colony of Gambia and then, when the death rates turned out to be unconscionable, discovering the solution of Australia. But even transportation to Botany Bay could not serve as the centerpiece for punishment. As the colony flourished, it lost some of its deterrent effect — rumor had it that some offenders actually pleaded to be sent there, and tales about debauchery and drunkenness at Botany Bay were circulating widely. However convenient it might appear to export the deviant, some other solution would have to be devised.

The one last institution associated with punishment, as well as with the confinement of the "furiously mad," namely the jail, was more a part of the problem than a potential answer to it. Well into the eighteenth century, these facilities were holding stations. The majority of inmates were debtors awaiting a forgiveness of their obligations by creditors, although confinement, of course, made it impossible for them to earn the sums necessary to pay them back. The jails also held accused felons awaiting trial or convicted felons awaiting the execution of their sentences. Mixed in with them were the insane (particularly those whose disorders made them aggressive) and a variety of misdemeanants and petty offenders (generally coming from the ranks of apprentices, prostitutes, and servants) confined for short periods to undergo corrective discipline.[16] By universal agreement, jails were such disorderly places as to be altogether unsuitable for any purpose. In the history of the prison, the jail was a negative reference point, not a prototype.

The displeasure, really the disgust, with jails had many sources, for they were places of both physical and moral contagion, spreading fever and vice. The quarters were almost always makeshift. Some English jails (like the infamous Newgate) were lodged inside the gatehouses of city walls (where soldiers or watchmen had once boarded); or within castle keeps (the Tower of London held a jail); or in abandoned chapels and churches, and in one case a synagogue; or in stables and taverns. The jail routine (if it could be so called), whether in the American colonies or in Europe, was casual to the point of chaos. The custom everywhere was for the jailer to levy a charge for every service and provision — for food, drink, and lodging — and, in English jails particularly, his desire to make the most handsome returns from inmates as well as visitors made many jails indistinguishable from taverns or bawdy houses. The great novel of the jail, Daniel Defoe's *Moll Flanders* (1722), captured its essence well; Moll's descent into corruption began when she had to carry food and other necessities to a kinswoman confined to Newgate. She witnessed, and later succumbed to, the "wicked practices in that dreadful place" and learned, firsthand, about "how it ruined more young people than all the town besides. . . . There are more thieves and rogues made by that one prison of Newgate than by all the clubs and societies of villains in the nation."[17] All the while, the jails, typically damp, dark, and badly ventilated, were perfect breeding places for "gaol fever," what we know as typhus, and thus they subverted not only the moral but also the physical well-being of the community. Debauchery and disease combined to make the jail the most abject of institutions.[18]

And yet, astonishingly enough, when viewed from the eighteenth century forward rather than the twentieth century back, the shared response to the problem of the care and correction of the deviant and dependent, in the United States as in Europe, became a system of confinement. Why so extraordinary a practice was begun is the question that this book, and a now extensive historical literature, attempt to explain. But even before recounting the variety of answers that have been proposed and vigorously debated, it will be useful to enumerate the essential features of the prisons, mental hospitals, reformatories, and almshouses. However different the approaches to the matter of causality, there is a consensus among historians about their major characteristics.

First, incarceration became the prime mechanism for punishment and treatment. There is no disputing the fact of a revolution. Confinement was the common, and the preferred, response to the deviant and dependent.

Second, the new institutions, regardless of their official and purported function, whether they were to correct the behavior of a felon or to cure the insane, adopted the same pattern of organization. Although most of the recent histories analyze only one type of institution (either the prison or the insane asylum or the reformatory) and the more inclusive character of this book has not been duplicated (only Foucault has written about the prison as well as the mental hospital), still, the authors often acknowledge that their particular analysis is consistent with what they have learned about other incarcerative institutions. Thus, historians have confirmed the validity of Erving Goffman's concept of "total institutions," which minimizes the differences in formal mission to establish a unity of design and structure.

Third, the permeability of eighteenth-century institutions gave way to sealed-off space. The new institutions were in every sense apart from society, bounded by sturdy walls and by administrative regulations that self-consciously and successfully separated inmate from outsider.

Fourth, all the institutional routines were segmented into carefully defined blocks of time, scrupulously maintained and punctuated by bells. There was nothing casual or random about daily activities.

Fifth, at the core of the routine was a dedication to the principles of work and of solitude, of steady labor and of isolation. These mechanisms promised to transform the inmate's character so that he would leave the institution a different person. The reformatory regimen would alter not only behavior but also personality.

Sixth, most institutions in their first decades of existence managed to translate blueprints into practice. The early asylums were to a notable degree ordered and orderly. With the possible exception of the almshouse, their designs came close to fulfilling the ambitions of their founders. But then, over the course of their second and third generation — in the United States, for example, by the 1850s and still more clearly by the 1880s — they became overcrowded, corrupt, and brutal.

Seventh, almost all the institutions, with the exception of a handful of private insane asylums, confined the lower orders of society. They housed the laboring classes and those toward the bottom of the social scale.

That such a consensus marks the recent research (and is consistent with the chapters that follow) is important to recognize. So, too, the notion that the core purpose of the asylum can be entirely encompassed by invoking the humanitarian spirit of the founders has few proponents. An interpretive scheme that rests entirely on the idea that asylums represent the progress of mankind, whether through the advance of science or benevolence, has little appeal outside of the more dogged defenders of the mental hospital and psychiatric wisdom.[19] This is a minority voice, almost never heard in the literature on prisons, reformatories, and almshouses. What is at dispute are the motive and purpose behind the introduction of the asylum. What led the United States and European countries to create, and perpetuate, institutions of confinement?

Humanitarian impulses must have a place in the explanation. However irresistible the urge to make rigid dichotomies in historical interpretations, neither *The Discovery of the Asylum* nor most of the other books that follow its approach dismiss such considerations or denigrate the motives of reformers. Indeed, the new literature analyzing pre-asylum modes of punishment makes it clear that the degree of brutality of earlier practices was even more stark, not only in the descriptions of torture and executions but even in the sentences to transportation. The accounts of the convict origins of Australia are replete with heartbreaking stories of what it meant to men and women, often guilty of no more than petty thievery, to be separated forever from spouses, children, and other relatives. Nevertheless, benevolent motives take us only part of the way to understanding the origins of asylums. No matter how empathetic one may be to the impulse to find a substitute for garroting the condemned or chaining the mad to basement floors, the fundamental question still remains: why invent a system of incarceration, why substitute confinement in segregated spaces and invent a routine of bell-ringing punctuality and steady labor? Why channel the impulse to do good into creating something as strange as prisons and mental hospitals — a system that more than 150 years later can still prompt an inmate to want to meet the man who dreamed it all up, convinced that he must have been born on Mars?[20]

The "made on Mars" character of the asylum provides a useful clue to understanding its origins. The nineteenth-century asylum, whether in Europe or in the United States, did not replicate an already existing institution within the society. It was not a faithful re-creation of the army or the church monastery or the factory, although bits and pieces of each of these organizations entered its design. The pre-modern jail was the town writ small, a reassemblage within a city gate or tower keep of the tavern, the bawdy house, the artisan shop, and the family household. There was nothing imagined about the jail. But in confronting the asylum, we leave the real for what historian Robin Evans has so aptly called the fabricated. Or in the words of another historian, Robert Castel, the asylum presented the need "to construct from nothing a new social laboratory in which the whole of human existence could be programmed."[21] In effect, the asylum first had to be imagined and then translated into reality.

One of the most daring, albeit not altogether successful, efforts to identify the ideational sources of the prison is John Bender's book, *Imagining the Penitentiary*. Finding the essence of the prison in its ordered environment, Bender locates the inspiration for that order in the new literary form and structure of the novel. It was the novelists, especially Daniel Defoe, who imagined the penitentiary before there was such a thing as the penitentiary. As Bender writes, "The earlier eighteenth century novel bore the form within which the seeming randomness inside the old prison boundaries would later be restructured into a new penal order." First, the literary depictions of the prison, which were so common an element in the new novel (foreshadowing the day when the depictions of poverty would be so common an element in the new form of photography), helped engender a self-consciousness about, and subsequent dissatisfaction with, the old prison. The dissoluteness of the prison emerged with especial clarity not only in the investigatory accounts of a reformer like John Howard but also in the intrinsically ordered narrative of the novel. Second, and perhaps even more important, the form of the novel suggested and incorporated the vision that became fundamental to the prison. Not that Defoe or any other novelist actually described the new prison the way a science fiction writer of the 1920s might "describe" space travel. Rather, the novel "banished chance and fortune — the providential order of things — in favor of human planning and certitude imagined in material terms. . . . 'Reform' assumes rationally ordered causal sequence and conceives human intervention as capable of reconstructing reality," which is precisely what a novel does. In short, the novelists' imagination animated the reformers' imagination. To be sure, Bender never does document the precise nature of the cause-and-effect relationship, and it seems the more probable that both the novelist and the prison reformer, quite independently, shared a still more general cultural mind-set. But his analysis vividly demonstrates the power of the imagination in the creation of the prison.[22]

A still more persuasive and detailed explication of the originality of the asylum emerges from Robin Evans's history of English prison architecture from 1750 to 1840. Evans demonstrates how the effort to translate reformers' concepts into a brick-and-mortar structure required exceptional inventiveness. The principles intrinsic to the idea of the prison posed starkly conflicting demands. The prison was intended to isolate and segregate the inmates and yet do so in an environment that was healthful, allowing for the free circulation of light and air. The first requirement, however, presupposed an enclosed space; the second, an open space. By the same token, the prison in its ideal form was meant to fulfill a deterrent function (to strike the fear of law into the hearts of offenders and the general populace) and a rehabilitative function (to reform the deviant). To accommodate both demands required novel solutions, and the architects faced up to the task. They surrounded the prison with a massive and fortresslike wall, whose very dimensions and design represented visually to insiders and outsiders the full authority of the state; at the same time, the presence of the wall allowed the architects to construct cell wings at a distance from its perimeter, thereby maintaining the seclusion and security of the cells while letting in light and air. (It is no coincidence that the designers of the mental hospital also confronted what one historian has called a "design dilemma," that is, "how to create an institutional environment that was simultaneously awe-inspiring and comfortable, one that would bring order to disordered minds without repelling their families."[23]) Indeed, in the course of the effort to fabricate a space that would help men become virtuous and healthy, architecture would, "for the first time, take full advantage of its latent powers. A new role had been found for it as a vessel of conscience and as a pattern giver to society, extending its boundaries way beyond the limits customarily ascribed to it either as an art or as a prosaic utility."[24] The mission that architecture first pursued in the prison was later expanded into a still broader role in the design of schools, hospitals, new-style tenements, and, eventually, new-style towns.

Although these accounts help us to understand the degree to which the asylum was imagined and fabricated, we are still left with the question of origins and purposes. In the language of architecture, who were the architects' clients and what were their goals? Or in novelists' terms, who set the plot and what denouement did they have in mind?

Some of the most compelling answers to these questions share the premise that underlies this book, namely that the idea of the asylum took form in the perception, in fact the fear, that once-stable social relationships were now in the process of unraveling, threatening to subvert social order and social cohesion. These approaches have been grouped together and labeled, clumsily, a "social control" school of history. Rather than attempt to substitute a more apt phrase, it will be better to review some of the major texts and the concept of social control itself, to the end of identifying their major strengths and weaknesses.

The Discovery of the Asylum argues that Jacksonian Americans experienced a crisis of confidence in the social organization of the new republic, fearful that the ties that once bound citizens together — the ties of community, church, and family — were loosening and that, as a consequence, social disorganization appeared imminent. Their fears were confirmed and exacerbated by the extent of the crime, poverty, delinquency, and insanity that they saw around them. In response to these perceptions, to an anxiety about the stability of the social order and an alarm about the extent of deviancy and dependency, they discovered the solution of the asylum. This institution would at once rehabilitate the inmates, thereby reducing crime, insanity, and poverty, and would then, through the very success of its design, set an example for the larger society. The good order of the asylum, its routine of punctuality and steady labor, would act as both a cure and a preventive — reforming its charges and serving as a model to the community. It was a grand and almost utopian vision, one that sought to ensure the safety of the republic and promote its glory.

Michael Ignatieff, analyzing the origins of prisons in England, and Andrew Scull and Robert Castel, analyzing the origins of insane asylums, one in England and the other in France, each put their own gloss on this approach, but all of them link the design and popularity of the asylum to a wider societal mission, an effort to restore stability where disorganization seemed rampant.

Ignatieff hinges his account on a sharp increase in crime, pauperism, and unrest in England after 1815, the result of a disintegration of traditional ties and relationships in agriculture (in the southeast), in the new factories (in the north), and, most visibly, in London.[25] "The massive investment in institutional solutions," writes Ignatieff, "would have been inconceivable unless the authorities had believed that they were faced with the breakdown of a society of stable ranks and the emergence of a society of hostile classes." This perception affected a diverse group of constituents, including evangelical philanthropists, manufacturers, secular reformers, and public officials; and all of them, for their own particular reasons, promoted the development of a prison system that would segregate the offender and subject him to a routine of discipline and labor. For some, the main attraction of the new arrangement was that it would divide the criminal class from the working class and thereby reduce a propensity to riot or rebellion. Others welcomed the prospect of demonstrating that the state was powerful even as it was merciful. Still others believed that the prison would promote religious reformation within and without its walls, and some hoped it would instill an internal discipline of order and regularity not only in those who arrived at the prison but also in those who arrived each morning at the factory gate.[26] The motives of asylum proponents, then, were varied and not easily sorted out or ranked by weight of influence. In the end, the prison satisfied a variety of agendas, all of which had as their initial inspiration an effort to bind together a fragmented society.

Andrew Scull is also convinced that a crisis swept over England in the late eighteenth and early nineteenth century as it lurched "from a social order dominated by rank, order, and degree to one based on class." The chief agent of change was "the development of national and international markets [that] produced a diminution, if not a destruction, of the traditional influence of local groups (especially kinship groups), which formerly played a large role in the regulation of social life." Scull finds a number of reasons that this breakdown should have stimulated the growth of the asylum. He notes the contributions of both Evangelicalism and Utilitarianism. For the religiously motivated, an ordered asylum was a way to make certain that "those who had lost their reason should not also lose their souls." For secularists, the filth, cruelty, and neglect that the insane suffered was "a powerful argument against the haphazard, amateurish, social policies of the past" as well as an opportunity to impose a new rationality and order. At the same time, marketing and manufacturing activities demonstrated how raw materials could be transformed through human intervention, thereby emboldening some of the new capitalists (most notably the Quakers) to dare to consider transforming the mad. The new industrial activity sensitized still others to the need to impose a new order of discipline on the working class and then, by extension, on the mad: "Lunatics, too, were to be made over in the image of bourgeois rationality." [27]

For Robert Castel, the social crisis underlying the adoption of the insane asylum in nineteenth-century France was the tension between the pre- and post-Revolutionary orders. "Madness posed a challenge to the society that had arisen as a result of the convulsions of the fall of the *Ancien Regime*."[28] Before 1789, the confinement of the insane was accomplished mostly through the arbitrary exercise of state authority, by the issuance of a royal order, the lettre de cachet. After 1789, the representatives of the new order, in essence the bourgeoisie, had to find a way to exercise guardianship without subverting the sanctity of the contract. They had to devise procedures that would deprive the insane of their liberty without endangering the liberty of all, that would segregate the mad without opening the door wide to the abuse of executive discretion.

The asylum resolved the dilemma by introducing a quid pro quo: in return for giving up their liberty the insane received treatment. ("It is a happy coincidence," announced one contemporary, "that . . . the application of rigorous measures causes the wellbeing of the sick person to accord with the welfare of all."[29]) Moreover, the physician superintendents of the new asylums became the intermediaries between the state and the insane. By establishing medical approval as a precondition for confinement, they helped to remove madness from the realm of civil politics, to make it the exceptional case. The physicians' expertise and power to heal legitimized their, but only their, exercise of authority. The doctor in charge, as Castel puts it, was a kind of philosopher-king, a position that at once sanctioned and contained the exercise of unbridled discretion. The doctor's despotism was confined to the mad in the asylum and as such did not contaminate the exercise of power in the civil society.[30]

The strength of these several approaches rests first in their ability to explain the widespread appeal of the asylum solution. An amazingly diverse group of constituents lined up in support of an undertaking that was exceedingly expensive and complex, and without appreciating the larger goals of the project, the extent of the investment in the asylum and the degree of enthusiasm for it cannot be understood. If the incapacitation of the inmate had been the exclusive concern, it would have been unnecessary to invest so extravagantly in asylums or to organize such elaborate and disciplined routines. To punish the criminal through service on some form of a chain gang or to relieve the poor, insane or not, by paying for their support in neighboring households would have been considerably cheaper and more efficient. To be sure, there were naysayers to the asylum, easier to identify in Europe than in Jacksonian America. Some among them did not want to see the burden of taxation increased, others did not want to empower doctors to make commitments over and against the family, and still others were convinced that the only punishment that criminals respected was capital punishment. But a shared sense of crisis and emergency overrode these objections. Too much was at stake to postpone action; something had to be done lest republican order, or, as Ignatieff, Scull, and Castel would have it, bourgeois order, be subverted.

Although the interpretive framework of *The Discovery of the Asylum* does not share the more class-based analysis of the other texts, it is important to note that they all agree on the need to reckon with the concerns of asylum proponents for buttressing the social order. Moreover, the emphasis that others place on the role of the bourgeoisie is not narrow or one-dimensional. They do not make a case for the asylum as a simple translation from the factory or argue that the asylum was born in the factory. In England, as Ignatieff demonstrates, the appearance of the prison preceded the organization of the factory, and it stretches common sense to believe that the entire mission of the asylum can be summed up in the need for employers to discipline factory workers; surely the manufacturing enterprise had sources of recruitment broad enough to ignore the hapless mad, the determined felon, and the aging poor. It seems far more likely, as Ignatieff concludes, that to the degree that prisons and factories resembled each other, it was "because both public order authorities and employers shared the same universe of assumptions about the regulation of the body and the ordering of time."[31] In the United States, as we shall see, the vision that animated the asylum looked back, nostalgically, to the eighteenth-century community, not to the new factories of the nineteenth century; and the spread of asylums through the nation proceeded without regard to the extent of a state's economic development. One recent quantitative analysis of the growth and the spread of reformatories finds that neither rates of manufacturing nor of urbanization nor of immigration are valid predictors of change: "The reformatory is not efficiently explained either as a functional outcome of modernization or as a simple instrument of class control and industrial discipline."[32]

Moreover, all of the authors appreciate the contributory role of philanthropists and humanitarians. Some are more apt to emphasize the secular impulse to do good and are less convinced of the centrality of the role of evangelical Christianity; *The Discovery of the Asylum* falls into this camp.[33] Others attribute more importance to the Quaker or the Methodist vision. But no one contends that good intentions are irrelevant — only that taken alone, they are not sufficient to account for the process of change. Without an appreciation of the social crisis that underlay the asylum movement, one cannot account for the peculiar design that was incorporated into all of the asylums, whether they served the insane, the criminal, the delinquent, or the poor. The shared emphasis on order and regularity, the insistence on uniformity and punctuality, the devotion to steady labor and habits of discipline, are most persuasively explained by linking the values that the asylum sought to inculcate with this larger social agenda. The felt need for order and discipline that affected psychiatrists, wardens, and superintendents had a common root outside the asylum, that is, in a society deeply apprehensive about the prospect of disorder.

Were these fears justified? Was the social crisis real or imagined? Here again, some differences emerge, and so do some uncertainties. It may be that England experienced a degree of social disturbance more severe than anything found in the United States or perhaps even in France. But the data to resolve these questions are very difficult to gather. American historians, for example, have not been confident about plotting changing rates of crime in the antebellum period, when the gathering and recording of statistics were as primitive as the policing mechanisms. Any generalization about changing rates of mental illness is even more hazardous, because the very application of the label is socially determined. Thus, it has been suggested (by way of attempt to justify the resort to insane asylums) that mental illness

(particularly schizophrenia) may have been on the increase —
but whether an actual increase occurred or whether society was
more prepared to identify and label as mental illness a wider
range of behaviors cannot be established. Nevertheless, the issue
of rates and measurement is ultimately not the determining
question in the origins of the asylum. Whatever the reality, the
fact of a subjective vision of disorder is indisputable. More, the
numbers cannot help us to understand the form that the response took. Even were crime and madness increasing, why turn
to the asylum and devise its special routine?

The books under discussion here also help to account for the
grim subsequent history of the asylum, its degeneration after the
mid-nineteenth century into warehouses that were understaffed,
overcrowded, harsh, and corrupt, without a semblance of treatment (in the case of mental hospitals) or of training (in the
prisons and reformatories). For one, confinement was simply
too convenient a solution to social problems. Even as the crisis of
order lessened in the United States and scandals about substan-
dard institutional conditions proliferated, the asylum population increased, testimony to an unflagging readiness to keep the
deviant out of sight and out of mind. For another, the original
program contained the seeds of its own destruction. An emphasis on discipline and order all too easily degenerated into a punitive routine, and the unbounded confidence in the ability of a
structured environment to make men over slipped, ever so
smoothly, into a belief that hospitalization or incarceration
would in and of itself bring benefits.

To view the degeneration of the asylum, as some historians
do, as the unintended consequence of benevolent motives, as a
series of incremental changes that unexpectedly and unpredict-
ably produced a horror show, is to avoid the challenge of historical analysis. To insist on the moral purity of state intervention
and psychiatric paternalism, to absolve them of all responsibility
for the decline (on the grounds that human institutions are inevitably fallible), is to sidestep the important historical questions:
Why did the state and the profession fail to recognize the falli-
bility of their creations? Why, even decades later, did asylum
proponents maintain their positions and continue to legitimize
the practice of confinement even in the face of declension? To

resolve these questions by ascribing blindness to asylum superintendents and randomness to the social process, or, as Andrew
Scull astutely remarks, to the Manichaean nature of the universe, is to avoid the very issues that historians must confront.
What is required is an analysis of the functional character of the
asylum, the inherent weaknesses of the first design, and the
society's definition of what it can exact from and what it must
provide to the deviant and dependent.[34]

The interpretations that locate the origins of the asylum in a
profound uneasiness about the fragility of the social order are
often joined under the rubric of a school of social control. That
they do share similarities of outlook is indisputable — one need
only note the repetition of such words as *social order, disorder,
regulation,* and *discipline* in their titles and subtitles. Nevertheless,
the social control label is an ill-suited one, obfuscating more than
it clarifies and oversimplifying a complex historical analysis.

The term "social control" had its origins in sociology in the
1920s and 1930s, in the writings of men like George Herbert
Mead and E. A. Ross. They invoked it in order to promote a
sharper appreciation of the role of subjective and qualitative
values in binding social groups together. Rather than assuming
that the good order of the society rested on the regulatory authority or police power of the state, they sought to connect it to
commonly held values and principles, to make social order the
result not of fiat and force but of ideas and sympathy. Accordingly, the institutions of social control that concerned them were
not the police or the army but the family, the church, and the
school. In fact, they searched so broadly for the agents that
instilled social harmony that they made social control indistinguishable from socialization. Convinced that America in the
opening decades of the twentieth century exemplified an ordered society and that Americans shared a value system that
bound everyone together (think, for example, of the implications of the metaphor of the melting pot), they found social
control everywhere and applauded its exercise.[35]

Not until the post–World War II period did the term change,
and actually reverse its meaning. Sociologists like Richard Cloward and Francis Piven and left-leaning Marxist scholars made

it synonymous not with persuasion but with imposition of state or class authority over the lower classes. Social control was equated with repression and coercion, with the formal and informal mechanisms intended to obscure realities (generally defined as evidence of class repression) and, that effort failing, to compel order and obedience. It was with this negative connotation, not with its Progressive roots, that social control came to the attention of historians.

At first appearance, the concept served a highly useful purpose, stimulating a series of novel questions and serving as a useful corrective to the prevailing idea on "reform." Although "social control" was never clearly defined and one never knew what did or did not come under the rubric, it encouraged a group of historians to stop taking claims of benevolence at face value and to start investigating the purposes, benign or not so benign, that a purported reform might fulfill. (That the need for this exercise was not already self-evident testifies to the power within the discipline of a reformist, or what the English call a Whig, interpretation of history.) The result was to promote fresh questions about the asylum, and fresh answers as well. Indeed, this new perspective had a liberating effect also on the historians of the family, of education, and of social welfare.

But this prodding function completed, the term, for all its popularity, has little to commend it. It is not always evident whether social control is being invoked as a statement of fact (this organization or institution is charged to maintain social order) or being invoked as a proposition (this is an organization that attempted to buttress the social order by coercing or deceiving the lower classes). Social control may be the equivalent of the formal exercise of state power — in the sense that the police are agents of social control duty-bound to maintain public order — or it may be used in a more sweeping, if ill-defined, manner, to make it a weapon (secret?) in the arsenal of the ruling class. In the case at hand, to label interpretations of the asylum "social control" might reflect the self-evident fact that the authors employing this term are writing about institutions charged to maintain order or, more likely, to refer to their willingness to go beyond a paean to reform. In all events, the term in present usage neither advances knowledge nor clarifies subtle differences. The strong case that can be made for banning the word "reform" from historians' vocabulary applies with equal force to "social control."

Notwithstanding their many advances, the new histories of the asylum have left unresolved a number of significant issues. There is a tendency among the texts to obfuscate the identity of the historical actor, to fail to identify with precision who carried forward the asylum design and how they reaped political as well as cultural success. *The Discovery of the Asylum* often refers to "Americans" without becoming more explicit about the social identity of the agents of change; others are only seemingly more precise when they invoke the bourgeoisie and attempt to make the essence of the asylum story the imposition of the values of one class on another.[36] Some among the recent investigations have introduced welcome refinements. Robert Castel's study of French developments on occasion lapses into a Foucault-like appeal to the spirit of the capitalist age, but it more successfully sorts out, camp by camp, the composition of the pro- and anti-asylum forces in the national debate over the watershed law of June 1838 concerning the insane. In the struggle to define the administrative and legal responsibilities for their care, Castel finds an old guard (determined to protect the prerogatives of the family in matters of commitment and local departments in matters of fiscal expenditures) forcing compromises upon a new guard (prepared to give far greater authority to both the psychiatric profession and the national government). The divisions, then, had to do with class, family, inherited status, professional orientation, and vision of the nation — not well captured by the simple resort to the term "bourgeoisie."

In the American case, the politics of asylums was not only reserved to the separate states but does not appear to have sparked open confrontations between supporters and opponents. The consensus was broad, undoubtedly because the idea of the asylum had something for everyone. There were those who supported it because they thought the new prisons would strike terror into the hearts of the offenders (and juries would not hesitate to convict the guilty if they knew a prison sentence, not the gallows, awaited them); others advocated confinement certain of its rehabilitative potential. (In the twentieth century, the effects of this coalition on Progressive innovations is more evident, and with this theme in mind, my sequel study to this volume is entitled *Conscience and Convenience*.[37]) In the Jacksonian era, however, the asylum's appeal was so diffused through the society that to give proponents a class label belies the nature of the coalition as well as its motives. That the asylum was the creation of those with standing in the society is clear — but their position came as much through education and a concern for the well-being of the republic as from their economic identification. Moreover, their fear of disorder was far more a fear of moral dissoluteness than of class warfare: it was the weakened authority of the family and the community, not the aggressive demands of a submerged laboring class, that frightened them most. Thus, their solutions as exemplified in the asylum routine looked more to individual reformation (in a secular sense) than to an altered group consciousness. This characterization may still appear, at least to some, too imprecise, but to convey greater specificity through the imposition of class distinctions is not consistent with the American context.

No less important in the ongoing research is the need to map the lines of influence that spread the asylum across national boundaries. The new research makes apparent that the asylum was not a uniquely American invention. *The Discovery of the Asylum*, some commentators have suggested, appears to exaggerate the uniqueness of the American experience and overemphasize the peculiarly American circumstances that entered into the adoption of a system of confinement. There is no doubt that had the research on European developments been available earlier, the text would have devoted more attention to English precedents (particularly the experiments in the 1790s with both the prison and the mental hospital) and to the French experience (the post-1789 dissatisfaction with the treatment of the criminal and the insane). But the point acknowledged, the problem of sorting out and defining the impact of the European influences still remains.

We now know that the fear about social order that swept over the United States in the 1820s and 1830s had its counterpart in England and in France. Louis Chevalier's compelling analysis of how the French gave an entirely new meaning to the concept of the "dangerous classes," identifying them with the lower orders, points to a process that, if not quite identical to the one that went on in Jacksonian America, certainly is of a kindred spirit.[38] We also know that the principal elements of the new asylum system, its reliance on rigid segregation and the discipline of work and time, as well as its confidence about the rehabilitation of inmates, were intrinsic to European as well as American institutions and, in the case of England, preceded the American experience. But what do these similarities and precedents suggest? What weight should be accorded to the European developments?

Although the issue is far from resolved, the new findings are more suggestive of a parallel discovery of the asylum among western nations than a heavy debt of one country to another. One question often asked of *The Discovery of the Asylum* by European readers was why Jeremy Bentham's 1791 design for the Panopticon was not given greater prominence; surely his emphasis on the need for the segregation, employment, and surveillance of the criminal offender inspired the American prison. But however logical the expectation, the debt was actually minimal. Few Americans (and not very many Englishmen) read Bentham, and even fewer took him seriously. Bentham had a genius for spinning off ideas and trying, almost desperately, to give them a practical bent, but there was always something fantastic about his schemes. One must also remember that his grand penitentiary design never left the printed page; despite early parliamentary enthusiasm, the institution, which would have had Bentham both as its superintendent and owner, was not constructed. The English prison that might be thought to represent his ideas, Pentonville, did not open until 1842 and by then reflected forty years of English developments and the impact of the American experience as well.

In still more general terms, the first English experiments with prisons in the eighteenth century did not command great respect, either at home or abroad. The British were suffering their own crisis of confidence in confinement by the 1810s and were hardly about to serve as a point of inspiration on this side of the Atlantic. Although the American rejection of eighteenth-century practices toward the criminal and the insane had similarities with the European, it was never as intense, mostly because the experience had not been as brutal. The colonists did make public executions central to criminal justice and often treated the insane shamefully, but they avoided the worst excesses of Europe.[39] The torture that the French practiced, and the deportations that the British instituted, had no counterpart here. In sum, it must be appreciated that while European precedents did exist for the Americans' discovery of the asylum, they would not have been binding unless they suited peculiar American conditions and needs. These institutions were not some sort of fruit that, once propagated in one country, was reflexively transplanted to another. The American asylum was essentially homegrown, whatever the resemblance to European counterparts.

The new research has also brought the perspective of the inmate to bear on the history of the asylum. It is not difficult to imagine the agonies of life in the tomblike environment of the prisons of the 1830s or in the brutal atmosphere of the insane asylums of the 1880s. But some historians, by dint of good fortune in locating archival materials and of creative interpretations, have moved beyond such observations to provide insights into the very dynamics of institutionalization. They afford us a keen appreciation of how the inmate subculture undermined the reformatory ideal of the prison. Patricia O'Brien demonstrates unequivocally the existence of an inmate subculture in French prisons in the nineteenth century that was powerful enough to thwart efforts to superimpose an official culture, with its values and habits. Drawing on several remarkable contemporary surveys of French prisoners, including one by an investigator who went from facility to facility to count, describe, and classify the tattoos that inmates sported, O'Brien rightly concludes that "prisoners were not an inert mass, a passive population on which the new disciplinary system acted without reaction or resistance." Moreover, as many prison investigations confirmed, the inmate subculture had its own sexual mores, with regular recourse to homosexual relationships. Although prison officials considered the sin unspeakable, in contravention of every value they wished to inculcate, they were helpless to contain or stifle it. Thus, it was not only external considerations — the unwillingness of the state to invest more in prison programs or hire a better class of guards — but also internal ones, the power of the inmate subculture, that undercut the stated mission of the prison.[40]

In similar fashion, Nancy Tomes, drawing particularly on the correspondence of patients' families with Thomas Kirkbride, superintendent of the highly regarded Pennsylvania Hospital for the Insane, persuasively illustrates how families turned to the asylum to resolve their own crises, in the process helping to stamp a functional, as opposed to reformatory, character on the institution. The very act of confining a troublesome or danger-ous relative satisfied the entirety of their needs, regardless of the prospects for cure. Tomes shows that families were slow to in-stitutionalize a relation, no matter how emphatically psychia-trists declared that the insane should be committed in the early (and ostensibly curable) stages of illness: "Patrons waited for months, sometimes years, before applying to the asylum as a last resort." But once the family's tolerance was exhausted, they gave their burden over to the asylum, grateful for the relief it pro-vided. The net effect of these individual decisions was to help make the asylum into a repository for the most chronic and unruly patients, those who were least likely to respond positively to its routine. But all the while, by relieving the family of the onus of care, the asylum was fulfilling a vital function, respond-ing to a general anxiety about social order and a particular anx-iety about one or another disorderly individual. Indeed, the design of the asylum seemed responsive to both demands. The families relished its very separate and isolated character, for through commitment, "they expected to put an end to embar-rassing public displays and discussions of their relative's insan-ity." So, too, they encouraged the asylum to administer an ordered, even overly ordered routine. Since the patient's intrac-tability had been the cause for commitment, the families ex-pected that the asylum would, in their words, "keep him from roaming off," or "keep her within bounds," or compel her "to conform to certain rules in the first place." Hence, an appreci-ation of all that the asylum meant to the social order should not obscure its usefulness to the family, whether or not it realized a rehabilitative ideal.[41]

Tomes goes on to make an even more critical point: the legitimacy accorded the asylum lowered the standard of behavior considered sufficiently troublesome to justify confinement. "The *level* of violence, disruptiveness, or intellectual impairment deemed necessary to merit confinement had certainly fallen since the eighteenth century. Increasingly families sought asylum care for patients who could still be managed at home without resorting to extreme measures." The result was "a broadening of the asylum function . . . in the types of mental disorders considered suitable for treatment," a widening of the cohort of those considered appropriate for asylum care.[42]

An appreciation of this dynamic should underlie any final consideration of the success or failure of the asylum in the nineteenth century. Such an evaluation is rendered especially complex not merely because of the number and variety of institutions but also because of an uncertainty as to how to frame the inquiry. The asylum was a success or failure as judged by what? By reformers' dreams, or by families' needs, or by what might have come in its stead, or by the practices it actually replaced? If the question is whether the asylum lived up to the expectations of its founders, the answer is an unequivocal no. But then one must immediately ask why the failure persisted, why the asylum lived on long after the dream turned into a nightmare. The likely answer is that it was fulfilling the needs of those outside, if not inside, its walls. Their wish was to be rid of the deviant and dependent, to put them out of sight and out of mind, and in that regard the asylum was a notable success, functioning ever so effectively.

But surely the asylum should be considered a success when compared with the practices it replaced. Was it not an improvement over the gallows, the whip, and the dank cellar hovels in which the insane lived out their lives? Even this seemingly self-evident judgment, however, must be qualified, for the asylum extended its reach and brought into its orbit many who would have been spared punishment or confinement in an earlier era. It is likely that some among the mad undoubtedly suffered less because of the asylum, but some may have suffered more; and a number of prisoners spent years in a cell who in an earlier day would have been shamed before their neighbors and then left to resume their lives. The calculus of benefits and losses is too finely balanced to render an unambiguous verdict.

Finally, is the history of the asylum relevant to our understanding of the present and our imagination of the future? Are there lessons that we should draw from the record? Clearly, the past is no predictor of the future, and the fact that asylums failed to deliver on their promise is no warrant to find that they have outlived their usefulness and should now be abandoned. At the same time, we would be foolhardy not to raise our level of skepticism. The closing paragraphs of *The Discovery of the Asylum* constitute a plea not for "simple moral judgments," but for recognizing that "proposals that promise the most grandiose consequences often legitimate the most unsatisfactory developments." In light of the history, surely the burden of proof falls on those who would claim that confinement can serve all ends, benefiting the inmate and the society.

But the history serves another purpose as well. The last paragraphs hold out a vision of history as a liberating discipline, for it reminds us that there is nothing inevitable about the institutions and procedures that surround us, that "we need not remain trapped in inherited answers." It was right to close a book on the asylum with that message in 1970, and it is right to do so today.

The Discovery of the Asylum

1

The Boundaries
of Colonial Society

The colonial attitudes and practices toward the poor and the criminal, the insane, the orphan, and the delinquent were in almost every aspect remarkably different from those Americans came to share in the pre–Civil War decades. Almost no eighteenth-century assumption about the origins or nature of dependency and deviancy survived intact into the Jacksonian era, and its favorite solutions to these conditions also became outmoded. In fact, the two periods' perspectives and reactions were so basically dissimilar that only a knowledge of colonial precedents can clarify the revolutionary nature of the changes that occurred.

Eighteenth-century Americans did not define either poverty or crime as a critical social problem. They did not interpret the presence of the poor as symptomatic of a basic flaw in the citizen or the society, an indicator of personal or communal failing. Compared to their successors, the colonists accepted the existence of poverty with great equanimity. They devoted very little energy to devising and enacting programs to reform offenders and had no expectations of eradicating crime. Nor did they systematically attempt to isolate the deviant or the dependent. While they excluded some persons, they kept others wholly inside their communities. At times they were generous with the needy, fully understanding their plight, and at times they were willing to allow offenders another chance; but they could also show a callousness and narrow-mindedness that was utterly cruel. From the viewpoint of nineteenth-century critics, their ideas and behavior seemed careless and inconsistent, irrational and injurious. But within their social and intellectual framework, the colonists followed clear and well-established guidelines. A distinct set of principles existed in the preasylum days.

The eighteenth-century use of the term "poor" encompassed a wide variety of conditions. When colonists discussed the poor or legislated for them, they included widows along with orphans, the aged along with the sick, the insane along with the disabled without careful differentiation. The fact of need, not the special circumstances which caused it, was the critical element in the definition. Thus, ministerial sermons on charity usually set down communal obligations to the poor without bothering to delineate exactly who fit into the category. Assembly codes were equally imprecise. New York, for example, in its first province-wide legislation on the subject in 1683, simply charged local officials to "make provision for the maintenance and support of their poor," and succeeding acts did not add more explicit instructions. New Jersey legislators passed "An Act for the Relief of the Poor," in 1709, but did not specify which townspeople ought to be included. Declaring that "it is necessary that the poor should be relieved by the public where they cannot relieve themselves, and are not able to work for their support," they turned immediately to describing who should administer the act, not to whom the law should be applied.[1]

Occasionally, in the course of the colonial period, some assemblies passed laws for a special group like the insane. But again it was dependency and not any trait unique to the disease that concerned them. From their perspective, insanity was really no different from any other disability; its victim, unable to support himself, took his place as one more among the needy. The lunatic came to public attention not as someone afflicted with delusions or fears, but as someone suffering from poverty. In this spirit a Massachusetts law, frequently copied elsewhere, established that "when and so often as it shall happen any person to be naturally wanting of understanding, so as to be uncapable to provide for him or herself," then the town, in the absence of relatives and personal property, was to provide for his relief.[2] The colonists, in brief, were concerned with the financial effects of all adverse conditions, not their idiosyncratic attributes. They made a variety of cases all part of the definition of "poor."

Yet, despite the latitude of this definition, not everyone who was not self-supporting qualified automatically as one of the poor. The colonists refused to support some individuals, those whom they classified as rogues and vagabonds. Here very different attitudes prevailed. To some extent the two categories represented a division based on moral character. Some dependents were honest men who had fallen on hard times and therefore warranted support, while others had lived a corrupt life or were not actually incapable of work, and therefore should be punished. But the distinction also reflected the element of settlement, differentiating between resident and nonresident, townsman and outsider. Dependent neighbors made up the ranks of the poor. The town recognized a clear obligation to them and officials were not especially concerned with possible malfeasance. The lazy and shiftless among them could be easily identified, without the aid of intricate codes or elaborate precautions. Local communities, however, did not accept responsibility for the needy outsider, no matter what his moral condition, and they drew up complicated statutes to exclude him. Poor relief was a local system, towns liable for their own, but not for others.

These attitudes were intimately related to a broad range of social and religious considerations. Colonial ideas were in part a response to prevailing religious teachings, in part to secular definitions of the proper functioning of the social order, in part to English traditions, and in part to a special sense of community.

To explore first the position of the poor, these several influences gave eighteenth-century Americans a distinctive perspective on poverty: first, that it was not symptomatic of a critical defect in the social order, and second, that the community could handle what need there was without acute strain.

These two judgments did not result simply from an absence of dependency among the colonies. For despite the casual observations of European visitors, the colonists expected to find, and did find, poor in America.[3] As the fragmentary records of local officials make clear, urban and rural communities gave a good deal of attention and, in comparison with the rest of their expenditures, large sums of money to poor relief. For example, the Boston almshouse in the 1760's relieved an average of two hundred and fifty persons annually — of which less than one-quarter were children — and at least three to four times as many inhabitants probably received some public assistance. Moreover, churches, mutual aid societies, families, and neighbors supported many others. As early as 1735 Boston appropriated £2,500 to the poor, one of the costliest items on the budget. In relative terms, the figures are not staggering in a community of fifteen thousand; but in absolute terms, the numbers are large enough to dispel the notion that the absence of dependency accounts for colonial equanimity. Agricultural communities also had their poor. Virginia's St. Paul's parish, one of the colony's wealthier settlements, almost half of whose approximately two thousand inhabitants were slaves, provided extensive public assistance to fifteen to twenty persons a year; unrecorded others received small funds from overseers and benevolent citizens. Public relief in this parish alone in the 1740's rose to fifteen to twenty thousand pounds of tobacco annually, making it a principal expense. From every indication, the poor were with the colonists.[4]

One of the most influential organizations in dictating American attitudes toward the poor was the Protestant church. The clergy successfully took poverty and its relief for their special province. At religious services, they often preached about the poor; at annual meetings of benevolent societies they were the main speakers, regularly publishing their sermons to reach a still wider audience. They made the treatment of the poor as much a religious as a secular matter. They established the importance of their standards, so that biblical injunctions demanded consideration along with material calculations in setting the poor-tax rate. The balance, of course, did not always tip to their side. Sunday's lesson could be ignored not only by those who did not go to church but also by those who conveniently forgot its moral. Nevertheless, religious precepts were vitally significant in the eighteenth century. Religion defined the presence of poverty in the world as natural and just, and its relief as necessary and appropriate. It neither feared nor ignored the poor. And while the clergy did not maintain its hegemony for very long into the nineteenth century, in the colonial era it dominated the discussion.

At the root of the religious position was the premise that the existing social order had divine approbation, that its form was not accidental or fortuitous, but providential. A higher design made some men rich, eminent, and powerful and others low, mean, and in subjection. The postulates that John Winthrop had presented to his shipmates on board the *Arbella* were expounded by clergymen through the eighteenth century. But while Winthrop at least had wondered whether the Puritan community might alter this division of society, his successors shared no such vision and bound themselves firmly to the prevailing order of things.[5] In so doing, they left themselves open to the obvious question: was it really God's intent that children should suffer hunger and widows cold? Was the presence of poverty evidence of a flaw in God's work? To which the colonial clergy replied emphatically, no; they then went on to offer the necessary and traditional rationales for the existence of poverty. In their interpretation it was not a necessary evil but a positive good. Its presence benefited persons at all levels of society.

The task of making poverty seem right and just was not as difficult as one might think. Ministers conceded at the outset that the poor would always be with us, certain that need would no more cease out of this land than out of any other. But rather than bemoan a possibly tragic truth of human organization, they serenely asserted that the presence of the poor was a God-given opportunity for men to do good. The relief of the needy, explained Boston clergyman Samuel Cooper, was the highest Christian virtue. "It ennobles our nature, by conforming us to the best, the most glorious patterns. . . . Charity conforms us to the Son of God himself." Poverty actually made money a blessing, for it permitted men to act as the stewards of God's wealth.[6] Minister after minister proclaimed this doctrine, teaching that "he who is most favored in regard to temporal things is but a steward," that God was "pleased to make you the stewards to his bounty . . . generously conferring on you the privilege of doing his work."[7] The steward, however, was not to strip himself of his worldly possessions to fulfill his charge; such zeal might disrupt the hierarchical order of society and therefore had no place in this lesson. Rather, only after making due allowance for profession, office, and rank was the steward to relieve the poor. The wealthy "are bound to *remain* the stewards of God. A visible distinction between *them* and others is proper. . . . Order is heaven's first law; some are and must be greater than the rest."[8]

Ministers enumerated the rewards of stewardship to vindicate the discrepancies in the condition of men. Philanthropists escaped the burdens of the sin of pride because they were able to rise above self-interest to an interest in others. The society benefited, for charity brought neighbors together and by balancing self-love with social love strengthened the bonds of cohesion and order.[9] Benevolence also justified the pursuit of wealth, sanctioning commerce, trade, and the other bustling economic activities of growing towns. As Boston's Benjamin Colman assured his parishioners, charity made the "merchandise of people a holiness to God." When cities grow rich and opulent, Colman warned, "they also grow *sensual, profane* and *insolent, unjust* and *unrighteous.*" Boston would be spared this fate by remembering that divine blessing brought prosperity and by dedicating "a due part of our substance, together with our selves, to the glory and service of God." And, of course, the returns were to be spiritual. Clergymen invariably linked the relief of the poor to winning salvation. The absence of philanthropy, Colman insisted, "is a sad and dark testimony to the poverty of grace." Even into the opening decades of the nineteenth century, his colleagues preached that "our past conduct in reference to the poor and our present determination, will show whether we are beloved by God. The criterion are manifest." No good works were more important than caring for the needy.[10]

The pervasiveness and import of these doctrines helped prevent men from fearing and distrusting their poor neighbor. Pity, sympathy, yes — but not fear when the needy provided an ideal moment for adorning secular achievements with religious sanctions. Clerical preachments, to be sure, did not eschew all discrimination among the poor. Medieval churchmen had distinguished between the deserving and undeserving poor, and the differences were certainly not lost on Calvinists. Charles Chauncy, the staunch Old Light clergyman and articulate foe of Jonathan Edwards, delivered a charity sermon around the lesson: *The*

Idle Poor Secluded from the Bread of Charity by Christian Law.
Chauncy left no doubt that the idle among the poor, those
who would not work, ought not to be relieved.[11] Yet the colonial
clergy spent little energy clarifying or insisting upon this distinction. Ministers like Samuel Seabury taught that the poor were
"every one who is suffering for want. And no matter how their
suffering come on them, whether by accident, by idleness, by
vice — while they suffer they are entitled to relief." Seabury did
add that those guilty of vice should be assisted only in modera-
tion and until the emergency passed. But still they belonged in
the camp of the poor. As other ministers explained, Christians
would be foolhardy to insist that the "idle and even intemperate
. . . shall suffer before our eyes, because they do not actually
merit our charity." After all, "what if God were to refuse his
mercy to those of us who do not deserve it. . . . We deserve
nothing but hell; and shall we refuse to supply the poor with a
little portion of God's property in our hands of which he has
made us the stewards?" The best policy was not to discriminate
too carefully in matters of charity.[12]

But these were ultimately secondary issues. The clergy devoted
a minimum of time to the poor themselves, taking their usual
angle of vision and focus from the top looking down, identifying
with the better sort and urging them to do good. The number of
idle who could be found among the needy was a minor consideration. Indeed, whether the poor profited as the rich did from the
divine plan was hardly ever discussed. Here and there a minister
declared that the poor should thank Providence for the generos-
ity of their donors: "They should religiously accept the Gift of
Heaven in those whom they must call their benefactors. They
should look through and above men unto God, who gives by
their hands." And Cotton Mather in his volume, *Bonifacius: An
Essay upon the Good,* briefly noted: "A mean mechanic, who can
tell what an *engine of good* he may be, if humbly and wisely
applied unto it!"[13] But most often the clergy focused on the
doer and his deed, disregarding the needy. The poor were the
pawns in a divine game where the better sort made the moves.
There was no reason to fear a pawn, and no reason to alter the
rules of the game. The ministerial perspective rendered the poor

impotent and safe, necessary and not dangerous, part of the social order, not a threat to it.

The secular definition of the social order in the eighteenth century also helped buttress this Christian acceptance of poor neighbors. The colonial image of society was hierarchical, with a series of ranks, upper to lower. Each segment enjoyed a fixed place with its own particular privileges and obligations. From this perspective, the community's poor, at the bottom of the scale, were a permanent order, integral to the system and not a perpetual source of danger to it. As members of society, they were to respect the hierarchy and their place within it and pay proper deference to those above them. In return, they could expect assistance in time of need. Reciprocal obligations were carefully spelled out, that is, while the poor were not among society's respected members and no one thought permanently to ameliorate their condition, at the same time, they were neither feared nor repressed. Social philosophy as well as theology gave them a standing within the community. And if as a result a neighbor's poverty was that much easier for the middling and better sorts to bear, at least they did not totally ignore, harshly punish, or isolate him.

The hierarchical interpretation of the social order was so axiomatic to eighteenth-century society that it was not frequently expounded. Colonists' comments on social rankings were usually random and brief, assertions that one or another level — usually the middle — predominated in a given town or province.[14] A moment of crisis, however, such as the Great Awakening, did spark discussion, and even some debate, on this issue. The protectors of the religious status quo, Old Light ministers, articulately defended traditional social arrangements. The revivalists, for their part, occasionally attempted, but not very successfully or coherently, to define an alternative.

Ministers like Charles Chauncy found a grave threat to order in the New Light practices and denounced them for breeding chaos and conflict wherever they went. "There is indeed," contended Chauncy, "scarce anything so wild either in speculation or practice, but they have given into it." Above all, he blamed them for "leaving their own stations, and doing the work that was proper to others." Repeatedly he insisted: "Good order is the

Strength and Beauty of the World. The Prosperity both of *Church* and *State* depends very much upon it. And can there be Order, where Men transgress the Limits of their Station, and intermeddle in the Business of others? So far from it, that the only effectual Method, under God . . . is, for *every one* to be faithful, in doing what is *proper* for him in his *own Place.*"

The penalties for disregarding these truths were frightful. Under the guise of what Chauncy called "vain conceit," the multitude in the German Peasant Wars "took up *Arms* against the lawful *Authority*," and then "were destroyed at one Time and another, to the Number of an HUNDRED THOUSAND."[15] Implicit in this message was the view that so long as the lower classes remained in their stations and fulfilled their proper roles, the system would function smoothly. In short, if the poor were no challenge to peace and security, they belonged to the community and could be treated nonpunitively, perhaps even decently.

New Light ministers responded with broad declarations on universal love and harmony, but little explicit social theory. They proclaimed the brotherhood of man, tacitly rejecting the notion of hierarchy. But their musings did not affect eighteenth-century social thought. Even at the outbreak of the Revolution, the idea of hierarchy in society was still a postulate among the most avid supporters of independence and republican government. Equality, one recent student of this period has concluded, did not mean social leveling; most revolutionaries did not wish to abolish the system of rankings.[16] In the end, they left the social implications of the new polity for succeeding generations to work out.

The colonists' attitudes toward their poor neighbors also reflected the wide scope of public authority and local responsibility. This outlook reinforced both the prevailing religious and secular definitions of social responsibility. In part, this development fulfilled English traditions. Economic and social legislation in the mother country frequently empowered local authorities to override personal privileges for the general welfare. The poor-law statutes, for example, over their long history made the care of the needy the public duty of the parish. Elizabethan codes ordered each parish to elect overseers of the poor to administer the program, and compliance, if not at first then by the eighteenth century, was widespread. This type of arrangement fit well with conditions in the new world. Americans found it appropriate to elevate public authority over private privilege and convenient to extend the prerogatives of local authorities. In the seventeenth century Winthrop had charged his followers to be "knit together," and not desert one another in face of the wilderness. And this advice continued to appeal to later generations.

Few men commanded the extensive resources that could free them from a regular dependence on their neighbors or allow them to satisfy, in the form of investment, community needs. This was immediately apparent in rural areas. Few families along the frontier owned a full complement of tools for clearing and building, or commanded the necessary labor for carrying out vital economic tasks; older farming settlements, which produced little more than subsistence, also found that men could do together what they could not accomplish individually. Urban areas had similar experiences. Entrepreneurs did not possess the large capital accumulations necessary to meet the many needs of growing towns. Rather, citizens had to combine their efforts to protect themselves against fire and spread of disease, to establish the most rudimentary water- and waste-disposal systems, to light the streets and to build harbors. Common goals demanded community action.[17]

Townsmen were frequently bound together by strong social ties that promoted joint action. This was most true in older settlements, and especially in New England. There, communities were usually small in size, with relationships among neighbors often intimate and intense. In Massachusetts, for example, as late as 1765, only fifteen of more than two hundred towns held over twenty-five hundred persons; a majority had fewer than one thousand. Residents regularly worshiped at the same church, and frequent marriages between townspeople made many neighbors into relatives. In numerous settlements newcomers did not usually intrude. Town lands were generally completely distributed after three generations, offering few incentives to outsiders and forcing younger sons to leave for newer areas. These circumstances often gave a quality of insularity to established communities that encouraged and facilitated an expansion of public responsibilities.[18]

Such conditions were not precisely duplicated throughout the colonies, and in fact may have been breaking down over the course of the eighteenth century in older settlements. In Middle Atlantic and southern colonies, particularly in the backcountry of Pennsylvania and the Carolinas, geographic mobility was frequent. Migrants constantly shifted from one area to another and newcomers regularly arrived to search out homesteads. Residents were not religiously homogeneous and did not necessarily share the same language. Concomitantly, seaboard towns were experiencing their first bursts of growth. By 1750, Philadelphia, New York, Boston, Newport, and Charleston were beginning to shed village characteristics for urban ones. Furthermore, a widening division of economic and religious interests in older New England towns was beginning to promote individual actions at the expense of community cohesion.

Nevertheless, eighteenth-century society was far from atomistic. Settlers often moved into virgin territories with extended families, with co-religionists, or with fellow immigrants, so that a core existed for community solidarity. In the Carolina backcountry, for example, bands of Quakers and Scotch-Irish, as well as fathers and sons, filled the land. Primitive surroundings and the threat of marauders also encouraged members of small and isolated villages to cooperate. Even expanding colonial towns were comparatively small in size, and not immune to the social influences apparent in outlying villages. In 1755, Philadelphia held twenty thousand residents, and Boston, New York, Newport, and Charleston, less than fifteen thousand. Perhaps most important, the traditional idea of cooperation remained intact, so that changing styles of behavior were still for the most part understood as departures from older norms, not the first steps toward establishing a new type of social order. Hence the colonists continued to think in terms of hierarchy and fixity, mutual interests and cohesion.[19]

This orientation was evident in many aspects of colonial life. One inherited and influential principle was the right of the government to interfere in the workings of the economy. It had the power to inspect, to set standards, to grant monopolies — all in the declared interest of public welfare. Should a town require a bridge, one company received an exclusive title to the enterprise. Unable to provide the necessary capital for improvements, the government depended upon the stratagem of monopoly and this procedure provoked few objections. In this way general needs took precedence over the privileges of property, and community welfare overrode other considerations.

In the field of education too, the colonists assumed that public well-being came before individual or family prerogatives. Ministers instructed their congregants not only to raise children to be God-fearing, but to make them "serviceable in their generation." And statutes sought to enforce the command. If parents neglected their duty, the community had the right and obligation to intervene, to remove the child and place him in another household. In Massachusetts, for example, the 1735 assembly, dismayed at the neglect of instruction, ordered local officials to take children found in "gross ignorance," that is, ignorant of the alphabet at the age of six, out of their own family and to place them in another to receive a decent and Christian education. The act was not unique to New England; churchwardens in Virginia received similar instructions in the same period. In concept, the family was not to be exclusive, insular, solely self-serving, and inviolable. To the contrary. It was to fulfill public needs, to fit children for community life.[20]

The care of the town's poor was one with these judgments. The attitude that gave the community wide powers over the economy and education also dictated a broad responsibility for the needy. Charged to oversee the general welfare, officials aided the poor in the same spirit that they granted a monopoly to build a bridge and worried about ignorance. It was as unthinkable to allow the destitute to shift for themselves as to let commerce flounder or children grow up untrained. Thus, without second thought, the colonists relieved the needy, the widows and orphans, the aged and sick, the insane and disabled. This customary and legitimate function did not require finely drawn or detailed legislation, great fuss or trepidation.

The colonists' attitude toward the rogue vagabond revealed the influence of the same social organizations and conditions that shaped their view of the poor. Although eighteenth-century Americans were far more apprehensive about deviant behavior and adopted elaborate precautions and procedures to control it, they did not interpret its presence as symptomatic of a basic flaw in community structure or expect to eliminate it. They would combat the evil, warn, chastise, correct, banish, flog or execute the offender. But they saw no prospect of eliminating deviancy from their midst. Crime, like poverty, was endemic to society.

The colonists judged a wide range of behavior to be deviant, finding the gravest implications in even minor offenses. Their extended definition was primarily religious in origin, equating sin with crime. The criminal codes punished religious offenses, such as idolatry, blasphemy, and witchcraft, and clergymen declared infractions against persons or property to be offenses against God. Freely mixing the two categories, the colonists proscribed an incredibly long list of activities. The identification of disorder with sin made it difficult for legislators and ministers to distinguish carefully between major and minor infractions. Both were testimony to the natural depravity of man and the power of the devil — sure signs that the offender was destined to be a public menace and a damned sinner.[21] This attitude underlies the heavy-handedness of eighteenth-century codes, which set capital punishments for crimes as different as murder and arson, horse-stealing and children's disrespect for parents. More direct and dramatic evidence of the equation appeared in the sermons preached on the morning of the execution days. While the condemned man stood facing his coffin, the clergyman expounded the moral of his fate. One Connecticut minister told his audience that the purpose of the execution sermon was to connect us all as sinners with the murderer; his crime was only a more heinous manifestation of the evil within all of us, of every man's proclivities for sin and wrongdoing. Another colleague, preaching before the execution of a prostitute found guilty of infanticide, hoped his sermon would be "a means to startle the rising generation and keep others from sinning"; through the fate of this criminal, "all frail might hear and fear, and do no more so wickedly."[22] By linking murder with sin and sin with every transgression against man and God, clergymen taught the colonists to find terrifying significance in even casual offenses. An execution was an ideal opportunity to alert the public to the dangers of all forms of deviant behavior.

To counteract the powerful temptations to misconduct and the inherent weakness of men, the colonists looked to three critical associations. They conceived of the family, the church, and the network of community relations as important weapons in the battle against sin and crime. If these bodies functioned well, the towns would be spared the turbulence of vice and crime and, without frequent recourse to the courts or the gallows, enjoy a high degree of order and stability. To these ends, families were to raise their children to respect law and authority, the church was to oversee not only family discipline but adult behavior, and the members of the community were to supervise one another, to detect and correct the first signs of deviancy.

Sermons and pamphlets thoroughly discussed the family as an institution of social control. Ministers like Benjamin Wadsworth, author of the popular child-rearing tract, *The Well-Ordered Family* (1712), charged parents to fit their offspring for community life, "to train up a child in the way wherein he should go," and carefully mark out the steps. The family was to teach the child to follow an honest calling, to earn his living and not to be a drain on the community. It was to inculcate good manners, so that youngsters would be civil, respectful, and courteous, not "riotous or unruly." Above all, it was to impart the fundamentals of Christianity, and "also the second table duties, namely to be sober, chaste and temperate." Ultimately, Wadsworth insisted, the town's good order rested upon family authority, and so parents had to "'govern their children well, restrain, reprove, correct them as there is occasion. A Christian householder should *rule well his own house.*" For the sake of obedience it might be necessary to use the rod, but the price of the alternatives, indulgence or inattention, was inordinately high. As Wadsworth warned his readers: "When children are disobedient to parents, God is often provoked to leave them to those sins which bring them to the greatest shame and misery. . . . When persons have been brought to die at the gallows, how often have they confessed that disobedience to parents led them to those crimes?"[23]

Execution sermons often reiterated this point. One Boston

minister told a young girl about to be hanged that her sins were the direct result of "your pride, your disobedience to your parents, your impatience of family government." On a similar occasion, a Connecticut audience learned how "shameful and unpardonable . . . is the almost universal neglect of family instruction and government. One of the most truly unhappy consequences of this neglect, we behold in the ignominious end of this poor girl." The moral was clear: "Let all children . . . beware of disobedience. . . . Appetites and passions unrestricted in childhood become furious in youth; and ensure *dishonor, disease,* and an *untimely death."* Early lessons in religion and obedience could protect the child from the fate of the gallows.[24]

The colonists were less articulate about the potential contribution of the church to social stability, but the link between God-fearing behavior and lawful behavior was obvious. They assumed that the clergy would set strict standards, preach on the need to observe them, and tie performance to eternal reward and punishment. Would-be offenders were to fear not only the local constable but divine wrath as well — and in the many towns where the official was not an imposing figure, it was useful to magnify the dangers of the hereafter. Also widespread in the colonies was the assumption that the church, through the watchfulness of its ministers, deacons, and members, would closely supervise its congregants' lives to detect and correct transgressions. Such scrutiny could be especially useful in the area of behavior most difficult to police, private offenses, both domestic and sexual. Thus church membership in the eighteenth century was an important sign of respectability. A large and flourishing congregation would be a major contributor to the order of the community.[25]

Still, the colonists did not anticipate widespread success in deterring people from wrongdoing. Their Christian sense of crime as sin, their belief that men were born to corruption, lowered their expectations and made deviant behavior a predictable and inevitable component of society. The causes of crime were not difficult for them to understand and the theory of its origin stirred little controversy. The standard interpretation pointed first to the errors of the family; its failure to train its charges to social and religious obligations had left depraved inclinations unchecked. The analysis noted next that the influence of the church was narrowly circumscribed, unable to reach those who most needed its warnings. But the explanation soon focused on the sinner himself, on his personal liability. "The natural man," announced one execution sermon, "defiles every step he takes, and the filth thereof redounds to himself."[26] The roots of deviant behavior were more internal than external; the fault rested more with the offender than with the society. To the colonists the presence of crime, like that of poverty, was not symptomatic of social breakdown.

Sin, of course, demanded retribution and eighteenth-century punishments were harsh and even cruel. Correction, as clergymen methodically explained, had many important functions. It could serve to intimidate the offender, thereby discouraging him from further depravities. When ministers occasionally spoke of "re-forming" the deviant, they meant only that severe corrections might terrorize him into obedience. Whippings, they believed, were apt punishments for the first offender; he "ought to look on them as warnings of more severe punishments to be expected if he refuses to be reformed." To demonstrate to citizens the wages of sin might help to keep them to the right path. Correction was also essential to public safety, part of the right of self-preservation. The large number of crimes calling for capital punishment was no cause for embarrassment; to cut off those guilty of serious or repeated offenses was the privilege of an embattled community. In a still more fundamental way, through such actions the society carried out God's law. To allow the criminal to escape was to implicate everyone in his crime. Offenders had to be severely disciplined: "Otherwise the judgments of God shall fall upon the land."[27]

These attitudes did not stimulate the colonists to new ways of controlling crime. The broad definition of potential offenders and improper behavior did not spur attempts to revise the patently inadequate formal mechanisms of law enforcement. Assemblies created a militia to contain mass disturbances and repel enemy forces but they did not intend it or use it for day-to-day supervision. Towns designated constables to protect their peace, but the force was inadequate both in the number and physical condition of its men. It was understaffed, poorly supervised, and filled with the elderly. Rather, the colonists' perspective on deviancy encouraged a dependence upon informal mechanisms which promoted a localism in many settlements. To an important degree the community had to be self-policing. The citizens themselves would be on guard to report and even apprehend the offender. Just as churchgoers were to be diligent about one another's salvation, so too residents were to protect one another's lives and property. And given the popular sense of man's proclivities to sin and crime, they expected to be busy.

Fixity and stability of residence therefore appeared to be assets to the social order. The longtime resident, related to a well-established family, known to be a regular attendant at church services, was an important prop of the community. The local ne'er-do-wells, of which there were certain to be some, were not especially difficult to control; as their reputations spread, the town could more easily oversee and, when necessary, punish them. But outsiders posed a more serious problem and warranted scrutiny. After investigation, those with certificates of good standing from their former church and town, or with property and occupational skills, were welcome. Having demonstrated their fitness in one place, they could be easily accepted in another. However, the poor stranger, the vagrant or the wanderer, without these credentials, was to be excluded. He might become not only an expense to the town, but a cause of disorder.

Competing considerations often prevented communities from taking a very close look at newcomers. The demand for laborers was frequently too pressing. In frontier settlements the bonds between the residents were often too new and fragile to allow them to examine others very carefully, and some of the seaboard cities were expanding too rapidly to keep track of all migrants. Hence, the scrutiny of strangers varied in intensity from place to place. In many New England towns the new settler may never have come to feel entirely comfortable. In some Middle Atlantic communities he was probably accepted in full after presenting his credentials. In frontier areas, no one may have questioned his presence at all. Nevertheless, this idea of the self-policing community, with a premium on residential stability and the examination of outsiders, remained an important ingredient in eighteenth-century thinking about social order. The colonists did not yet perceive the various challenges to it — that migration and urban growth were beginning to make the notion static and outdated. Rather, throughout this period they wrote and revised their statutes with this principle to mind.

The force and significance of this mode of thinking is apparent in the colonial poor laws. Most students of American welfare practices have tended to consider these codes to be unthinking duplications of English laws, and have judged them to be cruel and vindictive in their outlook toward all of the poor. But both of these premises demand correction. Although American statutes were firmly based on English precedent, they did not mechanically repeat every stipulation and faithfully duplicate the system. Rather, assemblies selected from the English corpus those sections that they found most consistent with their own attitudes and most relevant to their own needs, and in so doing they gave a discernibly American quality to the result. They paid little attention to British laws governing the establishment of charitable trusts or empowering municipalities to erect various kinds of hospitals or requiring towns to build almshouses and workhouses.[28] What they did carefully reenact were provisions that empowered local governments, that fixed their responsibility for the care of their own needy, and established administrative methods for excluding others. Indeed, the history of the colonial poor law is the story of the increasing sophistication and intricacy of these procedures. The codes were not monuments to an indiscriminate harshness and cruelty. Their most punitive sections were directed more at vagrants and dependent strangers than at the local poor.

In colony after colony, the most detailed and complicated parts of the poor law involved settlement requirements. The statutes established qualifications for residence and instructed municipalities on enforcement procedures. The succession of laws in New York, for example, exemplified both the concern and the results of legislative actions. The first province-wide code of 1683, "An Act . . . for Maintaining the Poor and Preventing Vagabonds," announced in its very title the goals for the next hundred years of poor-law legislation: to relieve the needy resident while cutting off and excluding the dependent outsider. To these ends, the assembly charged local officials to support the poor and then devoted two detailed paragraphs to "the prevention and discouraging of Vagabonds and Idle Persons to come into this province from other parts, and also from one part of the province to another." There was no need to spell out who were the poor, for townsmen easily knew which of their neighbors stood in genuine need. But how was one to erect barriers against the vagabonds and idle persons who might enter the community? The bill therefore required that ship captains supply administrators with the names of all passengers and transport back to their ports of embarkation anyone without a craft, an occupation or property. It also empowered town constables to return to "the county from whence they came," any vagabond or beggar who came into their jurisdiction. The first code did not organize elaborate enforcement procedures. It quickly assured newcomers who had occupational skills that the prohibitions were not aimed at them and allowed eight days to apply for residence. It established no mechanisms for bonding strangers and set down no rules about local families boarding newcomers. The lines were not yet drawn very heavily.[29]

The assembly tightened the regulations in 1721. The new law's preamble stated that "several idle and necessitous come, or are brought into this province from neighboring colonies . . . who have either fled from thence for fear of punishment for their crimes, or being slothful and unwilling to work." The act required that any householder who boarded a stranger not known to him as a person of "good substance," to notify the justice of the peace of the "name, quality, condition, and circumstances of the person so entertained." If the justice suspected that the boarder might eventually become a charge to the town, he was to expel him immediately. The penalty for housing a stranger without notification for forty days — the time needed to qualify for residence — was the posting of a bond against future expenses or a term in jail. The statute also provided that anyone once transported out of the province who later returned was to be sent on his way with a maximum of thirty-five lashes.[30]

In 1773, the colony passed a new law, because the existing codes "relating to the settlement and support of the poor, are very deficient and ineffectual for that purpose." But every provision in the new bill indicates that settlement, and not poor relief, was at issue. Legislators still felt no need to define the category of the poor but wanted to increase protection against the intrusion of unwanted outsiders. Therefore, any justice, upon complaint from local officials, could now summarily order a stranger out of the town. To prevent persons from concealing themselves and then claiming residence, settlement could no longer be earned until forty days after a newcomer officially notified authorities, in writing, of his arrival and intentions. And the law established a system of residence certificates. Anyone wishing to move to a new place could thus document his good standing in his previous town and demonstrate its willingness to assume financial responsibility should he fall into need. For those lacking certificates, movement became that much more difficult.[31]

Thus, over the course of the eighteenth century, New York's provincial laws devoted far more attention to the problems of settlement than to the poor. Safeguards against vagrants, not a fear of all dependents, stimulated harsh and rigid legislation. The acts affecting the local poor were brief and unspecific, concerned more with collecting than distributing the funds. But the codes for nonresidents were lengthy, explicit, carefully drawn and revised to insure clarity and efficiency. By the end of the colonial period, stringent procedures helped enforce the distinction between townsman and outsider. Those who satisfied the requirements passed easily from one category to another, but those who could not received all the hostility and suspicion that a Los Angeles policeman gives to a pedestrian in Beverly Hills. The eighteenth-century equivalent of, why are you not driving? was, why are you not in your own town?

The attitudes fundamental to New York's poor laws were found in even more pronounced form in New England. Legislation in the province of Rhode Island, for example, revealed a suspicion of strangers so intense as to seem almost paranoid. Here too the statement of the care of the poor was casual and generous; the assembly instructed towns to "provide carefully for the relief of the poor," and to appoint overseers to fulfill the obligation. But the codes governing the reception of nonresidents were ironclad, erecting the staunchest barriers against intrusion. The statute of 1727 was the important measure. This act, "Enabling the Town Council . . . to receive or reject any persons from becoming inhabitants," tried to prevent "diverse vagrant and indigent persons" from entering the towns and being housed by lax residents. Legislators were convinced that these sort all too often "by their cunning insinuation" prevailed upon some townspeople to post bonds for them, thereby satisfying the existing requirements for residence. The result was that "such profligate persons, by their corrupt morals, too often prove pernicious to towns, in debauching of youth, and enticing of servants to pilfer and steal from their masters." Even when bonded, newcomers still seemed to threaten social order and stability, for the 1727 act declared first that towns need not accept a stranger as resident even if someone posted security for him. Second, any newcomer intending to settle in a town now had to inform local officials within one month of his arrival, and failure to notify subjected him to removal at any time. Moreover, a tavern keeper, innkeeper, or any other townsman who housed a stranger for more than one month without informing town officials was liable for a forty-shilling fine.[32]

Succeeding Rhode Island statutes reinforced these requirements. A law in 1748 spelled out the information a would-be resident was to give officials with a specificity that was testimony to grave suspicions. He was to declare his intentions, his place of birth, his last legal residence, as well as the size of his family. Then, if he was not warned out — that is, told to leave town — in the course of a year, or if he purchased land to the value of £30, or if he successfully completed an apprenticeship, he qualified for residence. The statute also instructed authorities on the method for removing strangers — giving details for everything from town seals and investigations to judicial proceedings, in case two municipalities should disagree about someone's legal residence.[33] In 1765 the assembly reviewed the subject once again, raising from £30 to £40 the property necessary for gaining settlement and widening the towns' discretionary powers by allowing them to refuse settlement not only to strangers with bonds but even to those with certificates of residence and good standing from other localities. Communities were obliged to protect themselves from men "of bad fame and reputation, or such as the Town Council shall judge unsuitable persons to

become inhabitants."³⁴ Thus Rhode Island regulations governing relief remained informal and unspecific, intended for neighbors. But for outsiders, the community adopted some of the
paraphernalia of a bureaucratic society — notices in writing,
questionnaires, time limits and judicial proceedings.

Southern colonies established similar procedures. The Delaware assembly in 1741 passed "An Act for the Relief of the
Poor," and the code's preamble declared its dual purpose: to
provide for "the better relief of the poor," and "the prevention
of straggling and indigent persons from coming into and being
chargeable to the inhabitants." Again, the entrance of strangers
received almost all of the legislators' attention, not the methods
for supporting the needy. The statute first authorized the appointment of overseers of the poor whose primary duty was to
"make diligent inspection and inquiry . . . after all vagrant,
poor and impotent persons . . . coming to settle or otherwise."
It did not matter whether the stranger was a vagrant — able but
unwilling to work — or was poor or disabled — willing but
unable to find or perform work. All were either to post security
or quickly leave the county under the penalty of daily whippings
until they did so. The code next listed numerous restrictions and
penalties for inhabitants boarding a stranger. They were either to
notify local officials of a newcomer's presence — thereby sub-
jecting him to immediate removal — or pay a fine of five shillings
a day plus all the eventual costs of transporting him out of the
county. The law also fixed a one-year waiting period for newcomers to gain settlement, with the further proviso that during
this time they had to be employed or lease property worth at
least fifty shillings a year. Only after these details had been well
arranged did the legislators turn to the question of the poor.
Briefly and directly they empowered local officials to determine
who should receive what amount of public aid.³⁵

The first colony-wide poor law in North Carolina matched
those in other provinces so closely as to confirm the pervasiveness
of these notions. The title of the 1754 law, "An Act for the
Restraint of Vagrants, and for making Provision for the Poor,"
indicates how popular was the division between the outsider and
the local poor; and the preamble, "Whereas diverse idle and
disorderly persons . . . frequently stroll from one county to

another," defines the problem and priorities in the usual terms. The response was also typical. Officials were to whip and then convey the rogue vagabond to his last place of residence; a one-year waiting period was required for settlement; no inhabitant was to board, hire or employ any stranger who did not have a certificate from another county verifying his residence there. The one unusual thing about the North Carolina code was that it forgot to discuss the issue of the poor at all. But this bears testimony to the colonists' willingness and ability forthrightly to relieve neighbors in need.[36]

Most colonial communities relied upon the settlement and poor-relief laws to combat the rogue vagabond and support the needy. But a few of the more densely populated ones thought to equip themselves with two other devices, well known throughout England: the workhouse and the almshouse. Few of these structures for punishing the deviant and incarcerating the dependent were, as we shall soon see, actually constructed. In comparison to the English investment, Americans spent very small sums on them. Nevertheless, some towns and counties did seek and utilize legislative authority to erect the institutions, and their plans reveal a harsh and punitive element in their thinking about the poor. By no means, however, should the importance of this element be exaggerated. Students of this subject have sometimes made the workhouse-almshouse expedient so central to their discussion that they have reported only a repressive quality in eighteenth-century ideas on the poor. This formulation is distorted. Not only in practice but in theory institutions were a minor theme in the colonial story.

The primary function of the workhouse, according to the governing statutes, was to strengthen the provisions of the settlement laws. The threat of incarceration at hard labor was to discourage the needy stranger from entering the community, and to punish him should he be apprehended. The specter of life in such an institution might repel and keep away those who calculated that the returns from begging and pilfering were worth the risk of being warned out and whipped. Legislators also intended the workhouse for other uses. A structure equipped to force inmates to labor seemed an appropriate way to punish the petty criminal. Its terror might deter potential offenders, residents or not, from crime. Finally, the institution's designers believed it could be used for setting the idle among the local poor to work. But this provision came as an afterthought. It was another way to take advantage of the building, but was not the major reason for its construction.

The ranking of these priorities emerges clearly in the Massachusetts workhouse legislation. The assembly, in 1699, passed an "Act for Suppressing and Punishing Rogues, Vagabonds, Common Beggars . . . and Also for Setting the Poor to Work." The first section declared that rogues and vagabonds were to be punished and set to work in the house of correction. The second empowered local justices to send to the workhouse "to be there employed and kept to work, all persons belonging to the same town, being able of body, that live idly or disorderly." But the thrust of the statute went to a concern over the rogue vagabond. This was evident not only in the allocation of space — the first section was twice as long as the second — but in the crucial substantive clause — the bill directed officials to build houses of correction for the rogue vagabond in nondiscretionary language: these structures "shall be erected." But the statute changed tone when treating the town's able-bodied poor. Here the words became conditional: if the town set aside funds for a stock of goods on which the poor could work, then the overseers were to take charge of it. If the justices wished to, they might use the house of correction for the local poor also. This basic difference reflected the degree of seriousness with which the colonists faced the two problems. The first demanded clear and certain action; the second could be handled more or less as the towns saw fit. The one called for strict and severe procedures, the other, discretion.[37]

This distinction also shaped legislation in Connecticut. The assembly issued only the most general instructions for the relief of the poor, first in 1702 and then again, with almost no change, a century later in 1808. They were simple enough: the towns were to maintain their own poor by means of overseers disbursing "what shall be by them judged needful for the relief of the poor."[38] The lack of specificity and the incredible longevity of this law had its obverse in the codes governing settlement. Here,

explicit instructions and frequent revisions of hostile and punitive regulations were characteristic.

As early as the seventeenth century Connecticut had legislated
on strangers, although the first laws merely stipulated that anyone living in a town for three months without being warned out
became its responsibility. This broad provision was soon revised
when at the beginning of the eighteenth century the colony gave
detailed attention to the problem of the rogue vagabond. The
preamble to the act of 1713 makes the prevailing diagnosis and
prescription clear. It complained of the "frequently diverse persons who wander about, and are vagabond, idle and dissolute,"
who beg, insult, curse and lie "to the corruption of manners, the
promotion of idleness, and the detriment of good order and
religion." Carrying the germ of disorder and corruption into the
colony, they had to be effectively quarantined.

To solve the problem, the Connecticut assembly called for the
establishment of houses of correction that would restrain, set to
work, and punish these persons. As almost every section of the act
confirmed, the primary function of these institutions was to
prevent strangers from endangering the town's peace and security. Its preamble located a major source of disorder with "persons
who *wander about*." The text of the law put the rogue vagabond
first on the list of potential inmates for the house, followed by
"other lewd, idle, dissolute, profane and disorderly persons, *that
have no settlement in this colony*." The bill next described other
persons who might invade and injure the town: jugglers,
gamblers, those pretending to occult knowledge in palmistry and
medicine (the wandering quack), fortune-tellers, and those
claiming to be able to locate "lost or stolen goods." In short, the
penalty for running a traveling sideshow was to be the workhouse. Only at the end of the list were town residents named,
men who neglected their callings, who squandered their earnings, or who otherwise did not provide adequately for themselves
or their families. The statute allowed magistrates to commit local
miscreants, the unworthy poor, to the house of correction. But
given allocation of space and the order of listings within the
code, this authorization was probably incidental to the major
goals of the act. Here was another way to use the workhouse, but
certainly not the main reason for building it.[39]

The eighteenth-century statutes governing the almshouse expressed different motives and expectations. The poorhouse was not to be just another name for the workhouse. Its task was to lodge, feed, and perhaps employ the town needy. It did not reflect a new sensitivity to the social dangers posed by the mobile lower classes; rather, and the distinction is important, it revealed a concern for the financial costs of relief. Not that the colonists perceived the presence of poor neighbors as threatening enough to warrant institutionalization, but that they found their tax rates so annoying as to make it seem a useful expedient. In other words, the statutes did not define the needy as a threat to the security of the community but as a monetary inconvenience. The almshouse codes, detailed and precise, formulated administrative guidelines for the institution, not procedures for screening, identifying, examining, penalizing, or reforming the poor. The local dependents were not suspect — at worst they were expensive.

The Pennsylvania poor laws illustrated these viewpoints. Like its sister colonies, the Quaker province passed a series of settlement laws, which grew more stringent during the eighteenth century. In 1718, 1734, and 1771, the legislature made residence requirements more demanding. Not completely satisfied with these measures, it authorized in 1756 the construction of workhouses. In familiar terms the law explained that a "great number of rogues, vagabonds, and otherwise idle and dissolute persons, frequently come from neighboring provinces," and anticipated that a workhouse would at minimal cost protect the community from these dangerous elements.[40] That same year, the assembly empowered Philadelphia to construct a poorhouse, but for very different reasons. The "Act for the Better Employment, Relief, and Support of the Poor within the City of Philadelphia," declared that the care of the city's poor had become very expensive and costs would probably continue to rise "without affording them so comfortable a subsistence as might otherwise be supplied." An almshouse would benefit the poor and the taxpayer alike, giving better treatment at a reduced rate. And since "inhabitants were charitably disposed to contribute largely toward such a good work," the legislature happily encouraged Philadelphia in this venture.[41]

Legislation in other colonies did not always distinguish so

carefully between the workhouse and almshouse. In 1748, the New Jersey assembly, responding to a Middlesex County petition, empowered officials to build a workhouse and a poorhouse. The one would punish rogues, vagabonds, and petty criminals (including anyone who was unwilling to be examined about his settlement), the other would provide a place in which to relieve the poor. But a suspicion toward both groups marked the language of the law and blurred the differences between the two structures. The statute allowed one building to fulfill the two functions and permitted local officials, at their discretion, to employ the poor in the workhouse. Still, the legislators quickly reminded the county that dependents outside the institution had to be supported; and the assembly's role in this venture was passive and modest, not enthusiastic and encouraging. "If the said justices and freeholders of the said county," it announced, "shall think it expedient and necessary to build a Poor-House and Work-House . . . then . . . it shall and may be lawful." Here was legislative sanction but not eager support. This was hardly one of the legislature's pet projects, at the heart of a program of relief.[42]

With these distinctions to mind, we may now turn to the colonists' day-to-day treatment of the poor and the criminal. Although the law did not always correspond to the reality, and attitudes were not always in harmony with practices, Americans did act in predictable and coherent fashion. Their concept of poverty and crime was fundamental to charity and correction in the eighteenth century.

2

Charity and Correction
in the Eighteenth Century

Generalizations about the techniques of colonial relief must be advanced very cautiously. Not only are the records sparse — surviving from a small proportion of settlements — but they are fragmentary. A typical town document lists only the sum given to all the poor — and does not identify particular recipients or explain the cause of their need or the method of support. Or it names the poor and cites the amount of relief but gives no other details. Very occasionally one finds a more complete account, in effect a case history: name of recipient, how relieved, the sum, the causes of dependency, the outcome. Yet this record may be highly idiosyncratic. Perhaps only the unusually fussy community kept such meticulous listings; towns that gave relief more casually asked for less information. But these problems are unavoidable. In the colonial period, as in most other eras of history, materials illuminating the fate of the poor are in short supply.

The essential characteristics of the poor-relief system, if not all its details, can be established. Both the records of eighteenth-century overseers of the poor and the early nineteenth-century statewide relief surveys make clear that the colonial community typically cared for its dependents without disrupting their lives. Wherever possible, it supported members in their own families; in extenuating circumstances of old age, widowhood or debility, it boarded them in a neighboring household. Only a handful of towns maintained an almshouse, and they used it as a last resort, for very special cases; workhouses were even less common in the colonies. As late as 1820, two investigators, Josiah Quincy in Massachusetts and John Yates in New York, discovered that institutional care was still a rarity. Massachusetts, Quincy found, had very few almshouses, and existing ones had almost all been built after 1790. Yates, surveying some one hundred and thirty New York towns and cities, including all the larger ones, learned that only thirty of them maintained almshouses. They too, with few exceptions, dated from the nineteenth century.[1]

The colonists normally supported the poor in community households, not in separate institutions. They found little reason to penalize their needy — poverty seemed trouble enough without adding the pain of separation. A policy of exclusion seemed purposeless since the lower classes were not necessarily subversive of good order and stability. Furthermore, the colonists attributed no special virtues to institutionalization. They were not preoccupied with having an almshouse divide the worthy from the unworthy poor, and they certainly did not believe that incarceration could, or should, alter the character of the poor. Towns, to be sure, were not generous with relief funds. The amounts they allotted at best maintained subsistence levels, although private donations undoubtedly supplemented public aid. But still, if they did not give unstintingly to the needy, at least they did not make them outcasts. Communities dispensed relief straightforwardly, without long investigations or elaborate procedures, without severe discomfort or dislocation.

This outcome did not reflect the colonists' automatic adoption of British practices. An American would have had difficulty in defining the English system, for it followed an almost bewildering variety of procedures. Some poor there received home relief, others went to an almshouse, still others to a workhouse. Although historians have disagreed about the relative size of each of these groups, at least a sizable minority of English towns were anything but casual in dispensing relief.[2] By the end of the eighteenth century, almost four thousand workhouses were scattered through the realm, holding something like one hundred thousand inmates, and philanthropists for three hundred years had been endowing almshouses. Moreover, colonial governors did not insist on one solution, and assembly instructions were, as we have noted, brief and vague. Towns were to care for their poor, but the methods were discretionary. As a result, American practices varied and household relief, neighbor relief, auctions and almshouses were used in one community or another. Yet, as a rule, colonists responded to the problem of poverty in similar ways without being overwhelmed by a sense of danger. They were content to dispense support in the least burdensome manner and eager to avoid institutional solutions.

It is useful to examine closely the practices of a few communities, for the tone and style of the system emerge most clearly in day-to-day decisions. The Virginia parishes are a good beginning point. Their records, not too incomplete, demonstrate what some might doubt — that economically developed southern counties followed the same procedures as New England towns and subsistence agricultural settlements. They too relieved the poor without cautious bureaucratic techniques. In Tidewater as well as Piedmont parishes, whether slaves were a majority or a minority of the population, churchwardens, the overseers of the poor, almost without exception supported dependents at home or in a neighbor's family. An occasional county assigned a contractor responsibility for all the poor, but invariably discontinued the practice after one or two years; a few settlements built and maintained a small almshouse — holding less than ten persons — yet even a minimal investment was unusual. Most parishes, with little discussion or disagreement — if the silence of the documents can be trusted — were satisfied with household relief.

Procedures in St. Paul's parish, in the Piedmont section of the colony, were typical. By the mid-eighteenth century, Hanover County, of which St. Paul was a part, had a population of some 4,250 slaves and a slightly larger number of whites, among whom it could count its most famous son, Patrick Henry. The St. Paul relief registers, undoubtedly incomplete, give details on 97 cases of support between 1706 and 1749, and while they are not proof of the extent of need or the sum of public assistance, they do indicate the traditional methods of care.[3] Regardless of age or sex or condition, the poor of the parish characteristically remained in a community household. Most often, they boarded with a neighboring family. A few stayed in their own homes or with relatives.

The responsibility for lodging the needy did not fall upon one special segment of the population, such as those who were themselves at the bottom of the social ladder. The same names did not recur on the lists of those boarding the poor. Rather, many households assumed the obligation, keeping one of the needy until his departure or demise, and then discontinuing the practice. In almost every instance, fully constituted families, headed by men, performed this task; only infrequently did the poor go to live with a widow. Householders' names rarely reappeared in later years as themselves recipients of aid. Hanover County did have one such case: a Richard Cooper, who frequently received parish payment for digging a grave, normally housed two of the poor; when one died or left, he took in another. When Cooper himself died, his widow kept up the practice, until eventually she became one of the poor and went to board with a neighbor. But this was the proverbial exception. Usually those with some means, not those on the brink of poverty, fulfilled the charge.

Other regions in Virginia followed similar procedures. In some parishes, almost all of the poor boarded with neighbors; in others a large number were relieved at home. In St. Peter's parish, for example (a Tidewater area with close to sixty percent of its population slaves), practices varied from period to period. Between 1700 and 1710, eighteen of the twenty cases that churchwardens noted in their vestry book were supported in a neighbor's household; between 1740 and 1750, of thirty-five cases, sixty percent went to board, the remainder stayed with their family or relatives. Details are scanty, but in all likelihood officials made their decisions on purely pragmatic grounds. They chose the course of least resistance, trying to minimize inconvenience to all parties. A widow with decent lodging and strength enough to sustain herself, or a father temporarily disabled was relieved at home; children were encouraged to take in aged parents. When the poor were without relations, and sick or feeble, a neighbor was reimbursed for assuming the responsibility. Undoubtedly, the assembly had these options in mind when instructing local officers to relieve the needy as they saw fit, to choose the most workable alternative and arrange it.[4]

There are other indications, some more tantalizing than conclusive, of pragmatic treatment. A large number of recipients of public aid in Virginia were men, an unlikely result if fear and suspicion had been rampant. Of the 97 poor listed in the St. Paul parish register, almost half were men, a third were women, and the rest children; of the 60 dependents listed in Blisland parish, a heavily slave-owning area, forty-five percent were men, and a little over a third were women. To be sure, more men may have survived into old age — the toll that childbearing took raising women's mortality rates — and possibly women were more often relieved by private than public sources. Still, in comparison to later figures, these percentages are noteworthy.[5] When nineteenth-century officials exercised a diligent oversight of poor relief, women and children dominated noninstitutional relief rolls. They were, after all, safe to support, less likely to take advantage of relief or to be corrupted by a dole. The larger number of men who were aided at home in the eighteenth century points to a far more complaisant and relaxed attitude. Churchwardens gave greater attention to supporting the poor than to detecting abuses.

Furthermore, the recipients of public aid were not just the sick and the dying, persons whose genuine need would be apparent at a glance. The records suggest a variety of conditions among the parish poor. The St. Paul registers, for example, always designated by name and title the actual recipient of public funds and occasionally even described the service for which he was being reimbursed. In less than thirty percent of the cases was serious illness the cause of the problem. Only to this extent was a doctor reimbursed for treatment, a druggist for medicine, a townsman for digging a grave or covering a burial expense. In other words, less than one-third of the parish poor entered the rolls in clear need of medical assistance, or were buried soon after receiving their first relief. Unfortunately, churchwardens, in dispensing the rest of their funds, listed only the family name and the sum for "support of the poor." But this general description probably included many less obvious cases of need. Also, to judge by the frequency with which names reappeared on relief records, churchwardens responded to both permanent and temporary demands. In Blisland parish, a little over half of the poor received assistance for less than two years; one-third had support for three to eight years, and the remainder stayed on for up to twenty years.[6] Officials extended short-term aid in time of emergency and supported the chronic as long as necessary.

In this same spirit, churchwardens did not discriminate between men and women in methods of treatment. Similar percentages of both sexes received support at home or went off to a neighboring household. In fact, officials tended to reimburse families who took in adult males at a higher rate than those who boarded females; no acute suspicions upset the elementary calculation that it would usually cost more to feed a man than a woman.[7]

Finally, the poor relieved within their own families were generally supported for longer periods of time than those boarding with a neighbor. Here too officials followed the principle of convenience. In Blisland parish, the average period of home support was twice that of neighbor support; of the thirteen cases supported for one year or less, eleven boarded in the community. Had parish churchwardens made distributions reluctantly and suspiciously, they would have tended to keep the longest cases — where the question of malingering could arise — under the supervision of a neighbor, and given only short-term relief at home. But following the simplest procedures, they kept the poor, where possible, at home.

The eighteenth-century system of relief at once reflected the colonists' easy acceptance of the poor and itself encouraged this perspective. One did not, in the first instance, take suspicious persons into one's household, and the very act of boarding made it that much more difficult to conceive of dependents as a class to be distrusted and feared. Also, keeping the needy within the community made it that much less likely that they would be abandoned at a time of crisis. The poor in this era were not invisible. They were next door or, in emergencies, boarding in a neighbor's household. In this way, complacency and responsibility were self-perpetuating.[8]

These principles guided practices in two of the colonies' leading urban centers, New York and Boston. Cities too relieved the poor in the most convenient fashion, relying under normal circumstances upon the household. Unlike Virginia's parishes, and most other eighteenth-century settlements, they did make frequent use of an almshouse, but the institution fulfilled a very special function. It admitted the exceptionally burdensome cases from among the townspeople — those incapable of caring for themselves, without relatives, and so afflicted as to be an onerous responsibility for a neighbor. The almshouse also served as a place for confining the dependent stranger who for one reason or another — serious illness or sudden disability — could not be immediately transported out of the town. In short, the use of the institution in the colonial era was exceptional; few communities depended upon it and even where found, it served only the unusual case. The almshouse was a last resort, for residents who were desperately ill or maimed, and for strangers who could not yet be sent on their way.

The decisions of the New York Mayor's Court — the administrative unit of the city responsible for poor relief — demonstrated these priorities. In 1700, New York opened its first almshouse, a primitive and not very large structure that remained in service for almost a generation. Officials considered it the least preferred treatment. Between 1724 and 1729, the Mayor's Court directed local officials on the disposition of 51 cases, and its instructions took one of three forms: to support the poor at home (18 instances), to board them with a neighbor (19), to enter them in the almshouse (14).[9] The assignments were not haphazard, and each group had its distinguishing characteristics. Those relieved at home were members of a functioning household. They were couples where one of the partners had fallen ill, perhaps only temporarily, or mothers with children still physically able to maintain a household, or competent widows. In one instance, the court decided to give funds to the wife of an insane but harmless man to care for him and their children; it saw no need to use the institution when the household could fulfill the task. Dependents put to board with neighbors were usually unable to care for themselves and were without relatives to assist them. They were orphans, or abandoned children, expectant but unwed mothers, or those vaguely described as sick or old, who probably needed some care and supervision as well as money. Those whom the Mayor's Court sent to the almshouse had much more serious ailments. They were missing limbs, were lame or

1. The New York almshouse, 1735. Built in the style of an ordinary residence, the almshouse followed, internally and externally, the organization of the family.

blind, were already in a neighbor's house but deteriorating physically, were very sick or very old ("ancient," in the language of the day). Or they were the archetype of the stranger — sailors, or others without ties to the community — who had been injured or suddenly fallen severely ill and would probably perish on the streets if not relieved. In essence, then, the Mayor's Court kept the disabled husband with his family, sent the orphan to a neighbor, and institutionalized the decrepit outsider.

In 1735, New York opened a new and larger almshouse which remained in use, with several additions and frequent renovations, through the eighteenth century. Faced with mounting costs and numerous migrants, officials expected the structure to save the city both money and trouble. Between 1700 and 1735, New York's population had more than doubled, reaching 10,600, and its commercial growth was attracting a host of newcomers — from ambitious merchants to drifting sailors. In the same period, the sums allotted for poor relief also doubled, and while this was not disproportionate to the increase in settlers, still the larger expenditure prompted concern.[10] In a first burst of enthusiasm for the innovation, the town council passed a harsh, and unworkable law, ordering all the poor into the almshouse. Within the institution, officials were to separate "those who have been ancient housekeepers and lived in good reputation . . . from the other poor who are become so by vice and idleness," but only so "far as may be without inconvenience." Churchwardens were to assist only the needy who were "willing to be maintained in the Workhouse and Poorhouse of this city, and do forthwith repair thither to be relieved and maintained therein."[11] Yet despite these rigid and legalistic instructions, relief at home continued unabated, and the almshouse did not become the exclusive setting for support. Within a decade the inmates in the new structure closely resembled those who had filled the earlier one.

The surviving records of almshouse admissions describe some fifty cases between 1736 and 1746, from a total probably four times as large. This small sample makes clear that despite council regulations, the institution still served primarily as a place of last resort.[12] The great majority of inmates either suffered from major disabilities — and could not have been easily relieved within a household — or were strangers, not likely to be taken into a family. One-quarter of them were lame or blind, insane or idiotic; another quarter were not only very old but infirm, sickly, and weak — in all likelihood, senile and incapacitated. Some fifteen percent were young and parentless children — the orphaned and the deserted — who would remain until beginning an apprenticeship. At least another ten percent were unmistakably strangers — a mother and her children recovering from a shipwreck, an injured traveler. In fact, their numbers in the almshouse were probably much greater, but officials did not yet keep systematic records of residence. Among the rest, one finds elderly couples, with indications that both partners were seriously ill, and mothers with their children, either so incapacitated that they could not care for them, or caught in need as they were passing through the town. Even without evidence available on the comparable characteristics of recipients of neighborhood relief, it is apparent that the institution held the exceptional case. The New York poor did not live in constant dread of the poorhouse.

The Boston almshouse served a similar function. Indeed, this city, as the commercial center of the colonies, was the first to establish an almshouse in America. It began operating in 1664 although nothing is known about its original size or character. Its eighteenth-century successor, much less obscure, was neither a typical setting for relieving the poor nor a place of punishment. As an exceptionally complete roster of admissions makes clear, the institution held the unusual case — residents who did not fit into a system of household support and strangers caught in need. Institutionalization did not reflect a scrupulous oversight of the dependent classes or acute suspicions. The almshouse lodged residents who were incapable of caring for themselves, were without relatives to assume the responsibility, and would have greatly inconvenienced a neighbor. It also admitted strangers in need — to prevent them from perishing; but they, unlike the chronic poor of the town, were supposed to be soon on their way. There was, then, a highly pragmatic quality about admissions to Boston's almshouse.

It was a busy institution. Between 1764 and 1769, a period for which the records remain especially full, the almshouse admitted

174 men, 236 women, 25 couples, and 72 unattached children.[13] In most instances, obvious and compelling reasons dictated the overseers' decisions. Almost half of the men, at the very least, were strangers to the city; most often they were simply in need, occasionally they were also sick or injured. Their tenure was usually brief, as they moved on to another town or sometimes to the grave. The townsmen in the almshouse were the sick (with smallpox as well as other diseases) and the aged (typically in their seventies and fully deserving the designation of "ancient"). A small group of them were acutely disabled, crippled or blind. It is little wonder that neighbors allowed them to pass on to the almshouse.

The large number of women inmates also indicates that the institution served the most helpless and dependent classes. Once again, eighteenth-century figures reversed nineteenth-century ones. In the pre–Civil War period, women filled the outdoor relief rolls, men, the almshouse. But this was not true in the colonial era. And just as the proportions in the Virginia parishes suggested the lack of suspicion with which Americans dispensed relief, so the many women in the Boston institution were evidence of its nonpunitive character as a last resort. The women in its halls were the aged widows and the sick, those who had outlived their husbands, had not accumulated savings, and whose children or relatives had died or disappeared. Unmarried expectant mothers were numerous, with no place to go and incapable of self-support. Many mothers with children entered the institution — usually when they or their charges were sick. Finally, some of the women were strangers, but not nearly so many as among the men.[14] Few women took to the road alone in the eighteenth century, except for those of dubious character like prostitutes. But what was the community to do with that mother who, with two children in hand and a third all too obviously on the way, entered Boston? The almshouse was a useful place on such occasions.

The circumstances surrounding the admission of the handful of couples also demonstrated the special functions of the institution. Very sound reasons kept these people from being relieved at home. Thirteen of the 25 were strangers to the city, without a household of their own in which to receive aid. Some of them were soon discharged to continue on their way; the others were not only outsiders, but old and sickly, both over seventy, or with terminal diseases, and so they did not remain a charge within the institution for very long. The husbands and wives who were Boston residents were too severely ill or disabled — both suffering from smallpox, or over eighty years old and totally incapacitated — to maintain themselves or board conveniently in a neighboring household. These case histories can well symbolize the almshouse population.

The last group in the institution was also the most impermanent — orphans and deserted children, without families or relations. The older ones were temporary residents, waiting for the overseers of the poor to arrange an apprenticeship. The younger ones remained until they too were of an age to board out. Only the severely handicapped stayed on, so the younger permanent almshouse residents closely resembled the adults there: both were disqualified from taking a place in the community at large.

These findings are the more significant when compared with the number of poor receiving outdoor relief in Boston and those confined to the city workhouse. Although little precise information survives on the types of cases relieved at home, a 1757 petition to the Massachusetts assembly for tax relief declared that the total number of persons relieved that year in Boston was about one thousand; since the almshouse treated a total of 250 inmates annually, it is clear that three times as many persons were being supported at home as in the institution.[15] The great majority of the poor received relief within the community.

Hardly any of them entered a workhouse. Boston was one of the few places in the colonies to erect a workhouse — New York, for example, did not follow this practice. Even so, the building was of very restricted use, holding only forty people two years after its opening. Although its size may have increased over the next decades, it seems that many of its inmates really belonged in the almshouse proper. In 1751, overseers, attempting to explain why the workhouse was costing the city considerable money, blamed the high costs of maintenance on "the number of distracted, helpless, and infirm people supported therein." In short, the institution was not much else than an adjunct to the poorhouse.[16]

The Boston almshouse and its counterparts elsewhere did not

function as places of punishment or stand as monuments to warn the poor to mend their ways. Officials set their sights very low, at most hoping that the poor stranger would not return and endanger the community. They simply tried to provide a substitute household for those who lacked their own and could not easily fit in with a neighbor. Nothing better demonstrates this aim than the external appearance and internal routine of the eighteenth-century almshouse. It looked and was run like an ordinary household, and years after its founding, something makeshift and ad hoc remained about it.

The almshouse patterned itself upon the family, following this model as closely as possible. The structure, typically located well within town boundaries, lacked both a distinctive architecture and special administrative procedures. Some settlements did not bother to construct a poorhouse; instead, they purchased a local farmhouse and used it without altering the room divisions. The new buildings were also indistinguishable from any other residence, except occasionally by size. The New York City Common Council was only concerned that its almshouse be "a good, strong, and convenient House and Tenement," qualities that any homeowner would list. The one unique thing about the Baltimore almshouse was that it sat on "Almshouse Street"; otherwise the structure, with its two stories and two chimneys and symmetrical plan, resembled every other neighborhood building. It was a perfectly ordinary setting for any family to occupy, complete to the decent-sized garden in front. A passerby could not have identified the function of the building from its form.[17]

The model of the family also shaped the interior arrangements and the daily routine of the almshouse. The keeper and his family lived in the institution, and the requirements for the post were as minimal as those required of family heads. New York City officials wanted someone who was simply "able and sufficient"; they chose a married man from several applicants and set aside a first-floor room of the almshouse for living quarters for him, his wife, and child. The residents also lived as they would in a family. They dressed in everyday clothing, not in special uniforms; their shifts were of ordinary color and make, just what the lower classes would wear. They slept several to a room and to a bed, as crowded families did; they were probably segregated by sex, but certainly not rigorously. Whatever furniture or linen they possessed could be brought to and used in the almshouse. They ate their meals together, with the keeper and his family. They walked — not marched — about the house, and lived as free of discipline and organization as any member of a normal household. They joined twice a week, as good Christians would, in prayer. One finds occasional complaints that the poor were abusing these privileges: going into town, for example, to sell their clothing and buy beer. And some establishments regulated the hours for bolting the doors and going to bed. But ordinarily, the almshouse functioned like a large household. Even the terminology describing the structure and population pointed to the significance of the model. It was an alms*house*, not an asylum. The residents were a *family*, not inmates.[18]

Patterned after the family, yet considered a place of last resort, the almshouse was typical of all eighteenth-century service institutions. The insane were usually supported at home, their illness making them one of the poor; only when they were uncontrollable, threatening the safety of relatives and neighbors, did towns seek alternatives. Those equipped with an almshouse put lunatics in an empty attic or cellar, to suffer alone. A community that lacked this option sometimes devised a special structure, which however rudimentary or elaborate, was invariably designed as a substitute household. Thus, officials in the early colonial period at times confined the violent insane in shacks and huts set up for the occasion on the commons. One local Pennsylvania court directed a village in 1676 to build "a little block-house" for a dangerous lunatic; unfit to live in another household, he would have a crude one of his own.[19] Even more striking, the designers of the first hospital exclusively for the insane in the American colonies, opened at Williamsburg, Virginia, intended it for a last resort, when the family did not, or could not, take responsibility. The burgesses, concerned that "several persons of insane and disordered minds have frequently been found wandering in different parts of this colony," established in 1769 a lunatic asylum. Although it might help to cure those not "quite desperate," its primary task was to preserve the peace of the community, to keep the insane from roaming about. Accordingly, no insane would be admitted to Virginia's new

2. *The Friends Asylum for the Insane. Private philanthropic associations, like those formed by the Quakers, attempted to relieve the insane in casual, nonregimented settings.*

FROM THE COLLECTIONS OF THE LIBRARY COMPANY OF PHILADELPHIA

institution if relatives or friends agreed to look after his welfare and behavior. When no one would take the charge, the asylum served as a surrogate household.[20]

The first hospitals for the sick fulfilled a similar function. In many places, the almshouse itself became an infirmary, an unintended result of its admissions policy. Since the most difficult cases and the ones that the community had the least desire to accommodate were often the diseased, the sick made up a sizable proportion of the almshouse population. As the institution became a collection point for illness, doctors became regular and salaried attendants, and soon they were training students there. The structure remained, of course, the least preferred setting for medical treatment, and people with sufficient funds received care at home. But by the end of the colonial period, the almshouse had become a hospital for the poor.[21]

A few communities erected a separate institution for the sick, probably the most famous of which was the Pennsylvania Hospital, established in 1751 with public and private aid. The hospital, its founders explained, would first house the ailing poor who, coming to Philadelphia in search of medical care, had extraordinary difficulty in locating and paying for a lodging. The institution would also admit poor residents, who were all too often "badly accommodated in times of sickness." They could be far better treated if brought together "under one inspection, and in the hands of skillful practitioners." Finally, the hospital would take in the insane, those "unhappily disordered in their senses," who wander about "to the terror of their neighbors, there being no place (except the House of Correction) in which they might be confined and subjected to proper management for their recovery."

The hospital would help to train medical personnel and attempt to effect cures. But its designers, conceiving of institutions as substitute households, gave their attention to the sick stranger, the ill-kept resident, the wandering insane.[22] The value of the place rested not only on its recoveries — which undoubtedly were as welcome as they were rare — but on gathering in the homeless.

The colonists confronted deviant behavior with far more intricate and severe measures. The equanimity that marked their treatment of the poor did not carry over to the criminal. Under the influence of religious definitions and community perspectives, they relied upon punishments that ranged from warning out strangers to capital sentences for multiple offenders. Still, a fundamental similarity marked their policies. Just as the alms-house was not the typical place of support, so too the jail was not the ordinary mechanism of correction. Americans depended primarily upon noninstitutional mechanisms in treating both the dependent and the deviant.

The enforcement of settlement laws, which stood midway between poor relief and crime prevention measures, was one basic technique by which colonial communities guarded their good order and tax money. Towns everywhere used their legal prerogatives to exclude the harmless poor, who might someday need support, and suspicious characters, who could disturb their safety and security. Great variation existed in practice, with some officials more efficient and diligent, others more perfunctory and lackadaisical, in apprehending and dispatching strangers. But rural hinterlands and urban centers had frequent recourse to these measures in the eighteenth century. Town records often refer to constabulary actions, to rumors heard and decisions taken. Officials warned out widows with children and unwed mothers with bastards; the one would drain relief funds, the other would imperil morality. Overseers expelled poor but healthy strangers and others of bad reputation.[23] When a non-resident was ill or disabled, as well as destitute, towns like New York and Boston put him into the almshouse; but no sooner could he move under his own power, then they sent him on, if necessary paying for his transportation.[24]

It is difficult to make precise judgments on the efficacy of these measures. Often officials acted without notifying the town meeting or keeping a record, so that the number of men warned out cannot be known. It is also very possible that the real effect of settlement laws, as in New England, for example, was to discourage strangers in advance from entering a town. The silence of a document may be compelling testimony to the law's potency and the insularity of the community. But the frequent revisions of these codes, with their preambles complaining that the poor stranger was still wandering into towns, may point to the im-

3. *Colonial Philadelphia's public charitable institutions. The clustering of institutions oc-curred first in the larger eighteenth-century cities. As Philadelphia grew, each of the build-ings added wings to the original houselike frame structure.*

potence of legal proceedings. We know too little, however, about population movements to reach precise conclusions. Nonetheless, it is clear that one colonial response to the problem of deviancy was to try to maintain order through insularity, like a quarantine against a disease. Yet nowhere was this method enough. Some strangers entered every town, even the most self-contained New England community, to commit offenses, and residents also broke the law. Settlement laws could be just one part of the system of social control.[25]

Eighteenth-century criminal codes fixed a wide range of punishments. They provided for fines, for whippings, for mechanisms of shame like the stocks, pillor and public cage, for banishment, and for the gallows. They used one technique or a combination of them, calling for a fine together with a period in the stocks, or for a whipping to be followed by banishment. The laws frequently gave the presiding magistrate discretion to choose among alternatives — to fine or to whip — or directed him to select the applicable one — to use the stocks if the offender could not pay his fine. They included some ingenious punishments, such as having a convicted felon mount the gallows, remain for an hour with a noose around his neck, and then go free. Rarely, however, did the statutes rely upon institutionalization. A sentence of imprisonment was uncommon, never used alone. Local jails held men caught up in the *process of judgment,* not those who had completed it: persons awaiting trial, those convicted but not yet punished, debtors who had still to meet their obligations. The idea of serving time in a prison as a method of correction was the invention of a later generation.[26]

The two most widely used penalties in the eighteenth century were the fine and the whip, the one, according to the closest students of colonial law enforcement, "the sanction par excellence," the other, "the afflictive penalty most favored" in provincial justice. The fine was a comparatively sophisticated punishment, presuming that the offender had property whose loss would be chastening. If forfeiture was to discourage recidivism, the criminal had not only to believe that the accumulation of money was an important goal, but to have been successful at it. It could not, therefore, operate with equal effectiveness over the entire population. The whip, on the other hand, was a more elementary punishment that complemented the fine. It did not require that the offender have property or share common attitudes beyond the most simple desire to avoid searing pain. Hence, the statutes fixing a penalty of a fine often provided that persons unable to pay the costs were to be whipped. Where one punishment was inappropriate, magistrates had recourse to the other. No clear-cut division by type of offense distinguished those who received a fine from those who received a whipping. The circumstances of the criminal, not just the crime, determined the penalty.[27]

Another common sentence in the colonial codes was the stocks, prescribed as an alternative to the fine for minor crimes. To be painfully confined on public display for several hours seemed a fitting punishment for men without property who disturbed the peace or were drunk and disorderly. In Massachusetts, anyone guilty of cursing or drunkenness was fined five shillings; those unable to pay remained three hours in the stocks. A similar alternative faced those guilty in New York of violating the Sabbath.[28] Finding stocks convenient and useful devices, the colonists erected them quickly, even before a courthouse or a jail, and kept them in good repair. As early as 1662, the Virginia burgess ordered every county to build stocks, along with a whipping post and pillory, or be liable for a fine of five thousand pounds of tobacco. Almost one hundred years later, the North Carolina legislature still cautioned officials to maintain the structures properly.[29]

Stocks also fit well with the colonists' notions of a self-policing community. To sit cramped for several hours was certainly discomforting but if pain alone was the goal, townspeople could have relied exclusively upon the whip. The added expense of building and repairing such a device was unnecessary. But in fact, the stocks operated not only in a physical but in a psychological way, as a mechanism of shame. The offender was held up to the ridicule of his neighbors, a meaningful punishment and important deterrent where communities were closely knit. The colonists used several similar mechanisms. Offenders stood on public display in a pillory, their head and arms inserted through openings in a wooden brace; criminals were driven through the town in a cart and then whipped for good measure.

Branding was another variant — a letter imprinted or worn to signify the offense — a practice familiar from Hawthorne's *Scarlet Letter*. Such a punishment could be physically painful and also had a biblical, Cain-Abel quality about it. But it also presumed a society in which reputation was an important element in social control, where men ordered their behavior in fear of a neighbor's scorn.

This perspective was also at the root of another popular sentence in the eighteenth century: whipping and expulsion for the nonresident offender. The standard court response to a stranger guilty of a noncapital crime was to order him flogged and banished. In New York City, for example, the Mayor's Court between 1733 and 1743 set this punishment for practically every nonresident guilty of theft. Carefully noting that the criminal was a "wandering" or "strolling" vagrant, the magistrates ordered them to receive, regardless of sex, thirty to forty lashes, and then be on their way. The advantages of the whip lay with its cheapness, its speed, and its effect upon those without property. The element of exclusion reflected the community's narrow definition of responsibility and its attempt to be self-policing. If the deviant, by virtue of his legal residence elsewhere, was someone else's problem, if he was outside the nexus of local relationships, then the quicker he was gone, the better.[30]

A shortsightedness, however, marked this decision. The town was rid of the disease, but without concerning itself about the spread of the contagion to others. This punishment also increased the community's need and desire to scrutinize the stranger. By expelling nonresident offenders, each town increased the likelihood that men on the move might be criminals. Since every constable knew the kind of men he escorted to the town line, he had good reason to examine the credentials of newcomers approaching his domain. In brief, a system of banishment demanded a rigorous oversight of admissions.

Despite the colonists' efforts to fit the punishment to the criminal, fines and stocks, whippings and banishment were very tenuous and limited ways of enforcing the public safety. The system attempted to be flexible but to an exceptional degree, the efficacy of the punishment depended upon the active compliance of the offender. Although this is to some extent true of all corrections (that no one can force a deviant to become law-abiding, only penalize his behavior), in the eighteenth century, the agencies of law enforcement were so weak and undeveloped that the punitive and coercive aspects of the law bore an unusually heavy burden.[31] Communities faced an obvious problem: what if the whippings did not discourage the culprit or if he repeatedly ignored the order of expulsion? What if an offender considered the fine a risk worth taking in his search for higher, but illegal returns, or if he lost all shame and embarrassment before his neighbors? What recourse did citizens have against these contingencies?

The colonists' solution to these problems was to define broadly the number of capital offenses. The religious impulse to punish crime as sin encouraged this practice. But the gallows were also to compensate for all the other shortcomings and defects of the criminal codes. The result was imbalance and inflexibility, a vacillation between lenient and harsh punishment. The statutes defined a large number and variety of capital crimes, and the courts were not reluctant to inflict the penalty. The gallows was the only method by which they could finally coerce obedience and protect the community. In the absence of punishments in the middle range, they depended extensively upon the discipline of the hangman.

The New York Supreme Court in the pre-Revolutionary era regularly sentenced criminals to death, with slightly more than twenty percent of all its penalties capital ones. When magistrates believed that the fundamental security of the city was in danger, as in the case of a slave revolt in 1741, the court responded with great severity (burning to death thirteen of the rebellion's leaders and hanging nineteen others). Even in less critical times, the court had frequent recourse to the scaffold — for those convicted of pickpocketing, burglary, robbery, counterfeiting, horse-stealing, and grand larceny as well as murder. Most of the petty criminals were second and third offenders. The New York courts either pardoned the first offender, using the ancient formula of "benefit of clergy" for legal trapping, or prescribed the whip or the fine. But recidivism inevitably brought the gallows. It was the only recourse the colonists believed they had when more lenient discipline was inadequate.[32]

This progression in penalties was also built into the Massachusetts codes. Convinced that "the punishments already provided by law against stealing, have proved ineffectual," the assembly in 1736 ordered that a thief upon first conviction was to be fined or whipped. The next time he would pay treble damages, sit for an hour upon the gallows platform with a rope around his neck, and then be carted to the whipping post for thirty stripes. For the third offense, he would be hung. So too, a burglar would be initially branded with the letter B on his forehead; after his second crime, he would sit on the gallows platform, be carted and whipped; for the third, he was to "suffer the pains of death as being incorrigible."[33] The colonists' rationale was clear: anyone impervious to the fine and the whip, who did not mend his ways after an hour with a noose about him, was uncontrollable and therefore had to be executed.

Practice, of course, did not always follow so fixed a formula. As the career of one "notorious Isaac Frasier" well illustrated, events could take a more cataclysmic course. Just before his execution, Frasier recounted his life in crime to a group of Connecticut ministers eager to publicize his story as a warning to others. He told them how infrequently he was apprehended for his many thefts, how when convicted he would be only lightly punished. He would have to return the stolen goods and frequently leave town, but since his past record did not follow him from place to place, he never approached the gallows. Suddenly, one day, his reputation caught up with him, and a Connecticut court, fully informed of his history, passed the death sentence. Frasier's life in crime aptly demonstrated the fragility of eighteenth-century law enforcement. The criminal went undetected or was mildly punished time and again, until abruptly he ended up on the gallows. The colonists, however, saw no alternatives. Capital punishment, they believed, was an act of self-preservation.[34]

Local jails were found throughout the colonies, and in decent repair. Some towns utilized part of the courthouse building, others erected a separate structure. But regardless of form, these institutions had only limited functions. They held persons about to be tried or awaiting sentence or unable to discharge contracted debts. They did not, however, except on rare occasions, confine convicted offenders as a means of correction. The jails facilitated the process of criminal punishment but were not themselves instruments of discipline. They did not expand in function during the course of the eighteenth century to become a method for penalizing as well as detaining offenders.

The colonists might have adopted a penitentiary system in order to reform the criminal, or to terrify him, or simply to confine him. They could have attempted to mold him into an obedient citizen, or to frighten him into lawful conduct or, at least, to prevent him, if for only a limited period, from injuring the community. But given their conception of deviant behavior and institutional organization, they did not believe that a jail could rehabilitate or intimidate or detain the offender. They placed little faith in the possibility of reform. Prevailing Calvinist doctrines that stressed the natural depravity of man and the powers of the devil hardly allowed such optimism. Since temptations to misconduct were not only omnipresent but practically irresistible, rehabilitation could not serve as the basis for a prison program.[35] Moreover, local officials believed that a policy of expulsion offered the community some protection against recidivism. Institutionalization seemed unnecessary when numerous offenders could be marched beyond the town line and not be seen again.

The failure to broaden the functions of the jail also revealed the colonists' dependence upon the family model for organizing an institution. Since life in a prison would perforce duplicate that in a large household, they saw no reason to believe institutionalization would discourage the criminal or even offer the community a temporary respite. A household existence did not seem either painful or corrective. Had they looked about for other possible models, they might have come upon military ones, but to them it would have seemed foolhardy to adopt a discipline that insured maximum protection against external attack, when it was the community and not the inmates that stood in danger. They might have considered monastery procedures, the cellular and isolated existence of monks, but this appeared to be a

4. *The Walnut Street jail, Philadelphia, 1770. The colonial jail, like the other institutions, followed the household model. Its design fit well with its limited function; clearly this structure was not intended for the long-term detention of criminals.*
COURTESY OF THE PENNSYLVANIA PRISON SOCIETY

routine for the already committed and dedicated, men in every way different from criminals.

The institutions already functioning in the colonies did not substantially depart from the family model. The almshouse ran like a large household. Since officials appropriately considered admission a privilege, penalizing anyone who tried to enter it illegally, the poorhouse was hardly an inspiration for a prison system. The occasional workhouse was not a more useful guide; the few to be found in America had not established a disciplinary or punitive routine. In fact, a visitor to the Boston workhouse would have found it almost identical to the almshouse. Some minor regulations differed; the workhouse was to lock its gates, check callers, and question inmates who claimed to be sick. Over its entranceway a slogan suggested that steady labor might improve character. But in design, the workhouse was to be no more than the family at work, and it did not actually achieve even that standard. Its inmates were practically indistinguishable from those in the almshouse, almost all broken by age and disease; neither group could carry out a day's work.[36] In short, the colonists had little incentive to confine criminals in such a setting.

Eighteenth-century jails in fact closely resembled the household in structure and routine. They lacked a distinct architecture and special procedures. When the Virginia burgess required that county prisons be "good, strong, and substantial," and explicitly recommended that they follow "after the form of Virginia housing," results were in keeping with these directions. The doors were perhaps somewhat sturdier, the locks slightly more impressive, but the general design of the jail was the same as for an ordinary residence. True to the household model, the keeper and his family resided in the jail, occupying one of its rooms; the prisoners lived several together in the others, with little to differentiate the keeper's quarters from their own. They wore no special clothing or uniforms and usually neither cuffs nor chains restrained their movements. They walked — not marched — about the jail. The workhouse model was so irrelevant that nowhere were they required to perform the slightest labor.[37]

Jail arrangements so closely replicated the household that

some colonists feared that prisons would be comfortable enough to attract inmates. Far from striking terror, they would build a clientele willing to be decently supported in return for a temporary deprivation of liberty. This is why towns frequently required prisoners to provide their own food and "to use such bedding, linen and other necessaries as they think fit, without their being purloined, detained, or they paying [the jailer] for the same." So long as they did not cost the town money, inmates could make living arrangements as pleasant and as homelike as they wished. A few communities carried this logic to its end and simply dispensed with a jail, allowing those awaiting trial to post security and stay at home. Once assured that the offender would come to court, they saw no difference between the household and the prison.[38]

The colonial jails were not only unlikely places for intimidating the criminal, but even ill-suited for confining him. Security was impossible to maintain, and escapes were frequent and easy. Conditions were sometimes so lax that towns compelled a prisoner to post a bond that he would remain in the jail, especially if he wished the privilege of exercising in the yard. Some assemblies tried to tighten control by holding the jailer responsible for the debts of an escaped prisoner; others devised a variety of inducements for night watchmen to keep a sharp lookout for escapees, or decreed without worrying about enforcement that an escape was tantamount to a plea of guilty to the pending charge. Still others appointed a special guard for prisoners held on serious charges like murder, hoping that an ad hoc arrangement would compensate for the jail's general weakness. No one placed very much confidence in these structures.[39] Even at the close of the colonial period, there was no reason to think that the prison would soon become central to criminal punishment.

3

The Challenge of Crime

Eighteenth-century notions of dependency and deviancy did not survive for very long into the nineteenth, nor did its methods of dispensing charity and correction. The social, intellectual, and economic changes that differentiated the states of the new republic from the several colonies prompted a critical reappraisal and revision of the ideas and techniques of social control. Americans felt compelled to rethink inherited procedures and devise new methods to replace old ones. They devoted extraordinary attention to this issue, hoping to establish quickly and effectively alternatives to the colonial system.

Between 1790 and 1830, the nation's population greatly increased and so did the number and density of cities. Even gross figures reveal the dimensions of the change. In these forty years, the population of Massachusetts almost doubled, in Pennsylvania it tripled, and in New York it increased five times; border and midwestern states, practically empty in 1790, now held over three million people. At Washington's inauguration, only two hundred thousand Americans lived in towns with more than twenty-five hundred people; by Jackson's accession, the number exceeded one million. In 1790, no American city had more than fifty thousand residents. By 1830, almost half a million people lived in urban centers larger than that.[1] During these same years factories began to dot the New England and mid-Atlantic rivers. The decade of the 1830's witnessed the first accelerated growth of manufacturing in the nation.[2] At the same time, Enlightenment ideas challenged Calvinist doctrines; the prospect of boundless improvement confronted a grim determinism.[3] But these general trends are not sufficient to explain the very specific reactions to the issue of deviant and dependent behavior. To them must be added Americans' understanding of these changes. Under the influence of demographic, economic and intellectual developments, they perceived that the traditional mechanisms of social control were obsolete. The premises upon which the colonial system had been based were no longer valid.

Each change encouraged Americans to question inherited practices and to devise new ones. Inspired by the ideals of the Enlightenment, they considered older punishments to be barbaric and traditional assumptions on the origins of deviant behavior to be misdirected. Movement to cities, in and out of territories, and up and down the social ladder, made it difficult for them to believe that a sense of hierarchy or localism could now stabilize society. When men no longer knew their place or station, self-policing communities seemed a thing of the past. Expanding political loyalties also made colonial mechanisms appear obsolete. Citizens' attachment to state governments promoted a broader definition of responsibility, so that a sentence of banishment seemed a parochial response. The welfare of the commonwealth demanded that towns no longer solve their problems in such narrow and exclusive ways.

This awareness provoked at least as much anxiety as celebration. Americans in the Jacksonian period could not believe that geographic and social mobility would promote or allow order and stability. Despite their marked impatience and dissatisfaction with colonial procedures, they had no ready vision of how to order society. They were still trapped in many ways in the rigidities of eighteenth-century social thinking. They knew well that the old system was passing, but not what ought to replace it. What in their day was to prevent society from bursting apart? From where would the elements of cohesion come? More specifically, would the poor now corrupt the society? Would criminals roam out of control? Would chaos be so acute as to drive Americans mad?[4] All of these questions became part of a full, intense, and revealing investigation of the origins of deviant and dependent behavior. To understand why men turned criminal or became insane or were poor would enable reformers to strengthen the social order. To comprehend and control abnormal behavior promised to be the first step in establishing a new system for stabilizing the community, for binding citizens together. In this effort, one finds the clearest indications of how large-scale social changes affected thinking and actions of Americans in the Jacksonian period. And here one also finds the crucial elements that led to the discovery of the asylum.

In the immediate aftermath of independence and nationhood, Americans believed that they had uncovered both the prime cause of criminality in their country and an altogether effective antidote. Armed with patriotic fervor, sharing a repugnance for things British and a new familiarity with and faith in Enlightenment doctrines, they posited that the origins and persistence of deviant behavior would be found in the nature of the colonial criminal codes. Established in the days of oppression and ignorance, the laws reflected British insistence on severe and cruel punishments. The case of William Penn seemed typical. He had attempted to introduce mild and humane legislation into his province, drawing up the Great Law of 1682, but the crown, in the person of Queen Anne, had callously disallowed it. "The mild voice of reason and humanity," explained New York Quaker Thomas Eddy, "reached not the thrones of princes or the halls of legislators." The mother country had stifled the colonists' benevolent instincts, compelling them to emulate the crude customs of the old world. The result was the predominance of archaic and punitive laws that only served to perpetuate crime.[5]

A reading of the Enlightenment tract of Cesare Beccaria verified for Americans in the 1790's the link between barbaric laws and deviant behavior. The treatise, *On Crimes and Punishments,* first appeared in 1764, was quickly translated, and was already being quoted by John Adams as early as 1770 in defense of the British soldiers implicated in the Boston Massacre. Beccaria insisted, and American experience seemed to confirm, that "if we glance at the pages of history, we will find that laws, which surely are, or ought to be, compacts of free men, have been, for the most part, a mere tool of the passions of some." They were all too often not only inhuman but self-defeating. "The severity of punishment of itself emboldens men to commit the very wrongs it is supposed to prevent," Beccaria announced. "They are driven to commit additional crimes to avoid the punishment for a single one. The countries and times most notorious for severity of penalties have always been those in which the bloodiest and most inhumane of deeds were committed." Punishment, to be effective, had to be unavoidable. "The certainty of a punishment, even if it be moderate, will always make a stronger impression than the fear of another which is more terrible but combined with the hope of impunity." Beccaria's summary advice was succinct and his program straightforward: "Do you want to prevent crimes? See to it that the laws are clear and simple and that the entire force of a nation is united in their defense."[6]

The young republic quickly took this message to heart, for it fit well with its own history and revolutionary ideals. Americans fully appreciated that the laws could be a tool of the passions of a handful of men. Did this not explain almost every piece of British colonial legislation after 1763? They believed that they had also witnessed the self-defeating quality of cruel punishments. Had not colonial juries often let a prisoner go free rather than condemn him to the gallows for a petty theft? In this way, criminals had escaped all discipline, and the community had allowed, even encouraged, them to persist in their ways. But independence in this new world made the time and place right for reform. The rhetoric of the Revolution had prepared Americans to fulfill a grand mission, and now they would demonstrate how to uplift one part of mankind, the criminal class. With the Revolution, declared Eddy, fitting Beccaria's doctrine into an American context, "the spirit of reform revived . . . strengthened by the general principles of freedom." The criminal codes of New York had to be revised, for the state could not tolerate laws of "barbarous usages, corrupt society, and monarchical principles . . . [so] imperfectly adopted to a new country, simple manners, and a popular form of government."[7]

Independence made citizens increasingly appreciative of conditions in the new world. They were not Englishmen, and their setting was not England's either. In 1793, William Bradford of Philadelphia explained in a widely read pamphlet, *An Enquiry how far the Punishment of Death is Necessary in Pennsylvania,* that the new nation was the ideal place for enacting Beccaria's principles. "It is from ignorance, wretchedness or corrupted manners of a people that crime proceeds," declared Bradford.

"In a country where these do not prevail moderate punishments strictly enforced, will be a curb as effectual as the greatest severity." America, a New York reform society declared, was "a land where the theatre of experiment is boundless. The relations of civil society were few and simple, and the complex abuses of long existing systems, in social order, were unknown." Southern states heard the same message. One Virginia legislator urged his colleagues to revise and moderate the criminal laws to make punishments "comport with the principles of our government."[8] And Robert Turnbull, returning from a visit north, counseled the readers of the *Charleston Daily Gazette* that more lenient laws helped to prevent crime, especially here, when "the mind of man is once more accessible to the mild influence of reason and humanity."[9]

These conceptions had an immediate and widespread appeal. The reform seemed worthy of the new republic, and feasible, so that by the second decade of the nineteenth century, most of the states had amended their criminal codes. The death sentence was either abolished for all offenses save first-degree murder or strictly limited to a handful of the most serious crimes. Instead, the statutes called for incarceration, the offender to serve a term in prison. Construction kept apace with legal stipulations.[10] Pennsylvania led the way, turning the old Philadelphia jail at Walnut Street into a state prison. In 1796, the New York legislature approved funds for building such institutions, and soon opened the Newgate state prison in Greenwich Village. The New Jersey penitentiary was completed in 1797, and so were others in Virginia and Kentucky in 1800. That same year, the Massachusetts legislature made appropriations for a prison at Charlestown, and in short order Vermont, New Hampshire, and Maryland followed suit. Within twenty years of Washington's inaugural, the states had taken the first steps to alter the traditional system of punishment.[11]

In this first burst of enthusiasm, Americans expected that a rational system of correction, which made punishment certain but humane, would dissuade all but a few offenders from a life in crime. They located the roots of deviancy not in the criminal, but in the legal system. Just as colonial codes had encouraged deviant behavior, republican ones would now curtail, or even eliminate it. To pass the proper laws would end the problem.

This perspective drew attention away from the prisons themselves. They were necessary adjuncts to the reform, the substitutes for capital punishment, but intrinsically of little interest or importance. A repulsion from the gallows rather than any faith in the penitentiary spurred the late-eighteenth century construction. Few people had any clear idea what these structures should look like or how they should be administered — or even addressed themselves seriously to these questions. To reformers, the advantages of the institutions were external, and they hardly imagined that life inside the prison might rehabilitate the criminal. Incarceration seemed more humane than hanging and less brutal than whipping. Prisons matched punishment to crime precisely: the more heinous the offense, the longer the sentence. Juries, fully understanding these advantages, would never hesitate to convict the guilty, so that correction would be certain. The fact of imprisonment, not its internal routine, was of chief importance.

By the 1820's, however, these ideas had lost persuasiveness. The focus shifted to the deviant and the penitentiary, away from the legal system. Men intently scrutinized the life history of the criminal and methodically arranged the institution to house him. Part of the cause for this change was the obvious failure of the first campaign. The faith of the 1790's now seemed misplaced; more rational codes had not decreased crime. The roots of deviancy went deeper than the certainty of a punishment. Nor were the institutions fulfilling the elementary task of protecting society, since escapes and riots were commonplace occurrences.[12] More important, the second generation of Americans confronted new challenges and shared fresh ideas. Communities had undergone many critical changes between 1790 and 1830, and so had men's thinking. Citizens found cause for deep despair and yet incredible optimism. The safety and security of their social order seemed to them in far greater danger than that of their fathers, yet they hoped to eradicate crime from the new world. The old structure was crumbling, but perhaps they could draw the blueprints for building a far better one.

Americans in the pre–Civil War era intently pondered the origins of deviant behavior. Philanthropists organized themselves into societies to investigate the question, hoping to devise an

5. *Newgate, the first New York state prison. Begun in 1796, Newgate was modeled after the Walnut Street jail (illustration 4). Given the few architectural departures from the colonial design, it is not surprising that the prison suffered internal disorganization and frequent convict escapes.*

COURTESY OF THE NEW-YORK HISTORICAL SOCIETY, NEW YORK CITY

effective method of punishment. Legislators, no less interested in a theory for crime, prepared to amend the statutes and appropriate the funds for a new system. To judge by the numerous periodical articles, laymen were also concerned with a subject that had a direct and obvious bearing on their daily lives. Traditional answers were no longer satisfactory.[13]

One of the best examples of their effort appeared in the early reports of the inspectors of New York's Auburn penitentiary. These officials, charged with the management of the prison, attempted to understand the causes of deviancy by collecting and appending to their 1829 and 1830 reports to the state legislature biographical sketches of inmates about to be discharged. The purpose of these brief ten- to twenty-line vignettes, the inspectors explained, was to exhibit "facts which must be interesting, as well to the legislator as to the philanthropist and the Christian." Here, in the life stories of several hundred convicts, they could discover the origins of crime. Impatient with theology and disappointed in the law, they turned to the careers of offenders for the information they wanted.[14]

At first glance, these accounts are curiously naïve. Officials obtained the facts, we are told, in interviews with the convicts just before their release, and obviously made no effort to check the accuracy of the statements. When the sketches recount the events that led up to the prisoner's conviction, each convict emerges as the innocent victim of some misunderstanding. He sold goods he did not know were stolen, or passed bills he did not recognize were counterfeit, or took a horse he did not realize belonged to a neighbor. The investigators, however, did not contradict these assertions or declare their own skepticism. They were not trying to prove that the courts of justice always convicted the right man, that the legal system was infallible. Clearly their concern was different. No record survives of how interrogators conducted the interviews or how they phrased their questions, what kinds of suggestions they openly or covertly made to the convicts. But the finished products follow so set a pattern, and officials were so eager to publicize them, that undoubtedly they heard what they wished to hear, learned what they wished to learn. Their interest was not in the process of conviction, they were quite certain that a collection of criminals stood before them. No, they were preoccupied with the convicts' early years, their growing up in the family, their actions in the community. And of the reliability and pertinence of this information they were certain.

In their search for the roots of deviant behavior, investigators concentrated on the convicts' upbringing, devoting the most space to it in almost every one of these biographies. They focused their questions on the criminals' childhood, recording what they wanted legislators and philanthropists to learn. No matter at what age the deviant committed an offense, the cause could be traced back to his childhood. Prisoner number 315, discharged in 1829, had been convicted for forgery at the age of fifty-five. Until then, he had apparently "maintained a respectable standing in the society." Why had a man of property with no previous record been guilty of such an act? His history provided the answer:

> No. 315. — A.N., born in Massachusetts; father was killed at Quebec when he was very young; family soon after scattered, and he was bound out to a farmer, with whom he lived till of age; was a wild, rude boy, and early addicted to some bad habits, drinking, swearing, etc.

In the early years, if you looked carefully, were the origins of deviancy.

And look carefully they did. The 1829 and 1830 reports of the Auburn penitentiary contained 173 biographies, and in fully two-thirds of them, the supervisors selected and presented the data to prove that childhood made the man. Almost always a failure of upbringing — specifically, the collapse of family control — caused deviant behavior. In these sketches, one of three circumstances characterized the failure. First, the children duplicated the parents' corrupt behavior. Prisoner 339 was typical: "Brought up . . . under the influence of a bad example; says his father has been in the New York prison." Or case 317: "Father a very intemperate man, and brought him up to it." Second, the family disintegrated because of death or divorce or desertion, turning an undisciplined child loose on the community. Inevitably, the results were disastrous. H. L., "born in Vermont; after his father's death, when he was a mere boy, worked out for a living and had his own way." And M. R. R.: "His father went off before his remembrance, and never returned . . . his mother married again . . . to a very intemperate bad man, who drove his stepchildren off, and told them he would kill them if they ever came home again." And J. L.: "Parents separated when he was seven on account of his father's going after other women; was then bound out to a farmer . . . ran away from him." Third, the child, through no obvious fault of the parents, left home. M. H., a girl born in Massachusetts, "ran away from her parents at thirteen years of age, and went into Rensselaer county . . . where she . . . soon became a common prostitute."[15]

Investigators had no need to question the truth of these facts. The very presence of the convict at the interview made them self-confirming. They did not doubt that the common whore had run off from her family, that the father of a thief was a drunkard, that a counterfeiter had been on his own from an early age. The moral was clear to them and could not be lost on their readers: deviancy began with the family.

Officials had no difficulty in tracing criminal behavior directly to circumstances of family life. They were certain that children lacking discipline quickly fell victim to the influence of vice at loose in the community. Inadequately prepared to withstand the temptations, they descended into crime. To document this idea, investigators inquired into and reported upon convicts' drinking habits, and those of their companions, and tried to discover other corruptions to which they had succumbed. Once again, they assembled the right facts for the story. In these sketches, the vices permeating the society made the family's failure decisive.

The undisciplined youth typically began to frequent taverns, soon became intemperate, and then turned to crime to support his vice. J. A., a French Canadian, "lost his parents when young, and was thrown friendless upon the world; had troubles which led him to excessive drinking. . . . Convicted of grand larceny." J. T., who had the misfortune to serve an apprenticeship under a drunken master, also "fell into the habit of drinking too much himself; it was in a grocery where he had been drinking too freely, that he committed the crime [theft] that brought him to prison." The temptation of liquor was so great that occasionally those properly raised succumbed to it in time of crisis. J. M. "was a steady young man and continued so till after his wife died . . . when he broke up housekeeping and went about from place to place; soon got to drinking too freely, became very intemperate, and at length took to stealing." R. R., "a steady industrious and moral young man . . . has been worth $3000; on account of domestic trouble took to drinking, and followed it up till he came to prison." If the best of sorts might yield to vice, those without rigorous moral training were certain victims.[16]

Persons outside family government often began to wander, falling in with bad company and acquiring the worst habits. Some first became intemperate and then committed crimes, others went directly to theft and burglary. Predictably, M. S., having run away from his apprenticeship at age fourteen, then roamed "about the country, with no other business than stealing." In another common variation, those lacking family counsel took up an occupation that was almost certain to lead to vice and crime. Enlistment in the army was one such step. The authors of these sketches were convinced that military service was a "school for vice." T. L., in their estimation, had proved himself an "apt scholar": while serving with the British forces in Canada, he "gave himself up to drinking, stealing, etc. and was ripe for crime when he came into this state." The American situation was no different: J. L., born in Albany, New York, enlisted after running away from a local farmer. "Had previously been a sober, industrious boy but in the army became very intemperate and vicious; after his discharge, strolled about the country, drinking more and more till he came to prison." Soldiers suffered from too little supervision once they left the barracks. The trouble with the military was that it was not military enough.

The sailor's life also offered an education in immorality. At sea, J. H. "became excessively intemperate, and addicted to all sorts of vice; had no sense of moral obligation; lived without God in the world. When he quit the seas, came into this state . . . through intemperance was led to the commission of a crime." Officials believed it axiomatic that anyone who "has been in almost every seaport in the world," would be "addicted to every bad habit in the world." Some civilian occupations were equally dangerous — for example, digging New York's new canal. J. P., typical of those leaving home without parental consent, "came to work on the [Erie] canal; fell into vicious company, and consequently vicious habits; became intemperate." Soon the courts convicted him for passing counterfeit money. G. J. "had previously been sober and industrious." But on the canal, "he soon got into many bad habits, drinking, gambling, stealing, etc.," till he arrived at the Auburn penitentiary.[17]

These carefully designed, really contrived biographies, undoubtedly strike the modern reader as crude and simplistic versions of later, more sophisticated analyses. Yet when looked at from the vantage point of the eighteenth century, they are in many ways important and different. For one thing, they are highly secular documents. Officials were interested in crime, not sin, and had no inclination to view legal offenses as Lucifer's handiwork or the retributive judgment of an angry God. The accounting system of the colonial period — where crime rates reflected both the community's religiosity and divine judgment on it — was outdated. Officials, in fact, gave surprisingly little attention to the convicts' religious history. Occasionally they noted if someone was raised without family prayer or had never regularly attended church. But even then religious training was an indicator of the quality of his upbringing, and without intrinsic importance. It revealed in one more way how the family had failed to educate and discipline the child.

Nor did these vignettes show the Revolutionary War generation's concern for legal reform. Officials now looked to the life of the criminal, not to the statutes, in attempting to grasp the origins of deviancy. They presented biographical sketches, not analyses of existing codes. They did not bother to gather information about or report upon convicts' previous encounters with the law, what kinds of punishments they had received, or their feelings about them. Such questions were for the 1790's, not the 1820's and '30's.

In a still more crucial way the concept of deviant behavior implicit in these sketches signaled a new departure. Although the colonists had blamed inadequate parental and religious training for crime, they were preoccupied with the sinner himself. Convinced that the corrupt nature of man was ultimately at fault, they did not extensively analyze the role of the criminal's family or the church or the general society. Furthermore, they shared a clear understanding of what the well-ordered community *ought to* look like, and this too stifled any inclination to question or scrutinize existing arrangements. Their religious and social certainty covered the discrepancies between ideas and realities, obviating new approaches and theories. Americans in the Jacksonian period stood in a very different position. They learned that men were born innocent, not depraved, that the sources of corruption were external, not internal, to the human condition. Encouraged by such doctrines to examine their society with acute suspicion, they quickly discovered great cause for apprehension and criticism.

But why did they become so anxious in their concern? Why did they so easily discover corruption? They were, it is true, predisposed to this finding, yet it is puzzling that they located all that they looked for. Communities were not overrun with thieves and drunkards, prostitutes and gamblers; the rate of crime, for example, probably did not increase over these years.[18] Rather, Americans conducted this examination with grandiose expectations. Assuming that deviant behavior was symptomatic of a failing in society, they expected to ferret out corruption and eliminate crime. With the stakes so high, they could ignore no possible malfeasance.

Another consideration expanded their list of social evils. Many Americans in the Jacksonian period judged their society with eighteenth-century criteria in mind. As a result, they defined as corrupting the fluidity and mobility that they saw. Thinking that an orderly society had to be a fixed one, they judged the discrepancies between traditional postulates and present reality as promoting deviant behavior. Not having evolved an alternative to the colonial vision of society, they looked back both with envy and discomfort. They were embarrassed about the cruelty and shortsightedness of earlier punishments, and hoped to be humanitarian innovators. Yet they also believed that their predecessors, fixed in their communities and ranks, had enjoyed social order. But how were they now to maintain cohesion in so fluid and open a society? This ambivalence gave a very odd quality to their thinking. On the one hand, they aimed at the heights, about to eliminate crime and corruption. On the other, they doubted the society's survival, fearing it might succumb to chaos. They confronted, it seemed, unprecedented opportunity, and unprecedented peril.

Holding such a position, American students of deviant behavior moved family and community to the center of their analysis. New York officials accumulated and published biographies because this technique allowed them to demonstrate to legislators and philanthropists the crucial role of social organizations. Accordingly, almost every sketch opened with a vivid description of an inadequate family life and then traced the effects of the corruptions in the community. While many a convict may possibly have come from a broken home or been prone to drink, no one ought to take the inspectors' findings as straight facts. They had a prior commitment to gathering and publicizing this type of information to explain the origins of crime. Interviewers probably induced the convicts to describe, whether accurately or not, their early life in grim terms. Sympathetic questioners, letting the criminal know that they thought that much of the blame for his fate rested with his parents, would soon hear him recount his father's drinking habits and the attraction of the tavern around the corner. These sketches reflected the ideas of the questioner, not some objective truth about the criminal. The doctrine was clear: parents who sent their children into the society without a rigorous training in discipline and obedience would find them someday in the prison. The case of W. S. can summarize both the approach and the message: "Lived with his parents who indulged him too much for his good; was a very wild unsteady boy; fond of company and amusements; when he could not get his parents' consent, would go without it." The result? "Convicted of an attempt to rape . . . and sentenced to three years."[19]

The pessimism and fear underlying this outlook pointed to the difficulty Americans had in fitting their perception of nineteenth-century society as mobile and fluid into an eighteenth-century definition of a well-ordered community. Their first reaction was not to disregard the inherited concept but to condemn present conditions. Hence, in these biographies a dismal picture emerged of a society filled with a myriad of temptations. It was almost as if the town, in a nightmarish image, was made up of a number of households, frail and huddled together, facing the sturdy and wide doors of the tavern, the gaudy opening into a house of prostitution or theater filled with dissipated customers; all the while, thieves and drunkards milled the streets, introducing the unwary youngster to vice and corruption. Every family was under siege, surrounded by enemies ready to take advantage of any misstep. The honest citizen was like a vigilant soldier, well trained to guard against temptation. Should he relax for a moment, the results would be disastrous. Once, observers believed, neighbors had disciplined neighbors. Now it seemed that rowdies corrupted rowdies.

Yet for all the desperation in this image, Americans shared an incredible optimism. Since deviant behavior was a product of the environment, the predictable result of readily observable situations, it was not inevitable. Crime was not inherent in the nature of man, as Calvinists had asserted; no theological devils insisted on its perpetuation. Implicit in this outlook was an impulse to reform. If one could alter the conditions breeding crime, then one could reduce it to manageable proportions and bring a new security to society.

One tactic was to advise and warn the family to fulfill its tasks well. By giving advice and demonstrating the awful consequences of an absence of discipline, critics would inspire the family to a better performance. (The biographical sketches, then, were not only investigations but correctives to the problem.) One might also organize societies to shut taverns and houses of prostitution, an effort that was frequently made in the Jacksonian period. But such measures, while important, were slow-working, and by themselves seemed insufficient to meet the pressing needs of this generation. Another alternative then became not only feasible but essential: to construct a special setting for the deviant. Remove him from the family and community and place him in an artificially created and therefore corruption-free environment. Here he could learn all the vital lessons that others had ignored, while protected from the temptations of vice. A model and small-scale society could solve the immediate problem and point the way to broader reforms.

Almost everyone who wrote about deviancy during the Jacksonian era echoed the findings of Auburn's inspectors and many emulated their methodology. Officials at other prisons conducted similar surveys among convicts, validating the general conclusions reached in New York. Interested laymen, organized into such benevolent societies as the New York Prison Association and the Boston Prison Discipline Society, made their own investigations and then helped to publicize the same ideas among a still broader portion of the population. Well-known reformers, like Dorothea Dix, Francis Lieber, and Samuel Gridley Howe, concerned with a spectrum of causes, paid great attention to the problem of crime and its correction and further popularized the concepts. Family disorganization and community corruption, an extreme definition of the powers of vice and an acute sense of the threat of disorder were the standard elements in the discussions. A wide consensus formed on the origins of crime.

Prison officials everywhere informed state legislators of the crucial role of the family and community in causing deviant behavior. "The mass of criminals," explained the inspectors of Pennsylvania's Eastern State Penitentiary, "is composed of persons whose childhood and youth were spent in the uncontrolled exercise of vicious instincts." The warden of the Ohio penitentiary listed the breakdown of the household among the leading causes of crime. "Unhappy orphanage," he lamented, "leaves the susceptible youth without those restraints and safeguards which conduct to a life of probity."[20] To buttress this argument one official calculated that of the 235 men committed to the prison in one year, 86 were under twenty-five years of age, a sure sign that the failure of the family was at the root of the problem. Another appropriately conducted interviews and compiled case histories. His most important finding, he believed, was that 221 convicts from a sample of 350 had been "thrown out from under parental influence and restraint," before reaching the age of twenty-one; in fact, 89 of them were without guardians by the time they were twelve. They had "never learned to submit to proper authority," or to understand that "their own safety and happiness are secured by such obedience."

All observers agreed that the forces at work in the community aggravated the family's errors. The future convict, concluded the Pennsylvania group, "social to a fault," took his cues from his surroundings; predictably, "the vices of social life have heralded the ruin of his fortunes and his hopes." Ohio's officials shared this view: "Without the refining and elevating influences of the home, without parental restraint and example, they were thrown upon a cold and selfish world, and often wronged. . . . They have done as might have been expected."[21]

An identical interpretation appeared in the opening pages of the first annual report (1844) of the New York Prison Association. According to one of its founders, the Unitarian minister William H. Channing, the association was formed to aid persons awaiting trial, to help reform convicts, and to assist released prisoners. This commitment, he explained, was not only testimony to a Christian desire to have good triumph over evil and to avoid "the vindictive spirit," but also reflected the community's ultimate responsibility, because of its "neglect and bad usages," for "the sins of its children." The first part of this formulation needed little clarification, but the second did, and so he elaborated on the role of the family and community in the origins of crime.[22]

"The first and most obvious cause," began Channing, "is an evil organization derived from evil parents. Bad germs bear bad fruit." Although his language suggested that a biological process was at work, he did not consider heredity anything more than a predisposing force that could be "cleansed away by a healthful moral influence." A properly organized social system would "purify away what is bad," and shield its members "from the temptations beneath which they are peculiarly liable to fall." The existence of crime pointed to the community's inability to fulfill its task, not the influence of heredity. Channing went on to link the failure of family training directly to deviant behavior. Of the 156 inmates recently admitted to Pennsylvania's Eastern State Penitentiary, he reported, fourteen had been orphaned by age twelve, thirty-six were missing one parent or another soon thereafter, 143 had received no religious instruction, and 144 never attended Sabbath school. "Such statistics," affirmed the minister, "tell at a glance that early neglect was certainly, in part, probably in great part, the cause of after crime."[23]

Channing too believed that the corruptions pervading the community made early parental neglect so injurious; in fact, he was surprised that the power of vice did not debilitate still more people. "We seldom appreciate," he declared, "how easily, if left alone, unsustained by worthy example . . . we might become lawless and perverse. . . . Slight deviations, uncorrected, hurry the transgressor into a rapid downward course. . . . Tempters ensnare the inexperienced. . . . The spirit of mere adventure entangles the careless into a web of vile associations, from which there is no after escape. . . . How many a young man . . . took, almost without a thought, the first step in that path which ended in the gambler's hell, the plausible deceits of the forger and counterfeiter." Well-baited traps were so pervasive that the slightest miscalculation brought terrible consequences. "The sight of evil, as by contagion, awakens the desire to commit evil." Yet, for all his anxiety about society, Channing, like other Americans in the Jacksonian period, did not succumb to despair. "The study of the *causes* of the crime," he concluded, "may lead us to its *cure*." His environmental theory encouraged rather than stifled action.[24]

Succeeding reports of the New York Prison Association repeated these themes. Continuously stressing the critical role of the family, they reminded parents of the "importance of exercising careful supervision and wholesome discipline." Otherwise, the contagion of vice would be irresistible. Intemperance was "the giant whose mighty arm prostrates the greatest numbers, involving them in sin and shame and crime and ruin." And behind it, "never let it be forgotten, lies the want of early parental restraint and instruction." Readers even learned that "the loss of the father more frequently than that of the mother leads to criminal conduct on the part of the children"; for "mothers, as a general thing, are less able than fathers to restrain their sons."

The catalogue of seductions that led hapless youngsters to the penitentiary did not become thinner with time.[25] The 1855 association report devoted a lengthy appendix to the sources of crime, first paying due regard to the position of the family as the "bulwark against temptation," and then spelling out the social evils rampant in the community. There was the tavern and the brothel house — appropriately joined with a quote from Hosea, "whoredom and wine . . . taketh away the heart"; the theaters and the gambling houses were menaces, and so were the men who sold licentious books and pictures at the railroad station and boat landings. Still, no matter how lengthy the list, the organization assured its followers that "energetic and enlightened action of the people in . . . social and individual capacities" would effectively combat crime.[26]

A rival and perhaps more famous association, the Boston Prison Discipline Society, differed on many substantive issues with its New York counterpart, but both agreed on the sources of deviant behavior. Founded in 1825 by Louis Dwight, a onetime agent of the American Bible Society, the Boston group set down a very familiar creed. "This society," announced one of its early reports, "shows the importance of family government. . . . It is the confession of many convicts at Auburn [New York] and Wethersfield [Connecticut] that the course of vice, which brought them to the prison, commenced in disobedience to their parents, or in their parents' neglect." No one was probably surprised to learn that "youth, when unrestrained and neglected by their parents, find their way to the tavern and the grog shop."[27] This was the meaning of member Samuel Gridley Howe's pronouncement: "Thousands of convicts are made so in consequence of a faulty organization of society. . . . They are thrown upon society as a sacred charge; and that society is false to its trust, if it neglects any means for their reformation."[28] Those to blame for this state of affairs had the duty, and seemingly the power to effect reform.

Two of the most important figures in the New York and Boston organizations, Channing and Dwight, had first followed religious careers — the former was actually a minister, the latter had studied for it and then worked for the Bible Society. But one must define very carefully the religious influence in reform societies. The changes in Protestant thinking from the eighteenth to the nineteenth century had certainly increased the clergy's concern and attention to social reform, and because of their insistence that men were to do good by improving the common weal, many Americans participated in benevolent activities. Nevertheless, the prescriptions of what was right action, the definition of the policy that men of goodwill were to enact, revealed more of a secular than a religious foundation. Channing and Dwight echoed prevailing social anxieties; they did not

make a uniquely religious perspective relevant. Their vision of
the well-ordered society did not indicate the influence of their
special training. In this sense, they, unlike their predecessors,
followed the pack rather than heading it.[29]

Noted reformers and pamphleteers in pre–Civil War America
were keenly interested in the predicament of the criminal.
Francis Lieber was distressed by the treatment of offenders as
well as of slaves. "The history of by far the greatest majority of
criminals," insisted Lieber, "shows the afflicting fact, that they
were led to crime by the bad example of their parents." From
this first cause flowed a sequence of events, "a gradual progress in
vice, for which society often offers but too many temptations."
No effort to assist the deviant should be spared, he argued, for
"society takes upon itself an awful responsibility, by exposing a
criminal to such moral contagion, that, according to the necessary course of things, he cannot escape its effects."[30] A more
celebrated contemporary, Dorothea Dix, wrote about the convict
as well as the insane, publishing an important pamphlet, *Remarks on Prisons and Prison Discipline in the United States.* "It
is to the defects of our social organization," declared Dix, "to the
multiplied and multiplying temptations to crime that we chiefly
owe the increase of evil doers."[31] And like Lieber, she too
announced that the community had the responsibility and the
resources to confront and eliminate the problem.

The Jacksonians' conception of the causes of crime had an
obvious and precise relevance for understanding juvenile delinquency. The child offender, no less than the adult one, was a
casualty of his upbringing. The importance of family discipline
in a community pervaded with vice characterized practically
every statement of philanthropists and reformers on delinquency.
Both mature and immature offenders were victims of similar
conditions. Not that Americans, insensitive to an idea of childhood, unthinkingly made children into adults. Quite the reverse.
They stripped the years away from adults, and turned everyone
into a child.

The custodians of juvenile delinquents asked the same questions and drew the same conclusions as wardens in state prisons.
No sooner did New York, for reasons we shall soon explore,

establish a house of refuge in 1824 to incarcerate minors guilty of criminal offenses, than its managers collected and published case histories. Their inquiries, following a set form, indicated a common perspective on deviant behavior. How long had the youngster been under family government? How often, and how long, had he served as an apprentice? What was the moral character of his parents and his masters? Did the delinquent drink? Or have other vices? What about his companions? What was his first illegal act? His second and his third? The very thoroughness of the examination reflected how much the interrogators valued the information.

Refuge managers located in parental neglect the primary cause of deviant behavior. In typical instances: J. C., at fourteen, ran away from an inattentive and corrupt father. He soon returned, to steal six watches; his father helped to sell the loot. R. W., whose parents were intemperate, roamed the streets, and stayed away from home for weeks on end; he pilfered or begged his daily subsistence until arrested. J. L., another inmate caught stealing, recounted that after his father's death, his mother began drinking, "and then we all went to destruction, mother, brothers, sisters, all."[32] Each case was proof that the child who became "his own boss and went in the way that was right in his own eyes," was a prison convict in the making.

The sketches demonstrated the dire consequences of even minor acts of disobedience. The delinquent moved inexorably from petty to major crimes. W. O. first stole one shilling from his father, then some items of clothing from a stranger, later robbed a watch and some broadcloth from a shop, and finally wrecked, burned, and looted a house. E. M. began his career by pilfering small change from drunkards and graduated to highway robbery. J. R. went from pennies to dollars, and C. B. from fruits and cakes in the kitchen cupboard to cash in store registers.[33] What a careless parent dismissed as a comparatively harmless prank was a crucial event. A few pennies and some sweets, as these biographies revealed, were the first symptoms of a criminal life.

The vices at loose in the community invariably brought the unwary and untrained child to the prison gates. Delinquents' careers demonstrated the debilitating influences of the tavern, where they first began to drink, and the noxious quality of theaters and the houses of prostitution, where they learned other corruptions. Temptations seemed so omnipresent that when dedicating a new building at the New York refuge, the presiding minister reminded his audience that, had their parents been less vigorous or their training less thorough, they too might have become delinquent. "Who of us dare to say," he asked, "that if he had been exposed to the same influences, he would have preserved his integrity and come out of the fiery ordeal unscathed? The sight of such a group of children . . . in yonder gallery should fill us with humility and teach us lessons of mercy!"³⁴

Thus, Jacksonians located both the origins of crime and delinquency within the society, with the inadequacies of the family and the unchecked spread of vice through the community. The situation appeared bleak, almost desperate. What elements would now stabilize the community? What kind of social order would keep deviancy within bounds? But if the dangers were immense, so were the possibilities. Convinced that crime was the fault of the environment, not a permanent or inevitable phenomenon, and eager to demonstrate the social blessings of republican political arrangements to the world, Americans set out to protect the safety of the society and to achieve unprecedented success in eradicating deviancy. Their analysis of the origin of crime became a rallying cry to action.

4

The Invention of the
Penitentiary

Americans' understanding of the causes of deviant behavior led directly to the invention of the penitentiary as a solution. It was an ambitious program. Its design — external appearance, internal arrangement, and daily routine — attempted to eliminate the specific influences that were breeding crime in the community, and to demonstrate the fundamentals of proper social organization. Rather than stand as places of last resort, hidden and ignored, these institutions became the pride of the nation. A structure designed to join practicality to humanitarianism, reform the criminal, stabilize American society, and demonstrate how to improve the condition of mankind, deserved full publicity and close study.

In the 1820's New York and Pennsylvania began a movement that soon spread through the Northeast, and then over the next decades to many midwestern states. New York devised the Auburn or congregate system of penitentiary organization, establishing it first at the Auburn state prison between 1819 and 1823, and then in 1825 at the Ossining institution, familiarly known as Sing-Sing. Pennsylvania officials worked out the details of a rival plan, the separate system, applying it to the penitentiary at Pittsburgh in 1826 and to the prison at Philadelphia in 1829. In short order, the Connecticut legislature stopped using an abandoned copper mine to incarcerate offenders, and in 1827 built a new structure at Wethersfield. Massachusetts reorganized its state

6. The New York state prison at Auburn. European and American visitors flocked to this exemplar of the congregate system. While not as awe-inspiring in design as the Philadelphia penitentiary (illustrations 8 and 9), Auburn gave greater attention to economy in construction and the profitable use of prison labor.

COURTESY OF THE NEW-YORK HISTORICAL SOCIETY, NEW YORK CITY

prison at Charlestown in 1829; that same year, Maryland erected a penitentiary, and one year later New Jersey followed suit. Ohio and Michigan built penitentiaries in the 1830's, and so did Indiana, Wisconsin, and Minnesota in the 1840's.[1]

The results of all this activity deeply concerned Americans, so that annual reports to state legislators and popular journals as well contained long and detailed discussions and arguments on the merits of various enterprises. Europeans came to evaluate the experiment and the major powers appointed official investigators. France in 1831 dispatched the most famous pair, Alexis de Tocqueville and Gustave Auguste de Beaumont; in 1832 England sent William Crawford, and in 1834, Prussia dispatched Nicholas Julius. Tourists with no special interest in penology made sure to visit the institutions. Harriet Martineau, Frederick Marryat, and Basil Hall would no more have omitted this stop from their itinerary than they would have a southern plantation, a Lowell textile mill, or a frontier town. By the 1830's, the American penitentiary had become world famous.[2]

The focus of attention was not simply on whether the penitentiary accomplished its goals, but on the merits of the two competing modes of organization. The debate raged with an incredible intensity during these decades, and the fact that most prisons in the United States were modeled after the Auburn system did not diminish it. Even more startling, neither did the basic similarity of the two programs. In retrospect they seem very much alike, but nevertheless an extraordinary amount of intellectual and emotional energy entered the argument. The fervor brought many of the leading reformers of the period to frequently bitter recriminations, and often set one benevolent society against another. Periodicals regularly polled foreign visitors for their judgment or printed a vigorous defense by one school and then a critical rejoinder by the other. The roster of participants in this contest was impressive, pitting Samuel Gridley Howe (a Pennsylvania advocate) against Matthew Carey (for Auburn), Dorothea Dix against Louis Dwight, Francis Lieber against Francis Wayland. Every report from the New York and Pennsylvania penitentiaries was an explicit apology for its procedures and an implicit attack on its opponents. And as soon as a state committed its prison organization to one side or the other then it too entered the controversy with the zeal of a recent convert.

The content of the debate between the Auburn and Pennsylvania camps points to the significance of the ideas on the causes of crime to the creation of the penitentiary, and the zeal reflects the expectations held about the innovation. To understand why men became so passionate about internal questions of design is to begin to comprehend the origins and popularity of institutionalization in this era. Under the Auburn scheme, prisoners were to sleep alone in a cell at night and labor together in a workshop during the day for the course of their fixed sentences in the penitentiary. They were forbidden to converse with fellow inmates or even exchange glances while on the job, at meals, or in their cells. The Pennsylvania system, on the other hand, isolated each prisoner for the entire period of his confinement. According to its blueprint, convicts were to eat, work, and sleep in individual cells, seeing and talking with only a handful of responsible guards and selected visitors. They were to leave the institution as ignorant of the identity of other convicts as on the day they entered. As both schemes placed maximum emphasis on preventing the prisoners from communicating with anyone else, the point of dispute was whether convicts should work silently in large groups or individually within solitary cells.[3]

To both the advocates of the congregate and the separate systems, the promise of institutionalization depended upon the isolation of the prisoner and the establishment of a disciplined routine. Convinced that deviancy was primarily the result of the corruptions pervading the community, and that organizations like the family and the church were not counterbalancing them, they believed that a setting which removed the offender from all temptations and substituted a steady and regular regimen would reform him. Since the convict was not inherently depraved, but the victim of an upbringing that had failed to provide protection against the vices at loose in society, a well-ordered institution could successfully reeducate and rehabilitate him. The penitentiary, free of corruptions and dedicated to the proper training of the inmate, would inculcate the discipline that negligent parents, evil companions, taverns, houses of prostitution, theaters, and gambling halls had destroyed. Just as the criminal's environment had led him into crime, the institutional environment would lead him out of it.

The duty of the penitentiary was to separate the offender from *all* contact with corruption, both within and without its walls. There was obviously no sense to removing a criminal from the depravity of his surroundings only to have him mix freely with other convicts within the prison. Or, as Samuel Gridley Howe put it when composing a prisoner prayer: "In the name of justice, do not surround me with bad associates and with evil influences, do not subject me to unnecessary temptation, do not expose me to further degradation. . . . Remove me from my old companions, and surround me with virtuous associates."[4] Sharing this perspective, officials in the 1830's argued that the great mistake of the prisons of the 1790's had been their failure to separate inmates. Lacking an understanding of the forces of the environment and still caught up with the idea that humane and certain punishment would eradicate deviancy, they had neglected to organize or supervise the prisoners' immediate surroundings. Consequently their institutions became seminaries of vice. Now, however, reformers understood the need to guard the criminal against corruption and teach him the habits of order and regularity. Isolation and steady habits, the right organization and routine, would yield unprecedented benefits.[5]

As a result of this thinking, prison architecture and arrangements became the central concern of reformers of the period. Unlike their predecessors, they turned all their attention inward, to the divisions of time and space within the institution. The layout of cells, the methods of labor, and the manner of eating and sleeping within the penitentiary were the crucial issues. The most influential benevolent organization devoted to criminal reform, the Boston Prison Discipline Society, appropriately considered architecture one of the most important of the *moral* sciences. "There are," the society announced, "principles in architecture, by the observance of which great moral changes can be more easily produced among the most abandoned of our race. . . . There is such a thing as architecture adapted to morals; that other things being equal, the prospect of improvement, in morals, depends, in some degree, upon the construction of buildings." Those who would rehabilitate the deviant had better cultivate this science.[6]

As with any other science, the advocates of moral architecture anticipated that the principles which emerged from the penitentiary experiment would have clear and important applications to the wider society. An arrangement which helped to reform vicious and depraved men would also be effective in regulating the behavior of ordinary citizens in other situations.[7] The penitentiary, by its example, by its discovery and verification of proper principles of social organization, would serve as a model for the entire society. Reformers fully anticipated that their work behind prison walls would have a critical significance beyond them. Since crime was symptomatic of a breakdown in traditional community practices, the penitentiary solution would point the way to a reconstitution of the social structure.

Tocqueville and Beaumont appreciated how significant both of these purposes were to the first penologists. The institutions, Americans believed, would radically reform the criminal and the society. "Philanthropy has become for them," observed the two visitors, "a kind of profession, and they have caught the *monomanie* of the penitentiary system, which to them seems the remedy for all the evils of society." Proponents described the penitentiary as "a grand theatre, for the trial of all new plans in hygiene and education, in physical and moral reform." The convict "surrendered body and soul, to be experimented upon," and the results, as the Boston Prison Discipline Society insisted, would benefit not only other custodial institutions like almshouses and houses of refuge, but also "would greatly promote order, seriousness, and purity in large families, male and female boarding schools, and colleges."[8] Perhaps the most dramatic and unabashed statement of these views appeared in a memoir by the Reverend James B. Finley, chaplain at the Ohio penitentiary. "Never, no never shall we see the triumph of peace, of right, of Christianity, until the daily habits of mankind shall undergo a thorough revolution," declared Finley. And in what ways were we to achieve such a reform? "Could we all be put on prison fare, for the space of two or three generations, the world would ultimately be the better for it. Indeed, should society change places with the prisoners, so far as habits are concerned, taking to itself the regularity, and temperance, ,and sobriety of a good prison," then the grandiose goals of peace, right, and Christianity would be furthered. "As it is," concluded Finley, "taking this world and the next together . . . the prisoner has the advantage."[9]

It is no wonder, then, that Auburn and Pennsylvania supporters held their positions staunchly, eager to defend every detail. With the stakes so high and the results almost entirely dependent upon physical design, every element in penitentiary organization assumed overwhelming importance. Nothing less than the safety and future stability of the republic was at issue, the triumph of good over evil, of order over chaos. Intense partisanship was natural where the right program would reform the criminal and reorder the society, and the wrong one would encourage vice and crime.

The Pennsylvania camp had no doubt of its superiority, defining in countless pamphlets, articles, and reports its conception of the model institution. It aggressively insisted that the separate design carried the doctrine of isolation to a logical and appropriate conclusion. The arrangements at the Philadelphia prison, as partisans described them, guaranteed that convicts would avoid all contamination and follow a path to reform. Inmates remained in solitary cells for eating, sleeping, and working, and entered private yards for exercise; they saw and spoke with only carefully selected visitors, and read only morally uplifting literature — the Bible. No precaution against contamination was excessive. Officials placed hoods over the head of a new prisoner when marching him to his cell so he would not see or be seen by other inmates.[10]

Once isolated, the prisoner began the process of reform. "Each individual," explained Pennsylvania's supporters, "will necessarily be made the instrument of his own punishment; his conscience will be the avenger of society." Left in total solitude, separated from "evil society . . . the progress of corruption is arrested; no additional contamination can be received or communicated." At the same time the convict "will be compelled to reflect on the error of his ways, to listen to the reproaches of conscience, to the expostulations of religion."[11] Thrown upon his own innate sentiments, with no evil example to lead him astray, and with kindness and proper instruction at hand to bolster his resolutions, the criminal would start his rehabilitation. Then, after a period of total isolation, without companions, books, or tools, officials would allow the inmate to work in his cell. Introduced at this moment, labor would become not an oppressive task for punishment, but a welcome diversion, a delight rather than a burden. The convict would sit in his cell and work with his tools daily, so that over the course of his sentence regularity and discipline would become habitual. He would return to the community cured of vice and idleness, to take his place as a responsible citizen.[12]

The separate system of penitentiary organization promised to accomplish these ends with a minimum of distraction and complication. The ordinary guards would not have to be well-trained, for their contact with the inmates would be slight and superficial; prisoners continuously confined to their cells would not have to be herded to meals or supervised in workshops and common exercise yards. Security would be easily maintained, since escape plans would be difficult to plot and to fulfill. There would be little recourse to the whip — cruel punishment would be rare, since men in isolation would have little occasion to violate regulations. Finally, these arrangements would permit officials to treat prisoners as individuals, rewarding some with more frequent visitors and books for good behavior, depriving recalcitrant others of these privileges. The Pennsylvania penitentiary promised to be a secure, quiet, efficient, humane, well-ordered, and ultimately reformatory institution.[13]

Advocates of the separate system dismissed the competing congregate program as an incomplete and inconsistent version of the Pennsylvania scheme. The basic imperfection of Auburn, insisted critics like Samuel Gridley Howe, was a failure to maintain a thorough isolation of inmates. New York knew enough to separate prisoners at night, but for misguided motives allowed them to work together during the day. One result was that convicts came to recognize the other inmates, making it that much more likely that they would meet after release to resume a life in crime. They would also influence one another while still within the penitentiary walls. So many possibilities for conversation occurred during work and meals and exercise that guards could not eliminate all communication.[14] Auburn's procedures diabolically tempted the convicts. They were to sit together at mess tables and workbenches, and yet abstain from talking — an unnecessarily painful situation. Officials, compelled to enforce rules that were too easily broken, inevitably meted out frequent and harsh punishments without solving the problem. These basic defects, Pennsylvania's partisans concluded, made cruelty and corruption endemic to the congregate plan.[15]

For its part, the Auburn school vigorously defended the principle of separation and the reformatory promise of the penitentiary, fully sharing the axioms and optimism of its rival. But in reply to criticism, Auburn was necessarily on the defensive, for its arrangements did not so totally isolate the inmates or so studiously aim to prevent all chance of contamination. Auburn's supporters, therefore, spent more time picking fault with their opponents than advancing the superiority of their own procedures. Wherever possible they moved the debate from the ideal to the real, insisting that New York had the more practical scheme, a balanced combination of commitment and flexibility. They argued that Pennsylvania did not carry out its program perfectly, and then went on to contend that the very consistency of the separate design was itself a grave fault. Auburn's partisans answered complaints of frequent inmate communication in congregate prisons by contending that the walls of the Philadelphia prison were not thick enough and its sewer pipes not arranged well enough to prevent convict conversations. Charge, of course, prompted countercharge and before long intricate measurements of institutional walls and elaborate diagrams of the layout of pipes filled much of the penitentiary pamphlet literature.[16]

One main thrust, however, of the congregate school came on the issue of the effects of constant and unrelieved isolation of prisoners. It was unnatural, the New York camp insisted, to leave men in solitary, day after day, year after year; indeed, it was so unnatural that it bred insanity. The organization of the Philadelphia institution, argued Francis Wayland, was "at variance with the human constitution," and his supporters tried to marshall appropriate statistics. The comparative mental health of prisoners under the two arrangements, the causes and rates of death, the physical health of the convicts entered the debate. No accurate data allowed precise calculations of these phenomena and partisans did little more than set down subjective judgments in the guise of absolute numbers. But the Auburn attack did manage to cast some doubt on the wisdom of Pennsylvania's routine.[17]

After asserting that the separate system was no more effective or perfect than the congregate one, the New York school presented what proved to be its most persuasive point: the added expenses of establishing the Pennsylvania program were unnecessary. Auburn-type institutions, their defenders flatly, and accurately, declared, cost less to construct and brought in greater returns from convict labor. Since the two systems were more or less equal, with faults and advantages fairly evenly distributed, states ought not to incur the greater costs of the separate plan. By having prisoners work together in shops, Auburn's cells did not have to be as large as those at Philadelphia; also, a greater variety of goods could be efficiently manufactured in congregate prisons. The New York program provided the best of both worlds, economy and reform.[18]

The pamphlet warfare between the two camps dominated practically all thinking and writing about the problem of crime and correction. The advantages and disadvantages of Pennsylvania as against Auburn blocked out any other consideration. No one thought to venture beyond the bounds of defining the best possible prison arrangements, and this narrowness of focus was clear testimony to the widespread faith in institutionalization. People argued whether solitary should be continuous and how ducts ought to be arranged, but no one questioned the shared premise of both systems, that incarceration was the only proper social response to criminal behavior. To ponder alternatives was unnecessary when the promise of the penitentiary seemed unlimited.

The ideas on the origins of deviant behavior led directly to the formulation of the Auburn and Pennsylvania programs, and these in turn became the blueprints for constructing and arranging new prisons. The pamphlet literature exerted a critical influence on legislators' resolves to erect penitentiaries and officials' decisions on how to administer them. As the inspectors of the Auburn penitentiary aptly concluded in 1835: "The founders of this system relied almost entirely upon theory for the groundwork on the plan."[19]

There was a clear value and import to a program of incarceration that removed the deviant from one town without sending him to another. In a physically mobile society, the prison was a useful form of control. And undoubtedly some supporters were drawn to the program only because they believed that the terrors of isolation and silence would decrease crime. But the appeal of institutionalization was still broader. Its functionalism was part of the story of its origins but not all of it. If incarceration had been nothing more than a practical alternative to expulsion or to whippings, then a minimum of effort and expenditure would have been made on these institutions. The penitentiaries, however, in first appearance were elaborate and expensive structures, with peculiar and idiosyncratic routines that had no obvious functional quality. To understand why thick walls and individual cells and the isolation of convicts became standard one must look beyond the immediate needs of the community to broader considerations, to reform, to model-building, to an almost utopian program.

Earlier structures, erected soon after the Revolution, had operated in a very ad hoc fashion, providing few lessons worth following. By the 1820's there had hardly been any advances in prison design in the United States, and only scattered ones in Europe. In the 1790's, reformers anticipating the benefits of statutory revisions had devoted little energy to internal prison arrangements. Since laws, and not blueprints, captured their attention, the prisons erected at the end of the eighteenth century usually made only minor or confused departures from colonial arrangements. As a result, they did not provide the next generation with tested principles. "Reform in prison discipline," declared one participant, "was an experiment. They had no model prison to visit; no pioneers in the march of reform, to warn them of errors or guide them to truth."[20] The first encounter with institutions was so disappointing, in fact, that many observers considered them positively harmful and dangerous.

Officials in the 1790's avoided the problems critical to making

a prison the basic form of criminal correction, and the consequences, to judge by frequency of riots, escapes, and statements
of public displeasure, were disastrous. The architecture of the
institutions still commonly followed the model of the household.
The Walnut Street jail in Philadelphia, built in 1790 and
quickly copied in such cities as New York, resembled an ordinary, if somewhat large, frame house, indistinguishable from
other sizable dwellings. The New Jersey prison at Trenton,
opened in 1798, was a typical two-storied home complete with a
columned doorway, and set apart only by a low wall enclosing a
courtyard.[21] One departure from this pattern occurred in Massachusetts, where architects in 1800 carefully constructed a building to provide maximum security. The Board of Visitors to the
Charlestown prison was pleased with the results, especially with
the high wall of hard flint stone that surrounded the structure
and an arrangement that fronted two sides of the building on
water. "Competent judges," it happily reported, "pronounce this
to be among the strongest and best built prisons in the world.
. . . It can neither be set on fire by prisoners, nor be undermined." But for all this confidence, sixteen inmates soon escaped.
In fact, sensitivity to prison structures was so blunted during this
period that the Connecticut legislature in 1790 decided to use an
abandoned copper mine for a state prison. Prisoners served their
sentences in slime-covered caverns with water dripping from the
ceilings. Fortunately, no other state took over this model.[22]

The first prisons also failed to devise an alternative design to
the household for their internal organization. Prisoners still lived
together in large rooms and took their meals in one common
dining area; they mingled freely, without restrictions. Institutional life remained casual, undisciplined, and irregular. Occasionally, prison officers instituted a new procedure intending to
buttress the security of the institution. Thus in the 1790's,
convicts for the first time began to wear uniforms in order to
render it more difficult for an escaped inmate to disappear into a
town. Maryland and New Jersey prisons relied upon a coarse
brown suit; Massachusetts, among the more security conscious of
systems, devised a more bizarre one, half red and half blue. New
York compromised with coarse brown for the first offender, red
and blue for the second. The focus on recapture pointed to the

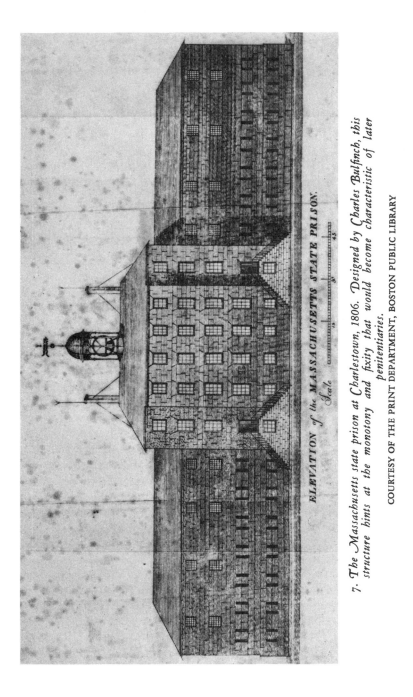

ELEVATION of the MASSACHUSETTS STATE PRISON.

Scale

7. The Massachusetts state prison at Charlestown, 1806. Designed by Charles Bulfinch, this structure hints at the monotony and fixity that would become characteristic of later penitentiaries.

expectation as well as reality of frequent escapes. The uniform did not signal the routinization of prison life but an effort to keep the convicts from leaving the institution at will.[23]

In the same spirit, wardens confronted the problem of coping with a refractory prisoner. The dilemma had not been acute when jails confined offenders only temporarily; but once convicts became more or less permanent residents, keepers had to search for additional powers of coercion. Most of them reverted to eighteenth-century practices, whipping or chaining an unruly inmate, as they once had the violent insane. Some officials, however, tried to devise solutions more in accord with republican ideals, seeking to avoid corporal punishment within as well as without the institution. Pennsylvania, New York, and Massachusetts corrected disobedient convicts by placing them alone in single rooms on a limited diet. This punishment was to strike terror in the heart of inmates, compel them to abide by the rules, yet not require bloodletting or a basic rearrangement of the style of penitentiary life. The confinement of a prisoner to a cell was convenient. Wardens did not intend for it to reform or elevate the criminal, or to have general applicability among all convicts.[24]

Prison officials in the post-Revolution period met other difficulties. By its very nature, a lengthy sentence entailed unprecedented expenses; feeding and clothing convicts for a period of years would swell costs. Then, some kind of daily activity was necessary, for otherwise inmates might come to suffer physical or perhaps emotional disability. The common solution in the 1790's was the most obvious one, as well as the least disruptive to the structure of the institution: to set aside several rooms and a garden for convicts to labor in. This tactic appeared to be an apt way to keep prisoners busy while reimbursing the state for the growing costs of confinement. And it would help to differentiate the prison from the almshouse, making it something else than a rest home between arrests. Some students of crime declared that the routine of labor might serve to rehabilitate the offender, transforming him into a hard-working citizen. Quaker reformers in Pennsylvania especially held out this prospect. But most officials were simply trying to save the state some money, to occupy the inmates, and to make clear that incarceration was a punishment.[25]

The results were not impressive. Officials made some of the adjustments necessary to carry out the logic of the decision, ending, for example, the colonial practice of having prisoners pay the jailer for their board, and deciding that even inmates with property would have to work while serving their sentences. But still they came up against unanticipated difficulties not easily resolved. The household model was not as appropriate to the organization of labor as they had believed. Prisoners were not kinfolk, and the institution was unable to order their actions effectively. Convicts worked slowly and sloppily, shirking whatever tasks they could. Lacking incentive and close supervision, they were neither reliable nor efficient.

Officials were ill-prepared to manage their side of the enterprise. They lacked experience in bulk purchasing of raw materials and in marketing procedures; they were uncertain as to whether the state should provide all the necessary goods or lease the entire operation to private contractors. Their ignorance together with prisoners' ill will made almost every prison ledger show a loss. Most institutions, rather then abandon convict labor, increasingly used it as a method of punishment. New Jersey legislators, concerned more with correction than with profit, instructed prison officials to institute "labor of the hardest and most servile kind, in which the work is least liable to be spoiled by ignorance, neglect or obstinacy." New York experimented with a treadmill, the prisoners turning it to exhaust and discipline themselves. But no one considered the introduction of labor a success.[26]

By 1820, the viability of the entire prison system was in doubt, and its most dedicated supporters conceded a near total failure. Institutionalization had not only failed to pay its own way, but had also encouraged and educated the criminal to a life in crime. "Our favorite scheme of substituting a state prison for the gallows," concluded one New York lawyer, "is a prolific mother of crime. . . . Our state prisons, as at present constituted, are grand demoralizers of our people."[27] Other critics issued harsh verdicts. A Massachusetts investigatory body and a group of Philadelphia reformers both labeled the prison "a school for vice," while a New York philanthropic society declared that it "operates with alarming efficacy to increase, diffuse, and extend the love of vice, and a knowledge of the arts and practices of criminality." Practically no one would have estimated that within fifteen years American penitentiaries would become the object of national acclaim and international study.[28]

The key to this transformation was the Auburn and Pennsylvania programs. Their concepts restructured the penitentiary, changing the popular verdict from failure to success. Little distance separated the ideas and the reality of the new penitentiaries; construction and organization to a considerable degree followed reformers' blueprints. The match, to be sure, was by no means perfect, and by the 1850's, abuses were undermining the system. But the states made an energetic and not unsuccessful attempt to put the programs into effect. These latest institutions were not the logical end of a development that began with the seventeenth-century house of correction, continued in the eighteenth-century workhouse, and improved in the post-Revolution prison. Of course various components in the system had roots in older ideas and practices, but the sum of the penitentiary was qualitatively different from its several parts. Europeans traveled to the new world to examine an American creation, not to see a minor variant on an old world theme. The antebellum generation could rightly claim to have made a major innovation in criminal punishment.

The new principle of separation was as central to penitentiary practices as it was to reformers' pamphlets. Officials repeatedly looked to it to solve specific problems (the rules governing letter-writing, how visitors should be treated), as well as to shape general policies (the inmates' daily routine, the overall design of the structure). It was never the only guideline — wardens and agents had financial obligations to fulfill, since state legislators anticipated that prisons would contribute substantially to their own upkeep. But the ledgers alone were not determinative.

The institutions rigorously attempted to isolate the prisoner both from the general community and from his fellow inmates. To fulfill the first charge, they severed almost every tie between the prisoner and his family and friends, and even attempted with some degree of success to block out reports of outside events. Pennsylvania went to the furthest extremes. The prison at Philadelphia prohibited any relative or friend from visiting the inmate and allowed only a handful of carefully screened persons, of whose virtue there could be no doubt, to see the convict in his cell. It banned all exchanges of correspondence and excluded newspapers to insure convicts' ignorance of external affairs. Partisans accurately boasted that a Pennsylvania inmate was "perfectly secluded from the world . . . hopelessly separated from one's family, and from all communication with and knowledge of them for the whole term of imprisonment." Throughout the pre–Civil War period, penitentiaries organized on the separate system made almost no compromises with these regulations.[29]

New York's practices were hardly less rigid. The state penitentiary rules in the 1830's declared that convicts were to "receive no letters or intelligence from or concerning their friends, or any information on any subject out of prison." Relatives were not permitted to visit with an inmate and he, in turn, was not allowed to correspond with them. "The prisoner," a Sing-Sing chaplain of this period recalled, "was taught to consider himself dead to all without the prison walls." And the warden himself repeated this analogy when instructing new convicts on their situation. "It is true," he told them in 1826, "that while confined here you can have no intelligence concerning relatives or friends. . . . You are to be literally buried from the world."[30] Officials somewhat relaxed these regulations in the 1840's, but the concessions were minimal. At Sing-Sing convicts were then allowed to send one letter every six months, and at the new prison at Clinton, one every four months — subject of course to the chaplain writing and the warden censoring it. They could also receive a single visit from relatives, in the presence of guards, during the course of their sentence. Throughout these decades the penitentiaries prohibited newspapers and books. The results were mixed, but if convicts often managed to smuggle these materials in, periodic cell inspections ferreted them out.[31]

Institutions in other states adhered to similar standards, all attempting, with varying degrees of success, to isolate the convict from society. New Jersey officials, for example, complained bitterly in 1830 that prisoners knew too much about public events. Convinced that "discipline is interrupted by a knowledge in the prison, among the convicts, of almost everything that is done abroad," they unhappily reported that inmates were learning through newspapers and conversations what was happening at the state capital, especially in regard to prison matters. The administrative reaction was predictable: more stringent isolation of the inmates from each other, from the guards, and from the community. Indeed, New Jersey soon decided to follow the more stringent procedures of the Pennsylvania system rather than the Auburn plan.[32] Maine's prison commissioner in this period, future presidential candidate James Blaine, was also certain that "information upon events of current interest, and glimpses of the outer world, have a tendency to unsettle the convict's mind and render him restless and uneasy." Distressed to find magazines and newspapers circulating in the state's congregate prison, Blaine charged officials to work still harder at "separating the convict from all association with the world at large," at banishing external influences from the penitentiary.[33] The thick walls that surrounded the penitentiary were not only to keep the inmates in, but the rest of the world out.

Just as critical to the organization of the penitentiary was the isolation of inmates from each other. The program was formidable, far more difficult than excluding visitors; still, wardens and keepers, especially before 1840, enjoyed a fair measure of success. The obstacles were greater in congregate than in separate institutions and the congregate system swept the states. But the popularity of Auburn was no less a triumph for the principle of separation. The prestigious Boston Prison Discipline Society announced that since congregate systems operated just as effectively as separate ones, it was senseless and wasteful to appropriate the extra funds. An influential pamphleteer like Matthew Carey also urged officials to adopt the New York plan, convinced that the separate system had no monopoly on proper discipline. Pennsylvania's defenders in rebuttal argued that no one ought to prescribe a particular medicine for the patient simply because it was cheaper. But their contentions carried little weight against the voluminous literature that legitimated the Auburn plan as a reform enterprise. Legislators deeply concerned with the issues of social control and rehabilitation, and yet tax-conscious, could honestly conclude that the New York plan promised success equal to that of its rival.[34]

In practice, Pennsylvania's institutions effectively prevented communication between convicts. The Philadelphia prison, for example, despite charges of faulty ducts and thin walls, did eliminate almost all inmate contact. Visitors' impressions, wardens' reports, and state investigations commonly testified to its success. "It is incontestable," wrote Tocqueville and Beaumont, "that this perfect isolation [at Philadelphia] secures the prisoner from all fatal contamination."[35]

The performance of Auburn-type institutions varied, more dependent than its competitor on skillful administration. Some prisons kept communication between convicts to an absolute minimum, with a single cell for every inmate at night and effective policing of workshops and exercise yards during the day. Others were more lax, understaffed, and overcrowded, operating with too small a budget or incompetent administrators. Prisoners lived two, three, or more to a cell, mingled freely in exercise yards, conversed openly at work. Still others enforced a silence but with such repressive and cruel tactics that even the most ardent defenders of the system had their doubts. Discipline also changed over time. The penitentiaries organized in the 1820's and 1830's largely satisfied the criterion of separation, particularly in New York, Massachusetts, and Connecticut. But in later decades control weakened. Older prisons became less rigorous while newer institutions in midwestern states frequently relaxed standards.

The early years at Auburn, the model for congregate prisons everywhere, were its most disciplined. The stillness that pervaded this prison was hardly less complete than that at Philadelphia. "Everything passes," Tocqueville and Beaumont noted after their 1831 visit, "in the most profound silence, and nothing is heard in the whole prison but the steps of those who march, or sounds proceeding from the workshops." After the convicts returned to their cells, "the silence within these vast walls . . . is that of death. . . . We felt as if we traversed catacombs; there were a thousand living beings, and yet it was a desert solitude."

Officials were able to maintain this silence by preventing

8. *The walls of the Eastern State Penitentiary, Philadelphia. The monu-
mentality of the design by John Haviland points to the importance of these
structures in Jacksonian America. The pastoral quality of the scene, with
the prison as castle, suggests how unbounded was the optimism with which
citizens greeted this innovation.*
COURTESY OF THE PENNSYLVANIA PRISON SOCIETY

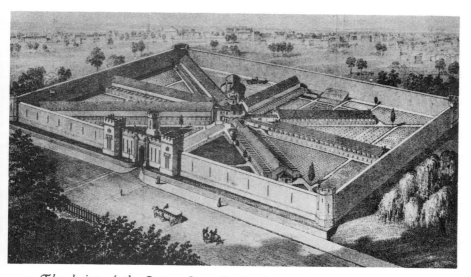

9. *The design of the Eastern State Penitentiary, Philadelphia. The commitment to isolation was so great that few costs were spared to attain it;
note, for example, the exercise yards, the honeycombed compartments along
each radial arm of the structure.*
COURTESY OF THE PENNSYLVANIA PRISON SOCIETY

overcrowding. As soon as swelling numbers imperiled the one-man-to-a-cell principle, they persuaded the legislature to appropriate funds to correct the situation. The state, rather than simply erecting higher walls and more strictly enforcing internal security, responded by adding cells to Sing-Sing in 1832, and to Auburn in 1833. Consequently, Auburn was able to satisfy the most basic prerequisite of the system and isolate inmates at night.[36]

Its wardens also policed convicts effectively during the day. The state-appointed prison inspectors were fully satisfied with Auburn's performance in the 1830's. Although the inspectors were not disinterested parties — having themselves selected the prison's top administrators — their reports were usually honest, candid, and to the point. When Auburn faced a crisis of overcrowding in 1830, they gave the legislature every grim detail; later, in the 1850's, when administrative diligence declined, their judgments were harsh and critical. But in these first years, they were ecstatic with Auburn's operations, convinced that internal regulation was effective. "The system of discipline which regulates this prison," they declared in 1835, "has advanced to a degree of perfection as desirable as it is difficult of attainment. . . . Our penitentiary system . . . has now become a model which the philanthropists of neighboring states, as well as of foreign countries, find it an object to follow. . . . It may now be said, without the charge of vanity, to be the best system of prison discipline in the world."[37] Even the Pennsylvania camp tacitly conceded Auburn's effectiveness. It criticized the frequency and severity of punishments and the temptations placed before the convicts, but did not contend that the prisoners were without discipline. From every indication, Auburn, like Pennsylvania, conformed to the principles of separation.

Success in the model institution did not guarantee faithful emulation, and Auburn's imitators often fell short of the program's goals. Still, they fully accepted the system's premises, and with different degrees of skill and concern enacted them. The Massachusetts and Connecticut institutions came closest to achieving Auburn's standards, rigorously enforcing the rule of silence and the separation of prisoners. Massachusetts moved quickly in the 1820's to adapt its prison at Charlestown to the congregate system, and for much of the next several decades, the solitary cell and the close supervision of inmates prevented most communication. Connecticut transferred prisoners from the wretched copper mine to a newly built congregate penitentiary at Wethersfield. Its wardens during this period, Amos Pilsbury and then his son Moses, were not without faults. But frequent state prison investigations usually agreed that Wethersfield was preserving silence and separation and was certainly no seminary for vice.[38]

Conditions degenerated as one moved westward. The Ohio penitentiary was intellectually committed to maintaining rules of silence with one prisoner to a cell. "The whole system of discipline," announced the directors in the prison rules, "depends upon non-intercourse between convicts." To this end, the legislature in the 1830's appropriated funds for a new institution that would not soon become overcrowded. But the structure proved superior to the administration and solitary cells did not insure an effective program. In the 1840's, convicts enjoyed an almost free run of the place, communicating at will and controlling much of their routine. Guards bribed inmates with food and clothing to secure compliance — a development that seems endemic to all prisons where administration is lax and permissive, and the convicts well organized. "At the start of my duties here," declared an entering warden in the 1850's with probably only slight exaggeration, "nearly all convicts were clamorous for what *they* claimed were their rights. . . . They acted as though they were martyrs. . . . Indeed the prison seemed a perfect bedlam." So, while the principles and the physical organization of the Auburn plan reached Ohio, the end product was hardly a triumph for it.[39]

The congregate ideology made headway at Illinois, but again the final result was mixed.[40] Iowa's officials also spread the congregate program. They erected a penitentiary in 1852 and then immediately dispatched a member eastward to survey the current methods of discipline, certain that "the subject of prison construction and discipline is a specialty . . . which mechanics and architects . . . generally do not understand." Impressed with what they learned, they set out to make the state institution "as perfect" as the ones in New York and Massachusetts. But although the institution was new, and the number of convicts was small, Iowa confronted disciplinary problems. The outbreak of the Civil War, however, turned attention elsewhere, putting to rest these ambitions for at least another decade.[41]

The problem of enforcement in the congregate system raised the dilemma of whether obedience was worth any price. Did the end of discipline justify every means of punishment? Was the cure more dangerous than the disease? The question had obvious relevance to an institution like Sing-Sing, which on the whole managed to curtail communication between convicts but with a type and frequency of correction that public investigators found cruel and sadistic. The issue, however, was not confined to one penitentiary or notorious warden. Prisons everywhere had to decide what punishments were proper for enforcing the system. Were the regular use of the whip, the yoke, the ball and chain, cold showers, or curtailed rations appropriate weapons in the battle to preserve order? Were offenders against prison law without rights, without protection from their keepers? The answer to this question offers evidence not only of the special administrative needs of penal institutions but also of the strength and implications of the concepts of deviancy and the reformatory program.

Sing-Sing officials in the 1830's were prepared to use every possible form of correction to enforce order, and justified their behavior by denigrating the whole notion of rehabilitation. Guards relied freely upon the whip, unhesitatingly using it for the smallest infraction, and their superiors defended this behavior vigorously. As Robert Wiltse, assistant to the warden, informed the state legislature in 1834: convicts "must be made to know, that *here* they must submit to every regulation, and obey every command of their keepers." Perversely insisting that most reformers had already abandoned the notion of a "general and radical reformation of offenders through a penitentiary system," Wiltse contended that a prison "should not be governed in such a manner as to induce rogues to consider it as a comfortable home. They must be *made* to *submit* to its rules, and this by the most energetic means; corporeal punishments for transgression, which to be effectual must be certain, and inflicted with as little delay as possible."[42]

Other institutions too were commonly far more intent on securing absolute obedience than on protecting convicts from cruel or unusual punishments. The whip was commonplace in Auburn and in Charlestown, in Columbus and in Wethersfield. Pennsylvania had recourse to the iron gag, Maine to the ball and chain, Connecticut to the cold shower. And officials wholeheartedly defended these punishments. Auburn's chaplain insisted that it would be "most unfortunate . . . if the public mind were to settle down into repugnance to the use of such coercive means." To isolate and rehabilitate convicts, corporal punishment was unquestionably proper and legitimate. "Only relax the reins of discipline . . . and a chaplain's labors would be of no more use here than in a drunken mob."[43] A Pennsylvania investigatory body justified using an iron gag on refractory prisoners. Convicts were "men of idle habits, vicious propensities, and depraved passions," who had to be taught obedience as the first step to reformation. Ohio's warden also considered the whip vital to a prison system. "For whenever the Penitentiary becomes a pleasant place of residence," he declared, "whenever a relaxation of discipline . . . converts it into something like an *Asylum* for the wicked, then it loses all its influence for good upon the minds of men disposed to do evil."[44]

Penal institutions' widespread and unembarrassed reliance on harsh disciplinary measures was due in part to the newness of the experiment. It reflected too a nagging concern that convicts might possibly join together to overpower their few keepers — no one was yet altogether confident that forty men could control eight hundred.[45] Yet even more fundamental was the close fit between the punitive measures and the reform perspective. The prevailing concepts of deviancy put a premium on rigorous discipline. The premises underlying the penitentiary movement placed an extraordinary emphasis on an orderly routine. Confident that the deviant would learn the lessons of discipline in a properly arranged environment, everyone agreed that prison life had to be strict and unrelenting. And with regularity a prerequisite for success, practically any method that enforced discipline became appropriate.

Reformers and prison officials agreed on the need for inmates to obey authority. Criminals, in their view, had never learned to respect limits. To correct this, the penitentiary had to secure absolute obedience, bending the convicts' behavior to fit its own rigid rules. Should wayward inmates resist, their obstinacy would have to be "broken," and as the word itself implied, the means were not nearly so important as the ends. Perhaps the most striking testimony to the influence of these ideas in legitimating disciplinary procedures came from Tocqueville and Beaumont. The visitors were under no illusions as to the nature or the extent of penitentiary punishments. "We have no doubt," they concluded, "but that the habits of order to which the prisoner is subjected for several years . . . the obedience of every moment to inflexible rules, the regularity of a uniform life, in a word, all the circumstances belonging to this severe system, are calculated to produce a deep impression upon his mind. Perhaps, leaving the prison he is not an honest man, but he has contracted honest habits . . . and if he is not more virtuous, he has become at least more judicious." Sing-Sing officials quoted these findings at length, and with obvious satisfaction.[46]

The commitment to a daily routine of hard and constant labor also pointed to the close correspondence between the ideas on the causes of crime and the structure of the penitentiary. Idleness was part symptom and part cause of deviant behavior. Those unwilling to work were prone to commit all types of offenses; idleness gave time for the corrupted to encourage and instruct one another in a life of crime. Proponents of a penitentiary training believed that the tougher the course, the more favorable the results. As one spokesman, Francis Gray, declared: "The object of prison discipline is to induce [the convict] not merely to form good resolutions . . . but to support himself by honest industry. The only effectual mode of leading him to do this, is to train him . . . to accustom him to work steadily and diligently from 8 to 10 hours a day, with no other respite. . . . The discipline best adapted to such men, is that which inures them to constant and vigorous toil."[47]

State legislators and wardens found these notions attractive and were eager to implement them. Secure in the knowledge that they were acting in the best interests of taxpayers and inmates alike, that they were simultaneously furthering financial and reformist goals, they had no objection to making some contracts with private manufacturers to lease convict labor or to establishing a prison routine of long hours with little relief. Hoping in this way to make the penitentiary a self-supporting, even profitable venture while rehabilitating the offender, they favored a schedule that maximized work. The results in New York were not unusual: convicts were up at five o'clock for two hours of work before breakfast, then back to it for three hours and forty-five minutes; lunch was at noon for one hour and fifteen minutes, then a return to the shop for another four hours and forty-five minutes. The weekly workday averaged ten hours, from sunup to sunset six days a week. A Christian Sunday and the lack of artificial lighting prevented a lengthening of the schedule.

But prison labor never brought great returns and in many instances was unable to meet the daily expenses of operation, let alone cover the costs of construction. Some of the first prisons did claim a profit in their annual reports, but often the figures were more testimony to the jugglings of the warden than to actual returns.[48] Officials gleefully cited a "profit" of ten thousand dollars at the end of the year, neglecting to mention that the costs of the institution's construction was two hundred thousand dollars. It would be decades before such a small return paid off the debt. Other agents published a favorable balance by not including officials' salaries or the cost of repairs.[49] The figures in the annual reports are generally too untrustworthy to allow firm conclusions, but it seems clear that if profit alone preoccupied the states, they could have found a better return on their investment elsewhere.[50]

External difficulties also arose constantly. Free labor bitterly and effectively protested against prison competition, and frequently secured the passage of restrictive legislation. In some states convicts were not permitted to practice a trade that they had not already learned and followed before confinement; in others the institution could not produce goods already being manufactured within the state's borders. Under these circumstances legislatures not only had to make up the deficits but bear the brunt of political protest as well. The widespread organization of convict labor was, therefore, not simply testimony to its economic rewards, any more than the persistence of penal institutions reflected their financial prowess. The idea of labor, even more than the calculations of profit and loss, made it central to the penitentiary.[51]

The doctrines of separation, obedience, and labor became the trinity around which officials organized the penitentiary. They carefully instructed inmates that their duties could be "comprised in a few words"; they were "to *labor diligently,* to *obey all orders,* and preserve an *unbroken silence.*"[52] Yet to achieve these goals, officers had to establish a total routine, to administer every aspect of the institution in accord with the three guidelines, from inmates' dress to their walk, from the cells' furnishings to the guards' deportment. The common solution was to follow primarily a quasi-military model. The regulations based on this model promised to preserve isolation, to make labor efficient, and to teach men lacking discipline to abide by rules; this regimented style of life would inculcate strict discipline, precision, and instantaneous adherence to commands. Furthermore, a military model in a correctional institution seemed especially suitable for demonstrating to the society at large the right principles of organization. Here was an appropriate example for a community suffering a crisis of order.

The first designers of the prison had few other useful models to emulate. In fact, the penitentiary was not the only institution in the 1820's and 1830's facing the dilemma of organization. Such a novel economic unit as the factory was also beginning to use rigorous procedures to bring an unprecedented discipline to workers' lives. Prison designers could find the factory an interesting but limited source of inspiration, appropriating that part of it which was most regulatory and precise. Both organizations were among the first to try to take people from casual routines to rigid ones.

Regimentation became the standard mode of prison life. Convicts did not walk from place to place; rather, they went in close order and single file, each looking over the shoulder of the man in front, faces inclined to the right, feet moving in unison, in lockstep. The lockstep became the trademark of American prisons in these years, a curious combination of march and shuffle that remained standard procedure well into the 1930's. Its invention and adoption exemplified the problems and responses of the first penitentiary officials. How were they to move inmates about? Prison officials with fixed ideas on convict communication and obedience, had to reject informal movement. Searching for greater discipline, they turned to the military march, crossed it with a shuffle to lessen its dignity, and pointed heads to the right, rather than facing straight ahead, to prevent conversation. The result, the lockstep, was an immediate success and became the common practice.[53]

Wardens organized the convicts' daily schedule in military style. At the sound of a horn or bell, keepers opened the cells, prisoners stepped onto the deck, and then in lockstep marched into the yard. In formation they emptied their night pails, moved on and washed them, took a few more steps, and placed them on a rack to dry. Still in line they marched to the shops. There they worked at their tasks in rows on long benches until the bell rang for breakfast. They grouped again in single file, passed into the kitchen, picked up their rations (regulations admonished them not to break step), and continued on to their cells, or in some institutions, to a common messroom where they ate their meal. (Regulations again instructed them to sit erect with backs straight.) At the bell they stood, reentered formation, and marched back to the shops. They repeated this routine at noon, and again at six o'clock; then they returned to their cells for the night and at nine o'clock lights went out, as at a barracks. Although some institutions were more exacting than others in enforcing these procedures, almost all of them tried to impose a degree of military routine on their prisoners.[54]

The furnishings of convicts' cells also indicates the relevance of the military model. A cot and pail and tin utensils were the basic objects. Prisoners now wore uniforms of a simple, coarse, striped fabric, and all had their hair cut short to increase uniformity.[55] The military example affected keepers as well as convicts. Several wardens came to their positions directly from an army or navy career, legislators obviously eager to have them apply their former training to this setting. Guards wore uniforms, mustered at specific hours, and kept watch like sentries. Regulations ordered them to behave in a "gentlemanly manner," like officers, without laughter, ribaldry, or unnecessary conversation while on duty. As Sing-Sing's rules put it, in only a slight overstatement of a general sentiment: "They were to require from the convicts the greatest deference, and never suffer them to approach but in respectful manner; they are not to allow them the least degree of familiarity, nor exercise any towards them; they should be extremely careful to *command* as well as to compel their respect."[56]

The military style also influenced the construction and appearance of the institutions. Some were modeled after medieval fortresses. An adaptation of a structure from the Middle Ages was necessarily monumental, appropriate in size to a noble experiment like the penitentiary, capable of stimulating a citizen's pride and a visitor's respect. It also had functional qualities, for thick walls promised security against prison breaks, and turrets became posts for guarding an enclosed space. Another popular alternative was to construct the prison along factory lines — a long and low building, symmetrically arranged with closely spaced windows, all very regular and methodical. Whatever it lacked in grandeur it tried to make up in fixity and order.[57]

The functioning of the penitentiary — convicts passing their sentences in physically imposing and highly regimented settings, moving in lockstep from bare and solitary cells to workshops, clothed in common dress, and forced into standard routines — was designed to carry a message to the community. The prison would train the most notable victims of social disorder to discipline, teaching them to resist corruption. And success in this particular task should inspire a general reformation of manners and habits. The institution would become a laboratory for social improvement. By demonstrating how regularity and discipline transformed the most corrupt persons, it would reawaken the public to these virtues. The penitentiary would promote a new respect for order and authority.

Reformers never spelled out the precise nature and balance of this reformation. They hoped that families, instead of overindulging or neglecting their children, would more conscientiously teach limits and the need for obedience to them. Assuming that social stability could not be achieved without a very personal and keen respect for authority, they looked first to a firm family discipline to inculcate it. Reformers also anticipated that society would rid itself of corruptions. In a narrow sense this meant getting rid of such blatant centers of vice as taverns, theaters, and houses of prostitution. In a broader sense, it meant reviving a social order in which men knew their place. Here sentimentality took over, and critics in the Jacksonian period often assumed that their forefathers had lived together without social strain, in secure, placid, stable, and cohesive communities. In fact, the designers of the penitentiary set out to re-create these conditions. But the results, it is not surprising to discover, were startlingly different from anything that the colonial period had known. A conscious effort to instill discipline through an institutional routine led to a set work pattern, a rationalization of movement, a precise organization of time, a general uniformity. Hence, for all the reformers' nostalgia, the reality of the penitentiary was much closer to the values of the nineteenth than the eighteenth century.

5

Insanity and the Social Order

One of the most articulate and elaborate statements of the social origins of deviant behavior appeared in the pre–Civil War analysis of the causes of insanity. Medical superintendents led the investigation and discussion, but the analysis was not an exclusively professional one. It spread from medical journals to popular magazines, from physicians to laymen. The *North American Review*, as well as the *American Journal of Insanity*, took up the issue, and reformers like Samuel Gridley Howe, as well as doctors like Edward Jarvis, pronounced their views. The terminology was to some extent specialized: "mania," "dementia," "melancholia" were technical terms with fairly precise definitions. But the concepts most critical to the interpretation of the origins of insanity were well within the comprehension of the ordinary public. For the analysis depended not on the lessons of anatomy, but on a critique of Jacksonian society.

The question of the etiology of insanity was a comparatively new one for Americans. The colonists had assumed that its cause, like that of other diseases, rested with God's will. The insane received public attention and sympathy as one group among the poor whose incapacitating ailment made them permanently dependent upon relatives or upon the community. But the biological or social agents of mental disease and the precise nature of the affliction prompted little reflection. In the aftermath of the Revolution, however, a spark of interest appeared, lit by Enlightenment ideology and an awareness of very dramatic events in Europe. Just as Beccaria had insisted that humane laws could eradicate crime, so men like Tuke in England and Pinel in

France insisted that kind and gentle treatment would help to cure insanity. The image of Pinel freeing the insane from their chains at Salpêtrière had an immediate and obvious appeal to men in the new republic.[1] They too had just emerged from bondage and intended to bring freedom to others.

The insane were an apt group for this experiment. Raising none of the domestic or international complications that were unavoidable in such issues as the abolition of slavery or the best policy toward the French Revolution, they presented a perfect opportunity to breathe new life into a downtrodden class. But once again, with the insane as with the criminal, the matter was not so simply solved. To provide them with warmth and clothing and remove their chains did not settle the issue, and by the 1830's, Americans calculated that insanity was increasing significantly in their society, not being cured. The problem then became not only to justify republican government in the eyes of the world, but to control what appeared to be an epidemic at home. Prodded by fear as much as by glory, Americans in the Jacksonian period opened an intensive exploration of the origins of the disease.

Every general practitioner in the pre–Civil War era agreed that insanity was a disease of the brain and that the examination of tissues in an autopsy would reveal organic lesions, clear evidence of physical damage, in every insane person. Isaac Ray, one of the leading medical superintendents of the period, when presenting the consensus of his discipline to the legal profession, confidently declared: "No pathological fact is better established . . . than that deviations from the healthy structure are generally present in the brains of insane subjects. . . . The progress of pathological anatomy during the present century has established this fact beyond the reach of a reasonable doubt." Should a particular autopsy reveal no physical changes in the brain, "the only legitimate inference" was that current skills were still too crude to insure accurate results.[2] Nevertheless, this view did not lead to intensive anatomical or neurological investigations to understand the etiology of the disease. Medical superintendents gave no room in their institutions to this type of research. They had no doubt that organic lesions existed, that insanity was a bodily ailment. But its first causes they assigned not to body chemistry but to social organization. The solution to the age-old ailment would be found not in the laboratory but in the society, not by looking into the microscope but into the community.

Medical superintendents carefully charted the likely causes of mental illness among their patients. The results seem if not bewildering, then at least woefully naïve and a bit foolish. One physician in New York, for example, listed 43 causes for the disease among 551 patients in 1845. They ranged from ill health (104), religious anxiety (77), and loss of property (28), to excessive study (25), blows on the head (8), political excitement (5), disappointed ambition (41), and going into cold water (1). A colleague in Tennessee attributed the ailment to such phenomena as ill health, disappointed love, pecuniary embarrassment, and "the present condition of the country." Another psychiatrist in Connecticut ranked ill health first, followed by intense mental and bodily exertion, and intemperance; important too were masturbation, Millerism, fear of poverty, and ridicule of shopmates.[3] Still, these categories were not absurd or arbitrary. The medical superintendents themselves were a little uneasy with them, always referring to the charts as the "supposed" or "probable" causes of the disease. Nevertheless, they were willing to compile and publish the results, for the particular findings fit well with the general theory by which they explained the origins of insanity.

Medical superintendents linked bodily ailments and injuries to mental illness. Since insanity was a physical disease, sickness or wounds could debilitate the brain. A blow to the head might impair the organ's functioning and bring on insanity. Similarly, disorders in one part of the body might in time adversely affect another; a stomach disorder could damage the nervous system and then attack the brain.

Psychiatrists' tables of causes, therefore, listed somatic problems ranging from burns, concussions, acid inhalation, and heart disease to suppressed menstruation and general poor health.[4] But a straightforward paradigm of bodily illness leading to mental illness accounted for only a limited number of cases. To understand the others, one had to look beyond such immediate and obvious causes to the workings of American society. Medical superintendents were convinced that social, economic, and political conditions exerted the crucial influence.

With a regularity that quickly rendered the idea as much a cliché as an insight, professionals and laymen alike attributed insanity to the course of civilization. Mental disorder, announced Edward Jarvis, a leading medical superintendent, was "a part of the price we pay for civilization. The causes of the one increase with the developments and results of the other. . . . In this opinion all agree." Jarvis did not exaggerate the consensus. Isaac Ray reported that "insanity is now increasing in most, if not all, civilized communities." And although some observers thought that "conservative" and "counterbalancing" forces might accompany the march of civilization, he was certain that they have "furnished only an insignificant check to the host of adverse influences" that produce the disease.[5] Another colleague, Pliny Earle, lectured to medical students on the "constant parallelism between the progress of society and the increase of mental disorders," pondering "whether the condition of highest culture in society is worth the penalties which it costs." And a reformer like Dorothea Dix, confident of the answer, rhetorically asked members of the Pennsylvania legislature: "Is it not to the habits, the customs, the temptations of civilized life and society" that we owe most of these calamities?[6]

A logical deduction from this doctrine was that primitive communities ought to be free of the disease, and so although writers cited only the crude observations of travelers and adventurers for proof, the popular idea went unchallenged. "As a general rule," announced Pliny Earle, "insanity is but little known in those countries . . . which are either in a savage or barbarous state of society." Dorothea Dix blandly asserted that "those tracts of North America inhabited by Indians and the sections chiefly occupied by the negro race, produce comparatively very few examples."[7] This perspective, of course, offered little comfort to the rest of America which, as a civilized nation — in its own eyes perhaps the most civilized of all nations — seemed especially liable to the disease. One medical superintendent, Samuel Woodward, rated the United States fourth among all countries in the occurrence of insanity. Another, William Rockwell, still more pessimistically contended that "perhaps there is no country in which it prevails to so great an extent as in these United States," while Isaac Ray agreed that mental illness was "more prevalent here, than it is in other countries." Laymen usually echoed the most dismal estimates. Both Dix and Samuel Gridley Howe put America at the very top of the list.[8]

The link between civilization and insanity was not first forged in the United States. The idea had its origins on the Continent and spread across the ocean. But to a surprising degree, Americans made it their own, grasping it with unrivaled intellectual enthusiasm and employing it in very special ways. The postulate became the base for a detailed critique of Jacksonian society, a specific and original analysis of the dangers of the existing social system.

Before the Civil War, practically no one in the United States protested the simple connection between insanity and civilization. Despite the tenuous quality of the evidence, Americans accepted the conclusion without qualification. The Europeans, however, were far more cautious. Samuel Tuke, one of the leading students of mental illness in England, considered the hypothesis unproven. Noting that some persons believed that British social conditions raised the proportion of the insane, he concluded that the evidence "must be noted as deficient, to an extent which, I believe, does not warrant us to decide." His well-known colleague, Henry Maudsley, was also very skeptical. Travelers' reports, he insisted, were inaccurate guides to the prevalence of the disease among primitive peoples; such informants would be neither competent nor learned enough to reach valid conclusions.[9] In Germany too, caution was widespread. Wilhelm Griesinger, in a leading textbook on mental pathology, contended that what seemed to be higher rates of insanity in more advanced countries simply reflected improved modes of treatment. Primitive states had probably just as much insanity but it remained hidden there for lack of proper care. Griesinger went on to insist that despite its drawbacks, civilization brought a higher standard of living and innumerable comforts, which "ought to compensate, at least to a certain extent, for any injurious influence of the spread of civilization."[10] Yet, American medical superintendents demonstrated none of the circumspection of their European counterparts. The connection of civilization to insanity fit well with their preconceptions and perspectives.

The postulate offered no firm guidelines to a social critique. A supposed relationship between insanity and civilization could promote the most conservative or radical conclusions. "Civilization" was a vague, almost meaningless term which did not dictate a well-defined response to particular religious or economic or political practices. A bias in favor of simplicity could inspire a revolutionary program or a reactionary one. In the name of simplicity one could call for aristocratic government — to leave the masses content and untroubled — or the most dramatic form of direct democracy — to eliminate all the superfluities of bureaucratic decisions.[11] This criterion in religion could support a John Calvin and Calvinism or a William Ellery Channing and Unitarianism. It could point to the need for the father to exercise unqualified authority or to the propriety of family counsels and democratic participation in the household. In other words, the theory was far too general to account for the explicit interpretations that Americans offered. The appraisal that emerged was ultimately their own and was not heavily indebted to Continental doctrines. The European and scientific literature made convenient and impressive footnotes, but the core of the medical superintendents' and laymen's analysis reflected a native outlook. Their understanding of deviant behavior had far more in common with compatriots' ideas on convicts and delinquents than with those of any Continental thinker or professor.

Medical superintendents' explorations of the origins of insanity took them into practically every aspect of antebellum society, from economic organization to political and religious practices, from family habits to patterns of thought and education. And little of what they saw pleased them. The style of life in the new republic seemed willfully designed to produce mental illness. Everywhere they looked, they found chaos and disorder, a lack of fixity and stability. The community's inherited traditions and procedures were dissolving, leaving incredible stresses and strains. The anatomical implications of this condition were clear: the brain received innumerable abuses, was weakened, and inevitably succumbed to disease. "There is no mystery in this," explained Isaac Ray. "As with the stomach, the liver, the lungs, so with the brain — the manner in which its exercise is regulated, determines, to a very great extent, the state of its health." Since American society made unprecedented demands on it, one had to expect that insanity would increase "at a rate unparalleled in any former period."[12] But the biological results were not nearly so critical to explore and clarify as the social origins. And to this consideration psychiatrists devoted the bulk of their attention.

The thrust of the argument was evident in medical superintendents' observations on the ethos and reality of social mobility. They were convinced that the startlingly fluid social order in the new republic encouraged and rewarded unlimited and grandiose ambitions. But rather than point with pride to these attitudes or achievements, they saw only the most pernicious effects. Here was one principal reason why Americans were especially prone to mental illness. "In this country," explained Edward Jarvis to a Massachusetts medical society meeting, "where no son is necessarily confined to the work or employment of his father, but all the fields of labor, of profit, or of honor are open to whomsoever will put on the harness," and where "all are invited to join the strife for that which may be gained in each," it was inevitable that "the ambition of some leads them to aim at that which they cannot reach, to strive for more than they can grasp." As a result, "their mental powers are strained to their utmost tension; they labor in agitation . . . their minds stagger under the disproportionate burden." How different were conditions in a more stable society. "In an uneducated community, or where people are overborne by despotic government or inflexible customs, where men are born in castes and die without overstepping their native condition, where the child is content with the pursuit and the fortune of his father . . . there these undue mental excitements and struggles do not happen." And without such tensions, "these causes of insanity cannot operate." So although Jarvis did not counsel his countrymen to adopt a despotic government or neglect education, he insisted that "a higher civilization than we possess would restrain these [ambitions] within the just limits of prudence and health."[13]

Isaac Ray fully shared Jarvis's outlook. It was "agreeable

enough to people of the old world," he contended, "to follow on in the same path their father trod before them, turning neither to the right hand, nor to the left, and perfectly content with a steady and sure, though it may be slow progress." But in the new world, all citizens struggle "to make, or greatly advance their fortunes, by some happy stroke of skill . . . chance, or some daring speculation." Sleepless nights, fears of failure, and extraordinary stress accompanied these efforts, rapidly consuming mental energies, and thus "strongly predispose the mind to insanity."[14]

William Sweetser, a physician of lesser note, popularized this message in a layman's guide to mental hygiene. "Our own peculiar circumstances," he wrote, "are especially favorable to the growth of ambition. . . . Every one sees bright visions in the future . . . our democratical institutions inviting each citizen, however subordinate may be his station, to join in the pursuit of whatever distinctions our forms of society can bestow." Yet, as a result, "the demon of unrest, the luckless offspring of ambition, haunts us all . . . racking us with the constant and wearing anxiety of what we call *bettering* our condition. The servant is dissatisfied as a servant . . . and so it is through all other ranks. . . . All are equally restless, all are straining for elevations beyond what they already enjoy." Relentlessly, "we go on toiling anxiously in the chase . . . until death administers the only sure opiate to our peaceless souls."[15]

To aggravate the problem, the achievement of success carried severe penalties. The change from a simple life to "the fashionable or the cultivated style," warned Jarvis, was not easily made. "There must be much thought and toil, much hope and fear and much anxiety and vexation to effect the passage and to sustain one's self in the new position." Since mobility strained every faculty, the price of transit frequently became insanity. Life in the world of commerce and finance took its toll. "Overtrading, debt, bankruptcy, sudden reverses, disappointed hopes," lamented Samuel Woodward in 1842, "all seem to have clustered together in these times, and are generally influential in producing insanity." Medical superintendents had little difficulty in accounting for the increase in the number of insane in 1858: the panic of 1857 had left its mark. Finally, as Jarvis explained, inflationary cycles, the risks of speculation and innovations in business techniques made fortunes in America especially precarious. Successful men were driven to "more labor, more watchfulness, greater fear and anxiety." Those perched on top of the ladder, as well as those trying to climb it, were liable to fall.[16]

A similar dynamic seemed to psychiatrists to operate in other facets of American life. Politics, like business, made citizens so frantic that outbreaks of insanity were common. Americans competed for power as they battled for wealth. Because men on every level of society considered a government office within their reach and appropriate to their talents, many of them paid the price of insanity for excessive ambition. "In this country," declared William Rockwell, "where all the offices of government are open to every man, and where the facilities for accumulating wealth are so numerous, persons even in humble life cherish hopes which can never be realized."[17] A well-ordered society, in which only those fit and able to rule sought position, or even a despotic government, in which the masses had no prospect of exercising power, avoided the pitfalls of so open a system.

American politics endangered the mental health of ordinary voters. Isaac Ray, distressed at the grave implications of "the practical workings of our republican institutions," pointed to the exceptional energy and attention given to political affairs as a case in point. "The public agitation which is never at rest around the citizen of a republic," he complained, "is constantly placing before him great questions of public policy, which may be decided with little knowledge of the subject, but none the less zeal." Every man had a voice in the affairs of the town, the state and the country. "It is not for him to suppose, in any national crisis or emergency, that the government will take care of the country, while he takes care of himself." One day he was in a frenzy over a proposed liquor law, on the next he debated the wisdom of supporting a public highway. And then he turned attention to the qualifications of the various office seekers in never-ending election contests. No sooner was the race for the legislature settled than the contest for Congress began. Ray could not resist a comparison to European conditions. "There, the public attention may be called once a year, to the election of a mayor, but it is an even chance whether the individual has any part or lot in the issue." Americans, he concluded, judged eternal vigilance to be the price of liberty, but they ought to remember all of its costs.[18]

Identical traits characterized the intellectual life of the country. With the same overzealousness with which Americans sought wealth and power, they pursued abstract study. Again, members from every social strata and with varying qualifications participated, not only the well-trained and capable. Part of the problem medical superintendents ascribed to the recent discovery of new areas and methods of study; work in these disciplines, whether phrenology or physiology, easily overtaxed the mind. But these general difficulties were especially acute in the United States. All sorts of people took up the burden of inquiry, and ambition soon outraced proficiency. "The number of those who are, or strive to be, highly educated," remarked Jarvis with obvious regret, "who undertake to be philosophers, chemists, mathematicians, who endeavor to fathom the mysteries of theology . . . who cease the labor of their hands and betake themselves to the labor of their brains . . . have increased in a much greater ratio, than the population of either State or Nation." Americans considered nothing so remote from their everyday concerns that they would resist playing part-time scientist or philosopher. The professional had no exclusive province. A specialist's judgment would not prevent others from conducting their own investigation or reaching their own conclusion.[19]

Citizens in the new republic rejected any bounds to their intellectual efforts. They would no more respect their fathers' ideas than they would rest content with his social status. Isaac Ray, with typical nostalgia, remembered that "people once thought they might sometimes abide by the wisdom of their fathers; that some things were considered as settled and others as confessedly beyond the reach of finite intelligence." Previous generations had been quite satisfied in "taking their opinions on trust, in the belief that others might be better qualified by education and experience to form them than they were themselves." In an obvious and deeply felt romance of the past, Ray described how "in the old days," work began at dawn and continued till evening, how people took cheer in modest goods and cultivated domestic affections, how sons and daughters never puzzled themselves over their mission in life but contentedly performed their duties at day and slept peaceably at night. Today, however, "we question everything; we pry into everything. . . . Subjects which once were supposed to be confined to the province of the learned . . . are now discussed by an order of minds which disdain the trammels of logic." The more complex the subject, the more active the speculation, and the greater the difficulties, the sharper the curiosity. The result, Ray would have it, was that Americans in unprecedented numbers broke their health.[20]

To these critics, the nation lacked all points of stability. Americans frenetically pursued wealth and power and knowledge without pause or concern for their effects. Imagine a film of a steeplechase race presented at several times its normal speed. Almost simultaneously one rider jumps over a barrier while another skirts a creek, a third topples on a row of hedges and a fourth dashes down the stretch, all moving at breakneck speed. Such was the critics' perspective on Jacksonian society.

Under these conditions, even the institutions which might have slowed the tempo and conceivably offered a sanctuary of security were either without influence or exacerbated the situation. Medical superintendents were hardly cheered by the state of religion. The problem, as they understood it, returned to Americans' unwillingness to accept doctrines on the basis of tradition or the status of their spokesmen. The church could not be an effective sedative in this overwrought society since few were willing to swallow the pill. Psychiatrists distrusted the more successful manifestations of religious enthusiasm in the revival. The subject was not altogether a comfortable one — for belief in God was not supposed to resemble financial or political ambitions, where too much was a dangerous thing. Still, medical superintendents regularly included religious excesses among the causes of insanity. And occasionally, a movement as extreme as the Millerites afforded them the opportunity to denounce "a popular religious error" for having produced "so much excitement in the community and rendered so many insane." The church did little to counterbalance prevailing trends, and at times even stimulated them.[21]

Still more disappointing — indeed, treacherous — was the performance of two critical institutions, the school and the family. It was within their potential to moderate the dangers so prevalent in the social order. But instead, according to medical superintendents, the classroom and the home were two of the chief villains. The frantic quality of American life owed much to the style of training the new generation. The school, for its part, ostensibly disobeyed every sound principle of mental hygiene. It admitted children at too early an age, between three and five, and kept them in the classroom too long, a minimum of six hours per day. It crammed them with information as rapidly as possible, piled lesson upon lesson, lengthened the hours of study, and considered recreation and rest as merely the loss of valuable time. The immediate damage inflicted on young and tender minds was only matched by the predisposition this regimen established for nervous disorders later in life.[22]

The classroom unhappily duplicated the pace and principles of the marketplace. Rather than offer an alternative to an overcompetitive and ultimately debilitating system, it reproduced in miniature the conditions of the larger society. "Discipline and development may be theoretically recognized as legitimate objects of education," observed Isaac Ray, "but practically they are regarded as subordinate to that which predominates over all others, viz., the means of distinction which it gives — the medals, prizes and honors." In other words, "we manage the education of our children somewhat as we often manage our capital, going upon the plan of quick returns and small profit." The students' accumulations were like the speculators', large, showy, but not solid. The close fit between the morality of the school and the society also infected children with the spirit of limitless ambition.[23] American education, contended Edward Jarvis, excited "expectations which cannot be realized and led their pupils to form schemes inconsistent with the circumstances that surround them." In the classroom students first learned to "look for success, honor, or advantages, which their talents, or education, or habits of business, or station in the world, will not obtain for them." Therefore, as adults, "they are laying plans which cannot be fulfilled, they are looking for events which will not happen. They are struggling perpetually and unsuccessfully against the tide of fortune." Without the ability, wisdom or power to satisfy "unfounded hope and ambition," they were "apt to become nervous, querulous, and despondent, and sometimes, insane."[24]

Medical superintendents ascribed to the family ultimate responsibility for perpetuating this educational system. "The plans of education proposed by many zealous instructors," argued Jarvis, "and adopted by many who are in authority . . . correspond . . . with the willingness of parents and children to carry them out."[25] The lessons that children first learned in their nurseries at home were repeated in the school, and parents would allow no other way. A mistaken ambition for the intellectual and social achievement of their children led parents to insist that teachers convey a maximum amount of information in the shortest possible time. And medical superintendents magnified the pervasiveness of this spirit of ambition: No sooner did a young man join the race for success than he not only received the approbation of his own conscience, but immediately became the pride of his parents, the honor of his school, the envy of his friends, and "the hope of the coming age" to commencement speakers.

The family was the one institution that psychiatrists believed might have calmed the frantic spirit at loose in the community. A well-ordered family could protect its charge from the disordered society, inoculating the child against the disease before he suffered exposure. Instead, it brought the germs right into the cradle. Whether indulgent or neglectful or hypersensitive to success, the family failed to discipline its charges. "The asceticism of our ancestors," claimed Ray with another fond look backward, "was infinitely less injurious than the license which characterizes the domestic training of their descendants." Children of this generation scarcely ever felt the authority of any will but their own, and obeyed "no higher law than the caprice of the moment." Family government exercised only "feeble and fitful rule," yielding to the slightest opposition, and encouraged, rather than repressed, children's selfish and indulgent inclinations. Almost from birth, Ray contended, youngsters contemplated life "not as a field of discipline and improvement, but a scene of inexhaustible opportunities for fulfilling hope and gratifying desire." Under this training, patience and perseverance "become distasteful to the mind which can breathe only an atmosphere of excitement. . . . It reels under the first stroke of disappointment, turns upon itself . . . and thus it is that many a man becomes insane." Mental illness, concluded Ray, will continue to increase until the time when the family transmitted "a higher culture" to the nation's children. But he saw little prospect for such a change.[26]

Medical superintendents broadly defined both the symptoms of the disease and its potential victims. They described in the widest possible terms the kinds of behavior that might constitute evidence of insanity, and repeatedly stressed that the ailment was not the special curse of one group or another, that anyone in American society could succumb to it. The barrier between normality and deviancy was very low. The preconditions for individual pathology so pervaded the society, and the manifestations of the disease were so broad that no one who stood on one side of it today could be sure he would not cross it tomorrow.

Official definitions did not limit insanity to a special style of behavior or restrict the range of possible symptoms. Psychiatrists did not attempt to label one specific mode of conduct deviant and indicative of mental disorder, another normative and therefore healthy. Taken alone, neither anger nor passivity, querulousness nor silence pointed to the disease. Any action could be a manifestation of insanity when placed in the context of the patient's life. At times the extravagance of the behavior made the diagnosis simple. Few skills were necessary for recognizing the insane suffering from delusions, thinking they were Alexander the Great or Christ. Similarly, a total loss of capacity to perform elementary acts without any corresponding physical disability — the unwillingness to eat, inability to talk or control muscles — pointed to the presence of the illness. But not all cases were so straightforward. And medical superintendents, conscious not only of their own needs but of those of lawyers and judges as well, attempted to explicate a more sophisticated guideline.

Isaac Ray's *Medical Jurisprudence of Insanity* was the clearest and most widely read effort. Ray conceded at the outset the difficulty of differentiating abnormal from normal behavior, "of discriminating . . . between mental manifestations modified by disease, and those that are peculiar, though natural to the individual." He found no fault, therefore, in allowing a jury of laymen, rather than a group of ostensible experts, to settle the question in criminal cases. Nevertheless, there were useful principles to guide verdicts. The Rhode Island medical superintendent cautioned against associating only the most outlandish behavior with the disease, and attempted to extend, rather than narrowly circumscribe, the possible symptoms. "Madness," he insisted, "is not indicated . . . by any particular extravagance of thought or feeling."[27] A patient could be quiet and insane, insane on some subjects and not others, able to make rational calculations and yet suffer from irresistible impulses, fit to reach logical conclusions but not moral ones. Insanity might be characterized by violence, as in mania, or by depression, as in melancholia, or by incompetence, as in dementia.

But these categories were abstract. There was, perforce, no master checklist that men could use to reach a decision. "To lay down, therefore, any particular definition of mania, founded on symptoms, and to consider every person mad who may happen to come within the range of its application," argued Ray, would only promote a "ridiculous consequence." Hence, "when the sanity of an individual is in question, instead of comparing him with a fancied standard of mental soundness . . . his natural character should be diligently investigated." Only in this way could an observer know whether his behavior was evidence of madness or merely idiosyncratic. "In a word," declared Ray, "he is to be compared with himself, not with others." When the methodical businessman became confused, when someone economical suddenly turned prodigal, when a jovial and communicative person became morose and withdrawn, when a conservative and religious churchgoer turned radical and freethinking, then there was cause for concern. Insanity was no longer the exclusive province of the raving lunatic or totally incompetent. Medical superintendents opened up the category and alerted the community to a whole new range of possibly deviant behavior.

Nor did the analysis of the origins of mental illness in any way restrict the category of those liable to the disease. Everyone, regardless of social class, might suffer its effects. The rich could not expect a higher standard of living to provide protection and the poor could not take consolation in believing that their misery offered immunity. Medical superintendents issued identical and unequivocal pronouncements. "Every person," stated one psychiatrist in Connecticut, "is liable to an attack of insanity." His counterpart in Kentucky confirmed: "Insanity is peculiar to no grade in life. There are none so elevated as to be beyond its reach. . . . It has dethroned the monarch, and deepened the gloom of the hovel." In brief, "the disease is as apt to attack the rich as the poor."[28]

The reasons for the vulnerability of the middle and upper classes were implicit in the postulates on the causes of the disease. By explicitly linking mental illness with keen ambition, hazardous speculations with the vicissitudes of social mobility, medical superintendents left no doubt that men of success might well have to pay the price of insanity for their achievements. They incessantly reproved "unnatural" and "artificial" habits, defining these vague terms as a luxurious, modish or refined style of life. "With the increase of wealth and fashion," admonished Jarvis, "there comes also, more artificial life, more neglect of natural laws of self-government, more unseasonable hours for food and for sleep, more dissipation of the open, allowable and genteel kind." There was no doubt which class he had in mind when warning about the effects of "luxury, self-indulgence, sensuality, and effeminacy . . . late hours, spent in vulgar or graceful dissipation." The combination of these two elements, the "exhausting and perplexing cares and toils of business," together with a "social life and fashion," led inexorably to insanity.[29]

The poor, not ones to experience these particular penalties of civilization, had their own special problems. As Samuel Woodward explained, the effects of poverty — the struggle for subsistence, the constant threat of ill health, the domestic squabbles and the temptations to vice — all helped to make the lower classes as susceptible to mental illness as the most reckless group of speculators. In fact, contended Woodward, the poor were "more to be pitied," for unlike the upper classes, they did not have the prerogative of reforming their ways. If unable to escape from need, they could not avoid its harsh consequences. Among them, "the causes [of insanity] are generally involuntary," and none the less powerful for being so.[30]

The medical superintendents' critique of the antebellum social order cannot be dismissed or denigrated as the idiosyncratic view of a group of disaffected Whigs and die-hard Federalists, well out of the mainstream of American life and thought, or as the special perspective of a handful of professional men, faithful to a medical doctrine. Their attack was basic, but they were not responding as bitter outcasts or eccentric scientists. They condemned the very facets of nineteenth-century life which at least in retrospect seem most American: high levels of social mobility and political participation, intellectual and religious freedom and enthusiasm. Invariably, their comparisons between the seeming disorder of their own society and the fixity and stability of more traditional ones, put American innovations in a poor light. Medical superintendents were unable to approve a design that they believed excited each individual, regardless of station, to pursue grandiose goals, that brought every citizen, no matter what his capabilities, into the political arena. Their complaints make them appear almost as reactionary as the most aristocratic French émigré of the old regime. And yet, they were active participants in the new system, eminent and successful men, not bound to one political party or another.[31] They helped to lead a reform movement that to most contemporaries, as well as historians, epitomized the Jacksonian spirit of humanitarianism. Instead of standing aloof and bemoaning conditions, they plunged in with great energy and commitment to try to set things right. They enjoyed warm personal relations with lay reformers, influencing their thinking in critical ways. Dorothea Dix and Samuel Gridley Howe, for example, accepted and popularized their explanations for the causes of insanity. Psychiatric theories, then, did not reflect the unhappiness of an alienated minority but the widely shared anxiety of antebellum Americans about the social order.

Just as the first penologists located the origins of crime within the community, so psychiatrists linked mental illness to social organization. The epidemic of insanity, like the prevalence of crime, pointed to the most fundamental defects of the system, from mistaken economic, political, and intellectual practices to grave errors in school and family training. The insane were victims of forces beyond their control, not to blame for their misfortunes. Medical superintendents did not magnify the influence of heredity. Unlike their post–Civil War successors, they believed that it might predispose an individual to insanity, but could not by itself, and without the confluence of other circumstances, bring on the illness. Heredity, declared Samuel Woodward, "never results in alienation of mind without the intervention of exciting causes. If the exciting causes of the disease are avoided, the strongest predisposition need not result in insanity." The "exciting causes" were the key to the problem, and these medical superintendents discovered in abundance in the style of American life.[32]

The discussions of insanity, like those of crime, conveyed a heightened, almost hysterical sense of peril, with the very safety of the republic and its citizens at stake. From the inquiry into the causes of crime, it seemed as if Americans faced danger at every turn, and frequently succumbed to it. Officials and reformers pictured streets crowded with taverns, theaters and houses of prostitution, like a western town in a grade-B movie. And the same grim picture emerged from the writings of medical superintendents. The individual was under siege, surrounded by pernicious conditions and practically helpless to defy them. In their estimation, not vice so much as the basic organization of society threatened stability. But the implications of the two critiques were almost identical — wherever the individual turned, some hazard awaited him. Either vice would turn him to crime or stress would bring him to insanity.

Why were medical superintendents so convinced that dangers were omnipresent in the community? Why were their predictions so direful? For one thing, they had been taught, according to the prevailing psychological theory, that the mind operated by association and not through inherited ideas. When the mind became diseased, the fault had to rest with the associations outside it, and psychiatrists, therefore, turned attention to external influences, to the phenomena that the mind was perceiving — in other words, to the society in which the individual lived. For another, medical superintendents were eager to cure mental illness, prodded on by Enlightenment doctrines and a faith in progress, and republic patriotism. Convinced that to identify the source of the problem would be to master it, they looked avidly for faults in society. Yet, why were they, like the first penologists, so remarkably successful in their search, able to write almost endlessly about the deficiencies in American life? After all, Jacksonian society was not verging on collapse and it is doubtful, for example, whether the rates of insanity were actually increasing. (Evidence is hard to come by, but one recent study, *Psychosis and Civilization,* argues convincingly that the rate of insanity in this country has remained constant from before the Civil War to the present.[33]) Rather, psychiatrists' anxieties were ultimately tied to their conception of the proper social order. Against the norms that they held, the American scene appeared chaotic.

Medical superintendents were certain that their society lacked all elements of fixity and cohesion because they judged it by a nostalgic image of the eighteenth century. Frightened by an awareness that the old order was passing and with little notion of what would replace it, they defined the realities about them as corrupting, provoking madness. The root of their difficulty was that they still adhered to the precepts of traditional social theory, to the ideas that they had inherited from the colonial period. By these standards, men were to take their rank in the hierarchy, know their place in society, and not compete to change positions. Children were to be content with their station, taking their father's position for their own. Politics and learning were to be the province of trained men, and ordinary citizens were to leave such matters to them. Family government was to instill order and discipline, and the community to support and reinforce its dictums. This was the prescription for a well-ordered society, one that would not generate epidemics of insanity.

As early as the colonial period, reality did not always fit with such a static theory. But the colonists, lacking intellectual and social incentives, had not been forced to confront the gap. Americans in the Jacksonian period, however, recognized the disparity and were frightened by it. The society was more fluid than before, and greater geographic and social mobility made it more difficult to maintain older theories. Enlightenment ideas and a faith in progress also opened up endless possibilities for achievement, and the prospect of bringing glory to the new republic made these opportunities all the more welcome. As a result, they looked closely and carefully at their society, and worried about what they saw.

Medical superintendents had little trouble comprehending the influences encouraging individualism in America. But they could not perceive what forces would prevent the separate atoms from breaking off and scattering in wild directions. Was there a nucleus able to hold these disparate elements together? This fundamental and troubling question ultimately revealed the difficulties in conceptualizing the kind of social structure that should accompany republican government. Officials and laymen alike were dubious whether a society so intent on promoting individual effort would be able to achieve cohesion. Could it withstand the strains of widespread physical and social mobility? Could it tolerate unprecedented political participation and a pervasive skepticism toward traditional ideas? Later, in the post–Civil War era, with a confidence born of survival and some measure of success, men would emphatically answer yes. The fear of the father would become the glory of the son. The self-made man would stand as a hero, not a potential madman, a fluid society would be the pride of the country, not the chief cause of crime and insanity. But to Americans in the Jacksonian period the matter was anything but settled. The danger that under continued stress the structure might collapse seemed not at all remote.

And yet, the effect of these conceptions was to promote a vigorous and popular movement for amelioration. Rather than abandon all hope before such a depressing analysis of the nature of American society, medical superintendents and laymen issued a call for action and sparked a revolution in the practices toward the insane. For one corollary of these doctrines held that since mental illness originated in the structure of society, not in God's will or individual failings, the community incurred an inescapable responsibility. Reformers themselves felt the burden that this contention imposed, and educated the public to it. As Edward Jarvis explained, "Society establishes, encourages or permits these customs out of which mental disorder may and frequently does arise." Therefore, it had the clear obligation "to heal the wounds it inflicts." Dorothea Dix, taking her cues from this formulation, demanded of innumerable state legislatures:

"Should not society, then, make the compensation which alone can be made for these disastrous fruits of its social organization?" In similar terms, Samuel Gridley Howe prodded his countrymen to make a broad commitment to the care of the insane. "This duty of society, besides being urged by every consideration of humanity," he declared, "will be seen to be more imperative if we consider that insanity is in many cases the result of imperfect or vicious social institutions and observances."[34] Having caused the pain, it was incumbent on the community to help relieve it.

An environmental conception of the causes of deviant behavior encouraged men to believe that such ailments as insanity were curable. The community not only had the moral obligation but the ability to correct the condition. Having located the etiology of the disease in social organization, medical superintendents were confident that a setting which eliminated the irritants could restore the insane to health. The diagnosis of the causes of the disease provided the clues to a cure. To be sure, the very magnitude of the problem ruled out a frontal assault. Where would one begin an effort to limit ambition and intellectual independence, to curb physical and social mobility, to alter the economic, political, religious, and social character of the new republic? Framed in this fashion, the question was unanswerable. But reformers devised a workable solution to this dilemma. Rather than attempt to reorganize American society directly, they would design and oversee a distinctive environment which eliminated the tensions and the chaos. They would try to create — in a way reminiscent of the founders of utopian communities — a model society of their own, not to test a novel method for organizing production or making political decisions, but to exemplify the advantages of an orderly, regular, and disciplined routine. Here was an opportunity to meet the pressing needs of the insane, by isolating them from the dangers at loose in the community, and to further a reform program, by demonstrating to the larger society the benefits of the system. Thus, medical superintendents and laymen supporters moved to create a new world for the insane, one that would not only alleviate their distress but also educate the citizens of the republic. The product of this effort was the insane asylum.

6

The New World of the Asylum

The sturdy walls of the insane asylum became familiar landmarks in pre–Civil War America. They jutted out from flat rural landscapes or rose above the small houses of new suburbs, visible for some distance and unmistakably different from surrounding structures. Their growth was rapid and sudden. Before 1810, only a few eastern-seaboard states had incorporated private institutions to care for the mentally ill, and Virginia alone had established a public asylum. All together they treated less than five hundred patients, most of whom came from well-to-do families. Few departures from colonial practices occurred in the first forty years after independence; the insane commonly languished in local jails and poorhouses or lived with family and friends. But in the course of the next few decades, in a dramatic transformation, state after state constructed asylums. Budding manufacturing centers like New York and Massachusetts erected institutions in the 1830's, and so did the agricultural states of Vermont and Ohio, Tennessee and Georgia. By 1850, almost every northeastern and midwestern legislature supported an asylum; by 1860, twenty-eight of the thirty-three states had public institutions for the insane. Although not all of the mentally ill found a place within a hospital, and a good number among the aged and chronic poor remained in almshouses and jails, the institutionalization of the insane became the standard procedure of the society during these years. A cult of asylum swept the country.[1]

The movement was not born of desperation. Institutionalization was not a last resort of a frightened community. Quite the reverse. Psychiatrists and their lay supporters insisted that insanity was curable, more curable than most other ailments. Spokesmen explained that their understanding of the causes of insanity equipped them to combat it, and the asylum was a first resort, the most important and effective weapon in their arsenal.

The program's proponents confidently and aggressively asserted that properly organized institutions could cure almost every incidence of the disease. They spread their claims without restraint, allowing the sole qualification that the cases had to be recent. Practitioners competed openly with one another to formulate the most general and optimistic principle, to announce the most dramatic result. One of the first declarations came from the superintendent of the Massachusetts asylum at Worcester, Samuel Woodward. "In recent cases of insanity," he announced in 1834, "under judicious treatment, as large a proportion of recoveries will take place as from any other acute disease of equal severity." In his own institution, he calculated, 82.25 percent of the patients recovered. Still, Woodward's tone was judicious and moderate in comparison to later assertions. Dr. Luther Bell, from Boston's McLean Hospital, had no doubt that all recent cases could be remedied. "This is the general rule," he insisted in 1840; "the occasional instance to the contrary is the exception." Performance ostensibly kept pace with theoretical statements. John Galt reported from Virginia in 1842 that, excluding patients who died during treatment, he had achieved one hundred percent recoveries. The following year, Dr. William Awl of the Ohio asylum simply announced without qualification one hundred percent cures.[2]

These statistics were inaccurate and unreliable. Not only was there no attempt to devise criteria for measuring recovery other than release from an institution, but in some instances a single patient, several times admitted, discharged, and readmitted, entered the lists as five times cured. At Pennsylvania's Friends' asylum, for example, 87 persons contributed 274 recoveries. It was not until 1877 that the first major attack on these exaggerated claims appeared, and only at a time when the widespread faith in curability had already begun to evaporate.

Before the Civil War, these extraordinary pronouncements

were widely accepted at face value, and no skeptical voices tried to puncture the balloon of inflated hopes. Psychiatrists, confident of having located the origins of the disease, were fully prepared to believe and to testify that the incredible number of cures was the just fruit of scientific investigation. Personal ambition as well as intellectual perspective made them eager to publicize these findings. The estimates were self-perpetuating; as soon as one colleague announced his grand results, others had little choice but to match or excel him. With supervisory committees of state legislatures and boards of trustees using the number of recoveries as a convenient index for deciding appointments and promotions, medical superintendents were under great competitive pressure to report very high rates. And professionals and laymen alike desperately wanted to credit calculations that would glorify American science and republican humanitarianism. A cure for insanity was the kind of discovery that would honor the new nation.[3]

The consistency of the claims quickly established their validity. With an almost complete absence of dissenting opinion, the belief in the curative powers of the asylum spread through many layers of American society. Given the hyperbolic declarations of the professionals, laymen had little need to exaggerate their own statements. The most energetic and famous figure in the movement, Dorothea Dix, took the message from Massachusetts to Mississippi. With passion and skill she reported in painful detail on the wretched condition of the insane in poorhouses and jails — "Weigh the iron chains and shackles, breathe the foul atmosphere, examine the furniture, a truss of straw, a rough plank" — and next recited the promise of the asylum. Her formula was simple and she repeated it everywhere: first assert the curability of insanity, link it directly to proper institutional care, and then quote prevailing medical opinion on rates of recoveries. Legislators learned that Dr. Bell believed that cure in an asylum was the general rule, incurability the exception, and that Drs. Ray, Chandler, Brigham, Kirkbride, Awl, Woodward, and Earle held similar views.[4] Legislative investigatory committees also returned with identical findings. Both Massachusetts and Connecticut representatives heard from colleagues that insanity yielded as readily as ordinary ailments to proper treatment. The most tax-conscious assemblyman found it difficult to stand up against this overwhelming chorus. One after another, the states approved the necessary funds for erecting asylums.[5]

The institution itself held the secret to the cure of insanity. Incarceration in a specially designed setting, not the medicines that might be administered or the surgery that might be performed there, would restore health. This strategy for treatment flowed logically and directly from the diagnosis of the causes of the disease. Medical superintendents located its roots in the exceptionally open and fluid quality of American society. The American environment had become so particularly treacherous that insanity struck its citizens with terrifying regularity.

One had only to take this dismal analysis one step further to find an antidote. Create a different kind of environment, which methodically corrected the deficiencies of the community, and a cure for insanity was at hand. This, in essence, was the foundation of the asylum solution and the program that came to be known as moral treatment. The institution would arrange and administer a disciplined routine that would curb uncontrolled impulses without cruelty or unnecessary punishment. It would re-create fixity and stability to compensate for the irregularities of the society. Thus, it would rehabilitate the casualties of the system.[6] The hospital walls would enclose a new world for the insane, designed in the reverse image of the one they had left. The asylum would also exemplify for the public the correct principles of organization. The new world of the insane would correct within its restricted domain the faults of the community and through the power of example spark a general reform movement.[7]

The broad program had an obvious similarity to the goals of the penitentiary, and both ventures resembled in spirit and outlook the communitarian movements of the period, such as Brook Farm and New Harmony. There was a utopian flavor to correctional institutions. Medical superintendents and penitentiary designers were almost as eager as Owenites to evolve and validate general principles of social organization from their particular experiments.

The central problem for these first psychiatrists was to translate the concept of a curative environment into reality. Rehabilitation demanded a special milieu, and they devoted almost all of their energy to its creation. The appropriate arrangement of the asylum, its physical dimensions and daily routine, monopolized their thinking. The term for psychiatrist in this period, medical superintendent, was especially apt. Every detail of institutional design was a proper and vital subject for his consideration. His skills were to be those of the architect and the administrator, not the laboratory technician.

The writings of Thomas Kirkbride, head of the prestigious Pennsylvania Hospital for the Insane from 1840 until his death in 1883, testified to the significance of this perspective. He published one of the leading textbooks on insanity, *On the Construction, Organization, and General Arrangements of Hospitals for the Insane, with some Remarks on Insanity and its Treatment;* and the title was ample evidence of the volume's intellectual focus and ordering of priorities.[8] Kirkbride gave the book over to the location of ducts and pipes in asylums, and to accounts of daily routines. He first discussed the proper size and location for the buildings, the right materials for constructing walls and making plaster, the best width for rooms and height for ceilings, the most suitable placement of water closets and dumbwaiters; then he analyzed how to group patients, to staff the hospital, to occupy the inmates during the day. This type of treatise, it is true, was very useful at a time when building and managing institutions was an infant skill. Still, the objective needs of the situation were only a part of the inspiration for a book like Kirkbride's. Far more important to him was the conviction that in settling these technical matters of construction and maintenance, he was confronting and solving the puzzle of curing insanity.

His attitude was not idiosyncratic. The Association of Medical Superintendents, organized in 1844, had a membership composed exclusively of heads of asylums. Institutional affiliation, not research or private practice, defined the profession; the association's committees were predominantly concerned with administrative and architectural questions. There was a committee on construction, on the proper number of patients for one institution, on the best role of chapels and chaplains in the asylum, on separate structures for colored persons, on the comparative advantages of hospital and home treatment. The association also published the *American Journal of Insanity,* a periodical devoted to a wide range of issues. But the primary focus of the group was on the structure of institutions. In 1851 it produced its first major policy statement, a definition of the proper asylum architecture. Resolution number eight, for example, declared: "Every ward should have in it a parlor, a corridor . . . an associated dormitory . . . a clothes room, a bath room, a water closet . . . a dumb waiter, and a speaking tube." In 1853 it issued a second declaration on administrative organization. Rule number seven captured its spirit: "The matron, under the direction of the superintendent, should have a general supervision of the domestic arrangements."[9] In fact, the association was never able to widen its concerns. In the 1870's, when new ideas begin to revolutionize the field, it remained unalterably fixed to its original program, becoming a stumbling block to experimentation and innovation.

There was a functional quality to this narrowness of perspective. Medical superintendents lacked any guidelines with which to design and administer the first mental hospitals. Never before had Americans attempted to confine large numbers of people for long periods of time, and the difficulties were all the greater since their goals extended far beyond simple restraint. Eighteenth-century practices had little relevance to nineteenth-century officials. The almshouse and the jail represented all that medical superintendents wished to avoid in an institution.

Contemporary European practices were not very much more helpful. American superintendents frequently crossed the ocean to examine Continental institutions, but their visits were usually unproductive. Pliny Earle, who first headed the Friends' asylum in Philadelphia and then Bloomingdale in New York, toured the Continent in 1838–39 and then again in 1845, and his reports illuminated the unique problems and special opportunities confronting Americans, who were at once more free to innovate and yet felt more keenly the lack of precedents. European asylums, Earle discovered, were frequently nothing other than a new name carved in an ancient doorway. Each structure had a long history of different uses — a fourteenth-century monastery became later a sixteenth-century fort, and still later an eighteenth-century almshouse, and finally a nineteenth-century mental hospital. Earle methodically noted how in Prussia the asylums at Siegburg and at Brieg and at Owinsk were all former monasteries; in Halle, the hospital occupied the quarters of the old prison. The Austrian town of Ybbs, he found, turned a building that had served successively as a barracks, a military hospital, and an almshouse into an asylum. So, too, the German town of Sonnestein converted a onetime castle into a place for the insane and the village of Winnental made over to them a nobleman's palace that had once been a monastery.[10] But Americans, in marked contrast, had to start from scratch. "There were no old halfruined monasteries," observed one Englishman, "to be converted into asylums for their insane poor. . . . Americans had to build their own asylums." They had the opportunity to create something new, and the predicament of precisely how to go about it.[11]

Medical superintendents received little assistance from their countrymen. No groups of specialists — architects, engineers, bureaucrats — possessed requisite skills for constructing and administering a mental hospital. There were no large-scale organizations in the country whose designs and procedures could be easily emulated. One result of these circumstances was that every new asylum became the immediate focus of attention for other officials. Medical superintendents and legislative investigatory committees from neighboring states seemed to have arrived at the door of a new institution along with its first patients. No sooner did New York State appoint a board of commissioners to construct an insane asylum in 1839 than the committee visited the institutions in Massachusetts, Pennsylvania, and other nearby states; two years later the first trustees of the new Utica asylum made an exhaustive review of procedures in all leading mental hospitals. The tour of inspection was as necessary as it was popular.[12]

But an even more important result of these circumstances was that the concepts shared by medical superintendents exercised an exceptional degree of influence in the actual construction and administration of the first insane asylums. With few precedents to guide them, they experimented with their own ideas; with no inherited structures to limit them, they built institutions according to their particular designs. Hence, reformatory theory and practical needs fit well together, perhaps too well. It may be that part of the enthusiasm for environmental solutions reflected the lack of experience. Still, this concentrated attention to institutional organization established the guidelines for translating confinement into cure.

The first postulate of the asylum program was the prompt removal of the insane from the community. As soon as the first symptom of the disease appeared, the patient had to enter a mental hospital. Medical superintendents unanimously and without qualification asserted that treatment within the family was doomed to fail. They recognized the unusual nature of their doctrine and its apparent illogic. Since families had traditionally lodged the insane, it might seem a cruel and wanton abdication of responsibility to send a sick member to a public institution filled with other deranged persons. But they carefully explained this fundamental part of their program. Isaac Ray, chief of Rhode Island's asylum, conceded that "to sever a man's domestic ties, to take him out of the circle of friends and relatives most deeply interested in his welfare . . . and place him . . . in the hands of strangers, and in the company of persons as disordered as himself — at first sight, would seem . . . little likely to exert a restorative effect." Yet he and his colleagues insisted that isolation among strangers was a prerequisite for success. Although the strategy might increase the momentary pain of the disease, it promised an ultimate cure. "While at large," Ray declared, "the patient is every moment exposed to circumstances that maintain the morbid activity of his mind . . . [and] the dearer the friend, the greater the emotion. . . . In the hospital, on the other hand, he is beyond the reach of all these causes of excitement."[13] How else, asked Edward Jarvis, could the insane escape "the cares and anxieties of business . . . the affairs of the town . . . the movements of religious, political and other associations. . . . Hospitals are the proper places for the insane. . . . The cure and care of the insane belong to proper public institutions."[14]

Second, the institution itself, like the patients, was to be

separate from the community. According to medical superintendents' design, it was to be built at a distance from centers of
population. Since it was dependent upon the city for personnel
and supplies, it could not completely escape contact. But the
institution was to have a country location with ample grounds, to
sit on a low hillside with an unobstructed view of a surrounding
landscape. The scene ought to be tranquil, natural, and rural,
not tumultuous and urban. Moreover, the asylum was to enforce
isolation by banning casual visitors and the patients' families. If
friends and relatives "were allowed the privilege they seek,"
cautioned Ray, "the patient might as well be at large as in the
hospital, for any good the latter may do him by way of seclusion." Correspondence was also to be strictly limited. Even the
mails were not to intrude and disrupt the self-contained and
insular life.[15]

But the most important element in the new program, the core
of moral treatment, lay in the daily government of the mentally
ill. Here was the institution's most difficult and critical task. It
had to control the patient without irritating him, to impose
order but in a humane fashion. It had to bring discipline to bear
but not harshly, to introduce regularity into chaotic lives without
exciting frenetic reactions. "Quiet, silence, regular routine,"
declared Ray, "would take the place of restlessness, noise and
fitful activity." Superintendents had to walk a tightrope, making
sure that they did not fall to the one side of brutality or the
other of indulgence. "So long as the patient is allowed to follow
the bent of his own will," insisted Ray, he exacerbated his
illness; outside the asylum, the "only alternative was, either an
unlimited indulgence of the patient in his caprices, or a degree
of coercion and confinement which irritated his spirit and injured his health." The charge of the asylum was to bring discipline to the victims of a disorganized society. To this end it had
to isolate itself and its members from chaotic conditions. Behind
the asylum walls medical superintendents would create and
administer a calm, steady, and rehabilitative routine. It would
be, in a phrase that they and their lay supporters repeated
endlessly, "a well-ordered institution."[16]

The asylum's designers often labored under severe financial
limitations, when legislatures and private philanthropists were

10. *The Worcester State Hospital for the Insane, ca. 1855. Although the structures and the scene seem orderly and placid, the Worcester asylum was beginning to suffer overcrowding and haphazard expansion, the result of the swelling number of chronic and immigrant patients.*

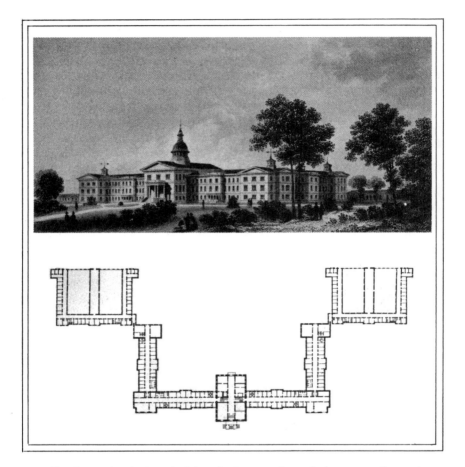

The Pennsylvania Hospital for the Insane. One of the outstanding private mental hospitals in the pre–Civil War period, the Pennsylvania institution revealed in its design the importance of uniformity and regularity in the treatment of the insane.

not generous with appropriations. Sometimes public officials interfered with their policies, setting down admission requirements that limited administrators' prerogatives. In Massachusetts, for example, the state hospital had to admit the most troublesome and least curable cases first; legislators were more impressed with the convenience than the effectiveness of the institution. And many superintendents were discontented with one facet or another of the asylum's architecture or procedures. Nevertheless, there was usually a close correspondence between founders' ideals and the asylum reality.

No principle was more easily or consistently enacted than the physical separation of the asylum from the community. Almost all the institutions constructed after 1820 were located at a short distance from an urban center. New York erected its state asylum one and one-half miles west of the town of Utica, and Massachusetts built its mental hospital outside Worcester, on a hill overlooking the surrounding farmland. In this same spirit, Connecticut's Hartford asylum went up one mile from the city, with a fine view of the countryside. In Philadelphia, the Pennsylvania Hospital, which had long kept a ward for treating the insane, decided in this period to construct a separate facility for them. The city now surrounded the old institution so that the conditions which made the move seem necessary also simplified the raising of money. The hospital sold off some adjoining lots, at a great profit, and used the proceeds to erect an asylum two miles west of Philadelphia on a one-hundred-and-one-acre farm. Midwestern states followed eastern practices. Ohio's officials, for example, located the mental hospital on the outskirts of Columbus, choosing a site that offered a broad natural panorama.[17]

There was, to be sure, a close fit between medical superintendents' desires and the more practical concerns of legislators and trustees. Land outside the city was not only more rural but it was cheaper. So, too, under this arrangement, no established community felt threatened by the intrusion of an asylum, or complained that a lunatic hospital would disturb its peace, safety, and real estate values. To the contrary, budding towns and growing suburbs competed for the right to have the institution in their midst, confident that the resulting income would more than compensate for any nuisance. By common agreement, and to everyone's satisfaction, the mental hospital secured its quiet and separate location.

The isolation of patients was more difficult to achieve. Medical superintendents had to balance a policy which was to the immediate benefit of the individual inmate with considerations of the long-range interest of mental hospitals in the nation. The asylum was a new institution, and citizens had to be assured that cruel practices would be prohibited. To exclude all of the interested and curious public from its buildings would not only keep distrust alive but even stimulate it. Under these conditions, legislative appropriations and charitable gifts would be curtailed and families would be loath to commit sick members. Some kind of balance had to be struck between isolation and publicity. Superintendents dared not seal off the institution from society.

The most common solution was to allow, and even encourage, tours of the asylum by the ordinary public while making every effort to curtail contact between patient and family. This arrangement would exhibit the institution to the largest number of persons at the least personal cost to the patient. The private Pennsylvania asylum explained to would-be visitors that "the visits of strangers among the patients, are often much less objectionable than those of friends and relatives." Managers would be "glad to show every part of the establishment, and to explain the details of treatment," to anyone genuinely interested in hospitals for the insane. But at the same time they carefully instructed relatives that "the welfare of the patient often demands that they should be completely interdicted." The presence of a family member could provoke an excitement that would take weeks to overcome and delay the recovery.[18]

A public institution, like the Utica asylum, opened its doors still more widely to strangers. Aware that many in the state were concerned about the institution's accommodations and management, officials uncomplainingly guided some twenty-seven hundred visitors around the grounds in a typical year, and even took special groups from different sections of the state through the patients' sleeping quarters. Yet they too asked relatives to avoid coming to the institution. The family, they noted, should not "throw any obstacles in the way of recovery, by frequent visits, or requesting friends and relatives to visit."[19] Medical superintendents also discouraged the exchange of letters, fearing that news from home might intrude on the calm and regular routine of the asylum and upset the patients' stability. They did not exclude all reading material, newspapers, and periodicals from the asylum. But they were eager to preserve the insularity of their domain. "Long and tender letters," warned Ohio's superintendent William Awl, "containing some ill-timed news, or the melancholy tidings of sickness and death . . . may destroy weeks and months of favorable progress."[20]

Superintendents' ability to enforce rigid rules was limited. If regulations were too stringent, the family might vacillate and keep the patient at home too long, or commit and then remove him too soon. The chronic and poverty-stricken insane were captive patients; but psychiatrists, convinced of their ability to cure the disease and eager to make the asylum a first resort, wished to treat the recently sick and those from comfortable households as well. Unwilling to frighten away potential patients, and yet determined to assert control, superintendents adopted two tactics. They discouraged but did not *forbid* relatives to visit and they insisted that a patient be committed for a minimum period — at least three or six months. This strategy was well conceived and in the best institutions, successful. Doctors calmed family fears and gained time to effect a cure, or at least to demonstrate progress. The detailed records of the Pennsylvania Hospital, for example, reveal the loss of only a handful of patients by removal annually.[21] Thus, once medical superintendents received a patient, they were usually able to separate him fairly systematically from the outside world.

To isolate the insane more rapidly and effectively from the sources of his illness, medical superintendents were also eager to leave commitment laws as simple and as uncomplicated as possible. Most superintendents preferred to allow relatives to bring the patient directly to the institution and arrange for commitment on the spot; only a few believed that prior judicial examination or jury decisions were necessary. The managers of the Utica asylum, for example, objected strenuously to legal formalities in its incorporation act that made the certification of insanity under oath by two "respectable physicians," a prerequisite for admission.[22]

Their attitudes were not difficult to understand. Confinement, they believed, was not a punishment but a cure, and hence there was as little cause to begin a legal proceeding before the insane entered an asylum as there was to require it for persons going to any other type of hospital. Furthermore, they found no need to rely upon legal processes when they themselves could easily differentiate between sanity and insanity and every cumbersome requirement might discourage someone from sending a patient to the asylum, a risk which medical superintendents wanted to minimize. Finally, judicial routines too often consumed valuable time, and the longer the delay in admissions, the less the likelihood of a cure. Better for the insane to sit in the asylum than in the courtroom.[23] These objections were generally persuasive. Managers were comparatively free to confine the mentally ill at their own discretion.

The internal organization of the asylum also represented medical superintendents' attempts to realize the idea of moral treatment. They designed and implemented an orderly and disciplined routine, a fixed, almost rigid calendar, and put daily labor at the heart of it. A precise schedule and regular work became the two chief characteristics of the best private and public institutions, and in the view of their managers, the key to curing insanity. The structure of the mental hospital would counteract the debilitating influences of the community. As one New York doctor explained, "the hours for rising, dressing and washing . . . for meals, labor, occupation, amusement, walking, riding, etc., should be regulated by the most *perfect precision.* . . . The utmost *neatness* must be observed in the dormitories; the meals must be *orderly* and comfortably served. . . . The physician and assistants must make their visits at *certain* hours."[24] Steady labor would also train inmates to proper habits, bringing regularity to disordered lives. "Useful employment, in the open air," explained the Vermont asylum superintendent, "affords the best moral means for the restoration of many of our patients." Luther Bell, head of the McLean Hospital, fully concurred: "*systematic, regular,* employment in useful body labor . . . is one appliance of moral treatment, which has been proved immeasurably superior to all others."[25] Precision, certainty, regularity, order — these became the bywords of asylum management, the main weapons in the battle against insanity.

From this perspective, the Pennsylvania Hospital arranged the patients' day. They rose at five o'clock, received their medicines at six, and breakfast at 6:30; at eight o'clock they went for a physical examination, and then to work or to some other form of exercise. At 12:30 they ate their main meal and then resumed work or other activities until six, when everyone joined for tea. They passed the evening indoors, and all were in bed by 9:30. This careful division of the day into fixed segments of time to rationalize the inmate's life was the creation of the nineteenth century.[26]

The procedures adopted at Pennsylvania were followed almost exactly in other hospitals. At the Worcester asylum, patients rose at 5:30 in the summer, 5:45 in the winter; after breakfast, according to the managers, "everything is put in readiness for the visit of the superintendent . . . which commences at precisely *eight* o'clock at all seasons." At Utica, patients awoke to a morning bell at five o'clock, ate at 6:30, and officials strictly instructed the attendants to be punctual. One typical rule: "Breakfast is always to be placed upon the table precisely one hour and a half after the ringing of the bells."[27] These regulations had some administrative advantages, enabling superintendents to oversee a more efficient operation. But they reflected even more the strength of a theory that ascribed a therapeutic value to a rigid schedule.

Of all the activities, asylums prized labor the most, going to exceptional lengths to keep patients busy with manual tasks. The Pennsylvania Hospital offered a choice of farming, simple workshop crafts, or household tasks; and superintendent Thomas Kirkbride boasted that many who previously "had unfortunately never been accustomed to labour, nor to habits of industry," were now regularly at work. He encouraged his private patients to do any task; it did not matter whether they planted a garden, husked corn, made baskets or mattresses, cooked, sewed, washed, ironed, attended the furnace or cleaned up the grounds. Outdoor chores were probably most healthy and pleasant, but the critical thing was to keep at the job. This regimen, Kirkbride and his colleagues believed, inculcated regular habits, precisely the trait

necessary for patients' recovery, and thus "rarely failed to contribute to the rapidity and certainty of their cure."

The proof for this was apparent in case histories, and so
exemplary tales abounded. One man, in a typical story, had
suffered violent fits at least once a month; he took up gardening,
applied himself vigorously, and subsequently was free of recur-
ring attacks. Indeed, medical superintendents sounded very
much like penitentiary wardens when claiming that their institutions succeeded, where the society had failed, in teaching the
virtue of steady labor. Kirkbride was certain that careful administration and a planned "monotony of the parlors and the
halls" (wardens talked about the dullness of cells), would lead
patients to regard work as a welcome diversion, a privilege and
not a punishment. At that moment, every student of deviancy
agreed, the inmate was well along the road to rehabilitation.[28]

Public asylums were even more eager to set patients to work.
Administrators' needs seemed to fit neatly with inmates' welfare.
Just as it was to the superintendent's personal interest to oversee
an economical and efficient operation, so too the patient would
benefit from a disciplined and fixed routine. The Worcester
asylum had the insane clearing the dining-room tables, washing
dishes, cleaning corridors, doing laundry, as well as tilling the
adjoining farm; and superintendent Samuel Woodward unhesitantly defended the hospital's right to utilize and even profit
from their efforts. After all, this schedule was the best mode of
treatment, and it was striking testimony to the asylum's "system
of discipline that the labor of this class of individuals can be
made available for any valuable purpose." The institution was
entitled to the reward for having brought the insane to this stage
of improvement. The managers of the Utica asylum followed an
identical course. They reported enthusiastically how patients
helped remove the enormous quantities of rubble that had
accumulated during the period of construction, how they cleaned
and scrubbed the institution daily, and how they raised some of
their own food. Their pride in keeping costs down and a belief
in the medical value of these tasks gave a self-congratulatory tone
to officials' remarks. The well-ordered asylum was a hard-working
one.[29]

The institution achieved its good order and enforced labor

discipline without frequently resorting to the coercion of physical punishment or chains, straitjackets, and other bizarre contrivances. Superintendents everywhere stressed the importance of avoiding harsh penalties and punitive discipline, and their public statements gave first priority to the importance of benign treatment. Of course, declarations of ideals did not always coincide with actual performance, and there were asylums whose professions had little relationship to the hard truth of their practices. Still, many institutions in their first years did live up to these principles. Private asylums in Philadelphia, New York, and Boston were able to avoid in almost all instances artificial restraints and unusual punishment, to maintain well the balance between laxity and cruelty. It demanded great diligence, skillful planning, and painstaking administration, but they achieved the goal.

Pennsylvania's first step was to classify the patient population, dividing the noisy and violent from the quiet and passive, and housing them accordingly. The most dangerous group, those who were most likely to need restraint, entered separate and specially designed buildings. Their rooms were constructed with windows high on the walls, beyond inmates' reach, and could be opened or closed only from an outside hallway. The furiously disordered could not annoy or threaten milder patients, or endanger their own lives. Superintendent Kirkbride chose his attendants well, employed a good number of them — roughly one for every six inmates — and indoctrinated them thoroughly. "We insist," he informed them, "on a mild and conciliatory manner under all circumstances and roughness or violence we never tolerate." A total patient population of about two hundred allowed Kirkbride to reserve for his medical staff the decision to use restraints. Convinced that attendants, no matter how rigorously trained or closely supervised were invariably too eager to apply them — thinking it would save them time and aggravation — Kirkbride gave them no discretion. The physicians, he expected, would first exhaust all other remedies. In fact, the staff usually secluded the violent or suicidal inmate in a guarded room and only if his life seemed in danger did it prescribe some form of restraint. Thus, through wise construction, expenditure of funds, and administrative regulations, Kirkbride minimized physical punishments. In a typical year, 1842, he happily reported that with the exception of one woman confined to her bed for a few nights, and seven men kept in wristbands or mittens for a few days, "we have found no reason for applying even the milder kinds of apparatus in a single one of the 238 cases under care."[30]

New York's Bloomingdale Asylum achieved a similar success through identical means. Classification was thorough and intricate for the 150 patients; there were six categories for men, four for women, and two separate buildings to lodge the violent of each sex. The superintendent, Pliny Earle, methodically schooled his attendants, and employed them in adequate numbers, one for approximately every seven inmates. A state legislative committee, after inspecting the institution in 1840, unhesitantly concluded: "The patients appear to have been remarkably well taken care of. There were none fettered, even with straitjackets. A pair of stuffed gloves for one patient, and stuffed chairs, with partial restraint for the arms, were the only restraints on any of the whole number in the establishment."[31]

In Boston, the McLean Hospital also managed to enforce discipline without harsh contrivances. Officials gave exceptional attention to classification, convinced that its importance "can not be overrated." They insisted that proper categorization together with "the extensive architectural arrangements . . . has enabled us to dispense almost entirely with restraining measures or even rigid confinement." With a dozen groupings to differentiate among the patients, and with such special facilities as a heated and padded room to calm frenzied inmates, McLean did not have to use mechanical constraints with even one percent of its population. Superintendent Luther Bell screened and selected the attendants very judiciously, considering himself especially fortunate not to "feel the want . . . of a proper kind of assistants." There were in New England, he declared, "a class of young men and women of respectable families, adequate education, and refined moral feelings," who were prepared to devote a few years to asylum employment. Bell hired them in large numbers, on the average of one for every four or five of his 150 patients. He carefully established precise regulations and severely circumscribed their discretionary powers. "No restraint, even of the slightest kind," announced the asylum rules, "should ever be applied or removed except under the direction of an officer." There is every indication that McLean followed both the letter and the spirit of the law.[32]

Public asylums attempted to emulate this performance. Superintendents, regardless of where they served, shared a revulsion against severe discipline, and tried to administer their institutions by the same standards as private asylums. State hospitals were generally less successful in this effort, unable to duplicate the record of Pennsylvania, Bloomingdale, or McLean. Nevertheless, their trustees and managers measured themselves against the criterion of a strict but not cruel discipline, organized a routine, and made necessary revisions to conform better to it. There were lapses and failures, but in the first years of the asylums they were not gross ones. Most mental hospitals in the 1830's and 1840's abolished the whip and the chain and did away with confinement in cold, dank basements and rat-infested cellars — no mean achievement in itself. And often they accomplished more, treating patients with thoughtfulness and humanity.

From its inception, the Utica asylum pledged to avoid corporal punishment, chains, and long periods of solitary confinement to control patients, and during its first years, it kept much of the promise. Managers delighted in describing how quickly they removed the rags and chains that so often bound a new patient, how they bathed and dressed him, and gave him freedom of movement. Almost invariably, they claimed, the patient became quiet, orderly, and responsible. To insure consistent treatment, Utica's regulations also reserved all disciplinary powers to the superintendent, requiring him to keep an official log of every restraint prescribed. Utica's managers instructed attendants precisely and explicitly in their duties: "Under all circumstances," they insisted, "be tender and affectionate; speak in a mild, persuasive tone of voice. . . . A patient is ever to be soothed and calmed when irritated. . . . *Violent hands are never to be laid upon a patient, under any provocation.*"[33]

Nevertheless, the organization and structure of the institution prevented full compliance. Attendants were too few — only one for every fifteen patients — to allow close supervision to obviate mechanical restraints. No separate buildings existed for noisy and violent inmates — just makeshift rooms — and patients were hardly classified. Not surprisingly, superintendents in the 1840's resorted to some odd forms of discipline, such as a warm bath immediately followed by a cold shower; and they themselves complained about overcrowding, tumult, and filth within the institution. These conditions did not go entirely uncorrected. A new manager in the 1850's introduced more intricate classification and abolished the shower-bath treatment. He, too, however, frequently utilized tight muffs and strapped beds to maintain order. If Utica was by no means a model institution, it did demonstrate a real dedication to the idea of mild punishment.[34]

The Worcester asylum had a similar record. Superintendent Samuel Woodward was intent on demonstrating that the influence of fear and brutal physical force were unnecessary in treating the insane. Despite his good intentions, the asylum did not enjoy consistent success. Performance in its opening years, the mid-1830's, was unsatisfactory. Woodward complained bitterly that the buildings were too few, that classification was impossible, and that attendants were difficult to train. To his extreme displeasure, convalescing patients mingled with violent ones, inmates damaged much of the asylum property, the atmosphere was disorderly, and the patients were clearly not under firm control. Soon, however, the institution entered a second stage, solving within the decade some of these problems. With greater experience and some new facilities, Woodward instilled a steady discipline, so that trustees, including such men as Horace Mann, could boast of "the kindness, the patience, the fidelity, the perseverance and the skill with which the officers and assistants have discharged their duty."[35]

But conditions again degenerated, and by the end of the 1840's trustees and managers were unhappy with internal procedures. Separation and classification became problems as the number of chronic inmates increased, and violent ones inflicted, in Woodward's opinion, "positive injury" on others, and themselves received inadequate care. But their dissatisfactions notwithstanding, they believed that their asylum represented a fundamental improvement over local poorhouses and jails for the insane. So certain were they of this judgment that they refused to discharge a violent or dangerous patient, even when he was unquestionably incurable, to such places. There he would be chained or handcuffed or locked in a dungeonlike cell. At Worcester, for all its faults, he would enjoy greater comfort and care.[36]

The ideals of other public institutions were no different. The directors of the Kentucky asylum insisted that restraints not be utilized, and the managers of the Indiana State Hospital for the Insane diligently instructed attendants to treat patients with "kindness and good will," to "speak to them in a mild, persuasive tone of voice. . . . Violent hands shall never be laid upon patients . . . and a blow shall never be returned." The superintendent at the Eastern Lunatic Asylum at Williamsburg, Virginia, pledged to establish a routine in which "kindness coupled with firmness, are the prominent characteristics." Practice often fell below these standards, but despite the lapses, the world of the antebellum asylum was a universe apart from local jails and almshouses. Medical superintendents' theories and responses brought a new standard of treatment to the insane.[37]

But the asylum system was highly regimented and repressive. Medical superintendents, carrying out the logic of a theory of deviancy, administered an ordered routine and hoped to eliminate in a tightly organized and rigid environment the instabilities and tensions causing insanity. Their program did resemble that of the penitentiary. Proponents of both institutions insisted on strictly isolating the inmates from society, on removing them as quickly as possible to the asylum, on curtailing relatives' visits and even their correspondence. They both gave maximum attention to matters of design, and both institutions organized their daily routines in exact and punctual fashion, bringing an unprecedented precision and regularity to inmate care.

Superintendents' language, it is true, retained many eighteenth-century usages. Their favorite metaphor was a family one, and they borrowed freely from family vocabulary to describe asylum procedures. The superintendent at the Utica hospital explained his classification system by noting that "our household" was divided into "ten distinct families." When the Worcester asylum was enjoying its most successful years, Samuel Woodward delightedly announced that his 230 patients "form a quiet and happy family, enjoying social intercourse, engaging in interesting and profitable employments, in reading, writing and amusements." At Blooomingdale, Pliny Earle reported that "the internal arrangements of the Asylum are nearly the same as those of a well-regulated family."[38] Patients, unlike convicts, wore ordinary clothing, and medical superintendents even instructed relatives to send along good items to bolster inmates' self-respect. There were no special haircuts, no head-shaving, no identification badges, no number-wearing in the mental hospital; patients walked from place to place, they did not march about or group in formations. By the same token, psychiatrists were very careful not to use penitentiary terminology. Pennsylvania's Thomas Kirkbride, for example, instructed attendants to avoid certain expressions: "No insane hospital should ever be spoken of as having a cell or a keeper within its walls." A household terminology, he assumed, would help to quiet the patients.[39]

Medical superintendents, however, had very special qualities in mind when they spoke about the family. The routine that they would create in the asylum would bear no resemblance to a casual, indulgent, and negligent household that failed to discipline its members or to inculcate a respect for order and authority. Convinced that the primary fault of the contemporary family lay in its lax discipline and burdensome demands — so that children grew up without limits to their behavior or their ambitions — medical superintendents were determined to strike a new balance between liberty and authority, in a social sense. They did not wish to abandon the benevolent side of family organization, but they hoped to graft onto it a firm and regulatory regimen. They took their inspiration from the colonial period, believing that they were restoring traditional virtues. But to a surprising degree, the result was more in tune with their own era. Regularity, order, and punctuality brought the asylum routine closer to the factory than the village.

If passersby might easily have mistaken an eighteenth-century institution for an ordinary dwelling, there was no confusing a nineteenth-century asylum with a private residence. "The slightest reflection will render it obvious," declared the officials planning the Worcester hospital, "that an edifice designed for the residence of the insane must be materially different, both in form and in interior arrangement, from ordinary habitations."[40] To protect, confine, separate, and treat the insane demanded special architectural forms. Managers looked hard for their answers, and since the search was unprecedented, solutions at times differed. But despite some variety, a common pattern emerged. Typically, a central structure of several stories stood in the middle of the asylum grounds, and from it radiated long and straight wings. The main edifice, and usually the most ornate one, was an administration building, fronted with a columned portico and topped with a cupola of height and distinction. Here the superintendent lived, and here the similarity between a fine home and the asylum was most complete. The wings, however, where the inmates resided, had bare and unrelieved façades. Along their length the windows of the patients' rooms divided the space into regular and exact sequences, giving a uniform and repetitious appearance floor after floor. The design of the Hartford Retreat, one of the better institutions of the period, seemed to one later observer exceptionally "plain and factory-like."[41]

There were alternative designs available to medical superintendents. They might have constructed a series of small houses or cottages, each sleeping five to ten patients. Classification would have been simplified, construction costs not significantly higher, and married couples could have supervised each lodging, giving a familylike quality to the units. But in fact, they welcomed the regimented quality of the wing design because it fit so neatly with their ideas on order and regularity. Its precise divisions, its uniformity and repetitiousness, symbolized superintendents' determination to bring steady discipline into the lives of the insane and to inspire private families to emulation. Since superintendents did not wish to re-create a prisonlike atmosphere, and wanted no one to confuse an asylum with a place of punishment, they carefully disguised window bars behind sashes and in a few of the more prosperous private institutions, carpeted the long hallways. They retained, however, regularity of appearance. This represented, in visual form, their faith in the ability of a fixed order to cure the insane.

Medical superintendents' confidence in the therapeutic effects of a rigid schedule also introduced a punctuality into the asylum routine. The institution brought a bell-ringing precision into inmates' lives. Officials' careful classification and supervision of inmates also gave the asylum a fixed and orderly quality. There would be no informal family government or easy mixing of its members here. The mental hospital grouped its patients, assigned them to different buildings, all men to one side of the wings, all women to the other, the noisy and bothersome to the outside, the calm and quiet to the inside. Each class of patients had its own particular obligations and privileges, and a hierarchy of officials watched their behavior, ready to move them from one category to another. Superintendents were determined not to impose a harsh system, but they saw nothing severe or unwarranted in regularity and regimentation. "Nothing is so important," wrote one psychiatrist, "as discipline and subordination, rules and order, in the government of an insane hospital." These virtues would enable patients to escape their disease.[42]

Thus the insane asylum, like other corrective institutions in the Jacksonian period, represented both an attempt to compensate for public disorder in a particular setting and to demonstrate the correct rules of social organization. Medical superintendents designed their institutions with eighteenth-century virtues in mind. They would teach discipline, a sense of limits, and a satisfaction with one's position, and in this way enable patients to withstand the tension and the fluidity of Jacksonian society. The psychiatrists, like contemporary penologists, conceived of proper individual behavior and social relationships only in terms of a personal respect for authority and tradition and an acceptance of one's station in the ranks of society. In this sense they were trying to re-create in the asylum their own vision of the colonial community. The results, however, were very different. Regimentation, punctuality, and precision became the asylum's basic traits, and these qualities were far more in keeping with an urban, industrial order than a local, agrarian one. The mental hospital was a rebuke to the casual organization of the household and a self-conscious alternative to the informality of earlier structures like the almshouse. It was, in essence, an institution — at its best uniform, rigid, and regular. This was the new world offered the insane. They were among the first of their countrymen to experience it.

7

The Paradox of Poverty

Americans in the antebellum era were as concerned and apprehensive about the presence of poverty as they were about the rates of crime and insanity, and gave unprecedented attention to the issue of poor relief. Dependency, like deviancy, became the subject of frequent discussion and detailed research, with legislators and overseers of the poor and philanthropists all attempting to fathom its causes, to estimate its effects, and to frame appropriate responses. Here, too, an acute sense of peril went together with the highest expectations. Observers feared that paupers were draining the nation's resources, demoralizing its labor force, and threatening its stability — and added these worries to a dread of crime and insanity. Yet, reformers also expected to be able to control and even to eliminate poverty in the new republic. The investigation into the nature of dependency, as into deviancy, promised great rewards for success, and awful penalties for failure.

The attempt to ferret out the causes of poverty and formulate a plan to combat it marked a clear departure from earlier practices. Eighteenth-century Americans had not devoted particular energy to these questions or tried to devise new methods of care. They did not interpret the presence of poverty as a social problem, view the dependent as a danger to order, or anticipate that somehow need might be eliminated from the society. Assuming that poverty was providentially caused, they found little to discuss or dispute, and by giving the poor neighbor a fixed rank in the social hierarchy, they forestalled further debate and analysis. In effect, this viewpoint assumed that the poor would always be found in America, that there was nothing exceptional about their presence. There was little reason to fear that they might disrupt the system or to ponder ways in which their condition might be improved. Few people questioned the community's responsibility to satisfy the pressing needs of dependents as directly and simply as possible or pondered alternatives to their methods of relief. To be sure, destitute strangers were not included in this consensus, and the colonists often worried about their intrusions and passed protective legislation to maintain the town's good order and protect its treasury. But throughout these decades, household relief seemed an equitable and reasonable way to carry out a traditional function. The poor were usually spared the animosity and suspicion as well as the ameliorative efforts of their neighbors.

In the 1820's and 1830's, however, Americans began to reverse each of these premises. They now considered the poor a social problem, a potential source of unrest and the proper object of a reform movement. Reformers' thinking became increasingly secular, so that God's will no longer seemed a satisfactory explanation for differences in social conditions. They were impatient with deterministic doctrines, refusing to believe that poverty was endemic to society, or that men were inherently depraved. In the new nation, physical mobility and wider political allegiances also helped to break down the relevance of distinctions based on residence. A system that took responsibility for the local poor but no one else now seemed excessively parochial. Further, the colonists' confidence in the power of a hierarchical organization of society to maintain order did not persist for very long into the nineteenth century. Americans recognized, with a good deal of anxiety, that ranks were not stable and ongoing, and this perception also put the issue of dependency in a new light. The poor not only lost their former status as neighbors in a stable community, but their position in a hierarchical order. As a result, they became suspicious and culpable characters, albeit persons whose condition might be elevated and improved through a rehabilitative and corrective program. The very influences which heightened a distrust of the poor also stimulated an awareness of the possibility of reform. Both of these attitudes reflected the loosening of the fixity of colonial views.

It is, therefore, not surprising that Americans shared an unprecedented interest in exploring and analyzing the condition of the poor and the efficacy of existing relief policies. Heretofore, townspeople had accepted both the vague legal charge to relieve the needy and the ministerial plea to give charity, without debating the origins of dependency or the wisdom of one kind of response or another. Beginning in the 1820's, however, public officials, philanthropists, and interested observers discovered the issue, removing it, as it were, from the church and bringing it to the legislature. In 1821, the Massachusetts assembly sponsored one of the first and most influential investigations, appointing Josiah Quincy chairman of a committee to report on the condition of the poor and the administration of relief throughout the state. The New York legislature in 1824 followed its example, charging a group under John Yates to carry out a similar task. Both Quincy and Yates corresponded with, polled, and questioned overseers of the poor, diligently surveyed and tabulated the number of persons receiving relief, the total expenditures, the methods of disbursement, sampled European opinion, and read whatever literature existed. They then composed thorough summaries of existing practices, attempted to explain the causes of poverty, and recommended new forms of action. In this same spirit, the city of Philadelphia in 1827 dispatched a committee to visit Baltimore, New York, Providence, Boston, and Salem, to study the problem and techniques for confronting it. So, too, benevolent societies actively took up the question, and such a group as the New York Society for the Prevention of Pauperism devoted itself to examining the sources of need and evaluating various responses. The complacency and consensus that marked the colonal decades were over. With the same energy and intensity with which Americans searched for the roots of deviancy, they pondered the origins of dependency.[1]

One more break with colonial attitudes intensified this new effort. Almost every critic assumed that given the natural condition of life in the new republic, dependency ought not to exist here. At this very time, England was also investigating the issue of poverty, and Americans were well acquainted with the critiques of traditional practices that emerged there. But observers in the United States did not simply repeat English judgments.

Their own case, they believed, was substantially different and they adopted a position held only by visionaries or cranks across the ocean. The centuries-old reputation of the poor as a permanent element in the society had been earned in the old world; that until now they had always been with us was testimony to the abuses of landlords and the oppressions of governments characteristic of Europe. Americans had no difficulty in accounting for the persistence of misery in that world against which their forefathers had rebelled. But how understand its presence in the United States? Surely a scarcity of labor and widespread availability of land ought to have eliminated it. And yet, despite these advantages, Americans too had so far failed to solve the problem. This was a puzzle and a challenge that they could not easily unravel or ignore.

The favorable position of labor in the United States impressed the members of the Yates committee as being fundamentally different from Continental conditions, and reason enough for expecting that the new world would escape the scourge of poverty. There was, they informed the New York legislature, "a wide and manifest difference between the character, habits, and manners of the population of this country and those of Europe." There, pauperism had become "truly frightful, and almost ruinous," while here it ought hardly ever to appear. A simple calculation explained the difference: "In this country, the labour of three days will readily supply the wants of seven, while in Europe the labor of the whole week will barely suffice for the maintenance and support of the family of an industrious labourer or peasant."[2] The report also quoted a similar estimate by an overseer of the poor from Oneida County, in the western part of the state. "In a country where labour is paid for in a ration double to that of any other," he insisted, "where all the necessaries of life are so abundant and cheap . . . there can be no danger of a meritorious individual being allowed to suffer." This attitude persisted through the period so that two decades later, New York City's poor-relief officials still contended that, "In our highly favoured country, where labour is so much demanded and so liberally rewarded, and the means of subsistence so easily and cheaply obtained, poverty need not and ought not to exist."[3]

The abundance of land prompted the identical conclusion. "Our situation is not, and cannot be for ages, similar to that of England," announced Cadwallader Colden, New York's mayor in 1819. "While we have so many millions of acres of uncultivated land, it is impossible that any portion of our population should want employment."[4] The managers of the Society for the Prevention of Pauperism extended this formulation. "Our territory is so expansive, its soil so prolific, that the American population, and the people of Europe cannot, for ages, bear the same ratio to their respective means of subsistence." In this nation, "the institutions were free and equal," there were no "distinctions of rank," laws of primogeniture, hereditary privilege, or confiscatory taxes. Americans enjoyed "ample scope for industry and enterprise, entire freedom from civil and political disabilities, and perfect security of natural and acquired advantages." Surely, it was reasonable to anticipate that "pauperism would be foreign to our country." And to any "political economist, philosophizing about this country, and comparing it with Europe, it would seem a strange paradox that pauperism, as a practical evil, should be known amongst us." Its appearance amid so many natural advantages would have to be "a matter of astonishment and regret." Theodore Sedgwick, one of the most noted social thinkers of the period, put the matter still more succinctly: "The people of the United States escaped from the poverty of Europe; now it is high time to inquire how they can, as far as may be, escape from their own poverty."[5]

But astonishing or not, these observers realized that poverty had established itself in the new republic, compelling them to confront the strange paradox. The Yates committee calculated that towns in New York State in 1822 relieved, in part or in full, a total of 22,111 paupers, at a cost of nearly one-quarter of one million dollars. It discovered that the burden was unevenly distributed, so that the area around the Atlantic coast and the Hudson River, with less than half of the state's population, supported far more than half of its poor.[6] Quincy's findings were very much the same; after sampling conditions in Massachusetts towns, he unhappily reported that Boston relieved as many as six hundred persons annually, while smaller communities maintained five to forty charges each. The Philadelphia committee also returned from its survey to complain of the expense of the poor. Philadelphia alone, it estimated, relieved in full some one thousand persons per year, dispensing almost one hundred thousand dollars.[7]

Nor were the poor found only in the cities. Their exact numbers are hard to estimate, given the absence of reliable and detailed statistics. But clearly the problem did not rest just with laying off industrial and urban workers in times of business depressions. Since only a minority of the labor force engaged in manufacturing pursuits before 1850, cyclical unemployment was not the exclusive issue. (In fact, according to one economist, the rate of unemployment in the antebellum period probably did not rise above five percent. Before 1840, it never exceeded two percent).[8] Rather, this was an agricultural society, and major causes of poverty were to be found in the low wages paid to the farm help, the seasonal layoffs, the absence of any protection against sudden disaster, illness or injury to those unable to purchase and settle a freehold of their own. The acute concern of Yates and Quincy and others with the question of dependency in part reflected an awareness of reality.

Nevertheless, their definition of the poor as a social problem and their fears of unrest from below cannot simply be understood in terms of the number of dependents. Their reactions seem exaggerated, for poverty was not rampant in antebellum society, and not of so great a dimension as to explain the reversal of colonial complacency or to generate a sense of crisis. The findings which so troubled Yates and the rest hardly seemed to warrant their rejection of traditional approaches. It would not have been surprising if these chairmen had argued on the basis of the returns that the republic was escaping the evils of poverty, since by ordinary standards the figures were exceptionally low. The 22,000 paupers in New York State, for example, came from a population of 1,372,000 — not a staggering percentage. The same was true of Philadelphia, where one thousand persons received permanent relief in a city of one hundred twenty-five thousand.

Some observers did view the situation calmly. New York's mayor, Cadwallader Colden, when questioned by the Yates committee, expressed a reasonable complacency. Colden contended that poverty was most acute in maritime cities, where a disproportionate number of foreigners congregated; in time, however, they would disperse, share in the munificence of American life, and escape their misery. Poverty, in his words, was a temporary situation, an "evil which will in a little while cure itself." Special investigations and elaborate precautions were unnecessary, concluded Colden, for "we did not have to fear that the English example will be repeated here."[9] But his remarks were idiosyncratic and few contemporaries were so sanguine about the future. Convinced that poverty ought not to enter their society, they found any evidence of it perplexing, disappointing, and frightening. Not only, it seemed, had Americans failed to eradicate crime and control insanity, but they were also unable to banish poverty. In each instance, higher expectations yielded greater frustrations.

The very attitudes which prompted the new investigations of poverty and its relief also promised that a dismal and fearful tone would characterize much of the results. The premise that need ought not to exist in America, when joined to a view that the poor were not full members of the community, could not help but breed distrust and suspicion, no matter what the size of the dependent classes. It was not the actual number of poor in antebellum society that logically and predictably altered the colonial perspective. Rather, nineteenth-century Americans judged the issue from a new viewpoint, so that he who had once been an accepted part of the community now became an odd and even menacing figure. Yet, at the same time, the public view of the poor as anomalous to America opened wide the prospect of change. The colonists, accepting the presence of poverty as normal, had made little effort to eliminate it. Their successors, perceiving dependency as abnormal, moved naturally and immediately to confront it. No wonder, then, that officials and philanthropists in the 1820's and 1830's began to explore the issue closely, anxious to understand how poverty had gained a foothold in the society and determined to design policies that would dislodge it.

One standard explanation for the origins of poverty blamed the poor themselves for their predicament. It is perhaps ironic but surely understandable that a basic faith in the prosperity of the new world frequently led to a conclusion that economic failure was due to moral failure. The more idyllic the description of fertile farms, the more stern the verdict on the needy; the more exalted the vision of the position of labor, the more severe the censure. Furthermore, once the sentiments of local responsibility had begun to weaken, and observers shifted the needy from the category of neighbor to part of the lower classes, and once the faith in the stabilizing effects of hierarchical organization had begun to decline, it became easier and more necessary to reprimand the poor. These several judgments joined to make the needy at least suspect, and often guilty.

From many quarters came unequivocal pronouncements on the culpability of the poor. Some respectable town burghers, serving a term as overseers of the poor, confidently declared that the great proportion of paupers were "voluntary," that is, made poor "in consequence of drunkedness, idleness and vice of all kind." There were local officials in New York certain that the prime causes of pauperism were found in "the constant use of spirituous liquors, and the consequent waste of time"; and counterparts who were equally confident that "idleness, improvidence and intemperance" produced the typical dependent. This attitude allowed one poor-relief overseer in western New York to dismiss the possibility of a "meritorious individual being allowed to suffer."[10]

The public surveys and benevolent associations' investigations frequently echoed these indictments. The Philadelphia committee affirmed that every stop on its tour had strengthened the conviction that "the poor in consequence of vice, constitute here and everywhere, by far the greater part of the poor." New York's Society for the Prevention of Pauperism announced in 1821 that "the paupers of this city are, for the most part . . . depraved and vicious, and require support because they are so."[11] These declarations were repeated throughout the period. In 1856, the newly formed Association for Improving the Condition of the Poor reported from New York: "Official data show . . . how large a part of the pauperism of this city and State is occasioned by indolence, intemperance, and other vices. . . . There is little pauperism among us not directly or indirectly traceable to these and kindred sources." The chief causes of poverty, insisted the association, were moral ones, and "they admit only of moral remedies." The poor, in brief, had to be elevated.[12]

The vice to which these critics usually devoted the greatest attention was drink. Here was the most convenient explanation as to why some men willfully ignored the natural advantages of the new world, yielding to corruption and need. "The case of pauperism, in this happy country," succinctly proclaimed one typical overseer of the poor, "is intemperance." The Quincy report put the matter just as narrowly. "Of all causes of pauperism, intemperance, in the use of spirituous liquors, is the most powerful and universal."[13] So, too, the A.I.C.P. informed its members that "the result of careful inquiries on this subject, show that the mechanics of this City expend as large a sum for strong drink . . . as their *employers annually save.*" Surveys even attempted to put these findings into statistical form. The resident physician at New York's almshouse hospital, for example, reported that ninety percent of the patients were intemperate.[14]

This particular formulation of the origins of poverty was appealing and useful in the Jacksonian period. It seemed to explain why some men and not others fell into vicious habits. Rum had power to corrupt the innocent — its pleasures were reason enough for succumbing to its influence. Such an interpretation confirmed everyday observations. Even the most casual visitor to the neighborhoods of the poor knew that grog shops and taverns were omnipresent, their numbers ample testimony to a flourishing business. The A.I.C.P., after surveying the situation, believed that "one astonishing fact on this subject should suffice." In the whole of New York City, there was one tavern for every eighteen families; but in the precincts of the lower classes, they were found "in double and treble this ratio, so that there is one grog shop for every five or ten families." Here was "a fact, unparalleled in the world!"[15] This doctrine exonerated citizens from assuming a primary responsibility for the poor, freeing them from a traditional obligation. Since vicious and unworthy dependents were hardly the sort to be included in a community or treated with solicitude, Americans could avoid a burden with good conscience. The poor had changed for the worse, not they.

To be sure, the least sentimental observer conceded that

worthy individuals were scattered here and there among the needy. The orphan, the widow, the sick, and the aged were not necessarily depraved, and many commentators attempted to differentiate between the "poor" — the deserving "who are wholly incapable of work," and the "paupers" — the unworthy who were able-bodied and lazy. But invariably, within a few minutes into the speech or after a few pages of the pamphlet, the distinction fell away, and the poor became synonymous with the idle and the degenerate. The dangers of indulging the vagrant and the shiftless, not the plight of orphans and widows, now captured the greater attention. Critics frequently insisted that the aged and the sick, although not dissolute, were foolish and imprudent. They ought to have saved for the proverbial rainy day; had they exercised prudent restraint and not carelessly squandered every cent, they would have accumulated funds against the contingencies of disease and incapacity. "If labor generally had a reserved fund to draw upon," declared the A.I.C.P., "there could be no suffering for there would be no poverty." But since the lower class was all too often "reckless of the future," spending as it earned, "of what avail, against a time of need, are plenty of work and good wages, or indeed, of any interposition in its behalf?" Really no one among the poor escaped guilt.[16]

In much of the writing on dependency, the category of the worthy poor was so narrow as to be practically irrelevant. The differences between dependency and deviancy narrowed, with the poor standing as potential criminals, as having almost crossed the divide. The same vices that caused their poverty would inevitably bring them to lawlessness. As one New York legislative investigation declared: pauperism, although "not in itself a crime . . . is not unusually the result of such self-indulgence, un-thrift, excess, or idleness, as is next of kin to criminality."[17] Vice, crime, and poverty were stops on the same line, and men shuttled regularly among them. Under the influence of these ideas, many Americans relinquished eighteenth-century attitudes. The colonists, assuming that the bulk of the local poor deserved support, had not let the potentiality for abuse, the possibility that loafers might profit from the arrangements, color their perspective on relief. To their successors, however, the chance of corruption overwhelmed all other considerations. Now that the poor were not brothers in the community but stood as next of kin to criminals, one could not be too careful to guard against dishonesty. Rejecting the slothful took precedence over relieving the needy.

These attitudes were not unqualified. Another critical element in antebellum thinking about the origins of dependency looked beyond the private guilt of the poor to public considerations. Just as the first penologists insisted that the failures of the family and community were basic to understanding the origins of deviancy, and medical superintendents posited that the structure of society was the primary contributor to the spread of insanity, officials and legislators also looked to the social order for the roots of poverty. The moral weakness of the poor was not a sufficient explanation; intemperance and laziness and the attractions of drink were part of the story, but not the sum of it. Why was it, critics asked, that the poor so readily yielded to noxious influences? Who licensed the grog shops? Why were churches and schools and families not preventing men from becoming the victims of vice, or helping them to escape it? If the natural advantages of America were unparalleled, did the fault for poverty rest with artificial arrangements? Starting with these questions, they went on to describe, with varying degrees of clarity, the role of the community in generating pauperism. They did not altogether deny or discount individual complicity. But their broader notions of responsibility significantly affected the response to poverty.

Beginning in the 1820's, and with increasing strength thereafter, a host of would-be reformers denounced the system of supporting the poor at home. For some observers the issue seemed simple: since the needy were vicious, the community ought not to maintain them within its bounds. But for others the matter was more complex. Benevolence appeared to be promoting the very evils it set out to combat. Outdoor relief, they believed, was a dole that sapped the energy and initiative of the poor, fixing them in their misery. It also gave the idle both the free time and the wherewithal to explore the vices pervading the community. These considerations shifted the causes of poverty from the character of the dependent classes to social practices and conditions.

The first and most important statements of this position, with an immediate impact on policy, appeared in the Quincy and Yates reports. Both committees insisted that outdoor relief aggravated rather than relieved poverty by encouraging the poor to rely upon a public dole instead of their own energy. Of all methods for supporting the needy, proclaimed Quincy, "the most wasteful, the most expensive, and most injurious to their morals, and destructive of their industrious habits, is that of supply in their own families." Yates reiterated this finding. The present poor laws, he informed the New York legislature, "tend to encourage the sturdy beggar and profligate vagrant to become pensioneers upon the public funds." Their provisions "operate as so many invitations to become beggars."[18] So too, the New York Society for the Prevention of Pauperism declared that since our country was "exempt from all the acknowledged causes of vagrancy and beggary in Europe," their origins must "exist in the enactments and artificial arrangements of the society." Pauperism in the United States "ought to be regarded as an evil [which] could not take place, unless by the fault of its laws and institutions," namely the perpetuation of the practice of outdoor relief. In 1827, the Philadelphia committee summed up the consensus on the traditional approach to the poor. "The whole system," they concluded, "is essentially founded in error, and all its parts are consequently defective."[19]

The roots of poverty, then, lay not so much with the moral depravity of the poor, as with the temptation that the community held out to them. Practically anyone would choose to avoid the burden of work if assured of support. If a member of the lower class had no option but to depend on his own exertions, he would surely search for — and given American conditions certainly find — employment. His instincts and his needs would make him a vigorous and diligent laborer. But once officials intervened and offered him a dole to be enjoyed at home, he very understandably preferred the handout to a job. Outdoor relief blunted his proper instincts, or in the words of various overseers of the poor, served to "relax individual exertion by unnerving the arm of industry," and weakened the "desire of honest independence." Since the habit of public alms was so debilitating, a recipient was unlikely to "ever again emerge from degradation, or elevate himself to respectability." The corruptions so obvious in the manners of the poor reflected not simply their own character, but the effects of an unwise policy. The verdict that "our numerous charitable institutions, however laudable . . . have the unhappy tendency of increasing the numbers of dependent poor," was inescapable.[20]

To admit of this kind of community complicity in the genesis of poverty might easily have led antebellum officials to the conclusion that they had better halt all efforts to ameliorate the condition of the poor and leave them to their own fate. If public relief funds created their own clientele, then it would be proper to abolish all poor laws, to remove the state completely from the business of charity, and allow a few private organizations to inspect and reinspect the credentials of the handful of deserving poor, and then give assistance. The Yates committee, for one, flirted with the idea, but finally decided that "the total want of a pauper system, would be inconsistent with a humane, liberal, and enlightened policy." The Quincy committee, for another, weighed this option, quoting with approval the remarks of such Englishmen as the Earl of Sheffield and Henry Brougham in favor of the step. Nevertheless, it too declared that "it had no intention to recommend . . . an abolition of those laws altogether in Massachusetts."[21]

The decision to urge public action in the field of poverty depended on other, more extended definitions of the community's complicity. According to activists, the poor suffered from more than the enervating influences of outdoor relief. They were the victims of economic emergencies beyond their control, and of more permanent and debilitating influences that kept them in need. Hence, some students of dependency, like medical superintendents and penologists, insisted that the community assume responsibility for healing the wounds it inflicted.

These observers, fearing that abstract principles did not cover every particular case, were unwilling to act consistently on the premise that all unemployment in America was voluntary. Convinced that at times the society was to blame by not providing the able-bodied with the opportunity to work, they balked at applying general notions too rigorously. Natural advantages did not preclude lapses, and some among the poor might be unemployed through no fault of their own.

Such sentiments were not as rare as one might think. Many officials were prepared to act upon exceptions to the theory of American munificence. No one, for example, blamed economic depressions on the laborer, and municipalities passed ameliorative measures. Public relief and public works seemed appropriate programs. Even in less critical moments, communities' failures might outweigh personal flaws. The A.I.C.P., one of the least sentimental of benevolent organizations, insisted that although "pauperism is an anomaly in our country, an exotic to our soil," that could "find no root except it be nurtured into baneful luxuriance by injudicious management," still poverty, "occasioned by sudden reverses or unavoidable calamities, may overtake the most prudent and prosperous." It was, they conceded, "an evil to which many in large commercial communities like our own, are peculiarly exposed." The effects of an "overstocked condition of the labor market," justified "charitable and philanthropic appliances."[22] An eminently worthy family could need support because of "insufficient employment and high price of family necessaries." A.I.C.P. reports also blamed the community for failing to protect the health of the poor. It was no coincidence that "epidemic and contagious diseases and infirm health most extensively and fatally prevail in those districts where the inhabitants are most densely crowded in badly arranged and ill-ventilated tenements amidst the accumulations of impurities." The fault rested with "imperfect drainage and sewerage," not the bad habits of the poor.[23]

Finally, the analysis of the A.I.C.P. indicated the limits to which some observers might go in apportioning the responsibility for poverty between the individual and the community. The association's managers were willing to grant that intemperance might be as much a symptom as a cause of dependency. Contradicting those who saw drink only as the great corrupter of the poor, the A.I.C.P. declared that intemperance was often the result of the wretchedness of the poor. It was "the lassitude consequent upon the foul atmosphere of their wretched homes, and the absence of domestic comfort which drives them to seek exhilaration and enjoyment in the tap room; their unimproved minds and tastes, without appropriate recreation, hard living and harder labor, that find in alcoholic stimulants a temporary relief."[24] Rather than condemn and neglect the poor, one had to attempt to relieve and rehabilitate them.

Society's responsibility for poverty went even deeper. To many observers, one of the most critical elements in generating dependency was the extent of vice in the community. The lower classes were the prime casualties. Whether idle by choice, because of a temporary shortage of employment, or because of the attractions of the dole of outdoor relief, they were especially prone to corrupting influence. They drank and gambled and ruined their lives not because of an inherent depravity, but because temptations were omnipresent and powerful. The poor were victims of forces beyond their control. The same image of the society that appeared in the literature on crime and insanity emerged here too. The correcting influence on the poor of such institutions as the family, the church, and the school could not offset the lure of taverns, gambling halls, and houses of prostitution.

This judgment emerged clearly in the Quincy and Yates reports. Officials in New York's Rensselaer County responded to committee inquiries by equating ordinary society with "the haunts of vice." If the poor could escape from an environment where they "live in idleness and dissipation . . . they become more healthy, and in fact more happy." Overseers in Dorchester, Massachusetts, repeated this argument. "Temptations [were] rendered less generous," as soon as the poor were not "suffered to remain in their own families."[25] The summary recommendations of the two committees also reflected this belief. Yates objected to outdoor relief in part because he found no institutions in the community able to control the poor, "restraining their vicious appetites and pursuits." In these circumstances, idleness inevitably led to vice, dissipation, and crime. Quincy, too, insisted that the inherent danger of relieving the needy within the community lay in exposing them to "the temptations to extravagance and dissipation."[26]

The image of Jacksonian society riddled with vice appeared even more sharply in the observations of those concerned with the youngest victims of poverty, orphans and destitute and vagrant children. To abandon them to the influences at loose in the community was to condemn them to a life of depravity and crime. "There is no lot as we all know," declared concerned officials in Cincinnati, "so hopeless and helpless as that of a destitute Orphan; its career of sin and ill, when neglected, is almost certain."[27] Unless some "restraining authority kept them back from the temptations of vice and pollution of the world," a minister in South Carolina told interested philanthropists, they would become "accustomed to crimes before they knew that they were evils," and in the words of another preacher, without fail suffer "the degradation of ignorance and almost inevitable vice."[28]

Destitute children were just as vulnerable. The goal of the Boston Asylum and Farm School was to take children from "abodes of raggedness and want," where "mingling with the cries of helpless need, the sounds of blasphemy assail your ears; and from the example of father and of mother, the mouth of lisping childhood is taught to curse and revile." Rather than allow them, with "the road to ruin before them," to go "hand in hand with beggary and vice, steering their downward course," the organization would intervene, "prepare a place of safety for them, where their eyes will be shut upon scenes of infamy and guilt . . . where temptations to evil shall be put far from them." The dangers were so great that nothing less would do.[29]

Perhaps most acute was the predicament of vagrant children. Roaming about at will, they were constantly exposed to the corruptions in the community. "The existing arrangements of society," explained a group of New York City philanthropists, did not curb "the true sources of vice and crime." As one of their members declared: "It is sufficiently difficult for the man of matured years, drilled in the hard school of active life, to contend against the innumerable temptations that beset him at every step and every moment. Who then can wonder that a mere child falls under the combined pressure of ignorance and evil example in the home where he was nursed and cradled . . . [in] the influences to which *the street* subjects him." The first priority then was to rescue the children from the burning house — "to remove them from dangerous and corrupting associations" in the society — and to leave it to others to try and extinguish the fires — to transform the community.[30]

Part of the source of some reformers' fright reverted to a distrust of the poor. Regardless of how few the taverns or how hidden the gambling halls, the poor would locate them, diligent in a way they had never been about finding a job. Some of the severity of their perspective also reflected a traditional concern with the effects of idleness — give men enough time and they would beat a path to the devil. Then, too, observers were often more distressed at the condition of the neighborhoods of the poor; not the entire community so much as its slums were corrupt. Nevertheless, a distinctly new view of the general community marked reformers' thinking. Like penologists and medical superintendents, they too had lost faith in the countervailing authority of inherited institutions of control. Although the colonists had feared the evil effects of idleness and worried over the power of demon rum, they had remained confident that the organization of society would order the actions of the local poor. This expectation many Americans no longer shared. They acknowledged that the eighteenth-century system had ended without leaving clear alternatives. A common allegiance to the ideal of social hierarchy, neighborhood ties, the supervision of the church and the family no longer could affect the behavior of the poor. But what would take their place? This question brought a note of panic and severity into the attempts to understand the origins of poverty and to evaluate the contributory role of the community.

The distrust of the poor and the sense of the pervasiveness of vice both derived from the same assumption: that the society had lost the stability and cohesion of the colonial period, that ideas and organizations that had once worked to bind members together were without effect. The poor stood as a separate, distinct, and hostile class. Rather than appear as brothers with a common bond of interest in the community, they became paupers, endangering the balance of the system. This same viewpoint led to the belief that the community was not only failing to inculcate order, but was actually encouraging men to disorder. As the authority of family and church and neighbors declined, the influence of the tavern and gaming house grew stronger.

Under these circumstances, reformers reconsidered the traditional methods of dispensing relief. When the poor had stood as neighbors, and vagrants as strangers, it made sense, they believed, to relieve the one at home and rely upon the constable to block the entrance of the other. But these techniques no longer seemed appropriate. Barriers around each town were both a parochial and, given the great amount of migration and immigration, not very workable solution. Similarly, the distribution of outdoor relief encouraged all of the poor in their corruption. What value or wisdom was there in keeping the family together if the idler would simply send his wife and children begging, thereby satisfying his own needs while corrupting the next generation as well? Convinced that vice was much more rampant and powerful in the community than virtue, the Jacksonians believed they had to formulate a new program of relief and correction.

The various elements that entered into the formulation and justification of this design were perhaps most clearly brought together in a lecture by Walter Channing to the Boston Society for the Prevention of Pauperism in 1843. Channing, brother to William Ellery, probably the outstanding Unitarian minister of his day, was a prominent Boston physician, and as Professor of Obstetrics and Medical Jurisprudence, lent distinction to the early history of Massachusetts General Hospital. Given the social origins of most obstetrical patients in medical institutions during these years — lying-in was unique to the lower classes — it is not surprising that he took a keen interest in the fate of the poor, read the contemporary literature closely, pondered alternatives, and then summed up lucidly and concisely the several strands of thought that we have been tracing here.

Channing spoke to the society on the causes of poverty. It was an effort of "no light labor," he told his audience; the issue "has taxed the strongest intellects of this, and all civilized times." Nevertheless, he too felt compelled to take up the burden of inquiry, convinced that the popular understanding of the question was woefully inadequate. "The pauper," protested Channing, "is forever looked to as the active, the sole agent in the production of his own misery. He is poor — he is squalid in dress and loathsome in his whole bearing. He is dependent upon others around him for that which he should obtain for himself. . . . He is in a state of willing slavery, and so he must be a degraded being."[31] But Channing insisted that such an image was grossly overdrawn and patently unfair. Americans committed the critical error of looking for the origins of poverty exclusively "in him or her who suffers it — in his or her faithlessness to human duty . . . in his or her voluntary dependence," as if the poor had been "in the possession of all human power, and surrounded with every opportunity for obtaining independent support." No matter how appealing this interpretation might be, Channing declared: "I for one protest against it in whole, and in part." Poverty was not an individual but "a social condition." Its causes "must be permanent. They must be out of the condition itself. *A condition can never be a cause;* and a voluntary, a moral, an intellectual being, can hardly be the sole agent in the production of his own deepest misery." Where, then, were we to look for the roots of the problem? Channing's response was unequivocal: "to SOCIETY ITSELF. It is here I look for the great and whole source of the whole misery of the social state."[32]

Part of the community's responsibility for poverty Channing attributed to the imperfect organization of the economy. Despite a generally favorable ratio of men to jobs and land, employment was not everywhere and always available. The state and federal governments were slow to act in times of emergency; believing themselves already too far in debt, they would not "carry on various important operations, which, while in progress, gave employment to vast numbers of men." Periodic crises reduced many laborers' wages below subsistence levels. The effect of "the sudden reduction of wages, extended to large numbers," Channing explained, "is not only directly injurious to wide interests, but produces pauperism." His medical practice also illuminated the community's role in the origins of poverty. Channing told his Boston audience how the severity of prevailing laboring conditions often ruined workers' health; physically unable to work, they soon became hopelessly dependent. Channing had no intention of attacking the general principles of laissez-faire economics, and was certain that strikes for higher salaries would not improve conditions. But like many of his contemporaries, he believed that the iron laws of the economy accounted for a large number of cases of poverty.[33]

Far more central to his analysis was a firm and vigorous

insistence that the ultimate roots of dependence lay in the faulty
organization of the *social* order. And he gave a dual meaning to
this notion. First, men who once had been considered brothers
were now depraved members of the lower class, isolated in their
misery. The shift in perspective had a self-fulfilling quality about
it, for by treating dependents as dangerous, more prosperous
citizens helped make them so. Angry rather than nostalgic,
Channing outlined the transformation. "By our modes of life —
our houses — our dress — our equipage; in short by what is
strictly external to us . . . men detach themselves from their
neighbors — withdraw themselves from the human family . . .
in its ever recognized relationship of brotherhood." His choice of
words was especially apt: neighbors, family, brotherhood, these
terms were prevalent in eighteenth-century discussions of the
poor. "Exclusiveness," Channing declared, had become the primary virtue. "It is not much disposed to go to the lower places in
society. If it attempts to aid Pauperism, it does so by delegation.
It knows too little of the detail of every day want and misery, to
feel that it can directly minister to its relief." The poor man had
practically ceased to be a man.[34]

Second, under these conditions corruptions had come to per-
vade the Jacksonian community. The poor, regardless of the
particular circumstances that made them so, inevitably succumbed to one vice or another; they were surrounded by
temptations, "the means of their sin," and the "opportunities for
crime," and so predictably turned vicious. The influence of the
tavern far exceeded that of the church. The one welcomed the
poor, the other practically excluded him. Heretofore, contended
Channing, all members of the community had mixed in the
church. But now, "social distinctions are most strongly marked.
Have we not churches for the rich, and churches for the poor?"[35]
(In truth, Dr. Channing had only to count the number of upper-
class parishioners in his brother's church to validate his statement. So perhaps he was indulging in more than a pun when
telling friends that William was the brother that preached, while
he, Walter, was the one that practiced.) The blame for poverty,
therefore, had to be diffused through the society and not concentrated exclusively on the poor.

The implications of these remarks were clear. A policy of poor relief, Channing concluded, was an inescapable obligation of the community. Just as medical superintendents and students of crime insisted that the society must heal the wound that it inflicted, so too Channing announced: "The public kindness here, is mainly a requital for great social defect and wrong."[36] A program to alleviate the needs of the poor and protect them from vice deserved the highest priority.

The career and pronouncements of Joseph Tuckerman, minister to the poor of Boston, also symbolized well the changes in American attitudes and responses to the poor between the colonial and the Jacksonian periods. In the eighteenth century, the clergy had dominated the subject, both in sheer output of statements and, far more important, in the quality of the discussion. The pulpit was the major forum for analyzing poverty, and the declarations accurately reflected the physical setting. The divine approbation of charity, the beauty of giving, the religious rewards for benevolence were among the primary considerations. The view was from the top down, with ministers giving little attention to the state and character of the poor. But if there was no superabundance of sympathy, there was no keen distrust either. The congregations were mixed, seating the poor, even if not in as many numbers as the better sort. And words like "brother" and "neighbor" flowed easily.

By the 1830's, however, the situation was fundamentally different. The congregation, reflecting community organization and interest, was now far more class-divided. Channing's description of the social exclusiveness of the church was fully warranted. Ministers were no longer the chief spokesmen on the issue. Pamphleteers, would-be reformers, local officials, and state legislators now almost drowned out the clergymen's voices. The perspective on what should be done for the poor shifted to a secular one. Ministers offered religious inspiration for social action, but the content of their program resembled that of lawyers or merchants. The clergy repeated the prevailing solutions for poverty, not adding a special one of their own.

Joseph Tuckerman's choice of ministerial duties pointed first to the new position of dependents in Jacksonian society. Since the poor were hardly ever to be found within Boston's established congregations, Tuckerman, with the prodding of William

Ellery Channing, began in 1826 to minister exclusively to the city's lower classes. Rather than occupy a fixed pulpit and lead a congregation in one residential district, Tuckerman devoted himself to visiting the poor in their homes, wherever they were to be found, and lectured to them from any podium, regardless of its location. Soon, under his leadership, mission churches for the poor opened all over Boston, and then spread to New York and other cities. Whatever the nobility of the enterprise, here was striking testimony to the real separation of the poor from the rest of the city. And religious leaders, rather than try to integrate them into the churches as neighbors and brothers, acknowledged the class gulf, and some pieties aside, accepted it. They sent out "missions" to the poor — forays into strange parts, to service an alien group.[37]

Tuckerman's writings and speeches showed little trace of eighteenth-century ministerial doctrines. He devoted unprecedented attention to the poor themselves and brought a new specificity and direct observation to his comments. In reporting to the Unitarian Association on his activities as Minister at Large in Boston, he painstakingly attempted to clarify the origins of poverty, the character of the poor, and the appropriate community response. His religious faith was no less intense than that of his predecessors. But his view on how religious sentiments should be expressed had changed. Rather than being preoccupied with the rewards of charity for the philanthropist and satisfied with vague statements on the condition of the needy, Tuckerman insisted that believers must further reform and improvement. He gave theological approbation to social betterment, and thereby provided a new and important impulse to reform activities. Yet, at the same time, his ideas on what ought to be done were usually indistinguishable from other, purely secular, diagnoses. Rather than bring a uniquely religious vision to bear on how society should be organized, Tuckerman reinforced and gave a religious sanction to the prescriptions of Quincy, Yates, and the others.

Tuckerman took as one task an accurate description of the dependent classes, looking to contradict any simple notion that blamed them for their circumstances. The poor, he cautioned, did not fit into a single category. Facile generalizations grouping them as "a class of society, a single body," with the intent of labeling them morally weak and corrupt, were the results of inexperience and ignorance. "Let us look at the poor as they are," the minister insisted, "a very mixed class — and comprehending as many varieties, both of condition and character."[38] They exhibited all shades of behavior, ranging from depravity to virtue, from improvidence to thrift. It was not their private character so much as the influence of forces beyond their control that accounted for the condition of the needy. There was, for example, the faulty functioning of the economy. "There are those who are sometimes compelled to beg," declared Tuckerman, "because they are wholly unable to work . . . to obtain employment by which they may live." Anyone doubting this claim, believing "they might obtain employment . . . if they would seek for it," ought to question the owners of the city's mills and learn that they were turning away hundreds of willing hands. Those with regular employment often had to try to exist on below-subsistence wages. "There is a vast amount of want and suffering," noted Tuckerman, "which is to be attributed to the low wages." Even those who had saved for a day of trouble soon exhausted their resources.[39]

Tuckerman went on, in tones reminiscent of Dr. Channing, to trace the origins of poverty to the social order. Positing that "society has caused — and who can doubt whether it has caused — a great amount of poverty," he focused upon the corruptions that seemed all-pervasive. For the idle poor the communities "furnish [the facilities] to the indulgence of the grossest appetites and passions," bringing them to "open shame and crime." Temptations to intemperance received special attention: "Has not society a large share of responsibility for this evil?" The ordinary citizen not only witnessed the swelling sale and disbursement of liquor with indifference, but even was ready to profit from it, unmindful that he was "ministering to the utter moral ruin of his fellow beings."[40] The children of the poor also suffered the same dismal fate. Destitute youngsters were ruined by parents all too ready to send them begging, and by the street, with its numerous taverns and theaters. No institution intervened to counteract these effects; the school, for example, was helpless so long as the child ignored the classroom for the company of "associates as idle as himself." Under these circumstances, Tuckerman noted, it was only to be expected that "the greatest part of the abject poverty and of the recklessness in crime, may be followed back to causes which showed themselves distinctly within the first fifteen or twenty years of life, and generally at a much earlier season." Clearly something had to be done to remove the poor, both young and old, "from the scenes and associates of the iniquity."[41]

Here again the grim view of the functioning of the community rested upon the notion that the colonial order had broken down, with no alternatives readily apparent. The forces that had moved the poor from brotherhood into the lower classes had also weakened the traditional mechanisms of control. Physical mobility and the concomitant growth of cities helped to destroy the nexus between citizens that had existed in the eighteenth century. "Men are not only divided and separated by great inequalities of their condition in respect to property," argued Tuckerman, "but by the very fact of the extent of their numbers. Every individual in the different classes may . . . be unknown to many even of the class to which they belong."[42] No wonder that suspicion was widespread, that the propertied distrusted the poor. By the same token, the network of community relationships could no longer check citizens' behavior, and institutions that had once influenced all members of the community were now unable to bridge the gap between classes. No sooner did the mechanisms of shame break down than the poor succumbed to "open" crime.

Thus the views of Boston's first minister to the poor coincided with the contemporary, and secular, understanding of the causes of poverty. The charity sermon now had shifted to an analysis of the structure of the community. Tuckerman's special ministerial interests could be detected in suggestions that Sunday schools could better extend the influence of the church to the lower classes, and he held out the hope that a rejuvenation of public spirit, "enlightened and wisely extended public sentiments," might improve matters.[43] But he took his place, comfortably and agreeably, with state legislators trying to frame a policy based on very different assumptions.

Given Tuckerman's analysis of the roots of poverty, it is not surprising to find the Massachusetts assembly appointing him in 1832 to a committee of four to review the findings of the Quincy committee. And predictably, the new group confirmed Quincy's recommendations. It too urged an end to public outdoor relief, insisting that the poor not be supported in the community. They too held out the prospect of reform, that the poor need not be always with us. But to this end, the dependents must be removed from the society, to a place where temptations to vice could be eliminated, and where their behavior could be controlled with appropriate rewards and punishments.[44] Here reformers, ministers, philanthropists, and elected officials arrived together at a program.

8

The Almshouse Experience

The reaction to the problem of dependency paralleled the response to the issue of deviancy. Just as the penitentiary would reform the criminal and the insane asylum would cure the mentally ill, so the almshouse would rehabilitate the poor. In the decades of the Jacksonian era, institutions for the needy spread through the country, as state legislatures, city and town councils, and county governments for the first time made incarceration central to a program of support. These structures, to be sure, did not monopolize the field of charity. Private benevolent associations and public officials dispensed limited amounts of food and fuel and petty sums of cash to the poor. But the door of the almshouse became the most important symbol — and reality — in the practice of relief.

The Massachusetts experience illustrated the dimensions of the change. In the eighteenth century only a handful of towns, and invariably the larger ones, had bothered to construct a poorhouse; most settlements straightforwardly relieved the local poor in a household. In the first decades after independence a few more communities invested in an almshouse, but not until 1810 did their numbers swell, and only after 1820, with the appearance of the Quincy report, did institutions become commonplace in the state. Between 1820 and 1840 some sixty towns constructed new almshouses and many others renovated and refurbished dilapidated ones. Legislative committees, attempting to keep track of the shift, frequently surveyed local practices. Their investigations were not always thorough and their statistics were sloppily gathered and inaccurate. Nevertheless, they pointed to

12. *The Boston House of Industry, 1821. The architecture of this institution exemplified the ideals of order and regularity. These virtues would bring a new discipline to the poor, transforming them into diligent, hardworking citizens.*

COURTESY OF THE PRINT DEPARTMENT, BOSTON PUBLIC LIBRARY

13. *The New York almshouse, 1825. The very close resemblance between the New York and Boston institutions points convincingly to the similarities in perspective on the need to regiment the relief of the poor.*

COURTESY OF THE NEW-YORK HISTORICAL SOCIETY, NEW YORK CITY

the revolution in treatment. In 1840 there were 180 almshouses in Massachusetts, valued at about $926,000, encompassing 17,000 acres of land. Even allowing for overstatement, it is evident that towns were investing heavily in caretaker institutions. Concomitantly, overseers of the poor expanded the majority of poor-relief funds for indoor rather than outdoor support. The first official returns, probably with some exaggeration, recorded a two-to-one ratio. But there could be no doubting the fundamental shift in procedures.[1]

There was some link between population and institutional innovation. Villages with only a handful of poor, less than ten, rarely went to the expense of constructing a poorhouse or, more accurately, converting a farmhouse into a poorhouse. Thus the western, Berkshire sections had many less almshouses than the areas around Boston and Worcester. And even in the most populated centers, caretaker institutions typically supported persons requiring full-time relief. The towns continued to dispense casual assistance, from a meal ticket to a bundle of wood, to meet momentary difficulties, and as a result, the number of poor receiving outdoor assistance was greater than the cases of full-time, indoor support. Nevertheless, for the hard-core poor, for those who faced permanent or long-term need, the almshouse was the critical institution. By the end of the Civil War, four out of every five persons in Massachusetts who received extended relief remained within an institution. Now the poor had to live with the specter of the almshouse before them.[2]

Events in New York followed a similar pattern. After the publication of the Yates report in 1824, almshouses proliferated. Surveying contemporary practices, Yates learned that only thirty in a sample of one hundred thirty New York towns (which included all the larger ones), maintained an almshouse; had he extended his examination to every community in the state, he would have found the proportion of institutions to settlements still lower. After this decade, however, the almshouse became the standard form of poor relief. By 1835 all but four of the state's fifty-five counties had erected a poorhouse. In 1830, the institutions together held 4,000 acres of land; by 1840 the figure almost doubled. In 1830 some 4,500 persons received indoor relief. By 1840 the number mounted to 8,225, and by 1850 it stood close to 10,000.[3]

The popularity of the almshouse in New York, as in Massachusetts, spelled the decline but not the eradication of outdoor relief. The comparative importance of the two systems was suggested in the first statewide-expenditure figures published in 1838. That year overseers of the poor gave approximately $380,-000 to indoor relief, about double the sum they allotted to outdoor relief. Although these percentages fluctuated over the course of the antebellum period, New York invariably spent considerably more funds on institutional than noninstitutional support. Thus by 1857, just a little more than three decades after the Yates report, the almshouse had become so basic to the state system that a new legislative committee investigating the plight of the poor gave it almost exclusive attention. The treatment of poverty had become synonymous with the condition of the almshouse.[4]

New England, Middle Atlantic, and Middle West states followed the example of New York and Massachusetts with varying degrees of speed and thoroughness. Rhode Island's major cities, Providence and Newport, quickly built large establishments, and although the villages did not emulate their practice, most of the state's hard-core poor faced institutional relief. When Thomas Hazard, on behalf of the legislature, surveyed the condition of the dependent classes in 1850, he published what was essentially a study of indoor relief policies. His first interest was with the almshouse — had the towns adopted one, what salary did they pay the keeper, what was the value of the land holdings, how much did inmate labor produce? His sample of fifteen institutions revealed that together they held 500 inmates, on property valued at $128,000; by comparison, fifteen settlements which did without an almshouse supported only 171 persons, and most of them relieved less than twelve cases each. Wherever the desperate poor were found in numbers, they entered an almshouse.[5]

Incarceration became basic to the system of support in Pennsylvania. In 1827, Philadelphia investigated the practices of Boston, New York, and other surrounding cities, and then decided to abolish all outdoor relief. Every one of the poor in the city, regardless of the extent or duration of his need, would receive aid only in the almshouse. After a decade of controversy, the state modified the law, and in 1839 the Philadelphia Guardians of the Poor again distributed outdoor as well as indoor relief. But this concession did not remove indoor relief from the center of the system. The overseers dispensed funds for household support grudgingly, suspiciously, and in very small amounts. Whenever possible, they dispatched the poor to the almshouse.[6]

In the pre–Civil War years midwestern states also adopted the poorhouse solution. Ohio, the first of the northwestern territories to enter the Union, duplicated the poor-relief statutes of eastern states, and then itself served as a model for Michigan and Illinois, which in turn influenced the laws in Wisconsin and Iowa. Given the low density of population, legislatures typically authorized but did not compel a county or town to construct an almshouse; yet they often encouraged a decision in favor of indoor relief. Thus in 1838 the Michigan assembly decreed that whenever possible the poor should be removed to an almshouse; persons needing temporary aid or those who "cannot be conveniently removed to the poorhouse," would be supported at home. The law insisted, however, that no sum greater than ten dollars be paid to any dependent without painstaking examinations and special permissions.[7]

Some cities, like Chicago, strove for all the rigid consistency of places like Philadelphia. In 1848 the Cook County commissioners resolved to abolish outdoor relief, making the almshouse the exclusive center for the care of the poor. Temporary support at home was, they believed, "a dangerous precedent"; allow one exception and applications for support would multiply. Here, too, however, the step was too drastic for public opinion to tolerate. In December 1858 the county commissioners relented, permitting outdoor relief in a few carefully screened cases; the next year they abandoned altogether the attempt to keep an almshouse monopoly over relief. So although institutionalization never became the sole method for caring for the poor, it did to an extraordinary degree dominate the public response to poverty.[8] In fact, throughout the Midwest, the appeal of this program was so great that one finds almshouses established in remote settlements with hardly anyone to occupy them. One student of the history of poor relief in Missouri, upon reviewing his findings, wondered why counties often insisted on establishing an almshouse when the number of dependents was so small. The same question occurs when one reads a traveler's description of visiting charitable institutions in Kentucky in 1845, and finding them empty. But these queries leave no doubt that the almshouse, like the penitentiary and the insane asylum, proliferated in the antebellum period.[9]

Another index of the popularity of the almshouse solution was the weakening of settlement laws and warning-out practices, and the reluctance of many states to press relatives to support their poorer kin. The New York experience illustrated the shift. Its revised statutes in 1827 dropped property qualifications for residence, and the new law not only prohibited the removal of dependents from county to county, but also from one town to another within the same county. In Connecticut, the history of the settlement law in this period, in the words of its closest student, was one of "steady progress toward liberality." Similar changes occurred in such midwestern states as Illinois, where the earliest codes established a twelve-month requirement for residence and where, by 1839, the period dropped to six months, by 1841, to thirty days.[10] Even where settlement laws remained on the books, practicalities forced officials to rely upon other stratagems. Thus Rhode Island's residential requirements were very strict throughout the nineteenth century — probably the toughest in the nation; yet officials in that state too recognized how exceptionally cumbersome were the procedures for removal. Providence ordered that since it was "in some cases utterly impossible to convey persons rejected by the said Town Council to the place of their last legal settlement," they should be sent to a workhouse and there "provided for and kept to labour."[11] In this same spirit, western states made little effort to compel relatives to support needy kin. Ohio, Indiana, and Tennessee, for example, put the burden of relief directly on the towns and counties, not the family. It is true that the newer states, fearful that they might become a dumping ground for the older regions and eastern states, worried about an influx of immigrants, kept settlement laws in their codes. But everyone realized that these statutes could not serve as a basis of a system of poor relief. A new departure was critical, and so all across the country institutionalization became as important to the care of the poor as it was to the treatment of the criminal and the insane.[12]

For many contemporaries the almshouse was an integral part of the movement that promoted the insane asylum and the penitentiary. Like these ventures, it would serve humanitarian and reformatory aims, and bring a new standard of treatment to the poor. The almshouse, however, did not generate the level of excitement and enthusiasm surrounding these two institutions. Few foreigners bothered to inspect a poorhouse, and Americans themselves did not devote to it consistent attention. Periodicals did not fill their pages with long and passionate arguments on the best methods for organizing institutions for the poor. Yet, to a significant degree the almshouse, the penitentiary, and the asylum all grew from the same sources. The backers of one institution often urged the adoption of the other; Dorothea Dix, for example, was certain that the almshouse was as proper a place for the poor as the insane asylum was for the mentally ill. Even more important, almshouse officials shared many premises with medical superintendents and penologists. They agreed on the elements responsible for deviancy and dependency and looked first to the reformatory potential of institutions to effect change.

Americans concerned with the issue of relief, whether overseers of the poor, state legislators, ministers, or interested laymen, considered support for the poor at home, the mainstay of eighteenth-century public charity, dangerous and debilitating. Outdoor relief not only encouraged the loafer in his dissipation but also corrupted the temporarily unemployed worker by robbing him of initiative. To leave men idle in a community pervaded with temptations was to condemn them to a life of vice and crime. One no longer expected that the family or the church or the network of social relationships could counterbalance the influence of the tavern and the gambling house.

The alternate systems of public charity that had grown popular in some communities in the decades after independence also were woefully inadequate. The practice of contracting all the town's poor to one local farmer, or auctioning them off to the bidder who would accept the burden of care for the lowest charge, seemed unnecessarily cruel. "The poor, when farmed out, or sold," declared the Yates report, "are frequently treated with barbarity and neglect by their keepers." In more than one instance, the committee asserted, "the pauper had suffered such cruelty and torture from his keeper, as to produce untimely dissolution." Clearly a new program was necessary.[13]

The plan which united practically all students of poverty put the almshouse at the center of public policy. At the very least, institutionalization would remove the poor from the corruptions sure to ensnare them within the community; it would also eliminate the abuses of auctions and contractors. More important, it promised to fit public response precisely to particular cases of need, to rehabilitate as well as comfort the poor. To the feeble, the old, the weak, and the sickly, the almshouse would offer care and attention, ministering to them with solicitude and compassion. To the unemployed, the able-bodied victims of hard luck, it would, either in its own quarters or in conjunction with a workhouse, provide the opportunity for labor, and thus dispense relief without enervating the recipient. To the vicious, the idle who wanted nothing else but a dole, it would teach the lesson of hard labor, insisting that anyone who received public funds spend his day at a task. The almshouse would serve all classes of the poor.[14]

The Jacksonian institution was to bear no resemblance to its eighteenth-century predecessor. The new almshouse would insist upon order, discipline, and an exacting routine. As various overseers of the poor in Massachusetts informed the Quincy committee, "order, regularity, industry and temperance" within the institution would bring a "hope of amendment to the vicious and assistance to the poor." The regimen would correct rather than confirm habits of idleness; inmates would learn "constancy and diligence," and "to obey and respect," in a setting which gave preeminence to "reformation (if any is necessary), health, cleanliness, acquiring industrious habits." The lives of the poor would be "more comfortable and happy," and above all, "temptations rendered less generous than if suffered to remain . . . in their own families."[15] An identical vision of the almshouse prompted the Yates committee to conclude that indoor relief alone would rescue the poor from "filth, idleness, ignorance and disease . . . vice, dissipation . . . and crime." Edward Livingston, a noted prison reformer, anticipated a similar result. In the well-run almshouse, "intemperance is wholly restrained, order is preserved, education diffused. . . . Is he able to work, but idle, intemperate, or vicious? His habits must be corrected by seclusion, sobriety, instruction, and labour."[16]

Other observers were no less enthusiastic about the innovation or less certain that it would inculcate industrious habits and preserve order. Speaking in a New Hampshire town in 1835 at the dedication of an almshouse chapel, clergyman Charles Burroughs roundly endorsed the new institution's procedures. "The infirm and helpless poor," he noted, "incapable of work, are here furnished with a most comfortable asylum." At the same time, "the able bodied paupers, before they can eat, are compelled to labor; and thus . . . brought into good habits." Therefore, Burroughs insisted, "relief should, if possible, be refused to all persons out of the almshouse. . . . No able bodied laborer should be entitled to relief from the overseers, unless he received it at the workhouse, and in conformity with its regulations." Only in this way can "order and strict discipline . . . be observed; and a full measure of work exacted from all, in proportion to their ability." "The reform of pauperism," Burroughs concluded, "should lie in the discipline of the workhouse."[17]

Another partisan of institutionalization, Walter Channing, celebrated these same qualities. "That noble [almshouse] establishment is for the comfort of the destitute," he told a Boston audience of philanthropists in 1843, "for the employment of those who will not voluntarily work." It would first isolate and then rehabilitate the inmates, for it was "a place where the tempted are removed from the means of their sin, and where the indolent, while he is usefully and industriously employed, may be removed from opportunities for crime, and by a regular course of life . . . be prepared for a better career when restored to liberty again."[18] Or in the words of Joseph Tuckerman, the almshouse would be "well-ordered," and "well-regulated," and thus effectively discipline its charges.[19]

Supporters charged the almshouse with the same tasks that penologists assigned to the penitentiary and medical superintendents to the insane asylum. Founders of all three institutions insisted that the removal of deviants and dependents from the community was a prerequisite for recovery. They also agreed on the importance of a strict and regular internal routine to order inmates' lives. A disciplined and precise schedule would train them to withstand the temptations at loose in the society. To each group, incarceration seemed the most effective response to a social problem.

The hopes for the institution were evident in the systems of relief planned in such cities as New York and Boston. Officials attempted to devise rules and regulations that would extend the benefits of institutionalization to the poor, so that the well-ordered almshouse could take its place alongside the penitentiary and the insane asylum. Overseers of the poor in New York, for example, devoted great energy to arranging a thorough program of indoor relief to meet these standards. There would be the almshouse proper, "a place of comparative comfort . . . a refuge from the evils and miseries of life," where the aged, the chronic sick, and the disabled would recuperate or, as the case might be, end their days in peace. Alongside it would be the workhouse for the able-bodied poor, both voluntary and involuntary, for men not guilty of a criminal offense but lacking other means of support. An orphan asylum and a nursery, as well as a hospital for those needing special medical attention would round out the scheme. One result of this organization, officials believed, would be an elementary but important degree of classification, the separation of inmates by age, health, and history. The decrepit poor would occupy one structure, the physically fit another, the young still another. Even more to the point, it would permit each institution to impose an appropriate kind of routine on its special class of inmates.[20]

The structures lodging the sick and feeble did not appear to require elaborate planning, since the bedridden did not need a special routine. But the workhouse, incarcerating the most suspect among the poor, demanded more careful design and administration. It was, founders insisted, the institution that could "revolutionize the entire system of Charity and Alms." The key to success lay in its ability to impose a disciplined routine that would bring new habits of industry to the idle and prevent the unemployed from succumbing to the corruption of a dole. Officials expected to keep inmates under close surveillance and steadily at work, to administer the routine "with strictness —

severity." Guards were to maintain a firm hand over their charges, unhesitantly coercing them into right behavior. "The officers," announced workhouse rules, "may rightly exercise . . . a measure of moral force upon the will of these persons, to induce them to do that which their own uncultivated understanding might oppose."[21] Inmates were to sleep in cells, albeit congregate ones, to eat from tin mess plates at large tables, and to wear tick shirts, tick chemises, and striped caps — almost, if not quite, a uniform. Regulations also specified the precise time for rising, for working periods, for meals, for lights-out. The external appearance of the workhouse was in keeping with this projected internal routine: a severe, unadorned exterior and long wings for inmates' living quarters, broken up only by very small, symmetrically spaced windows.[22]

Boston's officials grouped all of the city's needy into one structure, a combination almshouse-workhouse at Charlestown. They too made the heart of the program a rigid schedule and rigorous discipline. Exempting those under medical care from the several requirements, they expected all others to conform to a precise routine. An early morning bell would waken the inmates, another would signal the time for breakfast. Residents were to proceed immediately, but not in formation, to the dining hall, take their assigned seats, and finish their meal in the prescribed time; those guilty of wasting or pilfering food would be punished by a decrease in rations or, at the superintendent's discretion, solitary confinement. After breakfast they were to enter workshops, and again the threat of reducing provisions and solitary confinement hung over anyone who might be slothful or sloppy in his labor. No one could leave the institution without the manager's permission; no one could come to visit without his formal approval. Those almshouse residents who faithfully obeyed the regulations would be allowed to remain with friends for a few days once every two months. Habitual violators would suffer curtailed rations or confinement and repeated offenses would bring still more severe punishments. The essence of the institution was obedience to its rules.[23]

Other towns also followed this definition of the well-ordered almshouse and enacted the appropriate regulations. The almshouse at Warwick, Rhode Island, for example, devised procedures for a handful of inmates that were remarkably similar to those governing the much larger institutions of New York and Boston. Under its regulations the superintendent was to ring the morning bell at six o'clock; shortly after, he would sound a second bell and inmates would "in proper order, repair to the dining room; those not attending punctually, shall lose that meal. Half an hour shall be allowed for each meal." The same fixity marked working arrangements. "At the ringing of the [third] bell, all shall repair to their different employments." Officials would compel everyone who was physically fit to "diligently attend" to their tasks for the prescribed periods. Those neglecting their assignments, loitering, wasting materials, ruining tools, or violating any keepers' orders would be punished by the loss of meals, added tasks, and solitary confinement. The final bell rang at nine o'clock in the evening, signaling lights-out for the establishment.[24] The rules also regulated inmates' behavior as closely as their time. Residents could not leave the premises or receive visitors without official permission; any foul language or abusive behavior would be punished immediately with solitary confinement and a reduced food allowance. Those guilty of theft or drunkenness within the institution were to be imprisoned in a special cell for periods of up to five days. Clearly the officers of a small almshouse were no less eager to bring rigidity and regularity to their domain.[25]

The almshouse-workhouse, like the other institutions, tried to impose a regularity on inmates' lives to counteract the influences promoting and perpetuating idleness and vice. Unlike wardens and medical superintendents, however, almshouse managers were not very consistent. The routine of the almshouse lacked the quasi-military tone of the penitentiary or the less coercive but still regulatory quality of the insane asylum. It crossed the two, but not very effectively. Like the mental hospital it eschewed the lockstep, armed guards, and striped uniforms; but like the prison it established strict punishments for anyone violating the rules and was not at all loath to enforce obedience through physical coercion. At times, superintendents considered admission to the institution a privilege, warning residents that repeated violations of the rules would bring expulsion. Yet they also took in men whom judges had sentenced to periods of confinement, and bemoaned the event of their escape. Officials' terminology also pointed to this mixture. They referred to their charges as inmates — a term midway between patient and prisoner, who lived in cells, not rooms. But attendants, and not guards, supervised them.

Indeed, almshouse proponents seemed unable to decide what kind of institution they wanted. Their program lacked the careful balance of order without cruelty that was the goal of moral treatment, yet also lacked the efficient isolation of the Pennsylvania and Auburn plans; they had neither the regularity of the insane asylum nor the discipline of the penitentiary. Almshouse organizers who agreed that the fact of poverty in the new republic pointed to a social as well as a personal disorganization looked to institutionalization as an effective antidote. A well-ordered environment would transform the poor, like the criminal and the mentally ill, into hardworking and responsible citizens. But the gap between expectation and reality was considerable.

Part of the failure may be traced first to the fact that the founders of the almshouse lacked professional training. Unlike medical superintendents, they had no technical sense of their subject, no special terminology for conceiving of and presenting their ideas, no schools to refine and spread their findings. They were, in the words of one Michigan investigatory committee, "Uneducated . . . without the slightest training for such a management."[26] Almshouse managers — and note the absence of a better term for classifying them — were ill-equipped to formulate a consistent program and often unable to persuade the public of the rehabilitative potential of the institution. They also missed the opportunities that prison specialists enjoyed, regular contact with a dangerous and somewhat exotic segment of the population. Treating only the miserable poor, almshouse managers had less incentive to design rigorous programs and less opportunity to capture public respect. There was nothing very interesting, let alone exotic, about decrepit and unemployed men, and nothing that would confer a special status on those who managed them.

Their task was probably most difficult because the prejudices they had to confront were the most severe. Americans were less prepared to accept notions of community culpability for poverty than for crime or insanity, and therefore were less attracted to the reformatory promises of institutionalization. They estimated that the causes of dependency were less complex than those of deviancy. If one went to an extreme of conduct, in madness or lawlessness, then the fault could rest with community organization, with the breakdown of the eighteenth-century social order. But if one could not earn his daily bread in a land as prosperous as the United States, then the individual himself was primarily at fault. Proponents of rehabilitation did offer a rebuttal. But with a shortage of ideas about the structure of the almshouse, and without grand schemes to rival moral treatment or the Auburn and Pennsylvania programs, they could not generate excitement over the reformatory potentialities of the program. Each element reinforced the other. There was a lack of experts in a field in which the public believed expertise to be the least necessary. There was the least amount of innovation where the public demonstrated the least enthusiasm.

As a result, issues which played a minor part in the early history of other institutions assumed major significance here. Many of those urging the adoption of the almshouse program on state legislators and town councils were not convinced of the promise of reform, and neither were their audiences. Inevitably then, the ostensible financial benefits of the almshouse, the savings it would bring over a system of outdoor relief, became a primary consideration. The first thing Josiah Quincy said of the almshouse was that it was a "most economical mode" of relief.[27] To be sure, there was nothing unusual in introducing the issue of economy into such a discussion (certainly it entered the penitentiary and asylum literature as well). But the almshouse movement was so involved in cost accounting that other notions were blurred. Supporters devoted so much time to insisting that indoor relief would save localities tax money that they did not return to the possibility of rehabilitation. The reformatory quality of the almshouse was all too often lost in a maze of statistics on poor-relief expenditures.

The almshouse movement also gave disproportionate attention to the punitive quality of institutionalization. Not that penitentiary or insane-asylum supporters completely avoided such matters either. But once again almshouse proponents lost view of reformatory concepts. The influential Quincy report was filled with unqualified testimony on the power of the institution to terrorize the poor and thereby keep them off the relief rolls. Salem's overseers of the poor were certain that once incarceration became the only alternative to starvation, the able-bodied poor would quickly uncover employment opportunities: "Our institutions for the support of the poor . . . will have a direct and certain tendency to suppress them." Or, as Duxbury's officials counseled, make the poorhouse unpleasant enough and the needy will go to great lengths to avoid public support.[28] Many New York officials, questioned by the Yates committee, offered similar advice. Saratoga County selectmen insisted that the town's costs would be reduced through indoor relief, that dependents would prefer to work outside rather than inside an institution; colleagues in Herkimer County contended that the mere presence of the almshouse would intimidate gamblers and drunkards, and curb their squandering of money.[29] The notion that a specially designed environment could rehabilitate the poor was all too often drowned out in a chorus of voices proclaiming that the almshouse would frighten the poor into independence.

Taken together, these several elements kept the almshouse from duplicating the performance of other institutions. The founders' lack of professional credentials, the limits of their imagination, the failure of reformatory ideas to take hold, the concomitant centrality of considerations of economy and terror — and not just the fact that local communities rather than state authorities administered many of the almshouses — combined from the start to undermine an already fragile program. Some superintendents did manage to oversee a clean and orderly establishment, to occupy and relieve the poor. But more often the results were dismal, the poor suffering in decaying and sloppily run institutions. The almshouse had practically all of the vices of its sister institutions, and few of their saving graces.

The results of the almshouse experiment in Massachusetts disappointed even the most committed supporters of institutionalization. In 1833, a decade after the appearance of the Quincy report, another committee of the legislature toured the state to report on "the pauper system." Almost everywhere it found ample evidence of the popularity of indoor relief, together with grossly inadequate almshouse provisions. One of its first stops was the Boston House of Industry. The institution's structure, it noted, was sturdy, and like so many contemporary asylums, had at its center an administrative building, where the keeper and his family lived, with two long wings radiating out from each side, one for men, the other for women. But the committee found little to commend in the internal organization. The place was packed, with a population of 623 and an average of over seven inmates to a room; all kinds of persons were gathered there — from the aged, decrepit, and insane to abandoned children and expectant, unwed mothers — and no system of classification separated them. Only nine officials supervised the operation, and just three of them were free enough of household duties to look to the general discipline. The visitors found the name House of Industry especially inappropriate, for only a tiny minority of residents actually worked. The institution satisfied all too few of the criteria of a well-ordered almshouse.[30]

Conditions in the commonwealth's smaller towns were not any better. Salem constructed a two-wing, five-story structure, but aside from a segregation of men and women, no classification existed. Few inmates worked; apparently they left the institution as soon as they had sufficient strength. "We wink at their departure," confessed the officers, hoping that "the fear of punishment may deter them from returning." In more rural areas the almshouse was nothing more than an old farmhouse purchased by the community for the use of the poor. Ipswich, Andover, Groton, Taunton, Fairhaven, and countless other towns made a onetime homestead into a poorhouse. Since local officials institutionalized not only the needy but drunks and public nuisances as well, and since these structures did not permit any degree of classification, a motley assortment of persons mingled about.[31] No one regulated the daily routine of these institutions. There was little attempt to keep inmates at work, except perhaps for the occasional superintendent who held out the reward of liquor to those who would labor. (Not surprisingly, the visitors found this practice as reprehensible as the prevailing idleness.) In addition, many overseers of the poor insisted that anyone who absconded from the almshouse be placed in solitary confinement upon his return — a not very subtle attempt to discourage the inmate from coming back. Unlike the managers of the insane asylum or the penitentiary, they put no premium on the almshouse experience. In the end, the Massachusetts investigatory committee could not find one establishment to hold up to the others as an appropriate model.[32]

The catalogue of failures that describes the Massachusetts institutions also covers conditions in other states. In New York, the deficiencies of the almshouse were apparent both in the city, where the number of poor was large, and in the countryside, where the problem was much less pressing. For many years New York City maintained an almshouse near Bellevue Hospital, but as official reports revealed, it was very inadequate. Overcrowding was endemic, and officials desperately made lofts and basements into dormitories to find room for fifteen hundred residents. Almost every starting superintendent complained that inmates were idling about, never doing a day's work, and promised fundamental reforms. Yet each manager left the place in as disorderly a state as he found it.[33] When in 1848, the city established a new almshouse on Blackwells Island, conditions there too declined with incredible speed. The design was typical, a central structure with wings for inmates' quarters, and here officials erected two such buildings, one for each sex. Yet no other classification existed, so that the aged and the young, the sick, and the mentally ill, all mixed together in the house rooms and corridors.[34]

To make matters worse, these new structures soon deteriorated. Within a year of their opening, the warden complained that "the buildings are at present much out of repair, and gradually decaying, and require immediate attention. In many of the rooms, the walls and ceilings are much damaged, and in some places fallen down. The balconies or piazzas, in consequence of the floors not having a sufficient descent to carry off the water, are rapidly decaying, and fast destroying the ceilings and other work underneath." It takes little imagination to picture the leaks, drafts, dirt, and rubble that permeated the place; one later verdict fit the entire period: "One could hardly conceive a more neglected place," declared a superintendent on the eve of the Civil War. "Dirt, and vermin had been allowed to accumulate to such a degree as to almost discourage me."[35] Finally, no systematic provisions for work reduced this chaos. One of the reasons the city used Blackwells Island was to establish a separate workhouse facility, for no labor was carried on in the old almshouse. Blueprints, however, did not guarantee actual construction, and by 1850 the building was still far from completed. Put another way: thirty years after the Yates report, there was still no provision in New York for employing the poor within an institution.[36]

In 1857 a state legislative committee diligently inspected every city and county almshouse, and its conclusions were as harsh as its investigation was thorough. It is true that by this decade many leading asylums and penitentiaries did not maintain former standards; but this almshouse survey describes an ongoing condition. The 1857 report declared that almost all of New York's almshouses were "badly constructed, ill arranged, ill warmed, and ill ventilated." The able-bodied paupers were not at work, and classification was nowhere to be found. Old and respectable army veterans lounged about with the most degenerate characters; even the sexes were not separated, so that illicit relations and illegitimate births occurred regularly. Despite all these faults, supervisors and trustees rarely visited the institutions. "As receptacles for adult paupers," the investigators told the legislature, "the committee do not hesitate to record their deliberate opinion that the great mass of the poor houses . . . are most disgraceful memorials of the public charity. Common domestic animals are usually more humanely provided for than the paupers in some of these institutions."[37]

The committee hesitated to publish a detailed record of the gross neglect, reluctant to "disgrace the state and shock humanity." Still it offered enough particular accounts to substantiate its general conclusions. At Cayuga, in the rural, northwest part of the state, the poorhouse was an old and dilapidated frame building, where dependents, regardless of age, sex, or condition, lived in thirty tiny and often windowless rooms. "The ill and the maimed, the filthy and the diseased," reported the examiners, "are crowded in the same rooms, and in many cases lie on the floor together, wrapped in wretched blankets more like beasts than human beings." The house "is a disgrace to the county, and in no way fit for the reception of paupers." Conditions were no better in neighboring Oswego, where seventy-five young, old, sick, lame, idiotic, and insane paupers squeezed into a nine-room wooden house, to be supervised by one man and several pauper assistants. Was this, demanded the inspectors, to remain "the gauge and standard of philanthropy and Christian civilization?"[38]

They found glaring deficiencies everywhere. In Alleghany County, there was no full-time poorhouse keeper; in Broome, there was no bathing equipment. In Clinton, the poor had to subsist on a diet of pea soup and drink dirty water. Chautauqua crowded as many as thirty-two paupers into a room without ventilation: Montgomery had no way to heat the house in winter. The Sullivan County establishment had neither adequate space, nor ventilation, nor clean water.[39]

Interested citizens confirmed every bitter detail of this description. In the 1850's, one philanthropic New Yorker toured the almshouses and then presented his findings in open letters to New York's secretary of state. "I have not seen all the poorhouses in the State," he wrote, "but I have seen many of them, and I can most truly declare that I have never seen a well contrived building among them all." There was no semblance of classification: "The poor of all classes and colors, all ages and habits, partake of a common fare, a common table, a common dormitory." The poor widow sat beside the filthy prostitute, the old man next to the diseased drunkard. "As for ventilation, the thing is not thought of. . . . The dormitories early in the morning are dreadfully nauseous; I have often been surprised when I have smelled them, that they are not visited by the most malignant forms of pestilence." Inmates performed little work; the annual earnings of the average pauper in an institution, he calculated, amounted to about three dollars a year. By any standard the almshouse seemed a total failure.[40]

It is clear that cities in all sections of the country were unable to administer well-ordered almshouses. The institution at Philadelphia was well built and had decent and clean hospital facilities, but it too was unable to establish a system of classification or maintain regular labor. Officials in the 1840's attempted to organize a workshop for inmates, complete with machinery and raw materials. Very quickly, however, they abandoned the plan, sold the equipment, and left the poor to occasional household tasks.[41] Reports on the Chicago almshouse read very much like the conclusions of New York and Massachusetts legislative committees. A grand jury investigation in 1853 concluded that "the Poor House is entirely inadequate to the wants of this county for the healthful and convenient accommodation of so large a number [of poor]. . . . We find from 130 to 140 inmates. . . . From the number of inmates and the limited space in the buildings, we find the rooms literally filled with beds, and badly ventilated; the sick and the well necessarily thrown to-gether, making it extremely unpleasant for both." Smaller urban centers did no better.[42] Paterson, New Jersey, housed the poor in an old farmhouse, as dilapidated as it was filthy; no one usually bothered to inspect the place, leaving inmates to live under the most primitive circumstances. Louisville, Kentucky, supported a workhouse in which some fifty inmates congregated in a few dirty and practically bare rooms, idle day after day. There was no classification, so children mixed freely with drunks and public nuisances. As one visitor concluded: "This establishment, take it all in all, could hardly procure worse influences, or effect less in the way of reformation."[43]

The quality of the almshouse in less populated areas is more difficult to reconstruct, but some responsible and surprisingly thorough reports remain. Dorothea Dix, with remarkable energy and perseverance, traveled from town to town, investigating the predicament of the poor as well as the insane. Her several accounts are especially important for demonstrating that almshouses were not inevitably the shame of the community. As Dix made clear, individual initiative and social conscience often promoted comfortable and clean establishments for the needy. To be sure, her perspective was uncommon, affected by a knowledge of the far worse condition of the insane. After visiting lunatics chained in rat-infested cellars, any warm, whitewashed, and ventilated room could seem luxurious. But for all that, her descriptions still testify to some of the better records of indoor relief.

Take Dix's findings in New Jersey. Again and again in her travels there she visited well-administered almshouses. The Salem

County poorhouse was well conducted, its eighty inmates decently dressed and fed provisions of good quality. The Bridgeton poorhouse was "remarkably neat and comfortable throughout," serving sixty-two inmates well. The Cape May institution was "well regulated as regards the poor in general," and the one at Burlington was "well-ordered, all the apartments very neat, well scrubbed and white-washed." Only when one descended the steps into the basement, to visit the lunatics, did conditions take on a different quality.[44]

Dix's reports from Kentucky and North Carolina also revealed the adequacy of many local institutions. She was pleased with her findings in Kentucky. At Scott County, wrote Dix, "the appearance of the different rooms indicated the means of living with tolerable comfort, and the disposition of the citizens is benevolent and liberal." The Fayette County poorhouse "exhibited a comfortable appearance externally. . . . At present there is no deficiency, and the establishment seemed to be supplied with all the necessaries, and many of the comforts of the table." The Woodford County almshouse "seems to receive an unusual amount of care and attention. Fortunately for the good government of this establishment, there are several citizens in the county heartily interested in the best well-being of the inmates."[45] Conditions were more varied in North Carolina, but still Dix found many well-run institutions. The Rockingham almshouse, for one, was "singularly neat and well-ordered; the inmates sufficiently well-clad and very neat and respectable." The Iredall County poorhouse, for another, was "a model of neatness, comfort, and good order; having a most efficient master and mistress." There remained the example of New Hanover County, whose institution was "miserable and dilapidated. . . . Apparently the acting wardens are responsible for its decline." And the Stokes poorhouse was "extremely comfortless, the apartments are entirely too much crowded, and the arrangements are not suited to promote the comfort or good order of the inmates." Still the balance, Dix believed, tipped to the counties' consideration of the needs of the poor.[46]

Not every state investigation brought back the harsh judgments delivered in New York and Massachusetts. The Rhode Island legislature learned from Thomas Hazard in 1851 that most city and town almshouses met adequate standards. The Dexter Asylum at Providence, according to the Hazard report, provided the 136 inmates with "a fine and substantial building," well organized and administered. Newport's almshouse, holding seventy residents, "is large and substantial — is well arranged and furnished, and its affairs appear to be well conducted." There were some scandals. The town of Coventry kept sixteen paupers in an old and decayed house, with furniture "unfit for the use of the most degraded of savages," and with a diet of "unripe, watery potatoes" and bread. But these exceptions aside, Hazard and the legislature were satisfied with the neatness and comfort of the almshouse system.[47]

The spread of almshouses through the villages, towns, and cities of antebellum America at once established a uniformity of practice and a diversity of conditions. Institutionalization became the standard public response to the problem of poverty, but officials enacted the program with a wide variety of skill, sympathy, and diligence. The larger the institution, the more urban the setting, the more pressing the problem of poor relief, then the greater the likelihood that conditions would be unsatisfactory. A benevolent overseer of the poor was sometimes able to comfort a small group of dependents by carefully maintaining a handful of rooms and setting a decent table. But where administration rather than casual oversight was necessary, where more was required than a good heart, the results were generally unsatisfactory.

One finds in these circumstances the clearest evidence of the gap between the ideal and reality of the almshouse. Proponents who envisaged a strict and structured routine made little impact on the movement. At best, cities maintained fair hospitals, and towns fed the needy in a houselike setting. An unconverted farmhouse served as the institution, with the poor as boarders, in a style closer to eighteenth rather than nineteenth-century arrangements. At worst, dependents suffered innumerable indignities in swelling urban institutions. They lived in decrepit buildings, with meager provisions, under keepers who were more guilty of neglect than cruelty. But nowhere, not in the cities nor in the towns, did the almshouse classify inmates, put them to

14. *The Boston almshouse, 1849. Built on Deer Island, this almshouse has a fortresslike quality that points both back, to the importance in the Jacksonian period of a uniformity in design, and ahead, to the post-1850 period, when institutions would become more and more massive and unwieldy.*

COURTESY OF THE PRINT DEPARTMENT, BOSTON PUBLIC LIBRARY

work, or enforce discipline. It never stood as a well-ordered establishment.

Nevertheless, institutionalization remained the favorite form of public relief, not only for the economy-minded and for those eager to terrorize and punish the poor, but also for those seeking to rehabilitate them, who considered themselves humanitarian and concerned citizens. The attractions of the poorhouse as an instrument of punishment needs little explanation. Those who judged the poor to be guilty of most vices, and solely responsible for their own misery, were unwilling to support them within the community, to distribute outdoor relief. Town officials, however, could no longer banish all needy strangers or rely upon rigid settlement laws to exclude them. Not only was it difficult to guard railroad stations in the nineteenth century, but state regulations often prevented local communities from maintaining a high degree of insularity by prohibiting restrictions on intra-state movement. Hence before 1850, and as we shall soon see, even more so afterward, there was a functional quality to the almshouse.

But benevolent-minded citizens were also dedicated to a program of indoor relief. The most sensitive observer of the deficiencies of the poorhouse urged not its abolition but its transformation. That independent New York citizen who painstakingly reported glaring abuses throughout the state still wanted to perpetuate the almshouse. He did wonder whether the old and the feeble might not be better cared for at home, but for everyone else he was certain that indoor relief was most appropriate. At the end of his series of open letters he announced his willingness to reformulate guidelines for the almshouse — to devise new rules for admission and discipline — convinced that the only issue was one of internal reform. His faith in the potentialities of the almshouse, like that of many of his peers, was too strong to be diminished by evidence of particular problems.[48] The promise of a well-ordered asylum was reason enough to continue the experiment, no matter how mixed the first results.

Thus, the defects of the almshouse did not promote a movement for its abolition, and the history of poor relief through the nineteenth century reflected the implications of the first general consensus. Institutionalization at its moment of introduction, when attention was most focused upon it, received unanimous endorsement. The discovery of the almshouse ruled out even the consideration of alternate strategies. Observers debated the wisdom of one regulation or another, or the degree of monopoly that ought to be given to indoor relief. But no one questioned its centrality. Thus, in the 1850's and the decades that followed, when immigrants began to crowd these shores, when cities grew larger and unemployment mounted, the almshouse appeared as the perfect solution to new problems. Through the 1870's and 1880's, and well into the 1890's, most forums proclaimed the superiority of indoor over outdoor relief. Practically every participant in the national conference on charity and correction, as well as economists and social critics, voiced their approval. It was not until the Progressive era that the consensus reached in the Jacksonian period on the proper treatment of the poor began to splinter.

9

The Well-Ordered Asylum

No reformers were more confident of the advantage and success of their program than the philanthropists who founded child-saving institutions. For proponents, the movement to incarcerate the orphan, the abandoned child, the youngster living in dire poverty, the juvenile vagrant, and the delinquent promised enormous benefits while entailing few risks. Like their colleagues sponsoring insane asylums and penitentiaries and almshouses, they shared an intense faith in the rehabilitative powers of a carefully designed environment and were certain that properly structured institutions would not only comfort the homeless but reform the delinquent.

Child-care institutions, new to Americans, fundamentally altered traditional practices. In the colonial period, overseers of the poor, in the absence of responsible relatives and friends, typically had apprenticed the orphan to a local householder. In unusual circumstances, when the child suffered from a major disability, they might have recourse in one of the larger towns to the almshouse. The orphan asylum was all but unknown in the eighteenth century. There was one notable exception. George Whitefield in 1740 almost single-handedly organized an orphan house in Savannah, Georgia. This was the work of an Englishman primarily concerned with bringing young souls to Christ; moreover, he established the house in a colony whose peculiar origin and mission had weakened the stable ties of community and strengthened experimental philanthropic impulses.

After the Revolution, local officials perpetuated colonial precedents. In some of the larger cities, overseers had to dispatch a number of children to new and growing almshouses; this step was, however, an ad hoc solution to an immediate problem and not considered of special benefit to the child or the community. So, too, the fifteen privately sponsored orphan asylums that opened between 1800 and 1830 were not part of a systematic program but the work of dedicated yet idiosyncratic philanthropists, or of a religious minority, usually Catholic, eager to keep coreligionists within the faith and out of Protestant households. The dominant treatment of the orphan in the first years of the new republic remained noninstitutional.[1]

In the 1830's a basic transformation occurred as child-care institutions spread rapidly through the country. In this decade alone, twenty-three private orphan asylums began operating in various towns and cities, and the movement continued to grow in the 1840's with the founding of thirty more of them. They opened not only in New York, Boston, and Philadelphia — as usual, among the leaders in building institutions — but also in Bangor, Maine; Richmond, Virginia; Mobile, Alabama; Avondale and Cincinnati, Ohio; and Chicago, Illinois. By 1850, New York State alone had twenty-seven public and private child-care institutions. Within two decades they had become common structures, widespread and popular, with their own unique and important attributes, not just a last resort when apprenticeship was impossible.[2] Indeed, their promise seemed so great that trustees quickly spread their nets to catch a wide variety of dependent children. They admitted the abandoned as well as the orphaned child, and those whose widowed or deserted mothers, hard pressed to make ends meet, had little time for supervision. They accepted minors whose parents were quite alive but very poor, and those from families that seemed to them morally, if not financially, inadequate to their tasks. From an administrator's perspective, there was no reason to penalize the unfortunate child for the fact of his parents' survival.[3]

During these decades another type of caretaker institution became popular — the reformatory for disobedient children, the house of refuge. It took in several types of minors — the juvenile offender, convicted by a court for a petty crime, the wandering street arab, picked up by a town constable, and the willfully

15. *The first New York House of Refuge. One of the earliest reformatories constructed in the United States, this institution shows a gradual departure in the 1820's from a household model to a more regimented one.*

COURTESY OF THE NEW-YORK HISTORICAL SOCIETY, NEW YORK CITY

disobedient child, turned over by distraught parents. The reformatory, like the orphan asylum, maintained a flexible admissions policy, prepared to accept the commitment decisions of a judicial body, the less formal recommendations of overseers of the poor, or the personal inclinations of the head of a household. Its administrators expressed no fears about a possible miscarriage of justice and were disinclined to bring the protections of due process to these minors. A good dose of institutionalization could only work to the child's benefit.

Once again, the major eastern cities set the trend. New York philanthropists founded a house of refuge in 1825, and colleagues in Boston and Philadelphia followed suit within three years. The idea did not immediately spread to other urban areas, for most municipalities and state legislatures invested their funds first in multifunction orphan asylums. But by the 1840's specialization increased and houses of refuge appeared in Rochester, Cincinnati, and New Orleans; during the 1850's they opened in Providence, Baltimore, Pittsburgh, Chicago, and St. Louis as well. By 1857 the movement was broad enough to hold a national convention of refuge superintendents in New York. Its first committee on statistics calculated that seventeen reformatories now operated, with a combined inmate population of over 20,000, a value in land and buildings of almost $2,000,000, and total annual expenditures of about $330,000. Here was another sizable investment in institutionalization.[4]

Taken together, the admissions policies of child-care institutions were a catalogue of practically every misfortune that could befall a minor. The abject, the vagrant, the delinquent, the child of poverty-stricken or intemperate parents were all proper candidates for one or another asylum or refuge. Other practices did persist. One could still find minors confined to an almshouse or incarcerated in a local jail; smaller communities continued to rely upon apprenticeship to solve child-care problems. The new structures never won a monopoly. Nevertheless, they did become the model treatment for the homeless and delinquent. Like the mental hospital, penitentiary, and almshouse, they dominated the thinking of interested reformers, competing successfully for city-council, state-legislature, and philanthropic funds. The asylum and the refuge were two more bricks in the wall that Americans built to confine and reform the dangerous classes.

The founders of orphan asylums and houses of refuge shared fully with the proponents of other caretaker institutions a fear that anyone not carefully and diligently trained to cope with the open, free-wheeling, and disordered life of the community would fall victim to vice and crime. The orphan, robbed of his natural guardians, desperately needed protection against these dangers. Many children of the poor were in no better position, since their parents — at best too busy trying to eke out a living and at worst intemperate — provided no defense against corruption. The vagrant, by definition lacking in supervision, would certainly come under the sway of taverns, gambling halls, and theaters, the crowd of drunks, gamblers, thieves, and prostitutes. The nightmare come true, of course, was the juvenile delinquent, his behavior ample testimony to the speed and predictability of moral decline.

To counter these conditions, the asylum was shelter and sanctuary. Supporters pleaded vigorously and passionately for funds in order to snatch the child from the contagion of vice. The directors of the Orphan Society of Philadelphia asked patrons to endow a place where children of misfortune "are sheltered from the perils of want and the contamination of evil example." The Boston Children's Friend Society assumed the task of removing the sons and daughters of intemperate, depraved, and pauper parents as rapidly as possible "from those baleful influences which inevitably tend to make them pests to society, and ultimately the tenants of our prisons."[5] A state reformatory in New Hampshire also defined its function in terms of "the separation of the young convict from society; his seclusion from vicious associates." And the managers of the Philadelphia House of Refuge, appealing for funds, boasted that visitors would find "the orphan, deserted or misguided child, shielded from the temptations of a sinful world."[6]

But the asylum program had another, more important component — to train and rehabilitate its charges. It would not only shelter the orphan and delinquent, but discipline and reform them. Some philanthropic societies, it is true, limited their

16. The Philadelphia House of Refuge emblem. Used on membership certificates and public broadsides, this image captures the faith that Americans in the Jacksonian period held in the ability of institutions to transform deviants into respectable citizens.

activities to rescuing the child from his poverty and giving him over to others, to a sea captain going on a lengthy whaling voyage, or to a country farmer needing another hand. For them, removal was a sufficient program.[7] Many organizations, however, assumed a broader function, eager to carry out the tasks of child-rearing. Starting afresh, they would organize a model routine, design and administer an upbringing that embodied the highest standards. In a manner clearly reminiscent of the mental hospital and the penitentiary, and to some degree of the almshouse as well, they expected to demonstrate the validity of general principles through the specific treatment of deviants and dependents. The experiment would rehabilitate the particular inmate and by exemplification spark the reform of the whole society.

This perspective dominated the asylum movement. Proponents insisted that the discipline at the Philadelphia House of Refuge would provide delinquents with "a healthy moral constitution, capable of resisting *the assaults of temptations,* and strong enough to keep the line of rectitude through *the stormy and disturbing influences by which we are continually assailed."* This siege mentality united those attending the first national convention of house of refuge officials. They quickly formed a consensus around the sentiments expressed by Orlando Hastings, the delegate from the Rochester reformatory. Defining the fundamental purpose of the program, Hastings declared: "The object is not alone to make the boys behave well while in our charge; that is not difficult. . . . [But] any discipline . . . which does not enable the boy to *resist temptation* wherever and whenever he finds it, is ineffectual, and the whole object of houses of refuge is a failure."[8] An even more elaborate rationale emerged in the reports of the Boston asylum. "There are," its managers explained, "two ways to aid in the redemption of society — one is to remove the sources of corruption, and the other is to remove the young from the temptations that exist." While some reformers chose to follow the first strategy, they were determined to adopt the second, "to enlighten their [inmates] minds, and aid them in forming virtuous habits, that they may finally go forth, *clothed as in invincible armour."*[9] Let others try to weaken the force of vice in the society. They would gird the young to withstand temptation.

Once again, the analysis which diagnosed an ostensibly desperate state of things also promised a sure remedy. Since the root of the problem lay in a faulty environment, the means for improvement were ready at hand, and asylum proponents were even more confident than their counterparts in other caretaker institutions of the prospects for success. Although all reformers assumed a plasticity of human nature that gave a logic to their efforts, asylum supporters felt themselves singularly fortunate: their clientele was young, especially impressionable, and not fixed in deviant or dependent behavior. "Youth," happily reported the governors of the Philadelphia House of Refuge, "is particularly susceptible of reform. . . . It has not yet felt the long continued pressure, which distorts its natural growth. . . . No habit can then be rooted so firmly as to refuse a cure." In the same spirit, the Boston Children's Friend Society looked forward to rehabilitating those "whose plastic natures may be molded into images of perfect beauty, or as perfect repulsiveness." And managers of the New York House of Refuge assumed that "the minds of children, naturally pliant, can, by early instruction, be formed and molded to our wishes." If the young were highly vulnerable to corruption, they were also eminently teachable.[10]

Asylum proponents were not apprehensive about promoting the very vices they planned to eradicate. Overseers of the poor in this period anxiously wondered whether too comfortable an almshouse might inadvertently attract the lower classes, thereby promoting idleness; wardens also feared that a short sentence in a lax prison which coddled the criminal would increase recidivism. But child-care institutions were free of these concerns. Managers were confident that incarceration would not rob orphans of initiative — they were simply too young for that — or encourage their parents to avoid responsibility through commitment. And an indeterminate sentence to a house of refuge, for a term as long as the young offender's minority, could hardly be considered too lenient. Thus, without hesitation or qualification, they urged the new program.

At the core of the child-reformers' optimism was a faith completely shared by colleagues promoting other caretaker institutions: that a daily routine of strict and steady discipline would transform inmates' character. The asylum's primary task was to teach an absolute respect for authority through the establishment and enforcement of a rigorous and orderly routine. Obedience would bring reform. The function of the orphan asylum, according to Charleston, South Carolina, officials, was to train boys to a proper place in a community where *"systematic labor* of *order* and *regularity* established, and *discipline* enforced, are the social obligations." A strict training in accord with these virtues "disciplines them for . . . various walks of life," enabling them to become "practical men of business and good citizens, in the middle classes of society."[11] The Boston Asylum and Farm School for destitute and vagrant children was dedicated to the same means and ends. These classes, managers told would-be donors, "have been received within the walls of a Christian asylum, where they have listened to good counsel, and acquired habits of *order, industry* and *usefulness*. . . . We know not how anyone interested in the preservation of order or stability of government . . . can withhold his sympathy." Its annual reports regularly replayed this theme, noting that "it is almost astonishing how readily boys, hitherto accustomed to have their own way, and to dispute supremacy with inefficient or indulgent parents, are brought into habits of respect and order by a system of *uniformly firm discipline."* The Boston asylum directors recognized fully the affinity between their program and that of other contemporary caretaker institutions. "A hospital for the insane," they announced, "has hardly greater superiority over the private family in regulating its inmates, in this respect, than the Farm School over the mis-government or no-government of the weak and careless parent."[12]

The primacy of obedience and respect for authority in the process of rehabilitation was even more apparent in the institutions treating delinquents and vagrants. The New York Juvenile Asylum, serving these groups, put the matter aggressively. "We do not believe," announced its superintendent, "in the mawkish, sentimental and infidel philosophy of modern days, which discards the Bible method of disciplining the child into obedience. . . . It is manifest that but little good can be effected with all our appliances, unless order and obedience to established rules are vigilantly maintained. . . . What is needed for the children whom the law entrusts to us is the government of a well-ordered

Christian household."[13] Their neighbors at the New York House of Refuge agreed. Let inmates, officials declared, "be made tractable and obedient . . . [through] a vigorous course of moral and corporal discipline." With fidelity to this principle, the refuge superintendent argued that "the most benevolent and humane method for the management of children, is, to require prompt and implicit obedience." And to support his point he presented some sample cases. For one typical delinquent, the "discipline of the House was all that was requisite to make him obedient." For another, an especially refractory youngster bent on escaping, "it was found necessary to apply severe and continued punishments, in order to break the obstinacy of his spirit." Ultimately success came: "The discipline enforced had a most happy effect. He became submissive and obedient."[14]

All child-care institutions made this strategy basic to their procedures. In an 1826 prospectus, the founders of the Philadelphia House of Refuge promised to return delinquents to society after "a course of rigid but not cruel or ignominious discipline." There would be "unrelenting supervision, mild but certain punishments for any infraction of the rules, and habits of quiet and good order at all times." They described with obvious pleasure a recent tour through the New York House of Refuge, taking particular delight in one scene: the children silently marching in file into Sunday chapel, sitting attentively and quietly through the service, and then leaving in an orderly line. Here they found an achievement worth emulating.[15] A similar perspective won the general approval of the refuge superintendents meeting in national conference. As Orlando Hastings, the Rochester delegate, expressed it: asylum managers had to secure "the confidence and affection of those committed to their care"; otherwise they were not suitable governors. But this dictum had a very special meaning to Hastings and his audience, and he immediately explained it. "I am prepared further to say," he declared, "that the principle thing to be aimed at, and which must be secured, is obedience." Nothing was quite as pleasant to witness as "cheerful submission," compliance given with affection. However, there was no mistaking priorities; even if one had to resort regularly to punishing the child, obedience had to be won. And there was no need to worry about the possibly detrimental effects of such a policy. "After you establish the proposition in his mind that you are the ruler," Hastings complacently concluded, "he will look to you as his friend and benefactor, and you can cultivate his heart with ten-fold more effect." In this best of systems, authority bred friendship and admiration.[16]

The prescriptions for the well-ordered asylum embodied and reflected contemporary opinion on proper child-rearing techniques. The guidelines that superintendents established for institutional procedures fit closely with the advice that appeared in the new spate of child-guidance books. Indeed, the popularity of the asylum coincided with the proliferation of domestic tracts. The volumes first appeared in significant numbers in the United States in the 1830's, growing increasingly popular in the 1840's and 1850's. The best sellers, such as Lydia Child's *The Mother's Book*, Mrs. Sigourney's *Letters to Mothers,* Jacob Abbott's *The Rollo Code of Morals,* and Catherine Beecher's *A Treatise on Domestic Economy for the Young Ladies at Home,* went through many editions, becoming fixtures in American homes.[17] To be sure, there had always been some kind of literature giving advice to parents. In the colonial period, ministers' pamphlets had served the task — Benjamin Wadsworth's *A Well-Ordered Family* was an outstanding one — and there were reprints of English classics. In the pre–Civil War era, however, the tracts not only greatly increased in number, but were now almost all American in origin and were the work of laymen. Their style was a relaxed and homey one, and cautionary tales replaced biblical references. A new genre had appeared.

This change reflected the diminishing social importance of the clergy in this period, as laymen and doctors took over the advising function. It revealed a growing need for book instruction now that Americans' physical mobility often restricted intergenerational communication. When mother was half a continent away, daughter found Lydia Child a convenient substitute. But for our purposes, the most significant element in this literature was its tone of public crusade. These volumes, according to their authors, were not just a useful replacement for an absent parent, but a vital effort to perpetuate a responsible and law-abiding citizenry, to safeguard the future of republican institutions. There was a gravity to their message, an explicit warning that failure to heed their recommendations would bring disaster to individual families and the nation in general. The Abbotts and the Beechers defined themselves as reformers, and in fact they belonged in the company of asylum superintendents. The note of urgency, almost panic, in their writings can be understood only by recognizing their intellectual affinity with the various proponents of institutionalization. The child-rearing literature resembled the reports of asylums and refuges: the same critique of society, the same fears for the future, the same criteria for reform.

The guidebooks conveyed a clear sense of crisis, an image of the American community, and especially the family, confronting unprecedented challenges. The authors were a nervous group, one after another lamenting the "unhappy tendency of our age and country," the "alarming feature of this age," the need to ward off "the fearful crisis," to combat the "many influences which are in vigorous operation to corrupt the family."[18] Their analysis of the causes of the dangers was highly general, without delineation, and not as intricate as the critique of asylum reformers. But it repeated, albeit in briefer and somewhat more clichéd form, the same points. Some writers complained about the whirl of commercial activity and the concomitant lack of fixed social positions: others worried that political democracy bred a social libertarianism which often degenerated into license. Still others took alarm at the complex and artificial character of civilization. All of them agreed that antebellum America acutely suffered from a lack of order and stability. All feared for the cohesion of the community, finding in the swelling number of deviants and dependents dreadful confirmation of the dimensions of the crisis. Here was dramatic evidence that the very foundations of the republic were in imminent danger of collapse.[19]

Nevertheless, these authors were confident that the public crisis had a private remedy. Together with medical superintendents, penologists, and proponents of child-care institutions, they hoped to secure social stability through individual rehabilitation. They traced the origins of the problem to the decline of the community life and the weakness of family government, and found in their diagnosis a solution. If they could teach parents their correct role and encourage them to follow it, if they could define the components of proper family government and persuade readers to adopt them, then they would insure the nation's stability. In this sense, the child-rearing tracts were ventures in reform. Institutions treated those already in trouble; these authors would move back one step and try to eliminate the first cause of the problem. They wished to bring the rules of the asylum into the home, confident that as soon as parents became surrogate superintendents, the refuge, the penitentiary, and the rest could be eliminated. The well-ordered family would replace the well-ordered asylum.

The child-rearing volumes focused on obedience. No asylum manager devoted more attention to this trait than family counselors, and practically every guide to parenthood made it the cardinal virtue. "The foundation of all excellence of character," declared Artemas Muzzey in his widely read book, *The Fireside,* "consists in obedience. . . . It becomes important that we learn this lesson in our earliest childhood. The fact should be impressed on the very infant, that he has no alternative but obedience." A collection of open letters to young mothers by Ann Porter reiterated this theme. "The first, the second and the third requisite in family government," declared Porter, "is obedience. This must be secured; it is the helm to guide the ship."[20] Catherine Beecher's exceptionally popular *Treatise on Domestic Economy* also instructed parents to teach children "that their happiness, both now and hereafter, depends on the formation of *habits of submission, self-denial, and benevolence.*" And like the others she insisted on unqualified submission: "Obey, *because your parent commands,* is always a proper and sufficient reason." Or, as Jacob Abbott's *Rollo Code* explained: "Obedience . . . is doing what is commanded, *because it is commanded,* and not because we think it is best to do it ourselves. . . . It is very proper for children to like to know the reasons for their parents' commands; but they must never delay their obedience to inquire."[21]

The most serious parental failure in these tracts was indulgence, and cautionary tales rivaled one another in describing the awful scenes awaiting lax mothers and stubborn children. Mrs.

Sigourney told of a parent who denied herself many necessities in order to satisfy her child's whims; the result of this training was that he followed a debauched life as a sailor and died an early death from alcoholism. William Alcott warned of the calamities facing mothers who allowed their children free rein in the local candy store. The youngsters would surely go from these shops, "these places of pollution, *directly* to the grog shop, the gambling house or the brothel."[22] One volume, to illustrate the moral that "disobedience equals death," recounted how a willful boy, playing with matches, burned down the homestead and died in the fire; and there was the popular tale of the stubborn but sick daughter who protested so vigorously against taking her medicine that the parent gave in — and the child then died from the disease.[23]

The ideal mother in child-rearing literature was strict but loving, ever affectionate with her brood, but always successful in commanding their absolute obedience. The prototype runs through the pages of Lydia Child's *The Mother's Book:* the woman who combined firmness with gentleness, whose children cheerfully acted from the conviction that she knew best. John Abbott's *The Mother at Home* cautioned her not to depend exclusively upon the father to enforce discipline. It was "the efficient government of a judicious mother," that kept children from deception and disobedience. "The *mother* of Washington," he contended, "is entitled to a nation's gratitude. *She* taught her boy the principles of obedience, and moral courage, and virtue. She, in a great measure, formed the character of the hero, and the statesman."[24] The ideal father in this scheme reinforced maternal authority, intervening whenever a stronger or more consistent discipline was necessary. As one author explained, young boys often grew restive under a mother's rule; at such times, "a father's counsels, wisdom and firmness, and a father's authority, are demanded." Much of the child-rearing literature instructed fathers to keep somewhat aloof from their children, lest they compromise their ultimate authority.[25]

The guidebooks, to be sure, did maintain that the best way to achieve obedience was through the child's affections. In a model family the youngsters offered "cheerful submission," obeying their parents out of love. But again, there was no confusing priorities. For all the discussion, affection was never more than a means to a higher end — obedience — and by no stretch of the imagination, the goal itself. Without the slightest misgivings, therefore, every author urged parents to use the rod when all else failed: far better to punish the child than allow him to grow up disobedient. "Secure this great end," declared one of Miss Porter's open letters, "by love and gentle means if you can — try it long and patiently — but if that fail, do not hesitate to use the rod."[26] In a later period, in the beginning of the twentieth century, love and affection would move to the center of the child-rearing literature, to become important virtues in themselves and not just useful means for accomplishing other, more important ends. At that time, the cautionary tales would reveal a new twist; rather than kill off the child for disobedience, the mother would die for her sin, for not having recognized and returned the full love of the child. But in the Jacksonian period, the moral was very different. Counselors worried that too much affection would breed disobedience, not that the child might suffer from an excess of discipline.

At the root of this popular insistence on the primacy of obedience was a conception of individual respect for authority as the cornerstone of an orderly society. Like almost all others in this period who thought about deviancy and dependency, the authors of these tracts remained convinced that only a rigorous training in obedience could stabilize individual behavior and the social order. In their view, the community seemed to be in such a state of crisis that this message took on unprecedented significance. They saw change as declension, believing that the insularity of the community was now broken, its integrative functions having all but disappeared. Under these circumstances the family became the chief — really the last — barrier between the citizen and a life of vice and crime, between the nation and rampant disorder. The good order of the family had to promote the good order of the society. Hence this formula, basic to every eighteenth-century sermon on the family, appeared with special intensity in the nineteenth-century child-rearing volumes. The youngster had to learn obedience within the family or would all too predictably move from the candy store to the tavern and brothel, and then to a prison cell. The message of the tracts was clear, unqualified, and in accord with the dictums of asylum proponents. The well-ordered family, like the well-ordered institution, could not be too absolute in its discipline.

If fidelity to a doctrine could have guaranteed success, the antebellum orphan asylums and houses of refuge would have enjoyed remarkable achievements. Like the other caretaker institutions of the era, they too made isolation and order central to the design. Trustees and managers systematically attempted to remove and protect inmates from the corrupting influences of the community, to impose an exact and demanding schedule, and to enforce rules and regulations with strict and certain discipline. To these ends, they arranged admission policies and visiting rights, established daily activities, and meted out punishments. They translated a good part of prevailing theory into institutional reality.

The first element in the asylum superintendents' program was to abrogate parental authority and substitute their own. To bring the inmate under as absolute a control as possible, trustees characteristically insisted that the parent transfer to them all legal rights upon the child's admission. The requirement was a new one; the occasional colonial benevolent society that had housed dependent children did not attempt to erect legal barriers against parental intervention. Should a family's fortune improve, eighteenth-century officials willingly returned the youngster, at most asking for repayment for past expenses.[27] But nineteenth-century institutions typically would brook no actual or potential interference. The orphan asylum in Philadelphia, for example, compelled destitute parents wishing to institutionalize a child to sign a pledge declaring: "I do hereby surrender to the Orphan Society of Philadelphia, the child A.B. to be provided for. . . . I will not demand or receive any compensation . . . or in any way interfere with the views or direction of the said society." The District of Columbia asylum was just as rigid. Under its act of incorporation relatives and friends did not have the right to remove an inmate before he reached the age of twenty-one. Managers insisted upon having the time and the freedom to effect a reformatory program.[28]

House of refuge regulations were even more strict, and as ser-

17. *The Bloomingdale, New York, orphan asylum, 1840. Substantial and sturdy, this orphanage seems more a philanthropic than a correctional enterprise. Still, there is an architectural solidity to it that may well reflect the style of its keepers.*
COURTESY OF THE NEW-YORK HISTORICAL SOCIETY, NEW YORK CITY

vants of the courts, their powers were usually written into state laws. In New York, parents lost all prerogatives upon the child's commitment to the refuge; except for judicial directions, officials had sole discretion over delinquents until their majority. Other reformatory managers could not always gain as much authority as their New York colleagues, but they certainly tried. Meeting together in 1857 for the first time, the refuge delegates were reluctant to take formal positions on organizational matters, hesitant to announce policy statements that they might regret after greater experience. They made one important exception. The assembly unanimously approved a resolution declaring that the refuge should have unqualified control over the treatment and disposition of inmates for the length of their minority. This stipulation, they agreed, was a prerequisite for success and had to be immediately accomplished. While not all child-care institutions were so uncompromising in curtailing parental rights (some organizations provided a place for working mothers to leave their youngsters during the day and others offered temporary care in return for weekly payments, allowing the family to remain in legal charge), wherever the asylum provided full and continuing support, wherever it dominated the situation, there it almost always insisted on an unabridged freedom to act *in loco parentis*.[29]

In this same spirit, asylums minimized the intermittent contact of relatives with inmates, enacting regulations to curtail their rights to visit. The New York Juvenile Asylum permitted parents to see their children solely at the discretion of a special trustee committee; the Baltimore Home of the Friendless allowed family visitors only on the last Saturday of each month. Certain that such regulations were vital to the asylum's proper functioning, officials were not defensive about them. "It is proposed," announced the Boston Children's Friend Society, "that this shall be a place where the most respectable poor may feel perfectly safe in placing their children, as all intercourse will be cut off between the family, as such, and the connections of any that are otherwise."[30]

Houses of refuge enacted even more stringent rules, assuming that the more depraved the child, the more necessary his isolation. The New York House of Refuge allowed parents to see children only once every three months; and even the selection of visiting days — not at convenience or on a weekend, but only on Wednesdays and Fridays — reflected in yet another way the managers' distrust of outsiders. The Philadelphia refuge, reminiscent of many penitentiaries, provided separately for various types of visitors. Reversing the natural order of things, they established regulations whereby the closer a person was to an inmate, the less he was permitted to come. Foreign tourists had no trouble gaining admission; they could inspect the premises anytime with a ticket from the managers, the mayor, the ladies' committee, or a local judge. Interested citizens were slightly more restricted, entitled to admission on the first and third Wednesday of the month. But parents, guardians, and friends of the inmates, could visit only once in every three months. As a further safeguard, no one was permitted to converse with the children without special permission. Having rescued their charges from a foul environment, officials had no intention of bringing corruption to them.[31]

At least not until the institution had the opportunity to do its work. Asylum and refuge managers did not envision long periods of incarceration for inmates, and had no desire to isolate dependent or delinquent children from the community for the length of their minority. For one thing, they lacked the facilities; if the original group admitted stayed on till age twenty-one, the buildings would be too crowded to admit anyone else. For another, proponents expected asylum discipline to take effect relatively quickly. House of refuge trustees believed that confinement for one to two years would usually be sufficient for rehabilitation. "The inhabitants," declared the organizers of the Philadelphia refuge, "instead of being outcasts from society, with scarcely a possibility of return, will be withdrawn only for a season"; after proper training they could reenter the community and even "hope for its rewards." Others treating less depraved children were still more optimistic. "A month's stay in company with boys accustomed to systematic discipline and obedience," estimated officials of the Boston Asylum and Farm School, "with a sense that there is no escape from order and regularity, generally converts the most wayward into good pupils." The institution would sow the seeds, declared the New York Juvenile Asylum, and leave their cultivation to others.[32]

After short periods of incarceration, asylums dispatched inmates to an apprenticeship with respectable families in the country, where ostensibly vice was less prevalent than in the cities, or returned them to relatives or friends who, in the managers' opinion, were not totally depraved. Delinquents demonstrating no improvement were sent on a whaling voyage that at least would keep them out of the community if not out of trouble. But for all this, officials devoted a minimum of attention and energy to the problems of release. They did not diligently investigate the households to which they apprenticed inmates, or make a sustained effort to facilitate adjustment back into the society. They, like their contemporaries, focused almost exclusively on the organization of the institution, locating within it the hope for correction and reform. Asylum care, and not aftercare, monopolized their interest.[33]

The daily routine at the New York House of Refuge represented in slightly exaggerated form the kind of discipline and control that managers everywhere wished to exercise. Officials carefully organized a schedule for the 160 inmates, divided segments of time precisely, and used the house bells to announce each period. The first bells rang at sunrise to wake the youngsters, the second came fifteen minutes later to signal the guards to unlock the individual cells. The inmates stepped into the hallways and then, according to the managers' description, "marched in order to the washroom. . . . From the washroom they are called to parade in the open air (the weather permitting), where they are arranged in ranks, and undergo a close and critical inspection as to cleanliness and dress." Inmates next went in formation to chapel for prayer (it was the Sunday variant on this that so impressed the visitors from the Philadelphia refuge), and afterwards spent one hour in school. At seven o'clock the bells announced breakfast and then, a half hour later, the time to begin work. The boys spent till noon in the shops, usually making brass nails or cane seats, while the girls washed, cooked, made and mended the clothes. "At twelve o'clock," officials reported, "a bell rings to call all from work, and one hour is allowed for washing . . . and dinner. . . . At one o'clock, a signal is given for recommencing work, which continues till five in the afternoon, when the bell rings for the termination of the labor of the day." There followed thirty minutes to wash and to eat, two and one half hours of evening classes and, finally, to end the day, evening prayers. "The children," concluded the refuge account, "ranged in order, are then marched to the Sleeping Halls, where each takes possession of his separate apartment, and the cells are locked, and silence is enforced for the night."[34]

The institution's architecture was as monotonous as its time-table. Boys and girls occupied separate buildings, each structure of bare brick and unvarying design; as the refuge expanded, adding more wings, the repetition and uniformity increased. The buildings were usually four stories high, with two long hallways running along either side of a row of cells. The rooms, following one after another, were all five by eight feet wide, seven feet high, windowless, with an iron-lattice slab for a door and flues for ventilation near the ceiling. Each group of eleven cells could be locked or unlocked simultaneously with one master key; every aperture within an inmate's reach was guarded by iron sashes, every exit door from the asylum was made of iron. On the first floor of each wing was a huge tub for bathing, sizable enough to hold fifteen to twenty boys; on the fourth floor were ten special punishment cells. In keeping with the external design, all inmates wore uniforms of coarse and solid-colored material. No sooner did they enter the institution than they were stripped, washed, their hair cut to a standard length, and put into common dress. Managers appropriately claimed that the refuge's "main object, that of reformation, is never lost sight of, in any of its regulations, in all its discipline. From the entrance of the child, he becomes subject to a routine of duties. . . . *Order* and *method* it is the effect of this system practically to enforce."[35]

The founders of the Philadelphia refuge were undoubtedly sincere in admiring the New York experiment, for they emulated most of its procedures. They too arranged and administered an exacting routine with precise divisions of time. The inmates worked from seven-thirty until noon, and then from one o'clock until five; they sat in classes for one hour before breakfast and then again for two and one half hours after dinner. The bell ringing was constant, signaling each change of activity, and managers enjoined "the strictest punctuality . . . upon every person employed in the institution." Even more rigorously than the New York reformatory, it tried to prohibit any communication between the boys and the girls, and to keep to a minimum all conversation. The rules required silence of inmates at all times save for the brief exercise and recreation periods. The managers counted the children at regular intervals during the day, hoping in this way to keep everyone in proper place and prevent escapes. Every day at eight-thirty, two-fifteen, and three-thirty, the bells rang, and inmates filed out and grouped in ranks for a head count. Finally, there were few differences in physical appearance between the two houses of refuge; Philadelphia repeated the pattern of even spacing, long rows of cells, unadorned walls.[36] An outsider would have no doubt that he was looking upon an institution. His only difficulty would be in recognizing which one it was.

A visitor to the House of Reformation for Juvenile Offenders in South Boston in 1832 recounted in appreciative detail the strict authority and military precision of the administration. He told how the boys worked at their tasks without talking, using sign language and gestures as the sole means of communication, how they took their meals at prescribed periods at long tables and were forbidden to eat at any other times. He also described an exhibition that the superintendent organized to demonstrate the special qualities and achievements of the institution; the boys stood in military ranks at rigid attention, and answered in unison questions on various school subjects. Periodically the superintendent interrupted the quiz to have the inmates perform a series of exercises copied from West Point. After this part of the demonstration, the boys marched to the gymnasium, did more exercises, and then trooped to the chapel for a period of prayer. This, concluded the visitor, was a well-governed institution.[37]

The uniformity among houses of refuge, whether located in Baltimore or Chicago, in Pittsburgh or Providence, was so complete that there was great unanimity among superintendents discussing procedures at their national convention — and a notable absence of new or unusual ideas. With only minor differences, they all enforced an identical routine. Inmates everywhere spent the bulk of their day at work, had only a few hours for school, and even less time for exercise or recreation. The periods devoted to labor in all the houses of refuge, according to a statistics committee at the 1857 convention, were about the same, from six to eight hours. The time for schooling ranged from three to four hours, for exercises, from one and one-half to three hours. The institutions' physical arrangements were also alike. Managers typically followed what they called the congregate system. Rather than divide the children into small groups and supply each of them with a cottage and a caretaker, they lodged the inmates together, either in wings where cells followed upon cells, or in one central building, where dormitories stretched along either side of lengthy hallways. From all indications, a visitor to one house of refuge could be confident of having seen them all.[38]

The asylums for orphan and destitute children emulated in many essentials the style of the refuge. They too put a premium on order, obedience, and precision. There were, however, important differences in the design and conduct of these two types of institutions. The orphan houses, for example, did not to any significant degree use cells, and consistently devoted more time to classroom instruction. Nevertheless, a broadly similar tone pervaded both settings. The asylums, like the houses of refuge, typically adopted a congregate system, putting inmates into large central dormitories, rather than into smaller, more intimate quarters. The orphanage at Philadelphia had five sleeping rooms for one hundred children, while the asylum at Charleston maintained the same ratio, with ten rooms for two hundred children. The appearance of these rooms often prompted visitors to remark on how neat and evenly spaced the little beds were. Managers also administered a rigid and regimental daily routine. The morning schedule at the Philadelphia orphan asylum was not unusual. The children rose at daybreak, went to a chapel service thirty minutes later, and then marched quietly, two together and holding hands, to large dining halls for their meal. They ate at long tables, segregated by sex. Anyone wishing an extra helping raised his hand, the server came over, and if the request was proper, gave him what he wished. After the meal, the children filed out of the hall just as they entered, marching two by two.[39]

Managers arranged the rest of the asylum day with periods for school, work, and recreation. Where the majority of the institution's residents were older children who came from destitute families, as in the Savannah asylum or the Boston Asylum and Farm School, they usually spent their mornings in a classroom and their afternoons in the shop. Where the inmates tended to be younger in age and not vagrants or delinquents, as in the Baltimore home, the District of Columbia and Philadelphia orphan asylums, they remained in the classroom for most of the day, devoting only a few hours in the afternoons to learning the rudiments of a trade. All managers insisted on carrying out the routine in strict order.[40] Trustees charged the matron at the Baltimore home to keep it tidy and neat, to be sure that the children "have their meals at the *specified hour,* that they are industrious during working hours." She was also to impress upon them the need to listen carefully to every instruction, and "require from the children *unquestioning obedience.*" The managers of the Colored Orphan Asylum in New York City reiterated these rules. "The general discipline and regulation of the house," they declared, "enforce a wholesome restraint. A watchful eye and oversight succeeds." This same perspective led officials at the orphan asylum of Long Island to forbid all conversation in the dormitories. It also prompted the trustees of the New York Juvenile Asylum to go one step further and prohibit the children from talking not only in their sleeping quarters but in the shops and the dining room as well.[41]

Precision and regularity dominated other aspects of asylum life. Many institutions habitually drilled their inmates, organizing them in parade ranks and marching them up and down the field. "In one place," noted Lydia Child after a visit to the Long Island asylum, "I saw a stack of small wooden guns, and was informed that the boys were daily drilled to military exercises, as a useful means of forming habits of order." She discovered that this drill-like quality had infected other parts of the institution, the infant school, and even the chapel. "I was informed," wrote Child, "that it was 'beautiful to see them pray; for at the first tip of the whistle, they all dropped on their knees.'" Her verdict on this asylum may well stand for the others: "Everything moves by machinery, as it always must with masses of children never subdivided into families."[42]

The extraordinary emphasis of child-care institutions on obedience and authority was most apparent in their systems of classification and punishment. Houses of refuge in particular went to great lengths to enforce discipline, conceiving and administering elaborate programs. They depended first upon a highly intricate pattern of grading. Some institutions established four classes, others used seven — but the principle was constant. Superintendents assigned a new inmate to the bottom category and then, depending upon his subsequent behavior, promoted him. Every teacher, dormitory guard, and work supervisor had to file reports on each child's performance as a basis for rank, and the inmate wore a numbered badge on his arm to signify his standing. An obedient child at the Philadelphia refuge could move from class four to class one in seven months and win his tricolor badge. At Pittsburgh those who were well-behaved advanced one grade a month, and after spending three months in Class I were promoted to the Class of Honor. The Chicago Reform School put degrees within each of the four ranks, five levels for class IV, four for class III, seven for Class I; the perfect candidate would take fifteen weeks to pass each class and take his place in the Red Book of Honor.[43] The higher grades carried their own privileges, the lower ones, their penalties. At the Providence refuge, those in the bottom category were, by the rules, "excluded almost entirely from the others [in the house]; not being permitted to join them in sports, or hold any conversation with them." In New York the lowest rank lost Sunday supper and went to bed early, the top one gained extra recreation periods. The system had a convenient balance, for the disobedient were assigned extra periods of work, thus freeing the well-behaved for more leisure. The grading was also linked to discharge. Managers released those in Class I to parents, friends, or masters for an apprenticeship. Those unable to make it out of the bottom categories went over to a ship captain.[44]

Fundamental to the institutions' discipline was habitual and prompt punishment, so that inmates' infractions not only brought a mark in the grading system, but an immediate penalty as well. Corrections ranged from a deprivation of a usual privilege to corporal punishment, with various alternatives along the way. There was the loss of a play period, increased work load, a diet of bread and water, Coventry — with no one permitted to talk with the offender — solitary confinement in a special prison cell, wearing a ball and chain, the whip — and any one or two of these penalties could be combined with yet another and inflicted for varying lengths of time.[45]

Given their perspective on discipline and order, managers openly admitted and vigorously defended strict punitive tactics. They quoted with predictable regularity Solomon's warnings on spoiling the child, insisting that although the rod should be saved for a last resort, it still had to be used. A resolution of the convention of refuge superintendents set out the creed most succinctly: "The first requisite from all inmates should be a strict obedience to the rules of the institution; and where moral suasion fails to produce the desired result, the more severe punishments of deprivation of meals, in part, and of recreation, and the infliction of corporal punishment should be resorted to: the latter only, however, in extreme cases." The superintendent of the Western House of Refuge at Pittsburgh made the matter a precondition for remaining in his post. "I advocate the judicious use of the rod," he announced. "So well am I convinced of its efficacy . . . that I could not think of retaining my connection with such institutions, were the power of using it denied to me. . . . I never yet have seen the time when I thought the rod could be dispensed with."[46]

Refuge records do not often reveal precisely how superintendents exercised their authority, although there is little reason to expect that public statements were harsher than institutional practice. An occasional well-kept journal of daily decisions, however, does indicate the close correspondence between ideas and action. The first manager of the New York House of Refuge, Joseph Curtis, at a time when the institution was new, experimental, and a frequent stopping place for tourists and philanthropists, diligently recorded his decisions — and the result testifies to the frequency and severity of punishment. Few inmates in the course of their incarceration escaped the whip, the ball and chain, or solitary confinement. Some typical incidents from 1825 and 1826 case histories convey the tone and quality of the discipline:[47]

Ann M.: Refractory, does not bend to punishment, put in solitary.

William C.: Questioned guard's authority, whipped.

John B.: A few strokes of the cat to help him remember that he must not speak when confined to a prison cell.

Joseph R.: Disregarded order to stop speaking, given a bit of the cat.

William O.: Escaped. Returned, put in prison with irons.

Simon B.: Escaped. Returned, in handcuffs for 66 days.

John M.: No respect for rules of the Refuge; ball and chain for fifty-two days.

Edmund E.: Quarrelsome, in leg irons.

Samuel S.: Denied talking, given a little of the cat to assist his memory.

Curtis's daily journal also pointed to the regularity of punishments. The notes for the month of March, 1825, for example, read:[48]

March   1: Whipped J. T. for bed wetting.

March   3: J. P. whipped for talking last night; E. D. paddled, with his feet tied to one side of a barrel, his hands to the other.

March   6: M. Y. whipped for continuous disobedience.

March   8: D. S. never practiced obedience, boxed his ears; W. C. shamefully disobedient, put in the prison cell.

March 13: J. M. does not obey the orders for coming when called and neglects her work for play in the yard, leg iron and confined to House.

March 15: M. S. artfully sly, ball and chain and confined to House.

March 17: E. E. continually disobedient, locked in prison 1 day.

March 18: J. T. again wet his bed; certain he does it when awake, whipped.

March 19: J. P. released from prison, but keeps on ball and chain until he learns to be obedient.

March 20: M. S. still not obedient, despite ball and chain, so put in prison.

> March 30: Four boys in prison making noise so gave
> them the cat.

Curtis also arranged for a jury of inmates to try and to punish
offenders, and, as would be expected, they were no less harsh.
They sentenced E. E. and J. C. to three lashes each for leaving
work to play. T. B. received three lashes for frightening one of
the children, and L. S. the same penalty for using profane
language.

There was a great range in the personalities of refuge managers, with some tending to be overbearing and cruel, others,
considerate and gentle. But institutional norms maintained a
strict and severe discipline. Thus Joseph Curtis's replacement as
superintendent, Nathaniel Hart, enforced a very similar correctional system. As one recent student of the refuge has concluded:
When Hart "held sway, orderliness, regularity, and morality
dominated the life of the Refuge. . . . Hart did not hesitate "to
use corporal punishment." He even spoke of himself as "too
much of the old school" to accept a more lenient disciplinary
code. "In this refined and enlightened day," declared Hart,
"when people . . . insist that . . . the time has arrived when
no corporal punishment is necessary . . . I refer to the inspired
writer whom God in *His* wisdom had chosen to write for the
instruction, reproof and guide of his fallen creatures — Solomon."[49] In turn, Hart's successor, David Terry, maintained
these same attitudes and procedures. To choose but one example,
Terry argued that the best method for checking disobedient
inmates was "to take the largest and worst boy in the concern
and make an example of him, which we did by *hand-cuffing* him
in the presence of several others . . . and sent him to be locked
up on Bread and Water for a while." Finally, Terry's replacement, Samuel Wood, was equally severe in office. According to
the testimony of his assistant, the manager called the refuge
discipline "moral and intellectual," but in reality it was
nothing other than "physical and mechanical." "Corporal
punishments," noted this close observer of the Wood regime,
"are usually inflicted with the Cat or a ratan [*sic*]. The latter
instrument is applied in a great variety of places — such as the
palm and back of the hands, top and bottom of the feet — and
lastly, but not rarely nor sparingly, to the posteriors over the

clothes, and also on the naked skin. The ratan . . . is found in all parts of the premises, and liable to be used every where and at all times of day." From Curtis and Hart to Terry and Wood, reformatory corrections remained remarkably constant.[50]

Superintendents of orphan asylums undoubtedly exercised a more restrained authority than their colleagues in houses of refuge, dispensing fewer and less severe punishments. Their charges were younger and without records of delinquency, and therefore more easily prevented from breaking the rules, and the asylum placed lighter demands on inmates, reducing the need to coerce behavior and prevent escapes. The orphan did not have to suffer an eight-hour workday, and even the strictest classroom routine was considerably less onerous than that of the shop. Yet, here too one probably found little tolerance for disobedience and a predisposition to keep a steady and heavy hand over the inmates. The surviving records are too sparse to allow any firm conclusions, but managers' outlook and rhetoric not only sanctioned punishments but required them. Since every infraction, important as well as trivial, was a portent of a future crisis, since violating a rule of the institution was tantamount to breaking the most basic codes of society, superintendents had to respond quickly and punitively. There was simply too much at stake to do otherwise. Strokes of the whip or days of solitary confinement, no matter how painful to administer, were preferable to allowing the child to grow up in license. The asylum could not risk being a permissive place.

To follow the metaphors of superintendents of asylums and refuges, the family was the model for institutional organization. Whether serving the poor or the orphan or the delinquent, they repeatedly described their operations in household terms. The Baltimore Home of the Friendless, for example, announced a determination to "see that the order and decorum of a well regulated Christian family be strictly observed." The tougher the clientele, the more elaborate the family metaphor. The New York Juvenile Asylum insisted that "the government of the Institution has been strictly parental. The prominent object has been to give a home feeling and home interest to the children — to create and cultivate a family feeling . . . to clothe the Institution as far as possible with those hallowed associations which usually cluster about home."[51] The manager of the St. Louis Reform School was just as committed to this language. The refuge, he insisted, would succeed "by assimilating the government in Reformatories, as nearly as possible, to that of the *time-honored* institution which guided the infancy of nearly all the truly great and good men and women — that model, and often humble institution — the *family* . . . 'God's University' . . . the well-ordered Christian family."[52]

But as is readily apparent, rhetoric and reality had little correspondence. Except for these public declarations, one would not have considered the family to be the model for the asylum. Rather, from all appearances, a military tone seems to have pervaded these institutions. Managers imposed on their charges a routine that was to resemble an army camp. They grouped inmates into large companies under a central administration, rather than establishing small familylike units under the individual care of surrogate parents. Inmates slept in separate cells or on cots in large dormitories, all neatly spaced and arranged in ways more reminiscent of orderly military barracks than of households. They ate silently in large refectories, using hand signals to communicate their needs, in a style that was much closer to an army mess than a family meal. They marched about the institution, stood in formation for head counts and public quizzes, and carried wooden guns in parades for recreation. They followed an exact schedule, responding to bells like recruits to a bugler's call. They wore uniforms with badges for insignias and grades for ranks. They learned to drop to one knee at the sound of a whistle, even making prayer into a military exercise. They obeyed rules of silence or suffered punishment. They took the whip like disobedient soldiers being flogged. If anyone escaped, or went AWOL, the ball and chain awaited him upon his return.

As surprising as it may seem, the superintendents saw no contradiction between their language and actions, no opposition between parading children in ranks while paying homage to the family. For they believed that they were offering a critique of the conduct of the antebellum family, and an alternative to it. In their view the family had to emulate the asylum as constituted —

that is, put a greater premium on order, discipline, and obedience, not on domestic affections, pampering the child, or
indulging his every whim. The family did not need to march its
members from bedroom to kitchen or keep children silent
throughout a meal (although the adage did call for children to
be seen and not heard), but parents were to exercise a firm and
consistent authority and brook no willfulness. Thus, managers
found no real divergence between the well-ordered asylum and
the well-ordered family. The quasi-military quality of the institution was a rebuke and an example to the lax family. The
problem was that parents were too lenient, not that the refuge or
asylum were too strict. As long as the desideratum was order and
discipline, as long as the virtues most in demand in child rearing
were regularity and respect for authority, then the asylum was at
least as effective a training center as the home. To the extent that
the family neglected or overindulged or corrupted its members,
the institution was a distinctly preferable setting.

10

The Legacy of Reform

The American experiment with institutionalization was not a prolonged success. By the 1850's almost every type of asylum was losing its special qualities, and by the 1870's few traces remained of the original designs. In a majority of mental hospitals the careful balance of moral treatment gave way to custodial care; in almost every penitentiary the unique arrangements of the Auburn and Pennsylvania plans disappeared before wardens' preoccupation with peace and security. Almshouses, never very attractive places to begin with, became even more disorderly, while houses of refuge frequently came to resemble poorly run state prisons.

No fixed and inherent defect accounted for the asylums' degeneration. Their history might well have been different. The Civil War did strain their facilities: just when state funds were required elsewhere, the number of those dependent upon asylum care (because, for example, of the death or absence of the family head) increased. But the problems were long-term ones, and not the result of temporary dislocations. Many of the asylum's goals, it is also true, were so grand that some disappointment was unavoidable. Poverty, criminality, insanity, and delinquency were not eradicated, yet the nineteenth-century ventures could hardly be faulted if they proved inadequate to such a task. But even by less demanding standards the performances were disappointing.

Nevertheless, the growing irrelevance of a rehabilitative program to the asylums' daily routine did not bring about their dissolution. Despite their faults, they continued to dominate the care and treatment of the deviant and dependent classes in the middle decades of the century. It was not simply a matter of the states being lethargic and economical, and hence unwilling to dismantle the costly structures that they had just erected. Rather, legislators continued to invest in institutions, enlarging existing structures or constructing others. The appropriations were usually not sufficient to prevent overcrowding, but they were adequate for housing an increasing number of inmates. Not until the end of the century was there a marked change in practice and the beginnings of a noninstitutional response to the problems of poverty, crime, and insanity.

Both the failure of the asylums and their persistence had common causes. The elements that transformed the penitentiary and the mental hospital, the almshouse and the reformatory into places of custody also insured their perpetuation. The environmental concepts of the asylum founders at once helped to *promote* and *disguise* the shift from reform to custody. The post–Civil War asylum keeper all too predictably succumbed to the fallacy that in administering a holding operation he was still encouraging rehabilitation, that one only had to keep inmates behind walls to effect some good. Since the fact of incarceration was so easily confused with the improvement of the inmate, wardens and superintendents often relaxed their vigilance and allowed abuses to creep into the routine. Yet neither they nor the public at large confronted these changes.

More important, the asylums lost their reformatory design and remained in active use because of the character of their inmates. The people that filled the penitentiaries, insane asylums, almshouses, and to some extent, the reformatories as well, did not fit the expectations of the asylum founders, but officials and citizens were satisfied to incarcerate them even if only temporarily and without permanent effect. The first proponents of institutionalization had generally assumed that the recently insane would come to the mental hospitals, that those starting to follow a life in crime would enter the penitentiaries, that the able-bodied poor in sudden and perhaps unprecedented need would go to the almshouse — and that a system of discipline and order would have a quick and certain effect on all of them. These preconceptions proved woefully inaccurate. By the outbreak of the Civil War, the insane asylums were admitting great numbers of chronic patients, the poorhouses were taking in the aged and the decrepit, penitentiary cells filled up with hardened criminals and even the reformatories received teen-agers surprisingly advanced in a life of crime. The intricate designs of the asylum builders did not suit this clientele. Moral treatment had not been planned for the chronic insane, a system of steady labor for the senile, or the rules of silence and separation for the ten- to twenty-year convict. Under these conditions, superintendents were content to administer a custodial program.

The public accepted the decision. The inmates were a clear threat to safety and security, and also in many cases they were foreigners, and both considerations heightened the appeal of confinement, no matter how custodial the routine. The community would be spared the danger of their presence through a program that appeared to be especially appropriate for newcomers. A prison sentence would terrorize anyone, regardless of background, training, language, religion, or inclinations; the almshouse, despite its deficiencies, could still relieve at a minimal cost those who otherwise might starve or beg on the street. The mental hospital was a useful place for locking up lunatics, even without the prospect of a cure.

Once begun, the decline from rehabilitation to custodianship took on a self-reinforcing quality. As the community increasingly utilized asylum facilities to confine the hardened criminal, the incurably insane, and the decrepit poor, the recently insane from comfortable households or the able-bodied poor in need of temporary relief avoided them as best they could. In turn, the chronic and the helpless filled the vacancies and the institutions became even less attractive to anyone else. Superintendents then more easily accommodated themselves to the tasks of custodianship, and the notion of reform became irrelevant to the daily routine.

Convenience had always been part of the reason for the asylum's popularity. The institutional program had a pragmatic quality; the penitentiary and the almshouse were workable substitutes for stocks and edicts of banishment. Nevertheless, in the first formulation of the asylum idea, the prospect of improvement, both of the individual and the society, was far more significant, and the institutions' organization reflected this pri-

ority. The abundant evidence of the close fit between the reform
program and the actual appearance and arrangements of the
institutions testified convincingly to the founders' sense of priorities.

After 1850, however, the balance shifted, and subsidiary considerations became the primary ones. Urban areas now
held populations of unprecedented size, and industrial development had begun to alter the nation's economy; numerous immigrants entered eastern and midwestern cities, and the distinctions among social classes increased. Each change made the
traditional mechanisms for maintaining order less relevant.
Under these circumstances, incarceration became first and foremost a method for controlling the deviant and dependent population. The promise of reform had built up the asylums; the
functionalism of custody perpetuated them.

The history of the penitentiary illustrates the dimensions of
the change. By 1860, the state prisons were by no stretch of the
imagination reformatory, yet they continued to occupy the central place in the system of criminal punishment. Massive walls
still enclosed the prison space and heavy gates swung open
regularly to admit a stream of convicts. But inside little remained of a reform design or routine. Failure and persistence
went hand in hand.

Investigations of prison affairs revealed a common custodial
quality. Where once committees had surveyed neighboring institutions and reported back on the marvels of what they had seen,
now they returned subdued and disgruntled. Rather than
advise constituents to duplicate other states' designs, they urged a
vigorous effort to avoid their faults. The most thorough account
of the nation's prisons in this era — the 1867 report to the New
York legislature of E. C. Wines and Theodore Dwight, two
members of the New York Prison Discipline Association —
described clearly the disappointing conditions. The principal
finding of their *Report on the Prisons and Reformatories of the
United States and Canada* was that penal institutions no longer
made rehabilitation the central goal. "There is not a state
prison in America," they declared, "in which the reformation of
the convicts is the one supreme object of the discipline, to which

18. The Philadelphia jail, 1723. To compare this houselike colonial jail with the penitentiary of the 1850's makes clear the extent to which Americans in the pre—Civil War period invested in institutions.

COURTESY OF THE PENNSYLVANIA PRISON SOCIETY

19. The penitentiary at Blackwells Island, New York, 1849. This mammoth institution, extending monotonously window after window, corridor after corridor, points unmistakably to the increasingly custodial quality of correctional institutions.

everything else is made to bend." By this standard, "there is not a prison system in the United States, which . . . would not be found wanting. There is not one, we feel convinced . . . which seeks the reformation of its subjects as a primary object. . . . They are all . . . lacking in the breadth and comprehensiveness of their scope; all lacking in the aptitude and efficiency of their instruments; and all lacking in the employment of a wise and effective machinery to keep the whole in healthy and vigorous action." The old reformatory practices were passing and no new ones replaced them.[1]

State investigations of New York's own systems also presented a dismal picture of prison affairs. An 1852 investigatory commission declared that if the function of state prisons was to prevent a criminal from injuring society during the course of his confinement — if, in other words, its purposes were custodial — then the institutions succeeded tolerably well. While incarcerated, the convict had no chance to commit crimes. "But if," the committee went on, "the object is to make him a better member of society, so that he may safely again mingle with it . . . for with few exceptions all are again turned loose upon the world — that purpose cannot be answered by matters as they now stand." Two decades later another commission found conditions still worse. It not only uncovered instances of cruel punishments, such as hanging convicts by their thumbs, but many illegal transactions as well. Sing-Sing inmates regularly paid off guards to obtain a favorable work assignment; at Auburn there was an illicit but steady trade between contractors, convicts, and local farmers and merchants. The question was not whether the prison reformed the convict but the extent of its own corruption.[2]

Another common characteristic of penitentiaries in the Civil War period was overcrowding. By 1866 the institution most famed for maintaining the strict isolation of inmates, the Philadelphia penitentiary, confined more than one prisoner to a cell, and so did Sing-Sing, where the quarters were in fact much smaller. Wines and Dwight estimated in 1867 that at least one-third of all convicts did not sleep in individual cells.[3] Concomitantly, the emphasis on the rule of silence ended. Only a handful of wardens still made a serious effort to enforce this regulation, since subdued conversations between two persons in a cell could not be policed. And no one any longer paid much attention to restricting the flow of information, through letters or newspapers, into the prison.[4] Moreover, the institutions had difficulty in using labor efficiently and many among them could not pay their own way. The earlier efforts to establish manufacturing enterprises suffered from a combination of internal difficulties and external pressures against the threat of competition.[5] Finally, discipline was fitful, often brutal in its severity, sometimes incredibly lax. Few officials, in the opinion of observers and investigators, seemed able to strike a balance. An occasional officer managed to oversee a creditable program — but only for brief periods of time. The Charlestown, Massachusetts, prison was well administered in the 1860's, but a turnover in personnel and gradual overcrowding lowered its standards in the 1870's.[6]

The early reform principles had stimulated a popular and vigorous optimism about the prospect of rehabilitating criminals. But in the middle decades of the nineteenth century, this view was fast disappearing and the level of expectation was dropping sharply. At best, the shell of the original design remained, but without substance. Officials sometimes talked as if reform was still a primary goal, but the declarations sounded pro forma.

By the 1860's, the hold of the institutions on many penologists was also broken. Men taking their first look at the penitentiary establishment in this period had little patience with either the Auburn or Pennsylvania design. Rather than choose sides in the old debate, they lumped the two schools together, wondered why partisans had so fiercely debated one another when the programs seemed much more alike than different, and went on to indicate their common faults. Both systems, the new critics argued, were artificial, violating the most basic and valuable precepts of human nature. They had little sympathy for the idea that a properly structured environment could promote rehabilitation, that if the architecture was right, reform would certainly follow. And without this premise, the contrivances of the earlier programs seemed not only a bit foolish and unnecessary, but actually detrimental. Take, for example, the rule of silence. To later observers, the practice appeared to be a purposeless violation of a social instinct, a deleterious "departure from the laws of nature." As Wines and Dwight insisted, conversations between inmates could have the most beneficial effects; since sociability was "a fountain of moral strength in civil life," it would be "equally a source of moral strength in prison life." Invariably, "all attempts to carry out such a warfare upon nature must be productive of endless deception, and so far tend to corrupt and destroy what remains of virtue yet linger in the men." Wines and Dwight also criticized the exceptional rigidity of the earlier routine. "What we want," they announced, "is to gain the will, the consent, the cooperation of these men, not to mould them into so many pieces of machinery."[7]

This perspective bred dissatisfaction with the very idea of incarceration. Critics condemned large expenditures for elaborate structures as wasteful, insisting that prison buildings should be plain, simple, and not at all monumental. "A prison with a stately and imposing exterior," argued Wines and Dwight, "has a mischievous tendency . . . to give importance to criminals and dignity to crime."[8] They also attacked the penitentiary on a more fundamental level. Convinced that confinement was inherently unnatural, and therefore injurious, they wanted to return convicts, with appropriate precautions and supervision, to the community as quickly as possible. The sooner the criminal reentered society, the more likely that he would become law-abiding; the longer he remained secluded, the more incorrigible he would grow. The New York Prison Commission of 1852 was among the first to argue that "protracted incarceration destroys the better faculties of the soul," that "most men who have been confined for long terms are distinguished by a stupor of both the moral and intellectual facilities. . . . Reformation is then out of the question."[9] This contention became more popular in succeeding decades. Warren Spalding, secretary of the Massachusetts Board of Commissioners of Prisons, was certain that for most offenders incarceration was the "worst possible treatment." Prisons, he concluded, should be used "only as a last resort, when everything else has failed, and mainly for the incorrigible, who will yield to no other influence." Prison discipline societies also publicized and supported various proposals for minimizing the period of confinement. At first they promoted the Irish system of commutation and tickets of leave to allow convicts to reduce their sentences through good behavior; later they advocated probation and parole arrangements to shorten still further the penitentiary stay. To these ends they devoted new attention to prisoners' needs upon release. Now that institutions no longer seemed to answer the problem of crime, they shifted interest from architecture to adjustment back into society. They focused on lodging and employment opportunities, not the construction and arrangement of cells.[10]

Nevertheless, the penitentiaries remained central to criminal punishment. They continued to thrive long after their original rationale and practices were abandoned, and without many of them adopting a new reform program. An uncompromised reliance upon the sentence remained the rule. Neither the custodial quality of the treatment nor critics' insistence that incarceration diminished the likelihood of rehabilitation decreased its importance. For one thing, the reform theory encouraged a complacency that all too predictably made incarceration an end in itself, so that after a few decades officials interpreted the mere presence of men in cells as itself valuable. For another, the type of convict who entered the prison prompted wardens to define their task in terms of custody. As the institutions filled up with hardened and dangerous criminals, officials were satisfied just to prevent escapes and riots. Without great embarrassment they turned the penitentiary into a holding operation.

The fate of the prison illustrated well the dangers of a theory of thoroughgoing environmentalism. By positing that the origins of deviancy lay in the weaknesses of the criminals' early training and the corruptions at loose in the community, the founders made rehabilitation seem not merely a feasible but almost a routine matter. This viewpoint, however, fostered an attitude that ultimately deluded officials into believing that punishment and isolation were complete answers to the problem of deviancy. The first generation usually remembered that these were to be means to an end; their successors made them the sum of the program.[11]

The designers of the penitentiary, with significant and novel tasks to accomplish, had no trouble in preserving a sense of excitement and purpose. It was a difficult and challenging assignment, and they remained acutely sensitive to the broad goals of the movement. Their successors, however, moved into buildings already constructed, to administer a routine already established. They were from the start of their careers custodians — and not surprisingly the institutions under their care came to reflect this quality.

The doctrines of obedience and discipline were particularly susceptible to abuse. In the name of authority, wardens had an excuse to mete out the most severe punishments, while still believing that they were doing more than satisfying their own instincts. It was just a short step from positing that convicts should be the instruments of their own correction to assuming that the all-important task of administration was to safeguard the peace of the prison. Lackadaisical officials could ignore prisoners' welfare and administer the most aimless program, still thinking that they were overseeing a socially useful operation.

The very exuberance and optimism of the founders, their supreme confidence that rehabilitation would follow from institutionalization, also contributed to the decline into custodial care. The first claim soon seemed inflated and exaggerated. Neither Auburn nor Pennsylvania curtailed criminal behavior or sparked a reform of society; they had not even managed to end recidivism. Under these circumstances, wardens could hardly be expected to administer an idiosyncratic routine with particular diligence. Rather than defining themselves as the guardians of a reformatory design and making every effort to keep its principles alive, rather than being their own worst critics and using every available forum to publicize the deficiencies of the penitentiary, officials fell into a comfortable silence, and maintained it.[12]

This complacency contributed in still another way to making the penitentiary a holding operation. As the prison routine lost its special qualities, there seemed less reason to restrict potential profit-making ventures; contractors eager to lease convict labor now appeared as capable as prison officials of supervising the inmates' schedule. These types of arrangements, therefore, became increasingly popular, and although prisons probably did not become as a rule profitable operations, the cost of maintenance was not very onerous. Critics like Wines and Dwight protested vigorously what they considered to be the final corruption of the institutions — but without effect. The leasing arrangements were both symptom and cause of the general decline.

They reflected the loss of interest in reformatory routines, and made it that much more difficult to experiment with alternatives.[13]

Another element contributing to the decline of the reformatory system was the practice governing the admission and retention of inmates. The state prison indiscriminately housed all classes of convicts together, making no distinctions as to the nature of the crime or the history of the criminal. The amateur served his time in the same institution as the recidivist, the petty embezzler sat alongside the murderer. The prisons also held the most serious offenders for the longest periods, since the courts set the term of the sentence by the gravity of the crime. Wardens in the 1850's supervised a very mixed group of prisoners that contained at least a sizable minority of dangerous offenders — those serving ten- to twenty-year or life sentences. Having to enforce the same regulations on the first offender and the professional, they came to focus attention on the potentially most disruptive inmates, and framed general rules with them in mind. The fine points of a reform plan became irrelevant to security requirements.

The founders had not anticipated the extent of these developments. The prototype offender, for whom they had designed the system, was not the hardened professional but the good boy gone bad, the amateur in the trade. This prisoner would know how to read the Bible placed in his cell, prove able and willing to converse with benevolent visitors, and have the remnant of a conscience to torment him during his enforced solitude. The number of incorrigibles would be small and unimportant and not affect the institution's general administration. Moreover, the isolation of convicts would prevent contamination and obviate the need for intricate classification. This is why Auburn and Pennsylvania partisans urged the erection of one state penitentiary for all offenders.[14]

The designers proved mistaken. The state prisons from the start had a negative selection and negative retention of offenders. By legislative design and court action, penitentiaries received the toughest class among the criminals. Those guilty of minor offenses, from drunkenness to disturbing the peace, served in local jails. Embezzlers, forgers, and the like — not a dangerous or especially professional group — composed only a very small minority of convicts. Those guilty of crimes of violence — assault and battery, manslaughter, murder and attempted murder — and burglars and robbers — guilty of breaking and entering houses, particularly at night, or using force to extort property — were numerically much more important, and far more difficult to supervise. The largest bloc of offenders were guilty of grand larceny, and although the minimum sums defining this offense were quite small in some states, still many of these felons were veterans in crime and by no means easy to control.

The results of this selection appeared even in the early prison populations. Of the 839 convicts in the Connecticut state penitentiary between 1828 and 1840, sixty percent were guilty of crimes of violence and coercion. They were burglars and robbers (343), murderers and those who attempted murder (78), rapists (42), arsonists and prison-breakers (45). Only a minority of them received sentences for theft or embezzlement or forgery. At least half of them were functionally illiterate, unable to make use of that Bible in their cells.[15] The characteristics of Auburn's inmates were very much the same. Between 1830 and 1836, almost seventy percent of the some 1,000 men who entered the penitentiary were guilty of grand larceny (409), or of crimes of violence (269) ranging from murder and assault to burglary and robbery; only a third of them had committed petty larceny, forgery, or swindling. And here too, illiteracy was a common state; by the calculation of the chaplain in 1840, a little less than half the convicts were unable to read a book.[16] The Ohio penitentiary confined a similar class of inmates. In 1839, when the records were especially complete, twenty-eight percent of the four hundred eighty-six inmates were guilty of grand larceny, forty-three percent of crimes of violence; less than thirty percent were serving sentences for forgery and the like. Ten years later conditions were unchanged — grand larceny and crimes of violence were still the causes of conviction for seventy-two percent of the inmates. The literacy level was somewhat higher than elsewhere, but one-third of the convicts were illiterate. The situation was no different in the Virginia penitentiary. Of 193 inmates confined in 1849, forty percent were guilty of grand larceny, thirty percent of murder or intent to murder, seventeen percent of robbery and burglary, and only six percent of white-collar crimes.[17] In brief, most state prisoners from New England to the South were tough and professional.

A very detailed investigation of commitment patterns in Massachusetts at the close of the Civil War also pointed to the negative selection of penitentiary inmates. By comparing the criminals that the court sentenced to the state prison with those it dispatched to town and county jails, the report confirmed that the more dangerous the act, the more it was professional and violent in nature, the greater the probability that the criminal would go to the penitentiary. While only six percent of all Massachusetts offenders entered the state prison, seventy-seven percent of those guilty of manslaughter, sixty-eight percent guilty of rape or attempted rape, and fifty-three percent guilty of burglary or robbery did. On the other hand, those convicted of vagrancy, keeping a disorderly house, or some other petty offense almost always served in the local jail.[18]

Although this disturbing element was found in the prisons from the beginning, the first wardens did not quickly succumb to it. The strength of the ideology kept them from examining too closely the hardened character of the convicts and encouraged them to maintain the principles of silence and separation. For their successors, however, the diminishing attractions of the Auburn and Pennsylvania designs set off a self-perpetuating cycle of decline. As wardens looked more closely at the actual nature of the inmate population, they lost patience with the goals of reform; as they lessened their insistence on silence and separation, security became more of a problem. The result was that they gave still less attention to rehabilitation. In short order they were complacently administering a custodial operation.

The roots of this problem lay with the sentencing procedures. The original plan of a sentence, as formulated in the 1790's, had a compelling logic. Rather than rely upon the gallows to avenge a wide variety of offenses, legislators and magistrates could match correction to the severity of the act — for murder, execution or life imprisonment; for robbery, five to ten years; for petty larceny, one to two years. With juries no longer compelled to choose between humanity and justice, punishment would become certain and the futility of criminal behavior obvious. But the practice of passing a fixed sentence at the close of a trial persisted into the second stage of the reform movement, when the penitentiary experience, and not the predictable operation of the law, captured attention. And then the policy became much less appropriate.

The idea of rehabilitation was at odds with the stipulation that the criminal complete a predetermined and unalterable sentence. The sentencing regulations presented both inmates and officials with contradictory messages, but they easily learned which one to follow. On the one hand, the convict heard that the goal of confinement was reform and presumably wardens would judge him accordingly; they would reward cooperation and punish disobedience *as if* imprisonment was to continue until signs of improvement appeared, *as if* the convict could not rejoin society until demonstrating his moral fitness. On the other hand, the prisoner knew a much more crucial fact — that he only had to endure a period of detention in order to be released. Regardless of behavior he would gain freedom as soon as a fixed number of years passed. His proper concern, then, was with the calendar, not with his conscience. Officials could not arrange an early release for exemplary convicts or extend the confinement of recalcitrants. Thus one of the most fundamental principles of penitentiary organization encouraged prisoners, and their keepers, to think in terms of custody, of surviving a term of detention.

In still another way, sentencing procedures ran counter to the interests of a reformatory institution: they incarcerated the most hardened criminals for the longest periods of time. State codes and courts consistently fixed sentences according to the severity of the offense, unhesitatingly meting out lengthy terms for major crimes. The fate of inmates at the Ohio penitentiary illustrated the general condition: the average period of confinement for counterfeiting was four years; for assault, six years; for burglary with larceny, six and one-half years; for rape, twelve and one-half years; and for murder, life. At the Illinois penitentiary, those guilty of larceny served from two to four years; for assault, between five and nine years; and for robbery, between ten and fourteen years.[19] Under these conditions, state prisons, therefore, had the burden of confining murderers for life, rapists for over a decade, and robbers for nearly as long. The results were demoralizing to convicts and wardens alike. Facing an extended period of confinement, prisoners had little incentive to accommodate themselves to standing regulations. And officials found it difficult to preach moral reform to men who would spend a good part of their lives behind walls and in cells. These two elements reinforced one another to decrease still further the relevance of a reformatory program. As an inmate facing year after year of imprisonment turned uncooperative, wardens increasingly devoted attention and energy to the peace and security of the institution. They worried more about criminals actually completing the prescribed sentence than the prospect of rehabilitation. If the prison was in order, with no escapes or massive outbreaks of violence, and made some financial returns, they would be satisfied.

Once begun, there was no halting the process of decline. No sooner did officers relax the rules of silence than prisons suffered from an absence of a system of classification. The original design had assumed that the prohibition against communication obviated the need for other arrangements. But without such a regulation in effect, hardened criminals mixed freely with first offenders, and the institutions were once again open to the charge of being seminaries for vice. Furthermore, wardens became the captives of the prisons' weakest link. Since no one group of inmates could be treated differently from another, the best of convicts come under the rules regulating the worst of them. The end result was unmistakable: by the end of the period, the penitentiary served as a place of custody.[20]

The most active and discerning penologists of the middle decades of the nineteenth century, men like E. C. Wines, Theodore Dwight, and Frank Sanborn had little respect for the Pennsylvania and Auburn principles. Making no effort to preserve these standards, they contributed in significant measure to their loss of relevance. The critics found little evidence that the programs had fulfilled their grandiose promises and they were not intellectually committed to a theory of environmentalism. New doctrines stressing the powerful influence of heredity took their toll; so did a more general disillusionment with other unabashedly utopian experiments. And the threat of deviancy and dependency no longer seemed to menace the nation's welfare and security. Other considerations pushed this issue into the background; if the republic floundered, sectionalism and race relations, and not crime and poverty would be at fault. Critics were also escaping eighteenth-century conceptualizations of the proper organization of society, beginning to find cause for celebration in some of the very phenomena that had alarmed their predecessors. Social and geographic mobility, to take the chief example, now appeared to guarantee rather than to undermine stability. Mid-nineteenth-century Americans were far more confident than many of their predecessors that the self-made man and the open frontier would buttress social order, not endanger it.

The second generation of penologists contributed to the disillusionment with the Auburn and Pennsylvania schemes, but were unsuccessful in attracting a wide following for their own designs. Disenchanted with the potential benefits of institutionalization, they urged the adoption of commutation laws and conditional pardons to obtain the early release of well-behaved convicts and asked the states to create agencies for the aftercare of released prisoners. They demanded a separate institution for the young first offender and another for the worst class of criminals. "As in the world at large, so in a prison," declared Wines and Dwight, "it is found that the chief trouble is given by comparatively few persons." To segregate this minority would allow for much greater flexibility in administration. Yet reformers enacted little of this program. States were slow to establish parole systems and aftercare organizations, and were even less inclined to construct separate institutions for different offenders. Confinement, straightforward and unadorned, seemed sufficient.[21]

There was little discernible public opposition to the decline in penitentiary organization. The gap between the promise of the innovation and the later performance did not spark outcries or remonstrances. The excitement that reformers generated in the 1830's could not be revived thirty years later.[22] Part of the cause for this complacency may be found in the ephemeral quality of public interest in a particular program, especially when new and pressing issues assume importance; and it was undoubtedly easier to capture citizens' attention with predictions of success than with descriptions of corruption. Laymen may have accepted the notion that incarceration was in itself rehabilitative, also confusing confinement with reform. Yet the reasons for the silence and lack of indignation went deeper. Many members of American society, certainly the middling and upper classes, found in the social and ethnic composition of the prison population sufficient reason for upholding and supporting these institutions. The penitentiary, they believed, no matter how crude its internal procedures, was nevertheless performing a useful — indeed a critical — function.

The annual reports of the state penitentiaries made eminently clear that the overwhelming majority of inmates stood toward the bottom of the social ladder. By the 1850's, undoubtedly sensing the relevance of this information, wardens frequently asked convicts about their occupations prior to imprisonment and then presented the findings in table form. The identifications were brief and without detail — laborer or butcher or carpenter — based only on the prisoners' response. But the results indicated that in almost every state prison, laborers and semiskilled workers filled the rolls. Fully half of the criminals entering Sing-Sing prison in 1853 were ordinary laborers. Almost sixty percent of the inmates at New York's Clinton prison in 1849 were unskilled, as were sixty percent of those in the New Jersey institution, forty-one percent in the Eastern State Penitentiary in Philadelphia, fifty-two percent in Maryland, and forty-two percent in Ohio. The other convicts in these institutions bordered on the semiskilled — blacksmiths, bakers, tailors, carpenters, and the like. These labels do not indicate an exact position in the society — the blacksmith might have employed several others in a large shop or just owned a pair of tongs — but it is unlikely that a good number of them ranked above the lower middle-class, and many were probably below it. But whatever doubts the vagueness of these categories raise are quickly dispelled by the almost complete absence from prison lists of men of middle or upper-class occupations. The total number of professionals, merchants, shopkeepers, and farmers, in a sample of some eighteen hundred convicts in 1849 was less than three percent. Even without precise information, there is little question of the lower-class character of most penitentiary inmates.[23]

Official statistics also revealed that at least a large minority, and oftentimes a majority, of inmates were not natives to the states in which they were imprisoned. To judge by the tables on convicts' places of birth, the penitentiary always incarcerated a good many outsiders, but their character changed markedly over these years. At first, in the Jacksonian period, they were mostly Americans who had moved from one state to another; then, in the Civil War era, they became the immigrants. Between 1830 and 1835, only a little over one-half of Auburn's inmates were native to New York; most of the rest (thirty percent) had emigrated from other states, and a smaller number (twenty percent) were foreigners.[24] Of the 2,059 convicts who served in Pennsylvania's Eastern Penitentiary between its opening in 1829 and 1845, only fifty-eight percent were born in the state; thirty-four percent entered from other states, and just eighteen percent were aliens. In a more recently settled area like Ohio, Americans from other areas made up the bulk of the prison population (seventy percent in 1839), while native Ohioans and immigrants were evenly divided among the rest.[25]

Beginning in the 1850's, outsider and immigrant — in the person of the Irish — became increasingly synonymous. In New York in 1850, the foreign-born confined to the Auburn, Sing-Sing, and Clinton penitentiaries made up thirty-two percent of the inmate population; by the outbreak of the Civil War they were forty-four percent of the total. By then native New Yorkers had shrunk to a minority, composing only forty-one percent of the convicts. Conditions were much the same in Massachusetts. The 1859 report of the Charlestown prison revealed that almost forty percent of the inmates were aliens, and only one-third of the convicts were born in the state.[26] The Pennsylvania penitentiary was not so dominated by the foreign-born but their number was mounting. In 1853 immigrants were twenty-seven percent of the prisoners, and by 1860, thirty percent. Nor were these developments unique to the eastern seaboard. In Illinois, forty-six percent of the six hundred fifty-six convicts in 1859 were foreign-born. In short, the state-prison population became to a marked degree lower class and immigrant.[27]

This phenomenon helped to secure the place of the penitentiary in the system of criminal punishment, giving it a utility quite apart from the issue of reform. By the Civil War, inherited ideas and mechanisms of social order and control were irrelevant to the new society, and the character of the prison population indicated the nature of the problem. Little survived of the grandiose and nostalgic expectations of the earlier period. The passage of time not only revealed the inability of institutions to promote individual and social reform, but demonstrated how different nineteenth-century communities were from their predecessors. The social and ethnic composition of the penitentiary population represented the most important elements in this transformation. As the large percentage of immigrant and lower-class convicts made clear, homogeneity and insularity were things of the past; even if one could somehow exclude the foreign-born from the community, internal class divisions would remain troublesome.

These circumstances wiped away the last traces of the reformers' fanciful hopes for the penitentiary. But at the same time they supplied good reasons for defining the institutions as a useful and convenient, albeit temporary, method of criminal punishment. Incarceration was a certain penalty, not dependent upon the attitude or the experience of the offender. It worked as effectively against the Irish and the lower classes as anyone else. It offered the community a measure of security — at least for the period of the convicts' confinement. (To a society that was only beginning to evolve effective forms of policing, even a temporary respite was welcome.) Finally, it was an acceptable device for putting the offender out of sight and out of mind. The rhetoric in the Jacksonian period had justified confinement, and the next generation could resort to it without especial difficulty.

A holding operation was satisfactory to prison officials, state legislators, and ordinary citizens. Wardens no longer had to measure themselves by the demanding criteria of reform; regardless of how ineffective their efforts at rehabilitation, they could find in the task of guarding a tough class of convicts sufficient cause for satisfaction. Others, with more or less good conscience, found that institutionalization fit neatly with immediate needs. The structures, after all, were ready and certainly were suitable

20. *The Philadelphia House of Refuge, 1859. The reformatory became more rigid and custodial in the post-1850 period. Still, as the design makes clear, it was not as grim and unrelieved as the penitentiary.*

FROM THE COLLECTIONS OF THE LIBRARY COMPANY OF PHILADELPHIA

for restraining the foreign-born and lower classes. The handful of new reformers, dissatisfied with the course of events, attracted little support for schemes that would narrow the distance between the society and the penitentiary. This was not a good time to counter the appeal of custody.

The history of the house of refuge was in many ways similar to that of the penitentiary. Houses of refuge had difficulty in sustaining their original principles, and could not command wide support among the second generation of reformers. Nevertheless, abuses did not bring a quick end to the venture or loosen its hold on public policy. But there were also major differences in the fate of the two experiments. The decline of the refuge was not so precipitous. In fact, of all the caretaker institutions in the middle of the nineteenth century, the reformatories enjoyed the best reputation.

In the 1820's, the appeal of the penitentiary and the reformatory coincided. In this decade New York, Philadelphia, and Boston led the way in new prison construction and not coincidentally spearheaded the movement to erect structures for juvenile offenders. But in the 1850's the refuge enjoyed a second, and more widespread, burst of popularity that in part reflected the growing disillusionment with the penitentiary. As it became increasingly evident that the prison offered little prospect for reform, some officials and philanthropists, usually in large urban areas, devoted fresh energy to separating the youthful from the adult offenders; perhaps an institution devoted exclusively to juvenile delinquents could succeed where others, with an older and more experienced criminal population, could not.[28]

The results, however, were not altogether satisfactory. There were charges of overcrowding. "The institution," protested the managers of the New York House of Refuge in 1858, "suffers from this crowded condition of its inmates. The discipline of the House cannot be as well maintained; the classification of the delinquents, so highly important, is impossible." The state reformatory in Massachusetts, designed to hold three hundred inmates, contained on the eve of the Civil War twice that number. Inmates' unemployment was also a common problem. The depression of 1857 kept managers in both the New York and

Massachusetts institutions from finding work for the boys and the result was a good deal of idleness. Conditions did not improve through the war years and visitors continued to complain bitterly that many inmates sat about the house doing nothing.[29]

But the most serious and disturbing objection was to the discipline of the refuge. Critics believed it was harsh and senseless, sometimes indistinguishable from the corrections in the state penitentiary. An occasional observer declared that this resemblance was logical and not altogether unfortunate. The trustees of the New York Juvenile Asylum found the penal quality of the neighboring house of refuge obvious and practical. Conceding that by 1860 the New York refuge had assumed "the character of a penal institution," they insisted that "its usefulness would not be adequately felt unless it partook of this character." But most others deplored this condition. The members of the Massachusetts Board of State Charities, a body created in 1864 to oversee state and local institutions, charged that many reformatories were prisons, and the "pupils were in all essential respects prisoners"; in the same tones, the state's newspapers expressed shock when discovering in 1860 that in the reformatory "the method of treatment . . . was, in great part, the vulgar and harsh method of convict discipline, enforced by the carrying of bludgeons and loaded weapons by some of the officers."[30] Or as one participant bluntly told his colleagues at the 1857 conference of house of refuge superintendents, in judgment on all their efforts: "The great failure in these institutions is, not that we have not admirable men to take charge of them, but that we attempt to reform boys by prison discipline. . . . We have a prison discipline down even to the boys," and this "after we had failed in reforming men." The very name of the institution was misleading, bordering on the sham. "We call it by sweet names," he declared, "Houses of Refuge, Reformatories, etc., yet it is nothing but prison discipline."[31] If anyone was ever saved it was in spite and not because of the refuge routine. The indictment was severe but not inaccurate, and no one at the session rose to protest or refute it.

The disenchantment of reformers in the Civil War period with the refuge program was also linked to a sense of its penal character. In their view not only the discipline but every detail of the routine made the refuge indistinguishable from the prison and produced machinelike creatures. The leading exponent and publicist for this critique, as well as one of the first reformers to organize a placing-out program, was Charles Loring Brace. Author of numerous tracts as well as a minor classic in its time, *The Dangerous Classes* (1872), and one of the founders of the New York Children's Aid Society, Brace claimed that the prison atmosphere of the reformatories — and for that matter of many of the orphan asylums — was a predictable phenomenon. This tone, he insisted, was endemic to a system of institutionalization, an inevitable result of rigid punishments, large dormitories, a precise schedule, and the rest. "Let any of our readers, having a little fellow given to mischief," declared Brace, "imagine him suddenly put into an 'institution' for reform, henceforth designated as 'D' of 'Class 43,' to bed at the stroke of the bell . . . treated thus altogether as a little machine, or as one of a regiment." In brief, "the longer he is in the Asylum, the less likely he is to do well in outside life."[32]

The Brace position was by no means idiosyncratic. Something of a school formed about him, so that at practically every postwar convention of administrators and philanthropists, such as the National Conference of Charities and Correction, supporters urged and defended his views. They attacked the premises of institutionalization, insisting that orphan asylums and houses of refuge imparted the wrong kind of discipline, turning out children who marched and thought like automatons, incapable of individual initiative or responsibility. As the Massachusetts Board of Charities asserted: "Congregation in numbers, order, discipline, absolute powers of officers and entire submission of soldiers, are essential to the efficiency of an army; and are supposed to be so in reformatories; but the object of armies is to make machines; in reformatories it is to make men."

This school, however, did not win many converts. Asylum managers and trustees adamantly opposed the argument, insisting that their institutions were convenient, economical, and benevolent ways to care for dependent children.[33] The idea of revamping the reformatories won more adherents — at least to the extent that officials commonly paid lip service to the notion of cottage organization. This was the least original part of the

Brace program. Most delegates to the 1857 house of refuge convention had supported some version of this design, and so did
Wines and Dwight in their survey of penal institutions; and the
members of the Massachusetts Board of State Charities in 1866
were prepared to go further, proposing that reformatories become reception centers that quickly and efficiently boarded juvenile offenders with families.[34] Nevertheless, progress on all these
fronts was slow. Not until the Progressive era did noninstitutional procedures significantly affect the treatment of dependent
children; and the refuge was not much quicker to change its
ways.

The failures of the reformatory are not difficult to understand,
and Brace and his followers were essentially correct in identifying the problem with the founding ideology. The end of the
story was apparent in its beginnings. Here, as with the penitentiary, an environmental theory of the origins of deviant behavior
so strongly emphasized the wonders of institutionalization that
administrators — and the public also — could easily confuse a
holding operation with a rehabilitative one. The incredible stress
on discipline in the original program not only provided an
excuse for a coercive system but helped to promote it. These
notions did not merely supply officers with a plausible and
respectable rationalization for their harshest actions, they practically provoked them. It would not be a simple matter to
distinguish between the corrections of a sadistic keeper intent on
terrorizing his charges and the punishment of a benevolent
superintendent trying, in the fashion of the day, to rehabilitate
them.

The character of the inmate population was another element
in the decline of the reform program. The refuge, like the
penitentiary, received a negative selection among juvenile
offenders, so that managers, in a desire to maintain authority and
prevent escapes, sometimes lost sight of other goals. The New
Hampshire House of Reformation, beginning operations in Concord in 1860, confined a small but difficult class of offenders.
Although the maximum age for entrance into the institution was
sixteen, nearly half were between fifteen and sixteen years old.
Almost one-third of the inmates would have been sent to the state
penitentiary for terms over two years had not judges used the

option of the refuge; well over half of them were guilty of theft or arson or horse-stealing, while only a minority served for lesser offenses like vagrancy or begging. Sixty percent had been arrested at least once before, and of these, one-quarter had been apprehended more than four times.[35] The problem, explained the managers, rested with the decisions of local officials. Compelled by state law to pay the costs of the town's delinquents in the house of reformation, overseers were unwilling to assume the expense except in extreme circumstances. They often neglected first and second offenders, "suffering them to pursue," in the opinion of the refuge's officers, "a course of crime until they have become so advanced in years, and so dangerous to the community, that as the last resort, they are arrested and sent to the institution." This was the reason why "the Institution is not accomplishing what was expected by its friends," why superintendents behaved more like wardens than fathers.[36]

Yet institutionalization had an appeal beyond rehabilitation. Inmates in this period were typically lower class, foreign-born, and the children of foreign-born — a group that local officials and citizens found convenient to incarcerate. Like other caretaker institutions, the refuge began as an attempt to eliminate delinquency and ended up as a practical method for getting rid of delinquents.

The overwhelming majority of reformatory children came from the bottom layers of the social structure — from families of common laborers and semiskilled workers. Officials at the Philadelphia House of Refuge reported a preponderance of unskilled and semiskilled workers among delinquents' fathers — laborers, sailors, tailors, and blacksmiths — and only rarely did a lawyer or merchant appear on their lists. The managers of the New Hampshire House of Reformation calculated in 1860 that almost half of the inmates' fathers did not have regular employment, and Massachusetts state reform school officials a few years earlier set the figure at almost one-third.[37] As the statistics of the New York House of Refuge indicated, many of the children had not even experienced a stable lower-class existence. In case after case, one or both of the parents had died or deserted the family, leaving the youngster to his own devices. Of the two hundred fifty-seven children in the institution in 1847, sixty percent were whole or part orphans with most of them missing fathers. One recent student of the New York refuge, taking a sample of five hundred inmates between 1830 and 1855, found that only twenty-seven percent of them had lived with both natural parents prior to admission. Delinquents came to the refuge from the very margins of society.[38]

The national origins of the inmates confirmed this position, because the foreign-born pervaded the institution. In 1830, a substantial minority in the New York refuge was American-born; by 1850, native Americans had shrunk to a bare twenty-eight percent while the Irish now took up slightly over half of the places.[39] Nor was this development unique to New York. By 1855, only one-third of the residents of the Philadelphia refuge came from American families, while forty-two percent had parents born in Ireland; in Massachusetts in 1850, forty percent of the inmates were Catholics, most of whom were Irish, and this in a state where the foreign-born composed nineteen percent of the population. At the Cincinnati refuge in 1852, less than half of the residents came from native families. The Irish together with the Germans accounted for the rest.[40]

Hence, the refuge resembled the penitentiary not only to some degree in routine and style but in function. Just as the community found sufficient reason to incarcerate the adult criminal without the prospect of rehabilitation, it was willing to confine the young offender without a clear expectation of reform. In both instances, inmates represented incontrovertible evidence of the irrelevance of older ideas on community cohesion and mechanisms of social control. And in both cases, incarceration, even if only temporary, seemed an expedient solution. There seemed no reason to keep these dangerous classes within the community, especially when the reformatories stood there, fully legitimate, and proper to use.

Significant differences in the experiences of the two institutions also helped to explain the continuing public support of the refuge program. The juvenile reformatory commanded far more respect among observers in this period than did the penitentiary. It escaped the full pressure of the elements that so starkly transformed the prisons into places of custody. Dwight and Wines, after surveying the nation's penal structures, unhesitantly concluded: "There is no class of institutions in our country, connected with the repression and prevention of crime, that will bear a moment's comparison with [juvenile reformatories]. . . . Almost every one of them might be pronounced a model institution of its kind."[41] No part of the penitentiary system after 1850 received such an endorsement.

Several important advantages helped the refuge to earn this praise. Control over admissions defined the category of minor very narrowly. Almost all officials set the limit at sixteen, and kept incorrigibles from overwhelming the refuges. It was relatively easy to manage a tough fifteen-year-old and still preserve a benevolent routine. And reformatory officials determined the length of inmates' stay. The standard sentence for juveniles was indeterminate, that is, managers had responsibility for the term of his minority. Able to confine or apprentice or discharge him at will, superintendents exercised a wide authority over the composition of the institution. In most cases they maintained a very high turnover. The average term of confinement in antebellum reformatories was under two years, and practically no one remained for more than four years; in the 1850's the typical detention period at the New York refuge was sixteen months; at Philadelphia, twelve months; and at Cincinnati, fourteen months.[42] The great majority of inmates, who had demonstrated some responsiveness to the institution's rules and discipline, went to farmers' households or to semiskilled artisans as apprentices. Occasionally they returned to their own families. The New York refuge allowed this option where "parents are respectable, and are able to give the boy suitable employment . . . [and] he is so far reformed as to make it safe for him to be restored to liberty." But they actually followed it in only ten percent of the cases. Delinquents who showed no signs of improvement, who could not be trusted as apprentices, shipped out on extended whaling voyages. Thus managers, able to be rid of the most troublesome cases, did not have to suffer especially disruptive and disorderly inmates for very long.[43]

The refuge, therefore, avoided the worst excesses of the prison. Superintendents were not as frightened as wardens of their inmates and were less concerned with the possibilities of large-scale violence, disruptions, and escapes. (The internal policing was often lax enough to allow the very determined delinquent to escape — a phenomenon that also had the effect of reducing the number of recalcitrants in the reformatory.) Generally, managers were able to dispense milder punishments and administer a less custodial routine than their prison counterparts. They did not so often resort to beatings, or long periods of solitary confinement, or strange and terrifying contraptions. The other side of this coin was that they could organize a school and with some success teach illiterates to read, to learn arithmetic, and even acquire the rudiments of a trade. In practice the refuge was a refinement over the penitentiary, and the public could respond favorably to it as such.

But if the reformatory was not as brutal as the prison, it was also a less important and less total mechanism of social control — and the two characteristics were not unrelated. A program of confinement, as the refuge experience demonstrated, was most successful where it was least complete, where the distance between the institution and the community was narrowest, where movement between the two was regular and frequent. In other words, the refuge enjoyed some positive achievements because it did not have to hold all types of inmates for long periods of time. This freedom, in turn, was based upon the community's willingness to accept delinquents back into its midst — in this case as apprentices — and forgo the short-run advantages of confinement. Where the pressure to incarcerate deviants was most intense, as in the case of adult criminals and, as we shall immediately see, of the chronic insane, there the institution inevitably became custodial. But where the society perceived less of a danger, as with juvenile offenders, and was less committed to a solution of unqualified and extensive confinement, there the institution was able to fulfill a greater part of its original design.

11

The Enduring Institution

The insane asylums suffered the most dramatic decline from a reform to a custodial operation. By 1870 both the reality of institutional care and the rhetoric of psychiatrists made clear that the optimism of reformers had been unfounded, that the expectation of eradicating insanity from the new world had been illusory. The hospitals' daily procedures, as reported by medical superintendents and state investigators, revealed how inadequate treatment was; at the same time, professionals and laymen began to suggest that the disease was not as susceptible to remedy as they had once believed. Nevertheless, the insane asylum, like the penitentiary, remained central to public policy. The number of patients swelled and the size of the buildings increased. Once again an institution survived long after its original promise had dissolved.

The custodial qualities of the post–1850 asylums are easily described. The first and most common element was overcrowding and in its train came the breakdown of classification systems, the demise of work therapy, and an increase in the use of mechanical restraints and harsh punishments to maintain order. Structures designed in the 1830's to serve two hundred patients often held twice that number in the 1850's. Visitors to state and municipal institutions told of seeing beds strewn about the hallways, because the space in the dormitories had long since been exhausted. Simple arithmetic indicated the degree of overcrowding. The Worcester state hospital, for example, had a total of 285 rooms for sleeping, feeding and employing about 250 inmates. Between 1845 and 1860 as many as 532 and never less than 301 patients

filled them. Conditions were little better elsewhere. In 1871, the
New Jersey asylum at Trenton squeezed 700 inmates into buildings intended to hold 500.[1]

Not surprisingly, a general disorganization of routine accompanied this change. Superintendents made little effort to keep
inmates busy. When asylum officials gathered in 1862 to hear
Edward Jarvis report on employment for the insane in England,
almost all of them confessed an inability to put their charges to
steady work. The results, in terms of the appearance and tone of
the institutions, pleased no one. "One cause of sadness felt in
visiting our hospitals," declared a Massachusetts investigatory
board in 1867, "is the sight of so many persons of each sex, in the
prime or middle of life, sitting or lying about, moping idly and
listlessly in the debilitating atmosphere of the wards, and sinking
gradually into a torpor, like that of living corpses."[2] Under
these conditions classification disappeared. Some institutions
herded the most violent into special rooms, but without great
discrimination or thoroughness. The raving and furiously insane
usually mixed freely with the more peaceable and well-behaved
patients.[3]

Discipline was harsh and mechanical. Superintendents frequently kept unruly patients in line by using straitjackets, cuffs,
sleeves, bed straps, and cribs. When asked why they did not ban
such devices, as their English counterparts did, they insisted that
American patients were more excitable and tougher to control, or
that the British relied upon the brute force of attendants. More
embarrassing were the findings of the periodic state investigations. One committee found no "gross abuses" at the New York
Bloomingdale Asylum. But it had no doubt that "some instances
of the improper treatment of patients by attendants have been
fairly proven," and was convinced that a general laxity was to
blame.[4] Many asylums of the Civil War era illustrated all too
clearly the chief characteristics of a custodial operation: patients
listlessly dawdled about, with every bizarre or pathetic symptom
of the disease to be found in one room, while officials stood ready
to adopt the most convenient tactics to keep the peace.

Medical opinion on the benefits of asylum care at this time
also began to shift to a more hostile position. Superintendents
admitted that earlier claims for curability were exaggerated,

21. The Boston Hospital for the Insane in the Civil War era. There can be no doubt of the irrelevance of moral treatment of the insane to the conduct of such an institution as this.

while a growing number of physicians insisted that the drawbacks of institutionalization far outweighed its advantages. One of the most noted retreats from an earlier optimism appeared in the writings of Pliny Earle. In the 1870's, in a widely read article, "The Curability of Insanity," he methodically demonstrated how exaggerated were the asylums' first claims to success, revealing his own disenchantment with older formulas and shocking a good many readers into agreement. Through a careful attention to the mechanics of record-keeping, Earle disclosed that the antebellum figures on the number of cures were grossly exaggerated. The annual reports had estimated percentages of recoveries not on the basis of patients admitted but on those discharged; they had counted the same patient as cured many times over, with each release after a relapse put down as another recovery. Just when Americans were learning about watered stock, they received a lesson in watered statistics.[5]

Earle also downgraded contemporary asylums. The institutions of the 1830's and 1840's had offered patients better care with a greater likelihood of recovery than existing ones. Part of the reason for this decline Earle attributed to an increased number of chronic cases among the inmates. He also insisted that insanity, "as a whole, is really becoming more and more an incurable disease. . . . All estimates based upon the assumption that either seventy-five, or seventy, or sixty, or even fifty percent of the *persons* attacked with insanity can . . . be cured and returned to the class of permanent producers . . . are necessarily false, and consequently both 'a delusion and a snare.' "[6] He, and other superintendents like Edward Jarvis, convinced of "the inadequacy of hospitals to accomplish the desired end," recommended that the milder cases of mental illness be treated at home. The awe that had once surrounded the institution evaporated. It became a place of last resort.[7]

The dissatisfaction with the asylum was still more acute among neurologists. Convinced that medical care, as distinct from environmental manipulation, was basic to the treatment of the disease, they found little to support, and much to criticize, in a program of incarceration. William Hammond, professor of nervous and mental diseases at New York's Bellevue College declared the medical profession was "fully as capable of treating cases of insanity as cases of any other disease and that in many instances sequestration is not only unnecessary but positively injurious." Hammond contended that superintendents were usually ignorant of the anatomical roots of insanity and unable to provide the proper medical or surgical therapy. He also insisted that the effect of institutional living on most patients was detrimental. "The violent rupture of social and family ties is especially injurious . . . and the association . . . with lunatics far more profoundly affected than themselves cannot but have . . . a highly pernicious influence."[8] To make matters worse, "the system of inspection of such institutions, when there is any at all, is so inefficient that the greatest abuses may spring up, and the world will be none the wiser, till some day an exposure takes place; and then it is discovered that an asylum which has been the pride of the community is in reality a hot-bed of neglect and cruelty." Hammond reversed earlier perspectives and policies. "Asylums," he concluded, "are not curative any more than are other hospitals. . . . Hospitals of all kinds are to some extent evils." The appropriate course of action, then, was obvious: "Keep . . . mentally deranged patients or friends at home so long as this can be done with safety."[9]

Neither the pessimism of superintendents like Pliny Earle nor the fundamental objections of neurologists like William Hammond, however, led to the asylums' dissolution. State legislatures continued to support them, not appropriating sufficient funds to solve the problems of overcrowding, but not withdrawing support to the point where the hospitals might have to close. One crude index of survival can be found in the number of patients annually institutionalized: there were two thousand in 1840 and four times as many in 1860. Without great pretense that they were curing the majority of inmates or living up to the standards of moral treatment, asylums remained the keystone of the public response to insanity. Here, as with the penitentiary, the institution continued operating despite the irrelevance of the original design — and the causes of the one situation also help to explain the other.

Several external considerations, often beyond the power of medical superintendents to control, undermined the progress of moral treatment. A highly inflationary cycle in the post–1850 economy raised the costs of institutional construction and maintenance. Legislatures, dismayed by the price, were reluctant to appropriate funds for new facilities despite a swelling inmate population; under these circumstances, superintendents lacked the space to classify and employ their charges, to carry out a reform program. Furthermore, when states fixed the sum that a municipality was to pay the asylum for treating its pauper insane, they often set the figure at the moment of the institution's incorporation and later failed to raise the fee to meet escalating costs. The result was that superintendents were frequently short of funds and compelled to curtail expenditures on attendants, workshop materials, and the like. The first estimates of potential inmates were also too low, since committees had difficulties predicting the number of insane. The asylums, tied to faulty blueprints, all too quickly discovered that their facilities were inadequate. Finally, the state political parties in this period began to use the institutions' positions to reward the faithful. Superintendents complained with good reason that the spoils system was lowering the quality of the staff and making their own job more difficult.[10]

But other internal elements were more fundamental to the story. The organizing concepts of the asylum disguised and even subtly encouraged a custodial operation. The exaggerated emphasis on physical structure, on the benefits inherent in institutions, promoted an attitude that automatically identified an asylum with a therapeutic milieu. Many superintendents suffered a declining number of attendants together with a swelling number of inmates without altering their belief that the setting itself was ameliorative. Then too, the founding ideology placed such a heightened value on traits like obedience, respect for authority, punctuality, and regularity that superintendents, under the press of the number and type of patients, neglected considerations of humane and gentle management. The balance of moral treatment tipped to the side of repression, not indulgence.[11]

Another important cause for the degeneration of the reform program was the superintendents' inability and unwillingness to control the composition of the asylum population. The first proponents of institutionalization had expected to treat a cross-section of types of mental illness, the depressed as well as the violent; they anticipated caring for the recent insane, persons incarcerated immediately upon the appearance of the symptoms of the disease. But the inmates did not fit with these presumptions. They were to a large extent the manic, furiously insane, and worse yet, the chronic, with no prospect of meaningful improvement. It was difficult for officials to keep them neat, and almost impossible to administer the more sophisticated components of moral treatment. Some of the responsibility for this condition rested with the preferences and decisions of legislators and overseers of the poor. Yet superintendents and trustees acceded without challenging the choices or experimenting with difficult but necessary remedial measures. The alternatives were not without their own drawbacks; to dispatch chronic cases, for example, to special institutions might not be a clear gain. But beyond issuing an occasional complaint or protesting an appropriations cutback, officials did not energetically move to alter the situation.[12]

The history of the Worcester hospital illustrated well the dynamics of the process. In 1832, one year before the institution opened, the Massachusetts legislature established a series of priorities for admission. Its primary concern was with two classes among the insane: the violent, who heretofore had sat in local jails, and the paupers, traditionally confined to the almshouse. The law gave preference for commitment to the furiously mad, directing the courts to send all lunatics now imprisoned directly to Worcester and in the future to dispatch dangerous persons there immediately. Their threat to the safety of the community was greatest, and so was their discomfort. Next the legislature empowered local officials to confine the indigent insane to the institution, but the town was to pay the cost of support. After the jails were cleaned out, the poorhouses would be emptied. Any remaining room at the asylum would serve a third class of patients, those who were neither violent nor poor.[13] These guidelines seemed reasonable. But they frustrated early plans for a curative institution.

The state regulations deprived hospital directors of control over admissions, taking away from them the power to select or screen patients.[14] Superintendents were forced to admit every lunatic that the court dispatched and were at the mercy of overseers' decisions. Inmates with the least prospect of rehabilitation and the least affinity with a system of moral treatment were the first to fill the asylum. The furiously insane were at any time a serious challenge for superintendents, but when they had already spent years chained in a miserable cell, the prospect of a cure was minimal, and the problem of control basic. Similarly, the law encouraged overseers to send their most bothersome and expensive cases to the asylum. Compelled to pay hospital charges, local officials were likely to keep the most peaceable and manageable patients in their own facilities and dispatch only the most troublesome ones. When these types of inmates dominated the institution, respectable propertied families were loathe to incarcerate a relative upon the outbreak of the disease. Thus the very act of organization was at odds with a reform program.

The first years at Worcester demonstrated the full effects of these decisions. Of the 164 inmates admitted when the institution opened in 1833, one-half came directly from the jails and almshouses, and about one-third had already been confined for periods ranging from ten to thirty-two years. Sixty-five percent of them were, in the opinions of the courts, "so furiously mad, as to be manifestly dangerous to the peace and safety of the community." The trustees, in their initial report to the legislature, complained that the patients were "a more select class than were ever before assembled together; but unfortunately for success in regard to cures, it has been a selection of the most deplorable cases in the whole community." During the "dreadful period of their dungeon-life . . . systematically subjected to almost every form of privation and suffering," the inmates' "every regular process of thought had been broken up," so that now little prospect remained for improvement. "For years to come a large proportion of its wards must be filled with incurables," concluded Worcester's officials.[15]

The condition of incoming patients did improve in the 1830's. After the initial housecleaning of the state's jails and almshouses, the number of chronic insane among Worcester's admissions dropped to just a slight majority. In the 1840's, recent cases usually outnumbered old ones among entering patients — and not coincidentally the trustees in this decade frequently expressed satisfaction with the administration of the institution. With the backlog of chronic cases already taken up, and a more curable class of patients entering the hospital, Worcester at this time came closest to fulfilling the precepts of moral treatment. Unfortunately, the improvement was temporary and by the outbreak of the Civil War, the program had again degenerated. The number of chronic swelled and the refrain of custody rather than cure once more ran through official reports.[16]

The irrelevance of the reform design to the institution in the 1850's corresponded with an increasing number of foreign-born among the inmates — a situation that encouraged native Americans to keep all but the most troublesome cases at home, and medical superintendents to forget their ambitions. Legislative policy again had unintended effects. Since the newcomers were often without legal residence, the state, quite properly, assumed the costs of their confinement. The result was that immigrants entered the Worcester hospital without charge to their family or town, while others did not. Predictably, the percentage of foreigners in the asylum increased; by 1851 over forty percent of the patients were foreign-born. Given citizens' prejudices, it became more and more a place of last resort, a dormitory for difficult and incurable cases.[17]

At the same time, Worcester officials made no systematic effort to discharge the chronic cases. As the composition of the daily asylum population revealed, the recent cases of insanity moved relatively quickly from the institution back into the community, but a number of chronic ones remained. Since officials did not weed them out, they spread through the wards. Just as the toughest class of criminals dominated the penitentiary, so the group with the least prospect for rehabilitation took over the asylum.

Because of superintendents' reluctance to release the worst patients, the percentage of incurables was higher among the Worcester hospital daily residents than it was on the annual list of all persons admitted. On December 1, 1841, for example, inmates who had been ill for less than one year at the time of entrance composed a bare thirteen percent of the patients. Another thirty-seven percent of them had histories of one to five years, and fifty percent had cases of over five years upon admission. The situation was worse by the outbreak of the Civil War. On

December 1, 1857, thirteen percent of the residents had been insane for less than one year — a percentage equivalent to that of 1841 — but now sixty-one percent had histories of over five years. And as high as this figure was, it still underestimated the total number of Worcester's incurables. For almost one-third of the patients in December 1857 had lived in the hospital for five years or more — and while many of them arrived and would be counted as recent cases, they were chronic five years later.[18] Under these conditions the reputation and the administration of the asylum suffered. Citizens, where at all possible, would not send mild and new cases there. And superintendents, facing a group that was overwhelmingly incurable, had only custodial functions to perform.

Worcester's officials faced a choice of evils. They could send the hopelessly insane back into the community, ignoring the primitive conditions that would greet them there, or they could retain them, sacrificing the goals of moral treatment. Their dilemma was especially acute, for many of their patients were manic and if returned to the towns might end up chained in a local jail. An ordinary and decently administered almshouse, superintendents believed, might adequately house the insane who had degenerated to a state of "harmless imbecility." But lacking the proper facilities and organization it could not treat unruly inmates humanely; instead, "on the first exhibition of violence, resort must be had to severe modes of confinement — to handcuffs, to chains, and to dungeons." The decision taken at Worcester was in general to keep rather than discharge many of the chronic, but it paid a very heavy price for this. Officials set off a self-sustaining cycle: the more incurables they kept, the more they received. Inevitably custody and not recovery preoccupied the asylum.[19]

Other public institutions in this period followed a similar course. An intractable patient population in the state mental hospital at Concord, New Hampshire, made the administration of a rehabilitative design practically impossible. The chronic dominated the hospital. In 1847, one-third of the admissions were hopeless cases. By virtue of asylum policy, the chronic composed an even larger percentage of the daily inmate population. A census of the patients in 1849 revealed that less than one-third and probably only one-quarter of them had, in the estimation of the superintendent, a chance of recovery. The rest were at one stage or another of a permanent illness. In fact, the longer a patient was in the institution, the more likely that his illness had been chronic upon arrival, a reversal of the optimal situation for a curative institution. The greater the investment in the patient, the more probable that he was hopelessly insane.[20]

New Hampshire's superintendents consciously chose to retain the more difficult and dangerous chronic cases; and fully aware of the consequences of their decision, they defended it vigorously. Like their colleagues at Worcester, they insisted that community facilities were so grossly inadequate that the asylum could not in good faith discharge the incurable. As early as 1844, two years after Concord's opening, trustees were already rationalizing a custodial role. "There are yet many insane persons in the State," they reported, "now confined in misery and suffering, for whom there is now no hope but in death; and to collect all these, to cure many of them, to make *all* as comfortable as their disease will admit, is the object of the Asylum."[21] By 1846 the balance fell even more clearly to the side of comfort rather than cure. Certain that "the wards of the Asylum must in a measure be filled with cases which . . . must be regarded as hopeless," superintendent Andrew McFarland openly announced: "I can but consider this class among the most interesting that we can be called to treat. Humanity owes them a debt of fearful magnitude." Insisting that every mental hospital provide a retreat for this type of patient, he deplored the idea of discharging them from the wards. "I therefore regard it as a special duty," he concluded, "to view with consideration the numerous cases of *chronic* cases which commonly seek the mere shelter of the Asylum, without any expected curative advantages from its benefits. Though no such brilliant results are obtained . . . or long list of cures exhibited, as in cases of more recent occurrence, yet the great cause of humanity is as effectually served in the former as in the latter."[22]

New Hampshire officials continued to justify the presence of the chronic in these terms.[23] By the outbreak of the Civil War, the Concord asylum had moved from an experiment in curing the insane to a place for making the last days of the chronic as pleasant as possible. Every rationalization fixed the change more securely on the institution. There was a self-fulfilling quality about these pronouncements. Prepared to let the chronic take over the wards, superintendents put themselves in charge of custodial institutions.

In the South, the nation's oldest public mental hospital, the Eastern Lunatic Asylum at Williamsburg, Virginia, adjusted to a caretaker operation. In the 1840's superintendent John Galt was deeply concerned with the prospect of chronic patients monopolizing his wards, but he would not take the vital steps necessary to avert it. He complained, not without reason, that the opening in 1841 of a second asylum in the state's western section would deprive his own of recent cases. Because the incorporating statute compelled patients to seek admission to the institution closest to their place of residence, and the bulk of the population lived in the western rather than eastern region, Galt feared that the new hospital would pick and choose among its applicants, consigning the most hopelessly insane to Williamsburg. Then, as chronic inmates lowered the quality of treatment in the older asylum, patients who had an option would no longer seek admission, thereby creating room for more chronic cases. The more vacancies in Williamsburg, the more opportunity for the new institution to send over its undesirables; the more the west dispatched its undesirables, the more vacancies in the east to serve them.[24]

Nevertheless, Galt would not sponsor or support legislation permitting both asylums to discharge immediately all their chronic patients. He feared that they would eventually end up in his institution anyway, and he rejected in principle the idea of returning incurables to jails and almshouses where, he believed, they would suffer acute maltreatment. The effects of this decision were the same in Virginia as elsewhere: the Eastern Lunatic Asylum increasingly became a custodial institution. In the mid-1840's, one-third of the inmates were newcomers to the hospital, resident for less than one year; on the other hand, more than forty percent were old-timers, having been confined for over five years. By 1850 the situation had deteriorated to the point where only twenty-six percent of the patients had been in the asylum for less than one year; in 1860, the number dropped to an incredibly low fourteen percent. The one fault with Galt's forecast was his assumption that somehow the Western Lunatic Asylum would escape this fate. As its roster of admissions in 1860 made clear, it too served the chronic almost exclusively. Only thirty percent of entering patients were recent cases, and a full quarter of them had histories of the disease for over ten years.[25]

The Kentucky lunatic asylum, founded in the mid-1820's at Lexington, had also become a custodial institution twenty years later. Almost to a man its patients were incurable. In 1845, only six percent of the 285 inmates were recent cases; the next year, the superintendent classified only one of the inmates as definitely curable. In 1848 the asylum added a new building and expanded its facilities, but managers again confessed that among their charges "very few . . . were a class of patients affording any reasonable ground of hope of recovery."[26] Lexington's officials deplored this state of affairs through the 1840's, still hoping to attract and serve the recent insane. Yet they understood that as soon as the chronic predominated among the inmates, persons with a choice — whether because the symptoms were not flagrant or financial means allowed other options — avoided committing family members. Citizens, Kentucky officials conceded, "connect with the asylum the idea of a kind of comfortable prison, in which are collected a promiscuous assemblage, and view confinement in it as somewhat allied to penal expiation."[27]

Despite this awareness, the officials could not reverse the trend. In the 1850's they made peace with it. The superintendent at Lexington conceded that "our inmates are, with few exceptions, generally made up of cases of long standing, having accumulated here for more than twenty-five years, cures among them must be comparatively few." And then, like colleagues in other institutions, he elevated the function of custodianship. Although the asylum "is little more than a retreat for incurables," it was a noble charity and a worthy enterprise. "The filthy, ragged and disgusting objects brought here, from gloomy prisons and cheerless poorhouses would scarcely be recognized after a few days residence in the asylum." Men who had once expected to cure the insane now took pride in cleaning them up.[28]

Through the 1850's and 1860's, the annual asylum reports and state investigators commonly testified to the prevalence of this attitude. But perhaps more striking was the inability of many private asylums to avoid this predicament. Their policies and management unambiguously demonstrated the links between admissions procedures, the number of chronic, and the quality of the asylum routine. A few officials, able to control intake and eager to restrict the number of incurables, maintained the principles of moral treatment. But the majority could not or would not do this. Consequently, their establishments were often little better than the grimmest state hospital.

One notable example of failure was New York's Bloomingdale Asylum. Founded by Thomas Eddy and a group of Quaker-influenced philanthropists, it was one of the first mental hospitals in the nation. In 1816, through the efforts of Eddy, the legislature agreed to give the institution ten thousand dollars annually for a period of thirty years; for its part, both to justify the grant and fulfill its own sense of purpose, Bloomingdale agreed to accept all patients regardless of financial position, with a sliding scale of fees. It charged the wealthier patients between three and four dollars per week; the cost for the pauper insane, levied on the town, was two dollars per week. But these arrangements ultimately weakened the hospital's performance. It did not regulate all its admissions, with the result that a disproportionate number of chronic cases eventually dominated its wards. In 1840 conditions were still under control and the asylum maintained an acceptable level of care. But the problem was evident. The two-dollar patients were forty percent of all inmates, the incurable were half of the admissions lists. Town officials, as a resident physician explained, had once again proved unwilling to incur the two-dollar charge, preferring, especially when the disease was recent and mild, to keep the patient more economically in a local jail or almshouse. When some of the unfortunates "became incurably imbecile or so violent that they destroy more than their board [at Bloomingdale] will amount to," when "the disease becomes incurable, the conduct disorderly and the habits depraved, the patient as a last resort is sent to the Lunatic Asylum." As overseers increasingly defined the hospital as a dumping ground and acted accordingly, Bloomingdale became a place of custody.[29]

Since officials well understood the root of the problem, they devised solutions, and various suggestions appeared. (Under one remedy, the asylum would have charged the towns a reduced rate for recent cases and a higher one for chronics, thereby encouraging them to send the most curable patients.) But the trustees never adopted such proposals, and the situation continued to deteriorate. After 1840 the condition of entering patients and the level of treatment declined precipitously. In 1847 officials reported that "the House is filled with a mass of chronic and incurable cases," so that not even a dozen of its 142 patients were capable of improvement. The trustees themselves confessed that most inmates "were listless and indifferent and wholly unoccupied." And soon Dorothea Dix, visiting the institution, described the deplorable condition: the wards were overcrowded, the physical facilities inadequate, and the supervision deficient. Bloomingdale presented the dismal picture of a custodial institution.[30]

Other private institutions were also unwilling to exclude the chronic from among their patients. In the case of the Hartford Retreat, the decision was not very costly at first, for by keeping the incurables to a minority, the asylum could administer a program of moral treatment with fair success. In the first two decades after its opening in 1824, the retreat discriminated between self-supporting and charity cases. It admitted all paying patients, regardless of the type or duration of the disease; it also accepted some of the poor insane, but under entirely different provisions. The indigent, according to its regulations, were to compose only a small fraction, less than fifteen percent of the inmates at any one time; they had to be patients with brief histories of mental illness, less than six months, and would be discharged from the asylum, regardless of progress, after six months. With these stipulations in force, between seventy and eighty percent of the retreat's admissions in this period were recent cases. Since paying patients could remain so long as they met the fees, chronic cases made up about forty percent of the daily resident population. But the number was not large enough to discourage superintendents from administering a rehabilitative routine.[31]

But soon the retreat began to neglect these guidelines, lessening its control over admissions and discharge, and concomitantly increasing its custodial function. The turning point was 1843, when the asylum requested and received a state appropriation of ten thousand dollars to enlarge its facilities for caring for the indigent insane. The arrangement was a very practical one from the legislature's perspective, obtaining more space at a minimum cost; but for the retreat it meant leaving the idea of a curative institution for the safer role of custodian. Under this new arrangement, local officials had to contribute half the cost of maintaining the pauper insane and, predictably, they dispatched the most troublesome and querulous patients. The asylum population soon reflected the effects of this policy. Patients admitted with less than one year's illness dropped to around sixty percent, while those with long, over five-year histories of the disease, increased from around five to fifteen percent. Superintendents periodically complained of an accumulation of old and incurable cases, of so many "filthy, noisy or dangerous pauper lunatics" filling the asylum.[32] But rather than attempt to alleviate the condition, they compromised the principles of moral treatment.

In 1866, the legislature decided to erect a public institution, leaving the retreat once again free to select its clientele. The asylum, however, did not restore in full strength the idea of curability. Instead, officials complacently made the asylum into a resting home for the well-to-do, taking as their creed the notion that "no class of inmates should fail to find within its walls those liberal, refined and homelike accommodations which their habits, cultivations and sympathies demanded." They now took pride in renovations that created a "beautiful homelike structure, resembling a country residence of a private gentleman more than a public building or hospital." Just as state-supported institutions boasted of keeping the paupers clean, so too private ones found satisfaction in making the rich comfortable. Custody, not cure, preoccupied them both.[33]

An exception to this general deterioration of the asylum revealed the causal connection between admission and discharge policy and the quality of the program. No institution enjoyed greater prestige and success in exemplifying the precepts of moral treatment than the Pennsylvania Hospital for the Insane, and no institution was more rigorous about its intake procedures. Under the superintendence of Thomas Kirkbride, it usually managed to maintain a high degree of order and bring patients into a regular and disciplined routine without frequently resorting to mechanical restraints. Not coincidentally, it restricted, although it did not eliminate altogether, the entrance and retention of the chronic. The asylum was in an especially good position to carry out this program. Unlike most other hospitals, Pennsylvania was not dependent upon any form of state aid to fulfill its design. Its founders had purchased large amounts of cheap farmland around the original structure, and the subsequent expansion of the city increased its value many times over. When the asylum moved to the city outskirts, the sale of this property yielded large profits.

Financial independence helped to make the asylum in a real sense private. Its trustees were prepared to make use of their prerogatives, especially in regard to admissions. They decided to accept without charge a small number of charity cases, some ten to fifteen percent of the total, but by assuming the costs of confinement, they, and not local overseers of the poor or alms-house keepers, would select the inmates. They stipulated that only the recent insane from among the indigent would be considered for admission, and these patients would be discharged after six months if they showed no sign of improvement. "Without this provision," they insisted, "the list would long since have been filled with incurable cases." Officials adopted an unrestrictive policy toward paying patients, accepting and lodging any of them regardless of the duration or the nature of the disease.[34] The overall result of Pennsylvania's frankly discriminatory policy was to curtail the number of hopeless and unruly patients. In the opening year, 1841, when many inmates moved from the original building to the new asylum, the incurables composed almost sixty percent of the residents. But as the new regulations took effect, the situation improved dramatically. By 1843, and thereafter, recent cases predominated, almost never falling below seventy percent and occasionally making up as much as eighty percent of the total.[35]

The experience of the Pennsylvania Hospital was unusual in the Civil War period, and most asylums did not emulate its procedures. A private institution could limit the number of chronic patients. Public asylums would have faced a more difficult task. But almost none of them chose to do battle. They elevated the custodial task to a point of near equality with that of a cure, justifying their new roles in principle. During the

1860's and 1870's, medical personnel, as apart from asylum administrators, suggested erecting separate institutions for incurable patients. The American Medical Association and many private practitioners and members of state boards of charity believed that institutional treatment would improve if the chronic had their own establishments, in proximity to the state hospital but quite distinct from it.[36] The medical superintendents, however, steadfastly refused to sanction this policy, resolving in 1866, and periodically thereafter, that "insane persons considered curable, and those supposed incurable, should not be provided for in separate establishments." One of the most important reasons for the Association of Medical Superintendents' refusal to merge with the A.M.A. was the difference between them on this subject. The most prominent asylum chiefs, such as Thomas Kirkbride, Isaac Ray, Pliny Earle, and John Gray, steadfastly supported this proposition and kept the ranks solidly behind it. The two classes of patients had to be housed in the same structure.[37]

The superintendents feared that separate establishments for the chronic would rapidly degenerate into places as bad or even worse than the crudest almshouse. They may also have been wary about promoting a venture that would compete with their own for limited state funds. But they were also taking for themselves a function apart from cure, so as to base their task on less speculative and difficult grounds. Officials abandoned a high risk, high success operation for a minimum risk, minimum success one. Rather than rest the future of the asylum on an ability to rehabilitate the mentally ill, they assumed the failure-proof task of caring for the chronic. To observers who criticized the institution for not effecting cures, superintendents had a ready reply: it was a place of comfort and cleanliness, whose proper comparison was with the local jails and almshouse. Against the foul and primitive conditions existing in such structures, the asylums' merits were clear.

The abandonment of the reform design did not generate very much dissension either within the association or among laymen. A caretaker operation satisfied most asylum officials and, to judge by the willingness, indeed eagerness, of legislatures and courts to use the facilities in this way, the public also. To understand the general acquiescence to this change, one final ingredient must be added, the ethnic and class composition of the inmates. To a significant degree, patients in state and even some private institutions were lower class and foreign-born, and their presence in large numbers at once negated the original postulates of the asylum movement and gave a new logic and rationale to straightforward incarceration. Under these circumstances, officials and laymen abandoned the goals of the reform program but not its means. The convenience of confining these types of patients, even without the prospect of a cure, made the institution worth supporting. Here, as in other instances, the very elements which contributed to the erosion of a rehabilitative asylum helped to insure the perpetuation of a custodial one.

In the middle decades of the nineteenth century the foreign-born occupied a disproportionate number of asylum places, comprising a far greater percentage of inmates than their numbers in the general population. The heaviest concentration occurred, as would be expected, in the eastern institutions. At Worcester, over forty percent of the inmates in the 1850's were immigrants; whereas, according to the calculations of Edward Jarvis in 1854, only forty-three percent of the poor insane who were native Americans ended up in a state institution, almost every one from among the foreigners did. At the nearby Taunton asylum, opened by the commonwealth in 1854 to relieve the crowding at Worcester, the immigrants were still more numerous; in the first ten years of the hospital's life, half of the inmates were aliens, the Irish accounting for most of them.[38] Conditions were not very different in New York. The state asylum at Utica was less filled with the foreign-born, but only because the New York City Lunatic Asylum was completely overrun with them. This change spread beyond the eastern seaboard. In 1861, for example, sixty-seven percent of the patients at Ohio's Longview Asylum were immigrants; at the state asylum in Wisconsin, the figure reached sixty percent in 1872.[39] The swelling number of foreign-born not only rendered the ideas of moral treatment obsolete, but gave a new pertinence to a custodial operation.

A similar influence resulted from the predominance of lower-class patients. By the outbreak of the Civil War, the poor insane filled the asylums. Of the 107 patients admitted to the New

Hampshire asylum in 1860, sixty-two percent were, according to their occupations prior to hospitalization, unskilled laborers. Less than ten percent of them had followed middle-class pursuits, and the rest were at best semiskilled, blacksmiths, carpenters, and the like. At Worcester, officials tabulated that the number of state paupers — those without legal settlement and personal resources — in the asylum increased sixfold between 1842 and 1851, while the total inmate population only doubled. In 1842 they composed fourteen percent of the group, in 1851, forty-five percent. The situation was the same in Rhode Island; three out of four patients in Providence's Butler Hospital received state or city aid.[40] The Central Ohio Lunatic Asylum, as of 1852, would not admit anyone except the indigent insane; by regulation it served just the lower classes. At the Kentucky asylum too, paupers monopolized the places. Tennessee asylum officials, estimating that over sixty percent of the 390 patients had little or no schooling, concluded that the institution had become the province of the lower class.[41]

Under the press of these changes, many asylum officials, state legislators, overseers of the poor, magistrates, and, by implication, middle-class taxpayers as well, adjusted to a custodial operation. Superintendents lowered their sights, legislators tightened commitment procedures, and the public read wild accounts of allegedly sane people locked up in asylums.[42] Part of this attitude undoubtedly reflected common prejudices toward the immigrant and the pauper. When confronting such patients, officials were discouraged from administering a rehabilitative routine. The foreign-born, many of them declared in the 1850's, could not be taught discipline or almost any other trait vital to mental health. George Chandler, Woodward's successor at the Worcester state hospital, articulated these views. "The want of forethought in them," he reported of the Irish, "to save their earnings for the day of sickness, the indulgence of their appetites for stimulating drinks . . . and their strong love for their native land . . . are the fruitful causes of insanity among them. As a class, we are not so successful in our treatment of them as with the native population of New England. It is difficult to obtain their confidence, for they seem to be jealous of our motives." And a similar despair also marked his attitude toward the lower classes.

"When . . . the patients, instead of being partly drawn according to the original purpose from an intelligent and educated yeomanry, are drawn mainly from a class which has no refinement, no culture, and not much civilization even — that hospital must certainly degenerate."[43] Yet the issue went deeper than personal antipathies. It was not only ethnic and class biases that put an end to the ideas of moral treatment. The predominance of the poor and the immigrant in the institutions made observers question the reform program's basic assumptions about the character of American society.

The founders of the asylum had fully expected to bring order and stability not only into the lives of the patients but, through the power of exemplification, into society as well. Retaining eighteenth-century conceptualizations of social organization, they expected to re-create, both in and out of the asylum, a well-ordered, balanced, harmonious, and ultimately homogeneous community. By the Civil War, however, these expectations appeared unrealistic and irrelevant. There seemed to be unbridgeable gaps between lower and upper classes, between Catholics and Protestants, between newcomers and natives that would not permit the reestablishment of traditional social arrangements. Reformers in the 1830's had recognized the shift away from eighteenth-century conditions; but still hoping to reverse the trend, they set about inventing new forms to restore old patterns. The passage of time, accelerating the changes that they had tried to contain, made their goals and tactics seem fanciful. This awareness in the 1850's dampened the remaining enthusiasm for the precepts of moral treatment.

But rather than lead to the dissolution of the asylum, these circumstances heightened the attractions of a custodial operation. From the perspective of the community's officials, the pauper and the immigrant insane, especially the troublesome and dangerous ones, were a convenient and practicable group to incarcerate. The program had acquired a legitimacy in the Jacksonian period which did not quickly erode. The reform ideology not only sanctioned but encouraged isolation, so that later administrators could enforce it with good conscience. And to the degree that overseers and judges used the asylum instead of a poorhouse or a jail for the insane, they could better adopt a humanitarian pose.

Few countervailing influences worked to keep the pauper and the immigrant within the community. Reformers in the 1830's had already minimized the prospect of such organizations as the family or the church contributing to the deviant's welfare, and hardly anyone in the 1850's regarded immigrant associations as worth perpetuating.

Americans after 1850 were, therefore, free to follow what they considered an opportune and practical course. Convinced that the insane (especially the manic, but almost any among them) might at a moment commit some atrocious act or, less dramatically but no less seriously, spread their madness like a contagious disease, they found institutionalization a useful method for nullifying a fundamental threat. At the least, the asylum would shield society from disorder and contamination. Medical superintendents confirmed this view by devoting unprecedented attention to the dangers that the insane posed for the general public. Isaac Ray, in his widely read volume, *Mental Hygiene,* published in 1863, warned readers that "intimate associations with persons affected with nervous infirmities . . . should be avoided by all who are endowed with a peculiarly susceptible nervous organization, whether strongly predisposed to nervous diseases, or only vividly impressed by the sight of suffering and agitation." One of the great tragedies of insanity, declared Ray, was "that the poor sufferer cannot receive the ministry of near relatives, without endangering the mental integrity of those who offer them." The conclusion was inescapable: confinement of the insane was critical "not more for their own welfare than the safety of those immediately surrounding them." In a similar spirit, superintendents like Thomas Kirkbride warned that any lunatic, no matter how mild-mannered, might suddenly strike out at those around him; and such colleagues as John Gray and John Butler recounted one horror story after another to substantiate this assertion.[44]

From this perspective, it seemed just as well that an asylum serving as a dumping ground for social undesirables should have as its common denominator a lower-class and immigrant population. These groups, many observers believed, produced many of the dangerous lunatics and the lower the social standing of the inmates, the easier for other ranks to incarcerate their most troublesome cases there. Granted, this arrangement was not without drawbacks. By giving the asylum over to the least desirable elements, the middle and upper classes restricted their own ability to utilize it. They might well hesitate to incarcerate the peaceable but still bothersome relative in such a setting. But in the end they made their choice. The returns of a custodial operation seemed worth the price.

It is a more simple task to explain why, after 1850, the almshouse maintained a firm hold over public policy while its physical plant decayed and even the pretense of rehabilitation disappeared. From the outset, reform ideology played a less important role in the origins of this institution than in the others. The almshouse began with few accomplishments and confused designs. Poorhouse officials, lacking professional credentials and not confronting an especially dangerous group of inmates, did not formulate a consistent program; concomitantly, the public perspective on the pauper was especially rigid, depicting him for the most part as fully responsible for his own misfortune. Considerations of terror and economy, of how to operate the cheapest possible deterrent, assumed a crucial significance at the very start of the almshouse operation.

State investigations of the almshouses consistently returned a dismal verdict. Visiting committees found poor-relief institutions in the Jacksonian period in bad condition. After 1850, the situation continued to deteriorate. Reports from practically every region pointed to widespread and common deficiencies. According to the first survey of the Massachusetts Board of State Charities, almost all the almshouses, whether erected in the 1830's or the 1850's, were in sorry disrepair. "In the majority of the smaller almshouses," they declared, "the furniture is very scanty and very old, the beds are ancient pieces of property which have served the turn of generations of paupers, and the rooms frequently swarm with vermin." Pennsylvania's Board of Public Charities made a similar finding. "There is the strongest evidence, in many cases," they announced in 1871, "of gross incompetency and neglect," and "great defects." The almshouses did not separate the sexes by day or night, treat the sick in different wards, or prevent the insane from wandering through the buildings. Vagrants typically

stopped at one of these establishments, spent a day or two resting, and then went on their way to the next; none of the inmates
worked, and the children received instruction only in "vice and
indolence."[45]

Provisions were no better in midwestern states. One of the first
reports of the Michigan Board of State Commissioners described
the buildings as "inconvenient, poorly constructed, and without
any adaptation to the object to which it is appropriated. They
mixed the old and the young, the sane and insane, the sick and
the well . . . diseased, dirty men, and squalid women and children." Officials charged that "idleness is substantially the rule,"
giving the institution a tone of "listless indolence"; they were
certain that "children born or reared in the poorhouse are apt to
become paupers and vagrants for life. . . . Through the poorhouse, pauperism becomes hereditary."[46] The opening account
of the Illinois Board of State Commissioners reiterated almost
every one of these complaints. The cells for the insane and idiotic
were "dark, damp, cold, and filthy beyond description," medical
care for all inmates was "wholly insufficient," the common association of sexes led to "unmentionable evils," no attempt was
made "to impart either secular or religious instruction," and the
children had "little or no hope of ever being lifted out of the
pauper class."[47]

Nevertheless, despite the almshouses' obvious failings, there
were few attacks on the *principle* of institutionalization in the
post-1850 decades. The propriety of indoor relief was beyond
question. The general public seemed prepared to accept the
various flaws that boards of charities uncovered, in part convinced that life in the almshouse was less corrupting than life in
a slum, in part worried that unless the poorhouse was considerably less comfortable than the households of the lowest classes, it
would reward and encourage idleness. Some disrepair, dirt, and
general neglect, rather than reflect badly on the charitable spirit
of the community, were qualities proper to the almshouse.

State officials did not always adopt so complacent a view, but
they too stopped far short of recommending alternate arrangements. The only debate among them was whether to continue
public outdoor relief at all. The most avid friends of noninstitutional support asked that some provision for maintaining some of

the poor at home continue. But they were on the defensive in this period, never daring to suggest the abolition of the almshouse, no matter how many scandals investigators uncovered. At most they urged coexistence, proclaiming, as did Massachusetts charity commissioner Frank Sanborn, "wherever and whenever one of these methods has been wholly given up . . . evils have followed." In contrast, opponents of outdoor relief uncompromisingly insisted that support at home would rob the poor of their initiative, demoralize and corrupt them. No one wanted to see starvation in America, declared charity worker Josephine Shaw Lowell. But one had to be careful to place "such conditions upon the giving of public relief that, presumably, people not in danger of starvation will not consent to receive it." This stipulation the almshouse met — not despite, but because, of its defects.[48]

The tenor of the debate accurately reflected community practices. The almshouse was fundamental to public relief. True, most municipalities continued to dispense fuel, groceries, or petty sums to assist families for a few winter weeks, but the bulk of funds, especially in the largest cities, went to the almshouse.[49] One major experiment in public aid involved the abolition of noninstitutional relief. Brooklyn in 1878 and Philadelphia in 1879 adopted this policy, becoming laboratories for philanthropists and charity workers. Reports on this innovation were so commendatory — extolling the system for lowering costs, prodding the unworthy poor to find jobs, and increasing the comfort of the worthy — that it is clear why proponents of outdoor relief dared not request more than coexistence.[50]

For all the almshouses' defects, officials were deeply dependent upon them. As late as 1890, a committee in Hartford, Connecticut, having completed an investigation of the state of the poor, complacently advised the council to respect precedent and follow "the wisdom of our ancestors here." In 1822, it noted, the town had wisely stipulated that "all the poor whom this town is liable to support shall be placed in the almshouse, and in case any one who applies for assistance shall refuse to receive his support there . . . such refusal shall be *prima facie* evidence that he is not in want of aid." Seventy years later, they saw no reason to adopt a new procedure.[51]

The persistence of the almshouse pointed to an intensification of the attitudes and conditions that had first sparked its growth, and several decades of experience did not change the policy. Citizens found the program more than ever relevant to their needs. No matter that the almshouse had not promoted reform or terrorized the poor into hard work; overseers, legislators, philanthropists, and the taxpaying public still defined institutionalization as proper and useful. Their suspicion of the poor had grown more acute. The distance between them and the needy increased, both in a physical and an emotional sense, and the mounting number of dependents who were also immigrants widened the gulf. Officials did not attempt to differentiate carefully among the poor, to devise and administer one solution for the aged and another for the vagrant. Convinced that all the groups at the bottom were more or less bothersome, culpable, and unfit for extended relief at home, they continued to rely upon the almshouse solution.

The population of the poorhouse itself became compelling evidence of the need for institutionalization. Its corridors were filled with first- and second-generation immigrants along with the broken, aged, diseased, crippled, and dissolute. In northeastern states especially, "immigrant" and "poor" became synonymous terms. "Why has Massachusetts so many paupers?" demanded state officials in 1857. "Because we have a larger proportion of foreigners from which they are made." Corroborating evidence was ready at hand: "Our almshouse paupers are nearly all foreigners. . . . Aliens who have landed in this State and their children . . . aliens who have landed elsewhere and their children . . . embrace five-sixths of all who become chargeable." Part of this throng, they noted, were the old and infirm who, having outlived family and friends, were not without some claim on public sympathy. "But the greater portion," they argued, "consists of more recent arrivals. . . . Lazy, ignorant, prejudiced, and to the last degree unreasonable, receiving the charity of the State as a right, rather than a favor, they are most difficult to deal with."[52] For such a collection the almshouse was almost too generous a solution.

And the foreign-born dominated the institutions of other states. Slightly over half the inmates at the Providence poorhouse in 1851 were immigrants, almost all from Ireland. The Almshouse

Department of New York City reported in 1857 that aliens filled every one of its facilities: seventy percent of the patients at the Blackwells Island hospital were foreigners, as were seventy-five percent of those at the almshouse proper and the adjoining workhouse. The Pennsylvania Board of Public Charities' survey of local almshouses in 1871 revealed that the foreign outnumbered the native-born, even omitting Philadelphia's facilities from the calculation.[53]

Midwestern states reported similar statistics. In Michigan, fifty-five percent of the paupers receiving public aid in 1871 were aliens, mostly Irish and German; that same year the Board of State Commissioners in Illinois estimated that forty-nine percent of county almshouse residents were immigrants, and a large proportion of the remainder were of foreign parentage. "The foreign elements in our population," the commissioners concluded, "is far more apt to lapse into . . . pauperism than the native." The situation was even more stark in Chicago. Of the 610 almshouse inmates, only eight percent had been born in the United States; fifty-three percent were Irish, and this in a city where the Irish were thirteen percent of the population. Finally, a national study of the treatment of paupers, conducted in 1880 by federal labor commissioner Frederick Wines, estimated that almost forty percent of all almshouse inmates were immigrants; had Wines also included the children of the foreign-born in this category, the figure would have been still higher.[54] So, although the almshouse was by no means constructed for immigrants, it thrived after 1850 on their presence.

The other common characteristic of almshouse residents was an almost absolute helplessness. By every standard they were a forlorn, dismal, and desperate group, composed of the decrepit, demented, and insane, as well as friendless widows and orphaned children. A report of a visiting committee to one of Massachusetts's state almshouses depicted a prevalent condition: "One-half . . . of the inmates are little children, too young to work, many of them too young to even attend school. Of the other half, the proportion really fit to sustain any long-continued physical exertion is literally almost infinitely small. Such a motley collection of broken-backed, lame-legged, sore-eyed, helpless and infirm human beings one would not have supposed it possible to get together in such numbers."[55] The same qualities reappeared among the five thousand New York county almshouse residents. In the 1850's, children made up one-quarter of the inmates, and the deaf, dumb, blind, and insane another quarter. For the rest we have the testimony of an 1857 visiting state committee, describing a congregation of the "ill and the maimed, the filthy and the diseased . . . young and the old, sick, lame, vicious, unfortunate, the idiot, the lunatic." Twenty years later another New York investigation succinctly concluded: "The alms-house is full of broken-down and decrepit men and women and the old chronic cases from many of the other institutions are sent there to die."[56]

Western almshouses, as one observer informed a national charities convention in 1879, were strikingly similar to their eastern counterparts, filled with the refuse of the community. "These institutions," he declared, "have thus become the mere legalized cesspools or reservoirs of reception . . . of the most repulsive features of our social defects." In a typical poorhouse, with thirty to forty inmates, "the individual details usually include two or three foundlings or orphaned children; two or three half-grown boys or girls of feeble intellect . . . two or three adults with constitutional apathy to manual labor. . . . To all these add a few adult imbeciles and cases of destitute old age, these last being chiefly of foreign birth . . . and add also, with more or less frequency, homeless boys and girls . . . also cases of friendless men and women, forced by temporary or chronic illness to seek this refuge . . . and add the almost constant sheltering of several of those social outcasts . . . who . . . constantly pollute the very atmosphere of every place they occupy." The sum was a poorhouse population composed of people from the margins of society.[57]

The middling classes found this group so convenient to incarcerate that the abuses uncovered in periodic state investigations did not discredit the system. The practical advantages of having paid functionaries assume a very difficult and unpleasant task undoubtedly encouraged many citizens to make a quick peace with grossly inadequate almshouses. Feeling little kinship with the poor in general and the immigrant in particular, they happily shifted the burden of care to an institution.[58] No associations attempted to alter public policy or sentiments, to urge that these persons be relieved at home. The unfortunates were not only without political power but without the influence of moral suasion as well. Then, too, superintendents and towns-people, with an easy conscience, concluded that such a motley collection of residents precluded a well-ordered institution. Prepared to find ill treatment, they did not interpret evidence of it as cause for changing programs. Finally, the almshouse rosters ended the hope that the institution might restore the good order and homogeneity of the community. With no ideals against which to measure the real, propertied citizens accepted custodial care, however inadequate, as appropriate, even generous, for the immigrants and desperate poor.

In these circumstances, most communities did not maintain separate almshouses and workhouses. Despite a verbal commitment to the idea that one structure ought to serve the deserving poor and another the willfully idle, most officials and towns-people complacently allowed one institution to fill both functions. The vagrant slept alongside the aged, the public nuisance next to the sick. Even the urban areas which organized a workhouse did not attempt to distinguish between the worthy and unworthy in order to raise the standard of almshouse care. In New York — where in 1857 dual institutions operated in New York City, Buffalo, Brooklyn, and Rochester — the workhouse was the province of the police, an adjunct to the local jails, and the almshouse was the responsibility of the overseers of the poor. A drunk or vagrant picked up by a constable received a three-to-four-month sentence at the workhouse; those who applied for assistance, whether intoxicated or not, usually went to the poor-house. The division was administrative, and did not point to the community's willingness to distinguish among the poor or to ameliorate conditions for some of them.[59]

Nor did the distribution of outdoor relief reflect upon or promote a more discriminating view of the dependent classes. In the 1850-to-1880 period, few municipalities bothered to investigate thoroughly the family conditions and moral status of recipients of home support. Instead, they disbursed petty sums to minimize the risk of fraud, preferring to let the deserving go hungry than to reward the idle. A few bundles of wood and a meager assortment of foodstuffs, they believed, would not be very much of a temptation to the able-bodied and taxpayers would often be spared the larger expense of institutional care. This minimal assistance did not imply that the poor were any less to blame for their troubles, only that it was cheaper to tide them over a few winter months than to support them in an almshouse. Many private charities, it is true, did attempt to differentiate among the poor, distributing outdoor relief on the basis of need and virtue. But their funds were limited, their staffs small, their investigations lengthy, and a good number of them served only their own. They relieved a member's widow or his children, so that recipients were first and foremost part of a benevolent society and only incidentally one of the poor.[60]

In sum, officials and citizens in the post-1850 period let the needy live with the specter, and suffer the reality of, the alms-house. The poor took their place alongside the criminal, the insane, and the delinquent, as fit subjects for a custodial opera-tion. The public policy was to incarcerate all these groups, and the decision would not be quickly or easily changed.

Thus, the grim end of this Jacksonian reform leaves us with a curious ambivalence toward the entire movement. We in-stinctively shudder when passing a building surviving from a nineteenth-century institution, or a building of the twentieth century designed in this tradition. Yet we look back on the dis-coverers of the asylum with pride, placing them in our pantheon of reformers. We applaud the promotors of change, and are hor-rified with the results of their efforts.

This ambivalence is not surprising: the story of the origins of the asylum is too complex to lend itself to simple moral judg-ments. How far should one hold the first proponents responsible for the later uses of their designs? Might not a Samuel Gridley Howe or a Joseph Tuckerman or a Louis Dwight, had they seen the state of asylums in the 1880's, proclaimed themselves anti-institutionalists? And indeed, were the insane not somewhat more comfortable in a custodial hospital than in a filthy cellar, prisoners better off in a crowded cell than on the gallows or whipping post, and the poor happier eating the miserable fare of the almshouse than starving on the streets?

But one cannot easily accept these arguments. The reformers' original doctrines were especially liable to abuse, their emphasis on authority, obedience, and regularity turning all too predictably into a mechanical application of discipline. And by incarcerating the deviant and dependent, and defending the step with hyperbolic rhetoric, they discouraged — really eliminated — the search for other solutions that might have been less susceptible to abuse.

One cannot help but conclude this history with an acute nervousness about all social panaceas. Proposals that promise the most grandiose consequences often legitimate the most unsatisfactory developments. And one also grows wary about taking reform programs at face value; arrangements designed for the best of motives may have disastrous results. But the difficult problem is to review these events without falling into a deep cynicism. After all, one could argue, the more there was change, the more things remained the same; in this case, they may have grown a bit worse.

Still, there are alternative perspectives that can dispel some of this gloom. The history of the discovery of the asylum is not without a relevance that may be more liberating than stifling for us. We still live with many of these institutions, accepting their presence as inevitable. Despite a personal revulsion, we think of them as always having been with us, and therefore as always to be with us. We tend to forget that they were the invention of one generation to serve very special needs, not the only possible reaction to social problems. In fact, since the Progressive era, we have been gradually escaping from institutional responses, and one can foresee the period when incarceration will be used still more rarely than it is today. In this sense the story of the origins of the asylum is liberating. We need not remain trapped in inherited answers. An awareness of the causes and implications of past choices should encourage us to a greater experimentation with our own solutions.

Notes

Index

Bibliographic Note

POVERTY AND CRIME IN THE EIGHTEENTH CENTURY

PRIMARY SOURCES

The best beginning point for an exploration of colonial attitudes is with ministers' sermons. Students are especially fortunate to have the pamphlets listed in Charles Evans's *American Bibliography* readily available in microcard editions, and without difficulty I was able to read the many charity and execution sermons of the period. One of the best examples of this material is Benjamin Colman, *The Unspeakable Gift of God: A Right Charitable and Bountiful Spirit to the Poor and Needy Members of Jesus Christ* (Boston, 1739); a more cautious note is struck by Charles Chauncy, *The Idle Poor Secluded from the Bread of Charity by Christian Law* (Boston, 1752). Typical of the execution sermons are: John Rogers, *Death the Certain Wages of Sin to the Impenitent . . . Occasioned by the Imprisonment, Condemnation, and Execution of a Young Woman who was Guilty of Murdering her Infant begotten out of Whoredom* (Boston, 1701), and *A Brief Account of the Life and Abominable Thefts of Isaac Frasier* (New Haven, Conn., 1768). Reprinted too in this series are the constitutions and descriptions of colonial voluntary associations, giving a sense, albeit limited, of the scope of private philanthropy.

Another critical source for eighteenth-century attitudes and practices is the public law. Practically every colonial code is in print; and although the volumes are not often subject-indexed, or in one cumulative edition, still, legal research in the colonial period is not tedious to conduct. The best starting points for poor laws and criminal codes are with Massachusetts, which influenced New England practices, and with Virginia, which exerted a similar influence among southern colonies. Of course, the laws must not be used alone, and English precedents were of major importance. Still, colonial laws are an excellent indicator of prevailing attitudes, concerns, and procedures.

Town and court records form an indispensable guide to colonial measures to relieve poverty and punish crime. Many town records are reprinted; countless others are available in manuscript form. They are often fragmentary, especially with regard to reports by the overseers of the poor. Nevertheless, these materials shed important light not only on the study of poor relief but on the structure and functioning of the family and the community. As I attempt to demonstrate in Chapter 2, lists of the type, amount, form, and recipients of aid open up considerations that students of colonial society have heretofore neglected. Among the published materials, the records of Virginia parishes, under the editorship of C. G. Chamberlayne, are particularly useful, and so are those of New York City and Boston. More haphazard but still valuable are the town collections of New Jersey, Rhode Island, and Connecticut.

Some manuscript records from the larger settlements have been especially useful. The Massachusetts Historical Society has an unrivaled collection of materials on poor relief in eighteenth- and nineteenth-century Boston — one that has hardly been used. Its records on the Boston almshouse are unusually complete. So too, the New York Public Library and the New York Hall of Records have manuscript holdings by overseers of the poor that afford a close look into New York practices. These records exist too in Philadelphia, and a search of county courthouses would undoubtedly bring still others to light.

Finally, the court records setting down the punishments meted out to vagrants and criminals are important to this story. Here too, the records have not been used to their fullest in illuminating personal relations and community structures in the eighteenth century. An exploration of some New York City materials, the records of the Mayor's Court, was especially rewarding.

SECONDARY SOURCES

Many volumes dealing in part with colonial relief practices appeared in the 1930's, under the editorship of Sophonisba Breckinridge of the University of Chicago. Written by social workers, rather than historians, they relied exclusively upon the statutes, making almost no effort to use other materials. The result often is a sterile and unimaginative survey of the laws, without attention to colonial society. Among the better secondary studies of poor relief in the eighteenth century are: David M. Schneider, *The History of Public Welfare in New York, 1609–1866* (Chicago, 1938) and Margaret Creech, *Three Centuries of Poor Law Administration* (Chicago, 1942) ; a valuable and more recent survey with an excellent chapter on the colonial period is James Leiby, *Charity and Corrections in New Jersey* (New Brunswick, N.J., 1967). A non-interpretive but detailed account of the colonial poor laws is Stefan Riesenfeld, "The Formative Era of American Assistance Law," *California Law Review*, 43 (1955), 175–223.

Books treating colonial crime are not only in short supply but of low quality. They tend to be descriptive, with little effort at analysis as to why the colonists adopted particular forms of punishment. One exception, however, that stands as a monument to diligence and thoughtfulness in the use of legal sources is Julius Goebel Jr., and T. Raymond Naughton, *Law Enforcement in Colonial New York* (New York, 1944). It is only to be regretted that the volume has not spurred others to similar work. Also useful was a brief but interesting examination of religious views and court actions in Massachusetts before and after the Revolution: William E. Nelson, "Emerging Notions of Modern Criminal Law in the Revolutionary Era: An Historical Perspective," *New York University Law Review*, 42 (1967), 450–582. Our knowledge of legal and social history would increase if more studies of this sort were conducted.

The student of deviancy and dependency in the colonies will want to read closely the new community histories that unfortunately are limited to date to New England. Charles Grant on Kent, Connecticut, Richard Bushman on Connecticut towns, Kenneth Lockridge on Dedham, Massachusetts, Michael Zuckerman on New England towns, and Philip Grevin on Andover, Massachusetts, bring fresh insights to colonial society. Other volumes that assist our understanding of the poor and the criminal include: Sydney V. James, *A People Among People: Quaker Benevolence in Eighteenth-Century America* (Cambridge, Mass., 1963); Richard Shryock, *Medicine and Society in America, 1660–1860* (New York, 1960); Edmund S. Morgan, *The Puritan Family: Essays on Religion and Domestic Relations in Seventeenth Century New England* (Boston, 1944, rev. ed., New York, 1966); and John Demos, *A Little Commonwealth: Family Life in Plymouth Colony* (New York, 1970).

It is unfortunate that we do not have any studies of private philanthropy in the colonies comparable to the work of W. K. Jordan for England; nor do we know very much about geographical mobility, or the social origins and circumstances that brought men in the eighteenth century to crime, or for that matter, to poverty. One effort at interpretation that I do not believe succeeded is Kai T. Erikson, *Wayward Puritans: A Study in the Sociology of Deviance* (New York, 1966). While attention to theory is important, one cannot neglect research in the kinds of materials described above.

THE ORIGINS OF THE PENITENTIARY

PRIMARY SOURCES

The concepts of deviant behavior, the proposed remedies, and the operations of the penitentiary in the pre–Civil War era emerge clearly in the rich pamphlet literature written by the men who led the movement and interested observers. In the post-Revolution period, the statements of such men as Caleb Lownes, William Bradford, and Thomas Eddy make clear the expectations that Americans first held about legal reform. The ideas on crime and the reality of the penitentiary in the Jacksonian decades are well presented in the essays of Samuel Gridley Howe, Francis Lieber, Edward Livingston, Francis Gray, Matthew Carey, Francis Wayland, Francis Packard, and George W. Smith. Many foreign visitors described one or another state prison, but in most instances they were not perceptive commentators. One notable exception, fully deserving its fame, is Gustave de Beaumont and Alexis de Tocqueville, *On the Penitentiary System in the United States* (reprinted, Carbondale Illinois, 1964). It remains an excellent starting point for understanding the discovery of the penitentiary.

Another major source is the reports of reform societies. One of the earliest and most important of these organizations was the Philadelphia Society for Alleviating the Miseries of Public Prisons, issuing such publication as, *Extracts and Remarks on the Subject of Punishment and Reformation of Criminals* (Philadelpnia, 1790). Their manuscript records, together with the *Minutes of the Proceedings of the Committee on the Eastern Penitentiary,* are at the Pennsylvania Prison Society, in Philadelphia. In the later period, the two most influential groups were the New York Prison Association and the Boston Prison Discipline Society. Their annual reports illuminate both the expectations that reformers had of the penitentiary, and the day-to-day functioning of the institutions in all parts of the country.

Several types of state documents clarify the history of the penitentiary. When first appropriating funds for the construction of a state prison, many legislatures dispatched a committee to investigate conditions elsewhere. For one example of an investigatory committee's report, see R. Sullivan et al., *Report of the [Massachusetts] Committee, "To Inquire into the Mode of Governing the Penitentiary of Pennsylvania"* (Boston, 1817). States also conducted periodic investigations of their own institutions, usually in response to charges of brutality or corruption. Although the reports are difficult to use, since political pressures often prompted unfair criticism or unwarranted exoneration, they offer invaluable glimpses of life behind prison walls. Typical of these documents is *The Report of the Committee . . . on the Connecticut State Prison* (Hartford, 1833), and the rejoinder, *Minutes of the Testimony Taken Before . . . [the] Committee . . . on the Connecticut State Prison* (Hartford, 1834).

The most important official documents are, of course, the penitentiaries' annual reports to their state legislature. Here one finds descriptions of the structure, reprints of rules and regulations, accounts of the daily routine, biographical data on the convicts, from birthplace and degree of literacy to crime committed and length of sentence, as well as financial details. These are public statements, attempting to put the institution in the best possible light, but the information they include from the inspectors, the wardens, the agents, and the chaplains, is extensive. In the course of this study I examined the reports of most of the state prisons in this period; the Library of Congress and the New York Public Library were the most convenient places for locating these materials.

Of some use, too, are the memoirs of prison officials and their accounts of the institution. Two good examples are Gershom Powers, *A Brief Account of the Construction, Management and Discipline . . . of the New York State Prison at Auburn* (Auburn, N.Y., 1826), and James B. Finley, *Memorials of Prison Life* (Cincinnati, Ohio, 1851). In general, I did not find newspaper accounts especially rewarding; they tend to repeat information available in the annual reports or state investigations. Had my interest, however, been in the political battles that sprang up around the institutions' construction and administration, this source would have been more important.

SECONDARY SOURCES

Of all the institutions discussed in this book, the prisons have received the most attention from historians. Most of the studies tend to be long on facts and short on interpretation, but they do provide an important starting point for analysis. The most detailed account of this period is Orlando F. Lewis, *The Development of American Prisons and Prison Customs, 1776–1845* (Albany, N.Y., 1922); a broader survey is Blake McKelvey, *American Prisons: A Study in American Social History prior to 1915* (Chicago, 1936). The Pennsylvania system has been explored by Negley D. Teeters and John D. Shearer, *The Prison at Philadelphia, Cherry Hill: The Separate System of Prison Discipline, 1829–1913* (New York, 1957). Background is provided by Negley D. Teeters, *The Cradle of the Penitentiary: The Walnut Street Jail at Philadelphia, 1773–1835* (Philadelphia, 1935). A New York study which goes beyond administrative details is W. David Lewis, *From Newgate to Dannemora: The Rise of the Penitentiary in New York, 1796–1848* (Ithaca, N.Y., 1965). Some of the pioneering efforts of Harry E. Barnes in this field also remain of interest.

One of the few books to treat the subject of deviance is David Brion Davis, *Homicide in American Fiction, 1798–1860* (Ithaca, N.Y., 1957). And Roger Lane, in his study of the Boston police and rates of crime in nineteenth-century Massachusetts, has cast new light on this subject. But the field remains to a large degree unexplored. What we need most are studies that will relate the data to be gathered from prison records and from such other sources as court and police records to the general problems of crime, social control, and social organization.

Two works by sociologists helped me to organize my approach to the historical materials: Richard A. Cloward and Lloyd E. Ohlin, *Delinquency and Opportunity* (New York, 1960); Gresham M. Sykes, *The Society of Captives* (Princeton, 1958). These volumes provide excellent introductions to contemporary theories on deviance and on institutional structures.

CREATING THE NEW WORLD OF THE INSANE

PRIMARY SOURCES

Medical superintendents were a very literate group, turning out a large number of pamphlets and books on insanity and the asylum. One entry point to this material is the *American Journal of Insanity*, published by the Association of Medical Superintendents, organized in 1844. The *Journal*'s pages are filled with discussions of the origins of the disease, classification, European ideas and programs, and the work of the asylums. Among the writings of medical superintendents, I find the studies of Isaac Ray useful, especially *A Treatise on the Medical Jurisprudence of Insanity* (Boston, 1853, 3rd ed., reprinted by the John Harvard Library, Cambridge, Mass., 1960), and *Mental Hygiene* (Boston, 1863). So too, the work of Edward Jarvis is important; see such essays as *The Causes of Insanity* (Boston, 1851), and *Address Delivered at the Laying of the Corner Stone of the Insane Hospital at Northampton* (Northampton, Mass., 1856). For the asylum itself, one must begin with Thomas Kirkbride, *On the Construction, Organization, and General Arrangements of Hospitals for the Insane, with some Remarks on Insanity and its Treatment* (Philadelphia, 1880, 2nd ed.). I also relied upon the writings of Pliny Earle, Samuel Woodward, Amariah Brigham, and William Sweetser, among others.

The annual reports of the insane asylums are a crucial body of information. Even more frequently than wardens, medical superintendents used the occasion of the report to express views on the causes of insanity and the prospects for a cure; they also supplied detailed descriptions of the daily routine, biographical information on the patients, and the results of treatment. Although all are important, the reports of the Pennsylvania Hospital, the New York asylum at Utica, the Connecticut Retreat, Butler Hospital in Providence, and the New Hampshire asylum at Concord are particularly illuminating. Given the scope of this study, I did not often examine original manuscript materials of the institutions; the annual reports are full and accurate enough to obviate that. I did use the manuscript records of the Eastern Lunatic Asylum at Williamsburg, Virginia; while helpful, they confirmed how little distance separated the public and private pronouncements of superintendents.

State investigations supplement this material. Typical is: Philadelphia Citizens Committee on an Asylum for the Insane Poor, *An Appeal to the People of Pennsylvania* (Philadelphia, 1838); so is the *Report of the Committee on the Insane Poor in Connecticut* (New Haven, Conn., 1838). One of the most thorough and accurate compendiums of information on the pre–Civil War asylums may be found in the New York Lunatic Asylum, "Annual Report," *N.Y. Senate Docs.,* 1842, Vol. I, no. 20, Appendix A, 47 ff.

Of especial importance to the historian are the memorials of Dorothea Dix to many of the legislatures in this period. Dix traveled from state to state, investigating the condition of the insane poor and then reporting her findings and recommendations in the form of a petition to the state. These accounts not only illuminate the fate of the insane poor, but capture the spirit and ideology of the movement, and also testify to the remarkable energy and dedication of their author.

SECONDARY SOURCES

The history of the asylum and ideas on insanity have only recently begun to capture attention. A few older works, however, are useful references. Brief histories of all the nineteenth-century asylums can be found in Henry M. Hurd, *The Institutional Care of the Insane in the United States and Canada* (Baltimore, 1916, 4 vols.). A general survey is Albert Deutsch, *The Mentally Ill in America: A History of their Care and Treatment* (New York, 1949, 2nd ed.) .

A thorough account of ideas on insanity may be found in the recent study by Norman Dain, *Concepts of Insanity in the United States, 1789–1865* (New Brunswick, N.J., 1964) . The bibliography in this volume is exceptionally complete. Moral treatment has now begun to interest psychiatrists; a good summary is J. Sanbourne Bockoven, "Moral Treatment in American Psychiatry," *Journal of Nervous and Mental Disease*, 124 (1956) , 183–194, 299–309. Less successful in concept and research is Ruth Caplan, *Psychiatry and the Community in Nineteenth-Century America* (New York, 1969) . Other broad investigations include the American Psychiatric Association, *One Hundred Years of American Psychiatry* (J. K. Hall *et al.*, eds., New York, 1944) , and Mark D. Altschule, *Roots of Modern Psychiatry: Essays in the History of Psychiatry* (New York, 1957) .

There are very few histories of state or private mental hospitals. One study, with much detail, is William L. Russell, *The New York Hospital: A History of the Psychiatric Service, 1771–1936* (New York, 1945) . A more interesting and interpretive account is Gerald N. Grob, *The State and the Mentally Ill: A History of the Worcester State Hospital in Massachusetts, 1830–1920* (Chapel Hill, N.C., 1966) . We stand in clear need of research that will carefully and imaginatively relate the histories of these structures to the general society. There are also few biographies of the leading figures in this story. Helen E. Marshall, *Dorothea L. Dix: Forgotten Samaritan* (Chapel Hill, N.C., 1937) , is available but Dix deserves a fresh look.

SOLVING THE PARADOX OF POVERTY

PRIMARY SOURCES

Although the literature on poverty is not as rich as on crime and insanity, reformers did devote unprecedented attention to defining its causes and proposing remedies. The work of Theodore Sedgwick (*Public and Private Economy, Part First* [Boston, 1836]) , Walter Channing (*An Address on the Prevention of Pauperism* [Boston, 1843]) , and John T. Sargent (*An Address of Pauperism* [New York, 1846]) , suggests the nature of the response. So do the essays of Matthew Carey. The writings of socially conscious ministers not only shows how sharp was the break with eighteenth-century attitudes, but brings the new ideas into focus. The best introduction is Joseph Tuckerman, *On the Elevation of the*

Poor (E. E. Hale, ed., Boston, 1874). Of interest too is the work of George B. Arnold as Minister at Large in New York, and such sermons as Charles Burroughs, *A Discourse Delivered in the Chapel of the New Almshouse, in Portsmouth, New Hampshire* (Portsmouth, New Hampshire, 1835), and John S. Stone, *Considerations on the Care of the Poor in Large Cities* (Boston, 1838).

The annual reports of reform societies present nineteenth-century views and programs in rich detail. Two New York organizations were particularly important in this period, and I made frequent use of their statements. The earlier one was the New York Society for the Prevention of Pauperism, whose first annual report was issued in 1819. The later and equally influential one was the New York Association for Improving the Condition of the Poor, organized in 1843.

Annual reports of the almshouses are in comparatively short supply for the pre–Civil War decades. For reasons that the text makes clear, many almshouse keepers were not eager or equipped to make such reports, and officials did not insist on formal accounts of their operations. The records that are available are usually from institutions in large urban centers or under the direct supervision of the state; hence, I relied heavily upon the experiences of the New York, Boston, and Philadelphia alsmhouses. The other parts of the story, however, do emerge from other sources. As early as the 1830's, some eastern states compiled statistics on county and town almshouses, setting down the number of almshouses, persons receiving full- and part-time relief, the size of expenditures, and the goods produced by the inmates. The Massachusetts story is especially complete; see, for example, Commissioners of the [Massachusetts] Pauper Laws, *Report of 1833* (Boston, 1835), and Secretary of the Commonwealth, *Abstract of Returns of the Overseers of the Poor in Massachusetts, 1833–1855* (Boston, 1855).

The three path-forging state reports in the 1820's recommending the almshouse solution are of vital interest to the historian; not only do they clarify the thinking that went into program, but they offer an exceptionally thorough survey of prevailing attitudes and conditions. The report of John Yates appears in the *New York Senate Journal*, 1824, 95–108 and Appendix A; it is reprinted in the New York State Board of Charities, *Annual Report for 1900* (Albany, 1901), I, 937–1145; the Quincy report is bound separately as the Massachusetts General Court Committee on Pauper Laws, *Report of the Committee* (n.p., 1821). For Philadelphia see, Board of Guardians of the Poor of the City and Districts of Philadelphia, *Report of the Committee to Visit the Cities of Baltimore, New York, Providence, Boston, and Salem* (Philadelphia, 1827). Yates and Quincy, especially, solicited opinions from countless local officials, tabulated expenditures, and reprinted the settlement laws then in effect; their reports offer a generally complete picture of poor relief in their states.

State investigations that I found particularly useful include Thomas R. Hazard, *Report on the Poor and Insane in Rhode-Island* (Providence, R.I., 1851), and New York Select Committee, "Report of Charitable Institutions Supported by the State, and all City and County Poor and Work Houses and Jails," *N.Y. Senate Docs.*, I, no. 8, 1857. Valuable too are such documents as *Rules and Regulations for the Internal Government of the [Philadelphia] Almshouse and House of Employment* (Philadelphia, 1822). Although manuscript material on nineteenth-century almshouses is in short supply, the fragmentary records of the nineteenth-century Boston institution at the Massachusetts Historical Society are of use. The memorials of Dorothea Dix, while focusing primarily upon the insane, are also a storehouse of information about the poor.

SECONDARY SOURCES

The issue of poverty in early America is only now beginning to interest historians, so the available literature is not very extensive. A series of volumes on the poor laws in this period under the direction of Sophonisba Breckinridge have the fault I noted earlier — an excessive reliance upon laws. Breckinridge writes on Illinois; Aileen Kennedy on Ohio; Isabel Bruce on Michigan; Alice Shaffer and Mary Keefer on Indiana. One of the few historians to delve into this field is Bernard J. Klebaner; see especially, "Poverty and its Relief in American Thought, 1815–1861," *Social Service Review*, 38 (1964), 382–399, and, "The Home Relief Controversy in Philadelphia, 1782–1861," *Pennsylvania Magazine of History and Biography*, 78 (1954), 413–423. A general account is also to be found in Blanche Coll, *Perspectives in Public Welfare* (Washington, D.C., 1969). An interesting study of changing reactions to depression conditions is Leah H. Feder, *Unemployment Relief in Periods of Depression* (New York, 1936). One of the few people in this area to receive biographical treatment is Joseph Tuckerman, in a study by Daniel McColgan in 1940. We have no history of the almshouse in this country, and only a few scattered articles on the institution in one city or another.

A promise of the new work underway may be found in Stephan Thernstrom and Richard Sennett, eds., *Nineteenth Century Cities* (New Haven, 1969). The focus on social mobility will undoubtedly soon broaden to attempts to reconstruct the lives of the poor and to analyze further public attitudes toward them. In the post-1850 period, studies of the immigrant illuminate part of this field. But the earlier urban poverty and, incidentally, the later rural poverty, remain generally unexplored.

CHILD CARE

PRIMARY SOURCES

The pamphlet literature on deviant and dependent children in Jacksonian America is very thin, but the gap is more than filled by the annual reports of innumerable child-saving institutions. With an occasional exception, this literature has been untouched by social historians. The reports of the Boston Female Asylum, the Boston Asylum and Farm School, the Boston Children's Friend Society, the New York Juvenile Asylum, the orphan asylum at the New York almshouse, the Philadelphia Orphan Society, all reveal the character of child-care institutions and, equally important, the popular premises of the role of children and families, and the causes of poverty and delinquency. This is true of the reports of the Baltimore Home of the Friendless, the District of Columbia Orphan Asylum, the Cincinnati Orphan Asylum, and the Orphan House of Charleston, South Carolina. These subjects are also brought into clear focus in the reports of such institutions for deviant children as the New York House of Refuge, the Philadelphia House of Refuge, and the Providence Reform School.

A valuable document summarizing both the ideas of house of refuge superintendents and conditions in these institutions is, Managers and Superintendents of Houses of Refuge and Schools of Reform, *Proceedings of the First Convention* (New York, 1857). The manuscript records of the New York House of Refuge at Syracuse University Library are among the most useful collection of documents that I examined for this book. Materials there include case histories, the daily routine, administrative regulations, and the application of discipline.

The fit between the ideas of asylum superintendents and the advice in child-rearing volumes can be established by looking at the tracts of such authors as Catherine Beecher, Lydia Child, Lydia Sigourney, Herman Humphrey, Jacob Abbott, and Artemas Muzzey.

SECONDARY SOURCES

Two older volumes that treat this material, albeit sketchily, are Homer Folks, *The Care of Destitute, Neglected, and Delinquent Children* (Albany, 1900), and Henry Thurston, *The Dependent Child*

(New York, 1930). The recent study by Robert S. Pickett, *House of Refuge: Origins of Juvenile Reform in New York State, 1815–1857* (Syracuse, N.Y., 1969), is the first book-length account we have of a house of refuge, but it is far too narrow in conception to serve as a model for other studies. An interesting account of educational reform that devotes a chapter to the state reformatory in Massachusetts is Michael Katz, *The Irony of Early School Reform* (Cambridge, Mass., 1968).

Advice-giving literature has been surveyed by some historians, but the results invariably are limited, focusing on attitudes, with little or no attention to realities of family life. For one example see Anne L. Kuhn, *The Mother's Role in Childhood Education: New England Concepts, 1830–1860* (New Haven, Conn., 1947). For another, Bernard Wishy, *The Child and the Republic: The Dawn of Modern American Child Nurture* (Philadelphia, 1968). See too Charles Strickland, "A Transcendalist Father: The Child-Rearing Practices of Bronson Alcott," *Perspectives in American History*, 3 (1969), 5-73. A valuable collection of documents on children in this period is Robert Bremner, ed., *Children and Youth in America* (Cambridge, Mass., 1970), Vol. I, 1600–1865.

POST-1850 DEVELOPMENTS

In addition to the materials already discussed, the changes in attitudes toward and treatment of deviants and dependents in the middle decades of the nineteenth century are lucidly discussed and described in the annual reports of the National Conference of Charities and Correction. Beginning in 1873, the conference brought together those concerned with poverty, crime, insanity, and delinquency; the papers presented and the ensuing comments are reprinted in the yearly volumes. Another major source for developments in this period is the annual reports of the various state boards of charities. The Massachusetts board, for example, began investigating conditions in the state and local institutions in 1864; the Pennsylvania Board of Public Charities began operations in 1871, the same year as the Illinois Board of State Commissioners. The thoroughness of these reports stand in marked contrast to earlier ones, easing the task of the historian.

A few special studies deserve mention. The fate of the penitentiary innovation is described fully in E. C. Wines and Theodore W. Dwight, *Report on the Prisons and Reformatories of the United States and Canada* (Albany, N.Y., 1867). See also, New York State Prison Commission, *Investigations of the State Prisons and Report Thereon* (New

York, 1876). The writings of Franklin B. Sanborn are also important, not only to the prison story but to the almshouse history as well. The best starting point for the new attitudes on the insane is Pliny Earle, *The Curability of Insanity* (Philadelphia, 1887). The work of William Hammond (especially, *The Non-Asylum Treatment of the Insane* [New York, 1879]), E. C. Seguin and the National Association for the Protection of the Insane and the Prevention of Insanity (*Papers and Proceedings* [New York, 1882]), also illustrate the dimensions of the changes. Excellent too is Frederick Wines, *Report on the Defective, Dependent, and Delinquent Classes of the Population of the United States* (Washington, D.C., 1888). In the field of child care, one must begin with Charles Loring Brace; see the annual reports of the New York Children's Aid Society, and his account, *The Dangerous Classes of New York, and Twenty Years' Work Among Them* (New York, 1872).

GENERAL SECONDARY SOURCES

Some of the volumes not already mentioned that were particularly helpful in understanding the Jacksonian period include Marvin Meyers, *The Jacksonian Persuasion* (Stanford, 1957); Neil Harris, *The Artist in American Society* (New York, 1966); R. W. B. Lewis, *The American Adam* (Chicago, 1955); and Douglas North, *The Economic Growth of the United States, 1790–1860* (New York, 1961). A broad survey that takes the nature of the reform response for granted is Alice F. Tyler, *Freedom's Ferment: Phases of American Social History to 1860* (Minneapolis, Minn., 1944). For the religious element in reform, I began with Timothy L. Smith, *Revivalism and Social Reform* (Nashville, Tenn., 1957), and John L. Thomas, "Romantic Reform in America, 1815–1865," *American Quarterly*, 17 (1965), 656–681. One of the best biographies of a reformer in this period is Harold Schwartz, *Samuel Gridley Howe: Social Reformer, 1801–1876* (Cambridge, Mass., 1956). Robert Bremner, *From the Depths: The Discovery of Poverty in the United States* (New York, 1956), is a useful introduction to developments in the Progressive era.

For the European part of the story, it was valuable to read Michel Foucault, *Madness and Civilization: A History of Insanity in the Age of Reason* (New York, 1965) — despite the reservations I express in the introduction. So too, David Owen, *English Philanthropy, 1660–1960* (Cambridge, Mass., 1964); Max Grünhut, *Penal Reform, A Comparative Study* (Oxford, 1948); and Kathleen Jones, *Lunacy, Law, and Con-*

science, 1744–1845 (London, 1955), clarified nineteenth-century English practices.

Any student of institutions would profit by reading Erving Goffman, *Asylums* (New York, 1962). A recent bibliographic guide that serves social history well is Gerald N. Grob, *American Social History Before 1860* (New York, 1970).

Notes

1. For an explication of this link, and to bring the story of institution-alization and deinstitutionalization into our own times, see David J. Rothman and Sheila M. Rothman, *The Willowbrook Wars* (New York, 1984).
2. Michael Ignatieff, *A Just Measure of Pain: The Penitentiary in the Industrial Revolution, 1750–1850* (New York, 1978), xii.
3. Andrew T. Scull, *Museums of Madness: The Social Organization of Insanity in Nineteenth-Century England* (New York, 1979), 17.
4. Rothman, *The Discovery of the Asylum: Social Order and Disorder in the New Republic* (Boston, 1971), xiv–xv.
5. Andre Zysberg, "Galley Rowers in the Mid-Eighteenth Century," in Robert Forster and Orest Ranum, eds., *Deviants and the Abandoned in French Society* (Baltimore, 1978), 83–110. See also, in that same volume, Nicole Castan, "Summary Justice," 111–138.
6. Pieter Spierenburg, *The Spectacle of Suffering* (Cambridge, England, 1984), 82–83. See also 213–222 for his estimates on the frequency of capital punishment.
7. Michel Foucault, *Discipline and Punish: The Birth of the Prison* (New York, 1977), 3–6: Spierenburg, *Spectacle of Suffering*, 73–74.
8. Spierenburg, *Spectacle of Suffering*, 98.
9. Ignatieff, *Just Measure of Pain*, 88–89; Foucault, *Discipline and Punish*, 63–69: Spierenburg, *Spectacle of Suffering*, 94, 101–104, 108–109, 197.
10. Spierenburg, *Spectacle of Suffering*, 93, and also 98, 183, 190, 197.
11. The best entry point to this literature is Norbert Elias, *The Civilizing Process: The History of Manners*, originally published (in Basel) in 1939, and then translated and issued by Urizen Books, New York, in 1978. Probably as the result of feminist studies, a growing number of historians have been concerned with the history of the body, particularly with cultural definitions of gender differences. See, for example, Ludmilla Jordanova, *Sexual Visions: Images of Gender in Science and Medicine Between the Eighteenth and Twentieth Centuries* (Madison, Wisc., 1989); and Dorinda Outram, *The Body and the French Revolution* (New Haven, Conn., 1989), especially ch. 2.
12. For an elaboration of this view within the English experience, see J. M. Beattie, *Crime and the Courts in England, 1660–1800*

(Oxford, 1986); a very thoughtful survey on the new literature can be found in Joanna Innes and John Styles, "The Crime Wave: Recent Writing on Crime and Criminal Justice in Eighteenth-Century England," *Journal of British Studies* 25 (1986), 380–435.

13. Countess Harcourt, as quoted in William F. Bynum, "Rationales for Therapy in British Psychiatry, 1780–1835," *Medical History* 18 (1974), 319.

14. Michael Ignatieff, "State, Civil Society and Total Institutions," in Stanley Cohen and Andrew Scull, eds., *Social Control and the State* (New York, 1983), 90.

15. Ibid., 80–81.

16. Robin Evans, *Fabrication of Virtue: English Prison Architecture, 1750– 1840* (Cambridge, England, 1982), 19.

17. Daniel Defoe, *Moll Flanders* (Penguin edition, 1978), 100–101.

18. Evans, *Fabrication of Virtue*, ch. 1.

19. Among the avid defenders is Gerald Grob, *Mental Institutions in America* (New York, 1973). He has insisted that a less adulatory response to the rise of the asylum is designed to promote political ends, but to declare that an analysis of the limits of the asylum is ideology and a dogged defense of it is history is lame and barely in need of refutation.

20. For reasons of space and coherence, the discussion that follows concentrates on the prison and mental hospital and will not explore the new scholarship on reformatories, almshouses, and women's prisons. For the most part, the issues raised in this literature focus conceptually on the issues we will be exploring in the context of the prison and mental hospital. Note, too, that the emergence of a different incarcerative system for women occurs only after the Civil War. See, for example, the useful survey by Nicole Hahn Rafter, "Prisons for Women, 1790–1980," in Michael Tonry and Norval Morris, eds., *Crime and Justice: An Annual Review of Research* 5 (1983), 129–181. For an entry point into the new literature on reformatories, see Steven Schlossman, *Love and the American Delinquent* (Chicago, 1977), and John Sutton's book *Stubborn Children*, cited below. The almshouse has probably attracted the least attention from historians, but see Michael Katz, *Poverty and Policy in American History* (New York, 1983).

21. Robert Castel, *The Regulation of Madness: The Origins of Incarceration in France* (Berkeley, Calif., 1988), 74.

22. John Bender, *Imagining the Prison: Fiction and the Architecture of Mind in Eighteenth-Century England* (Chicago, 1987), 1, 3, 11, 34; see especially chs. 2–3. See also W. B. Carmochan, *Confinement and Flight* (Berkeley, Calif., 1977).

23. Nancy Tomes, *A Generous Confidence: Thomas Story Kirkbride and the Art of Asylum-Keeping, 1840–1883* (Cambridge, England, 1984), 14. Tomes borrows the term "design dilemma" from architectural his-

torian Dolores Hayden and links it as well to the term "moral architecture," which will be used here.

24. Evans, *Fabrication of Virtue*, 80.
25. Ignatieff, "Recent Social Histories," 88–89, and *Just Measure of Pain*, 154–156.
26. Ignatieff, "State, Civil Society and Total Institutions," 88–92.
27. Scull, *Museums of Madness*, 32, 47, 56–57, 72.
28. Castel, *Regulation of Madness*, 14.
29. Ibid., 168.
30. Ibid., 26–37, 73. See the perceptive discussion of Castel's argument (and of Scull and my own work as well) by David Ingleby, "Mental Health and Social Order," in Cohen and Scull, eds., *Social Control and the State*, 145–160. Readers will also find relevant Roy Porter, *Mind Forg'd Manacles* (London, 1987).
31. Ignatieff, "State, Civil Society and Total Institutions," 93.
32. John R. Sutton, *Stubborn Children: Controlling Delinquency in the United States, 1640–1981* (Berkeley, Calif., 1988), ch. 3, especially 119.
33. For an elaborate and persuasive analysis of the links between religion and social order, see also Paul Boyer, *Urban Masses and Moral Order in America, 1820–1920* (Cambridge, Mass., 1978), chs. 1–4.
34. See the essay by Andrew Scull, reprinted as ch. 2 of his book, *Social Order/Mental Disorder*, "Humanitarianism or Control?"
35. For a fuller explication of this position see Rothman, "Social Control: The Uses and Abuses of Concept in the History of Incarceration," *Rice University Studies* 67 (1981), 9–20, and reprinted in Cohen and Scull, eds., *Social Control and the State*.
36. Ignatieff, "State, Civil Society and Total Institutions," 92–95.
37. Rothman, *Conscience and Convenience: The Asylum and Its Alternatives in Progressive America* (Boston, 1980).
38. Louis Chevalier, *Laboring and Dangerous Classes in Paris During the First Half of the Nineteenth Century* (New York, 1973). For a sketch of the development of the prison in France, see Michelle Perrot, "Delinquency and the Penitentiary System in Nineteenth-Century France," in Forster and Ranum, eds., *Deviants . . . in French Society*, 213–240.
39. Louis Masur, *Rites of Execution: Capital Punishment and the Transformation of American Culture, 1776–1865*, chs. 1–2.
40. Patricia O'Brien, *The Promise of Punishment: Prisons in Nineteenth-Century France* (Princeton, N.J., 1982), 87, and ch. 3 *passim*.
41. Tomes, *Generous Confidence*, 109, 114–115. As Tomes notes, her conclusion fits with that of Richard Fox, in *So Far Disordered Minds: Insanity in California, 1870–1930* (Berkeley, Calif., 1978): "Insanity was not a threat to social order in the abstract, but in many cases to the 'public order' of their neighborhoods and the tranquility and financial survival of their families" (163). For a suggestive comment about how this same dynamic may have operated with laboring-

class families and commitment of children to the house of refuge, see Christine Stansell, *City of Women: Sex and Class in New York, 1789–1860* (Urbana and Chicago, 1987), 54.

42. Tomes, *Generous Confidence*, 119, 122, 125.

1. *Colonial Laws of New York From the Year 1664 to the Revolution* (Albany, 1894), I, 132. "An Act for the Relief of the Poor," in Samuel Nevill, *The Acts of the General Assembly of the Province of New-Jersey* [1703–1752] (N.J., 1752), 9. Codes in Massachusetts as well as in Virginia also failed to define the word precisely.

2. *Acts and Laws of His Majesty's Province of the Massachusetts-Bay in New-England* (Boston, 1742), 57; see too "An Act Providing for, and Ordering, Transient, Idle, Impotent and Poor Persons," *Statutes of the State of Vermont* (Bennington, 1791), 126–27.

3. Jackson Turner Main, *The Social Structure of Revolutionary America* (Princeton, 1965), 156–57, 194. Much of the limited information we have comes from New England. See Charles Grant, *Democracy in the Connecticut Frontier Town of Kent* (New York, 1961), ch. VI, especially Table 11, p. 96; compare too Kenneth Lockridge, *A New England Town: The First One Hundred Years* (New York, 1970), 151. The lowest fifth of the society at Dedham, Lockridge tells us, lived in "scrabbling inadequacy." Or, "One man in ten had as assets little more than his strong back."

4. *A Report of the Record Commissioners of the City of Boston, Containing the Boston Records from 1729 to 1742* (Boston, 1885), 121–122, January 1, 1736. (Hereafter cited as *Boston Town Records.*) *Boston Town Records, 1758–1769,* 275, April 4, 1769. *The Vestry Book of St. Paul's Parish, Hanover County, Virginia, 1706–1786* (Richmond, 1940), *passim*. A fuller discussion of these sources follows below in ch. 2.

5. Perry Miller, *The New England Mind: From Colony to Province* (Cambridge, Mass., 1953), 25, 400–401, argues well that eighteenth-century ministers lost this vision of reform.

6. Samuel Cooper, *A Sermon Preached in Boston, New England, Before the Society for Encouraging Industry and Employing the Poor* (Boston, 1753), 20.

7. James Milnor, *The Widow and Her Mites, A Sermon* (New York, 1819), 11; Anon., *A Sermon on the Blessedness of Charitable Giving* (Boston, 1817), 8. Cf. William Hollinshead, *An Oration delivered at the Orphan House of Charleston* (Charleston, S.C., 1797): "You are the Stewards of God to lay out as much of his bounty as

you can spare from yourselves for the needy part of his household." By giving charity, you "become God's substitutes on earth."

8. Elijah Parish, *A Sermon Preached before the Members of the Female Charitable Society of Newburyport* (Newburyport, Mass., 1808), 13. Not until the Jacksonian period, as we shall see below, was this ministerial message transformed.

9. Samuel Parker, *Charity to Children Enforced* (Boston, 1803), 14–18; Nathan Bradstreet, *Two Sermons on the Nature, Extent and Morality of Charity* (Newburyport, Mass., 1794), 39–40.

10. Benjamin Colman, *The Merchandise of a People Holiness to the Lord* (Boston, 1736), 2–3; Samuel Spring, *A Charity Sermon Delivered at the request of the Howard Benevolent Society* (Newburyport, Mass., 1818), 13–14. For a seventeenth-century statement of this, see Richard Bushman, *From Puritan to Yankee: Character and the Social Order in Connecticut, 1690–1765* (Cambridge, Mass., 1967), 24–25.

11. The Chauncy sermon was published in Boston, 1752. See also, Anon., *Industry and Frugality Proposed as the Surest Way to Make a Rich and Flourishing People* (Boston, 1753). These sermons do not fit well with the arguments of Brian Tierney, *Medieval Poor Law: A Sketch of Canonical Theory and its Application in England* (Berkeley and Los Angeles, 1959).

12. Samuel Seabury, *A Sermon Delivered before the Boston Episcopal Charitable Society in Trinity Church* (Boston, 1788), 14; Samuel Spring, *Charity Sermon,* 14–15.

13. Benjamin Colman, *The Unspeakable Gift of God: A Right Charitable and Bountiful Spirit to the Poor and Needy Members of Jesus Christ* (Boston, 1739), 14; Cotton Mather, *Bonifacius: An Essay Upon the Good* (reprinted, Cambridge, Mass., 1966), 32.

14. Jackson Turner Main, *Social Structure of Revolutionary America,* ch. VII, surveys this material. For a clerical statement, see Richard Bushman, *From Puritan to Yankee,* 11–13, quoting John Bulkley, *The Necessity of Religion . . .* (Boston, 1713).

15. Charles Chauncy, *Seasonable Thoughts on the State of Religion in New-England . . .* (Boston, 1743), quoted in Alan Heimert and Perry Miller, eds., *The Great Awakening* (Indianapolis, 1967), 299, 303. For a full discussion of the social implications of the Great Awakening controversy, see Alan Heimert, *Religion and the American Mind: From the Great Awakening to the Revolution* (Cambridge, Mass., 1966). See too Richard Bushman, *From Puritan to Yankee,* ch. XIII, esp. 264–265, 275.

16. Gordon S. Wood, *The Creation of the American Republic, 1776–1787* (Chapel Hill, N.C., 1969), 70–83.

17. Kenneth Lockridge, *A New England Town,* 141; Richard Bushman, *From Puritan to Yankee,* ch. II, VII–IX; even the most bitterly fought economic contests that Bushman describes in the later

chapters testified to a wide assumption about the rights and obliga-
tions of governmental interference in the economy. See too Joseph
Dorfman, *The Economic Mind in American Civilization, 1606–1865*
(New York, 1946), Vol. I, chs. 8–9.

18. For recent views on the centrality of the town, particularly in New
England, see Michael Zuckerman, *Peaceable Kingdoms: New Eng-
land Towns in the Eighteenth Century* (New York, 1970); Kenneth
Lockridge, *A New England Town;* Charles Grant, *Democracy in the
Connecticut Frontier Town of Kent;* and Richard Bushman, *From
Puritan to Yankee.* The town is also central to Philip J. Grevin, Jr.,
*Four Generations: Population, Land, and Family in Colonial An-
dover, Massachusetts* (Ithaca, N.Y., 1970). Unfortunately we have
few studies on settlements in other areas of the colonies. There is a
heated debate among these authors on how much change occurred
in the importance of the town in the eighteenth century. Zuckerman sees little change, Bushman an almost complete disintegration,
and Lockridge attempts to find a balance between the two. Support
for Bushman comes too in Edward M. Cook, Jr., "Social Behavior
and Changing Values in Dedham, Massachusetts, 1700 to 1755,"
William and Mary Quarterly, 27 (1970), 546–580. On the specific
issue of treatment of the poor and criminal, the attitudes that everyone agrees were present in 1690 survived through the next seventy
years, and while some practices may have been modified, no alternate procedures were established. Unfortunately, the above literature is often so focused on political matters, the nature of town
government, that it loses sight of social considerations.

19. Robert W. Ramsey, *Carolina Cradle: Settlement of the Northwest
Carolina Frontier, 1747–1762* (Chapel Hill, N.C., 1964), is one of
the few studies of migration in the colonial period. On urban life
the best beginning point remains Carl Bridenbaugh, *Cities in the
Wilderness* (N.Y., 1938) and *Cities in Revolt* (N.Y., 1955). See too
Sidney V. James, *A People Among People: Quaker Benevolence in
Eighteenth-Century America* (Cambridge, Mass., 1963), esp. chs.
2–3.

20. The Masssachusetts code, "An Act for Employing and Providing for
the Poor of the Town of Boston," appears in *Acts and Laws of His
Majesty's Province of Massachusetts-Bay in New-England* (Boston
1742), 303; for Virginia, see William Waller Henning, ed., *The
Statutes at Large Being a Collection of All the Laws of Virginia
(1619–1792)* (Richmond, Va., 1809–1823, 13 vols.), I, 336. Justices
of the peace "at their discretion" may bind out children, especially
where "such young children are easily corrupted, as also for the
relief of such parents whose poverty extends not to give them breeding." Bernard Bailyn, *Education in the Forming of American
Society* (Chapel Hill, N.C., 1960), traces the increasing role of
public authority in education. The Virginia magistrates could also

interfere where parents, particularly the poor, through "fond indulgence or perverse obstinacy" were unwilling to give up their children.

21. For the Puritan view see George L. Haskins, *Law and Authority in Early Massachusetts* (New York, 1960). For its persistence, William E. Nelson, "Emerging Notions of Modern Criminal Law in the Revolutionary Era: An Historical Perspective," *New York University Law Review*, 42 (1967), 450–482. Most criminal cases between 1760 and 1764 in Massachusetts, Nelson finds, were for offenses against God and religion; 210 of 370 prosecutions in Middlesex were for fornication (452).

22. Samson Occom, *A Sermon Preached at the Execution of Moses Paul, an Indian* (New London, Conn., 1772), 3–4. John Rogers, *Death the Certain Wages of Sin to the Impenitent . . . Occasioned by the Imprisonment, Condemnation, and Execution of a Young Woman who was Guilty of Murdering her Infant begotten in Whoredom* (Boston, 1701), n. p. in the preface, "To the Christian Reader." The title alone is indicative of colonial thinking on crime. See too Sylvanus Conant, *The Blood of Abel and the Blood of Jesus* (Boston, 1764), where the sermon was described as "like a flaming Beacon" warning us to avoid evil (26).

23. Benjamin Wadsworth, *The Well-Ordered Family or Relative Duties: Being the Substance of Several Sermons* (Boston, 1712), 44–59, 90–102. See too Cotton Mather, *A Family Well-Ordered, or An Essay to Render Parents and Children Happy in one Another* (Boston, 1699). Edmund S. Morgan, *The Puritan Family: Essays on Religion and Domestic Relations in Seventeenth-Century New England* (Boston, 1944, rev. ed., New York, 1966), reviews attitudes toward the family. The subject has begun to interest students. The Grevin and Lockridge studies cited above provide a good introduction to the literature. See also John Demos, *A Little Commonwealth: Family Life in Plymouth Colony* (New York, 1970); David J. Rothman, "A Note on the Study of the Colonial Family," *William and Mary Quarterly*, 23 (1966), 627–634.

24. Samuel Willard, *Impenitent Sinners Warned of their Misery and Summoned to Judgment. . . .* (Boston, 1698), 26, and the section entitled, "To the Reader." Henry Channing, *God Admonishing his People of their Duty, as Parents and Masters* (New London, Conn., 1786), 18.

25. On the exercise of church discipline, see Emil Oberholzer, Jr., *Delinquent Saints* (New York, 1956). See too Michael Zuckerman, *Peaceable Kingdoms*, 63, and Richard Bushman, *From Puritan to Yankee*, 15–16, 159, 229. Bushman sees church discipline as almost without effect after the Great Awakening, but most others consider this view extreme. Division of churches need not signal the end of the ability of the individual church to discipline its members.

26. John Rogers, *Death the Certain Wages of Sin,* 97.

27. Noah Hobart, *Excessive Wickedness, the Way to an Untimely Death* (New London, Conn., 1768), 9, 13; Samuel Willard, *Impenitent Sinners Warned*, 22.

28. The best introduction to the _ _glish experience is W. K. Jordan, *Philanthropy in England, 1480–1660* (London, 1959). A very precise account of the relationship between English and American poor laws is Stefan Riesenfeld's "The Formative Era of American Assistance Law," *California Law Review*, 43 (1955), 175–223. See too J. R. Poynter, *Society and Pauperism: English Ideas on Poor Relief, 1795–1834* (London, 1969).

29. *Colonial Laws of New York*, I, 131–133. See too David M. Schneider, *The History of Public Welfare in New York State, 1609–1866* (Chicago, 1938), chs. 2–5.

30. *Laws of New-York from the Year 1691, to 1751, inclusive* (New York, 1752), 143–145.

31. *Colonial Laws of New York*, V., 513–517.

32. *Laws and Acts of her Majesty's Colony of Rhode Island, and Providence Plantations* (Providence, R.I., 1896), 20, contains the 1663 code on poor relief. For the 1727 statute, see *Acts and Laws of his Majesty's Colony of Rhode Island and Providence Plantations in America* (Newport, R.I., 1730), 150–151. For general discussion of the problem, see Margaret Creech, *Three Centuries of Poor Law Administration* (Chicago, 1936).

33. "An Act directing a Method for gaining a legal Settlement in any Town in the Colony, and for Removal of Poor Persons," *Acts and Laws of His Majesty's Colony of Rhode Island and Providence Plantations, in New-England, in America* (Newport, R.I., 1752), 48–51.

34. *Acts and Laws of the English Colony of Rhode-Island and Providence Plantations, in New-England, in America* (Newport, R.I., 1767), 228–232.

35. *Laws of the Government of New Castle, Kent and Sussex upon Delaware* (Philadelphia, 1741), 208–215; quotation is on p. 209. See also the Virginia statute of 1727, "An Act for the Better Securing the Payment of Levies, and Restraint of Vagrant and Idle Persons," *Acts of Assembly Now in Force in the Colony of Virginia* (Williamsburg, Va., 1752), 108–110.

36. *A Complete Record of all the Acts of Assembly of the Province of North-Carolina Now in Force and Use* (Newbern, N.C., 1773), 172–174. See too Roy M. Brown, *Public Poor Relief in North Carolina* (Chapel Hill, N.C., 1928).

37. *Acts and Laws of his Majesty's Province of Massachusetts-Bay in New-England*, 22, 110–112. See also Robert Kelso's volume, *The History of Public Poor Relief in Massachusetts, 1620–1920* (Boston, 1922). George L. Haskins, *Law and Authority*, traces the Puritan codes on the poor.

38. Compare *Acts and Laws of his Majesties Colony of Connecticut in New-England* (Boston, 1702), 94–95, with *The Public Statute Laws of the State of Connecticut* (Hartford, Conn., 1808), Book I, 552–553.

39. *Acts and Laws of his Majesty's English Colony of Connecticut in New-England* (New London, Conn., 1750), 239 ff., 343 ff.; Edward W. Capen, *The Historical Development of the Poor Law of Connecticut* (New York, 1905).

40. *A Compilation of the Poor Laws of the State of Pennsylvania, from the Year 1700, to 1788 inclusive* (Philadelphia, 1788), 8–27, 54–81. The 1756 poor-relief act is reprinted there, 47–53.

41. *Ibid.*, 37–47.

42. *Acts of the General Assembly of the Province of New-Jersey* (1752), 408–418, quotation is on p. 409. See too James Leiby, *Charity and Corrections in New Jersey* (New Brunswick, N.J., 1967), ch. I.

CHAPTER TWO

1. These two famous reports are discussed below in ch. 7. They survey conditions in their states, and I have calculated the results. For the Yates report, see *New York Senate Journal*, 1824, 95–108, and Appendix A; it is more readily available in reprint in New York State Board of Charities, *Annual Report for 1900* (Albany, 1901), I, 937–1145. The Quincy report is available separately bound, Massachusetts General Court Committee on Pauper Laws, *Report of the Committee,* 1821 (n. p.).

2. The diversity of English practice is traced in detail in Sidney and Beatrice Webb, *English Local Government: English Poor Law History: Part I, The Old Poor Law* (London, 1927); see p. 215 for the 1815 estimate. There were workhouses, almshouses, weekly pensions, an allowance system, and methods for billeting out the unemployed, as well as settlement laws, vagrancy laws, and apprenticeship laws. The English relief practices were probably not as institutional in the eighteenth century as historians once believed. See Mark Blaug, "The Myth of the Old Poor Law and the Making of the New," *Journal of Economic History,* 23 (1963), 151–184. Still, in comparison to the colonial experience, the English relied far more heavily upon institutions. For the seventeenth-century investment in institutions, see W. K. Jordan, *Philanthropy in England,* Table II, p. 239. Workhouses were less successful than almshouses (270–272). David Owen traces much of the later story in *English Philanthropy, 1660–1960* (Cambridge, 1964). See too J. R. Poynter, *Society and Pauperism,* xx, 1, 14–15.

3. The instances of relief are found in C. G. Chamberlayne, ed., *Vestry Book of St. Paul's Parish, Hanover County, Virginia, 1706–1786* (Richmond, Va., 1940). After 1750, the records have little information on why persons were relieved; earlier, the name of recipient, how he was relieved, the sum, and the reason for the relief were regularly noted. Some of the findings more precisely: 42 men were relieved, 35 women, and 20 children. Of the men, 13 were listed as sick, or relief was given by a doctor; the rest were without information. Of the 35 women, 5 were widows and 9 were ill, the rest without information. Of the children, 7 were bastards, 2 orphans, one ill. Of 76 cases, 54 were relieved in a neighbor's house identified by a male name at the head of it; 2 of the needy went to women, 2 to widows; 10 stayed at home, 8 went to their parents, or were relieving their parents. On slaveholding figures, see Robert E. and B. Katherine Brown, *Virginia 1705–1786: Democracy or Aristocracy?* (East Lansing, Mich., 1964), 72 and Table 1. The parish records make clear that there was no difference in cost in supporting the poor at home or with a neighbor. Nor would a primitive almshouse have demanded a large capital expenditure.

4. C. G. Chamberlayne, ed., *Vestry Book and Register of St. Peter's Parish, New Kent and James City Counties, Virginia, 1684–1786* (Richmond, Va., 1937).

5. C. G. Chamberlayne, ed., *The Vestry Book of Blisland Parish, New Kent and James City Counties, Virginia, 1721–1786* (Richmond, Va., 1935). In sum, 67 percent of the needy were relieved in a neighbor's household, 26 percent in their own homes, and 7 percent with relatives.

6. Of 57 cases of relief in Blisland parish, 53 percent received support for less than two years, 32 percent for three to eight years, 15 percent for thirteen to twenty-one years. Those relieved in their own families were relieved on the whole for longer periods; the sex of recipient made no difference in the mode or length of treatment.

7. On the average, men received an allowance of 1000 to 1200 pounds of tobacco for a year's support; women and children received 600.

8. The evidence presented here is limited, but there are several reasons to give it importance. First, it is from a southern colony, where one might have expected the least persistence of community action. The non-Puritan character of the region and the presence of plantations did not, however, affect public relief policies. Moreover, by examining well-to-do areas, where formal procedures would have been most likely to occur, the prevalence of noninstitutional relief is again indicated. Since most of the writing about colonial poor relief, as exemplified in Kelso, Creech, and the others, rest almost exclusively on the codes, perhaps the type of analysis presented here will be extended to other parts of the colonies. The style and implications of outdoor relief have not been widely discussed.

9. *Minutes of the Mayor's Court of New York*, January 26, 1724 to

June 17, 1729, manuscript volumes, Hall of Records, New York City. For the entry on the first almshouse, see *Minutes of Mayor's Court,* 81–83.

10. For rising expenditures, see New York City, *Minutes of Churchwardens and Vestrymen,* manuscript volumes, New York Public Library (1694–1747). Compare February 11, 1701, p. 91; February 21, 1705, p. 139; January 22, 1706, p. 148; February 7, 1733, p. 205; February 5, 1735, p. 240. Payments ranged from two shillings sixpence to four shillings per week; thus it would take £8 per year for full support of one of the poor. By 1730, the sums expended annually on poor relief in New York were £300, so that the numbers receiving aid could not be very great, even allowing for part-time support. Nevertheless, the costs of poor relief were one of the largest items on the town budget, and therefore received close attention.

11. New York City, "Regulations by Justices and Gentlemen of the Vestry," *Minutes of Churchwardens,* April 13, 1736, p. 274; May 19, 1736, p. 279.

12. The entries for this period are found between pp. 240 and 597.

13. The records of the Boston almshouse are located in the Massachusetts Historical Society. For the inmate population see the manuscript volume, *Admissions, 1760–1812.* Because of the nature of the records, information for the year 1768 was not included here. Many of the inmates in the Boston almshouse were listed as "province poor," that is, people without legal settlement for whom the colony assumed the costs of relief. This arrangement, an exception to the general rule of local responsibility, was without clear legal authorization. The practice grew up to meet an unusual need in the eighteenth century, and as such remained outside the formal statutes.

14. Of the 236 women, 35 were mothers with children, 5 were widows, 24 were expectant mothers (usually unwed), 26 were aged, 10 sick, 9 listed as "poor," and 12 as strangers. The rest were not identified except by name.

15. Record Commissioners of the City of Boston, *Boston Town Records, 1742–1757* (Boston, 1885), April 20, 1757.

16. *Ibid.,* May 14, 1751. The workhouse, begun in 1735, was completed in 1739. See Record Commissioners of the City of Boston, *Selectmen's Minutes, 1736–1742* (Boston, 1886), May 20, 1735; July 20, 1739. In 1741 the workhouse held 10 men, 38 women, and 7 children; see *Boston Town Records, 1729–1742,* March 30, 1741; see also December 14, 1742; 110 persons were then in the almshouse and 36 in the workhouse.

17. *Minutes of the Common Council of the City of New York 1675–1776* (New York, 1905, 8 vols.), IV, December 20, 1734, p. 241. Douglas Carroll, "History of the Baltimore City Hospitals," *Maryland State Medical Journal,* 15 (1966).

18. *Minutes of the Common Council of New York,* IV, March 3, 1736, pp. 305–310; New York City, *Minutes of Churchwardens,* October 17, 1738, pp. 373–374.

19. The laws governing the insane in the colonial period clarified the priorities; see the 1694 code of Massachusetts, "An Act for the Relief of Idiots and Distracted Persons," *Acts and Laws of Massachusetts-Bay,* 57. Cf. Connecticut legislation of 1793, "An Act for Relieving and Ordering of Idiots, Impotent, Distracted, and Idle Persons," *Public Statute Laws of . . . Connecticut,* 386. The Pennsylvania incident is described in Henry M. Hurd, *The Institutional Care of the Insane in the United States and Canada* (Baltimore, 1916, 4 vols.), III, 380; for similar incidents, see too, I, 284.

20. William Henning, *The Statutes at Large,* VIII, 378–381, for "An Act to Make Provision for the Support and Maintenance of Idiots, Lunatics, and Other Persons of Unsound Minds." See too Vol. XII, 198–200.

21. Richard H. Shryock, *Medicine and Society in America: 1660–1860* (New York, 1960), covers this material. See too Leonard K. Eaton, *New England Hospitals, 1790–1833* (Ann Arbor, Mich., 1957), ch. 1.

22. [Benjamin Franklin], *Some Account of the Pennsylvania Hospital . . .* (Philadelphia, 1754), especially 3–5. So, too, smallpox hospitals were designed to function where the family, because of contagion, could not. See the 1701 Massachusetts code, "An Act Providing in Case of Sickness," *Acts and Laws of Massachusetts-Bay,* 148. In 1725 the colony also thought of establishing a children's hospital, "to train them up in christian knowledge and behavior."

23. For examples of warning out, see *Early Records of the Town of Providence, 1677–1750* (Providence, R.I., 1895), Vol. IX, entries of November 17, 1680; April 27, 1685; October 27, 1687; January 16, 1693; June 11, 1695. The Boston town records are filled with examples, as are the New York City *Minutes of Churchmen.* Josiah Benton, *Warning Out in New England* (Boston, 1911), argues that reliance upon this procedure weakened over the course of the eighteenth century. More recently, Michael Zuckerman, *Peaceable Kingdoms,* has disputed Benton, insisting that "town records continued to be studded with such warnings to the time of the Revolution itself" (113). See his footnote 52, pp. 304–305, for further examples of warning out. Given the problems I note in the text, no quantitative measure is likely to settle the dispute. But it is quite clear that settlement laws and warning out remained a bastion of defense in the towns through the eighteenth century. For examples from Virginia, see Howard Mackey, "The Operation of the English Old Poor Law in Virginia," *Virginia Magazine of History and Biography,* 73 (1965), 29–48, esp. p. 38. Edward Cook, "Social Values in Dedham," argues that warning out increased in Dedham over the eighteenth century (569).

24. New York City, *Minutes of Churchmen*, August 29, 1692; March 18, 1693; March 1, 1726; April 19, 1726; October 10, 1732; see too *Minutes of Mayor's Court*, September 19, 1729; October 31, 1727.

25. For one example see Kenneth Lockridge, "The Population of Dedham, Massachusetts, 1636–1736," *Economic History Review*, 19 (1966), 323, 344.

26. Julius Goebel Jr., and T. Raymond Naughton, *Law Enforcement in Colonial New York* (New York, 1944), 515, 709. "When a jail sentence was meted out," write the authors, "it was most often ancillary."

27. See the matching of punishment with crime in the Massachusetts legislation of 1692, "An Act for the Punishing of Criminal Offenders," *Acts and Laws of Massachusetts-Bay*, 11–12. Arrangements were very much the same in New York; see Goebel and Naughton, *Law Enforcement*, 703, 705, 709. They calculate that of the 446 punishments in the New York Supreme Court, 136 were fines.

28. *Acts and Laws of Massachusetts-Bay*, 9, 12; Goebel and Naughton, *Law Enforcement*, 707, note 151. They observe that although the use of the stocks does not often turn up in the court records, there are clear indications that they were kept in good repair. There is also evidence of some use of the pillory and carting (706). Cf. Michael Zuckerman, *Peaceable Kingdoms*, 242.

29. William Henning, *The Statutes at Large*, II, 75, act of March 1662; similar injunctions were kept on the law books at least through 1748. For North Carolina, see "An Act for the Building and Maintaining of Court-Houses, Prisons, and Stocks in every County within this Province," *The Laws of the State of North Carolina* (Edenton, N.C., 1846), 82–83.

30. Goebel and Naughton, *Law Enforcement*, 705; note the popular use of the whip. It was most frequently used in the Special Sessions Court, where most of the defendants were vagrants and/or without property. The Mayor's Court, also concerned with the problem of strangers, relied heavily upon it, along with the sentence of banishment (708, note 158). The Supreme Court used it most infrequently. In an attempt to make specific correlations between the punishment received and the status of the offender, I matched the Mayor's Court records with tax lists; the results, however, were not conclusive, for the number of those not appearing in the tax lists could reflect incomplete records rather than evidence of non-residence. Still, it is significant that wherever the evidence allowed a certain identification of the offender as stranger (when he was identified in the proceedings as from another colony or as a vagrant), then in almost every instance, the punishment was whip together with banishment.

31. Michael Zuckerman, *Peaceable Kingdoms*, 85–86.

32. Of the 446 cases between 1693 and 1776 where punishments were meted out by the New York Supreme Court, 87 called. for the

gallows. Goebel and Naughton, *Law Enforcement,* 702, note 139. Of 60 punishments in the Court of Oyer and Terminer, 15 were capital. The authors argue that there was probably less capital punishment here than in England, but the number of executions was still considerable. See too Lawrence H. Gipson, "Crime and its Punishment in Provincial Pennsylvania," *Lehigh University Publications,* 9 (1935), 11–12, and Hugh F. Rankin, *Criminal Trial Proceedings in the General Court of Virginia* (Charlottesville, Va., 1965), 121–122.

33. "An Act for the More Effectual Preventing and Punishing of Theft," *Acts and Laws of Massachusetts-Bay,* 310.

34. *A Brief Account of the Life and Abominable Thefts of Isaac Frasier* (New Haven, Conn., 1768).

35. Kai Erikson, *Wayward Puritans: A Study in the Sociology of Deviance* (New York, 1966), 196–197.

36. *Boston Town Records, 1729–1742,* October 12, 1739, 235–240.

37. William Henning, *Statutes at Large,* III, pp. 15, 214; Roberts Vaux, *Notices of the Original, and Successive Efforts, to Improve the Discipline of the Prison at Philadelphia* (Philadelphia, 1826), 26–30.

38. *Public Statute Laws of Connecticut,* 365, "An Act Regulating Gaols and Gaolers." See too a similar statute in Vermont, 1787, *The Statutes of Vermont,* 86. On bonding, see William Henning, *Statutes at Large,* III, 15. The provision was copied in North Carolina, so that whoever gave bond had "the liberty of the rules of the prison." *The Laws of the State of North Carolina,* 189.

39. In 1699 Massachusetts passed an "Act for the Regulating of Prisons, and to Prevent Escapes," *Acts and Laws of Massachusetts-Bay,* 121; see too *Public Statute Laws of Connecticut,* 367. The night watch was tried in New York, *Minutes of the Common Council,* III, January 9, 1725; March 24, 1727, pp. 362–363, 404–405. See too Virginia, *Acts of Assembly,* 187.

CHAPTER THREE

1. U.S. Bureau of the Census, *Historical Statistics of the United States, Colonial Times to 1957* (Washington, D.C., 1960), 12–14; George Rogers Taylor, *The Transportation Revolution, 1815–1860* (New York, 1951), 6–10, 141–144. The sophisticated studies of geographic mobility take their starting point with 1870, so we have no precise figures for the earlier period. However, gross numbers tell a good deal, and the very transportation revolution that Taylor writes about is another indication of the opportunity for mobility and the frequent use of the facilities. In 1790, the urban population was 5.1 percent of the nation; it rose to 7.3 percent in 1810, declined slightly to 7.1 percent in 1820, and thereafter increased steadily to

1860, reaching 19.8 percent. Some new and important efforts to examine migration patterns in this period may be found in Stephan Thernstrom and Richard Sennett, eds., *Nineteenth-Century Cities* (New Haven, 1969).

2. Douglas North, *The Economic Growth of the United States, 1790–1860* (New York, 1961), 167, 189 ff.; George Rogers Taylor, *Transportation Revolution*, chs. 10–11.

3. A good starting point for the intellectual history of this period is Perry Miller, *The Life of the Mind in America: From the Revolution to the Civil War* (New York, 1965). See too Charles I. Foster, *An Errand of Mercy* (Chapel Hill, N.C. 1960), for a discussion of the Protestant response to these changing conditions, how they equated movement with a return to barbarism.

4. One of the best accounts of the tensions that social change created in post-1820 America is Marvin Meyers's *The Jacksonian Persuasion* (Stanford, 1957). Meyers, however, seems to locate all the tensions within the Jackson camp. The materials I discuss in the following chapters show that the anxieties were far more broadly spread through the society. Another account, not as finely drawn as Meyers's, but sensitive to the darker side of the Jackson years is Fred Somkin, *Unquiet Eagle: Memory and Desire in the Idea of American Freedom, 1815–1860* (Ithaca, N.Y., 1967). For an incisive examination of these themes in the world of art see Neil Harris, *The Artist in American Society* (New York, 1966).

5. Thomas Eddy, *An Account of the State Prison or Penitentiary House, in the City of New-York* (New York, 1801), 5; this same argument is put forth by William Bradford, *An Enquiry how far the Punishment of Death is Necessary in Pennsylvania* (Philadelphia 1793), 14–20.

6. See the translation of Henry Paolucci (Indianapolis, 1963), 8, 43–44, 58, 94, for the several quotations.

7. Thomas Eddy, *An Account of the State Prison*, 9. Eddy was very familiar with the writings of Beccaria. See too the Philadelphia Society for Alleviating the Miseries of Public Prisons, *Extracts and Remarks on the Subject of Punishment and Reformation of Criminals* (Philadelphia, 1790), 3–4.

8. William Bradford, *An Enquiry*, 43. The Society for the Prevention of Pauperism in the City of New-York, *Report on the Penitentiary System in the United States* (New York, 1822), 12; for the influence upon them of Beccaria, see 9, 33. To appreciate how widespread these notions were, see E. Bruce Thompson, "Reforms in the Penal System of Tennessee, 1820–1850," *Tennessee Historical Quarterly*, I (1942), 293.

9. George K. Taylor, *Substance of a Speech . . . on the Bill to Amend the Penal Laws of this Commonwealth* (Richmond, Va., 1796), 23. Robert James Turnbull, *A Visit to the Philadelphia Prison* (Phila-

delphia, 1796), 3. The Philadelphia pamphlet was a reprint of a newspaper article. See 75–76 for the argument that certainty of punishment was the most critical element in criminal law.

10. Raymond T. Bye, *Capital Punishment in the United States* (Philadelphia, 1919), 4–9. Ohio, in 1788, was the first to limit the death penalty to murder; Pennsylvania followed suit in 1794. Few states abolished the death penalty altogether; by 1900, only six had done so. See too David B. Davis, "The Movement to Abolish Capital Punishment in America, 1787–1861," *American Historical Review*, 63 (1957), 23–46. A classic nineteenth-century statement is Edward Livingston, *On the Abolition of the Punishment of Death* (Philadelphia, 1831), originally a report to the Louisiana legislature in March 1822.

11. The first prison structures in the United States are discussed in Orlando F. Lewis, *The Development of American Prisons and Prison Customs, 1776–1845* (Albany, N.Y., 1922), chs. 1–8; less detailed is Blake McKelvey, *American Prisons: A Study in American Social History Prior to 1915* (Chicago, 1936), ch. 1.

12. The disillusionment with the first experiments appears in many pamphlets; see Thomas Eddy, *An Account of the State Prison*, 15–16, on the disappointment of "many citizens . . . [who] sometimes express a regret at the change . . . and returning to a system of accumulated severity and terror." Other expressions may be found in the Philadelphia Society for Alleviating the Miseries of Public Prisons, *A Statistical View of the Penal Code of Pennsylvania* (Philadelphia, 1817), 35; Stephan White, Sherman Leland, Bradford Sumner, *Report on . . . the State Prison at Charlestown* [Massachusetts], (Boston, 1827), 1. William Tudor, "The Penitentiary System," *North American Review*, 13 (1821), 417–420. Gershom Powers, *A Brief Account of the Construction, Management, and Discipline . . . of the New York State Prison at Auburn* (Auburn, N.Y., 1826), 64–69.

13. Jacksonian theories on deviancy have received little attention, but see David Brion Davis, *Homicide in American Fiction, 1798–1860* (Ithaca, N.Y., 1957). Davis's analysis is close to mine, but his interests are more in the literary expression of the problem than in the social origins of the ideas and their influence on social policy. There is also a discussion in W. David Lewis, *From Newgate to Dannemora: The Rise of the Penitentiary in New York, 1796–1848* (Ithaca, N.Y., 1965). Lewis argues that 1840 was a turning point, that after that date an environmental concern came to the fore; he finds the influence of phrenology vital to the story. There is, however, as the following discussion will show, much evidence of these ideas in the 1820's, and even more in the 1830's; furthermore, it was not phrenology that accounted for them, I believe, but a peculiar view of American society. For a concise survey of current theories of deviant behavior, see Richard A. Cloward and Lloyd E.

Ohlin, *Delinquency and Opportunity* (New York, 1960), chs. 2–4.

14. "Abstract of Brief Biographical Sketches as Taken From Convicts When Discharged from this Prison," "Annual Report of the Inspectors of the State Prison at Auburn," *N.Y. Senate and Assembly Documents,* 1830, I, no. 38, pp. 37–54. The second group of biographies is found in "Annual Report of Auburn Prison," *N.Y. Senate Docs.,* 1831, I, no. 15, pp. 32–63. All the cases below come from these pages and are identified by their number in sequence. The quotation is from the 1830 report, p. 5.

15. H. L. was case 433; M. R. R., 440; J. L., 319; M. H., 303. Of the 173 cases, 99 were explained directly in terms of parental failures. In 26, the parents set a bad example; in 27, they were absent by reason of death or desertion; in 32 cases, the child left home very young, in 11 he went to an apprentice. Two were at home but "wild," and one was in a "very poor" household.

16. J. A., was case 443; J. T., 444; J. M., 493; R. R., 352. Of the 99 cases which defined parental problems as critical, 27 children, according to the biographies, went directly into a life of crime; 13 first succumbed to a vice; 17 wandered and then began committing crimes. Twenty-one followed a corrupting occupation, such as sailor or canal-worker, and 20 ran away or had a bad apprenticeship. One suffered a series of misfortunes.

17. M. S. was case 492; T. L., 480; J. L., 419; J. H., 326; J. P. was case 339; G. J., 340.

18. Roger Lane, "Crime and Criminal Statistics in Nineteenth-Century Massachusetts," *Journal of Social History,* 2 (1968), 156–163. See also William Nelson, "Emerging Notions of Modern Criminal Law," 461–462; prosecutions for morality practically disappeared in Massachusetts after the Revolution.

19. W. S. was case 301. Note too that poverty as a direct cause of crime did not enter into this story very often. Others, as we will see below, ch. 7, made the link; but here it was a predisposing cause and not in itself a sufficient explanation for deviancy.

20. Inspectors of the Eastern State Penitentiary of Pennsylvania, *Seventeenth Annual Report* (Philadelphia, 1846), 58. *Annual Report of the Ohio Penitentiary for 1850* (Columbus, Ohio, 1851), 12–13.

21. *Annual Report of the Ohio Penitentiary for 1852* (Columbus, Ohio, 1853), 35; *Annual Report of the Ohio Penitentiary for 1858* (Columbus, Ohio, 1859), 40–41. Inspectors of the Eastern State Penitentiary, *First and Second Annual Report* (Philadelphia, 1831), 10.

22. New York Prison Association, *First Annual Report* (New York, 1845), 30–31. (Hereafter abbreviated N.Y.P.A.)

23. *Ibid.,* 31–33.

24. *Ibid.,* 34–35.

25. See, for example, N. Y. P. A., *Nineteenth Annual Report* (New York, 1864), 352. By that date, such views were no longer as popular as they had been in the 1830's, but were still expressed.
26. N.Y.P.A., *Tenth Annual Report* (Albany, N.Y., 1855), Appendix A., by James S. Gould, 61–117. Quotations are on pp. 61, 73, 93–94, 108–109, 116–117.
27. Boston Prison Discipline Society, *Fourth Annual Report* (Boston, 1829), 64. (Hereafter abbreviated B.P.D.S.); B.P.D.S., *Eleventh Annual Report* (Boston, 1835), 35. On Dwight, see William Jenks, *A Memoir of the Reverend Louis Dwight* (Boston, 1856).
28. Samuel Gridley Howe, *An Essay on Separate and Congregate Systems of Prison Discipline* (Boston, 1846), 79.
29. John L. Thomas, "Romantic Reform in America, 1815–1865," *American Quarterly*, 17 (1965), 656–681, notes a malaise but attempts to account for it as a crisis in church affairs; the argument here sees the crisis as far broader, touching all the society. So, too, I differ with the stress in Timothy L. Smith, *Revivalism and Social Reform in Mid-Nineteenth Century America* (Nashville, Tenn., 1957). Indeed, the evidence Smith brings forward on the actual social welfare work done by religious organizations, as apart from Bible distribution, is not very great.
30. Lieber's remarks appear in his translator's preface, reprinted in Gustave de Beaumont and Alexis de Tocqueville, *On the Penitentiary System in the United States* (Carbondale, Ill., 1964), 14–15. See too his *Remarks on the Relation between Education and Crime* (Philadelphia, 1835), 13.
31. (2nd ed., Philadelphia, 1845), 25.
32. Records of the New York House of Refuge, Syracuse University Library; for these biographies, see *Case Histories*, nos. 78 (December 10, 1825), 800 (September 30, 1830), 2657 (February 24, 1841).
33. Case no. 11 (January 1, 1825), case 55 (January 15, 1825), 1602 (July 30, 1835), 803 (October 8, 1830). To sample the many volumes of inmates' records, I examined the first 30 cases in the record book volume I, 1824–25, then the first 15 cases in vols. II (1825–27), V (1830–32), VIII (1835–36), XII (1841–42), XX (1851–52).
34. New York House of Refuge, *Thirtieth Annual Report* (New York, 1855), 55.

CHAPTER FOUR

1. Orlando Lewis, *The Development of American Prisons*, surveys this material. On the origins of the Auburn plan, see W. David Lewis, *From Newgate to Dannemora*, chs. 3–4; for Pennsylvania, Negley K.

Teeters and John D. Shearer, *The Prison at Philadelphia, Cherry Hill: The Separate System of Prison Discipline, 1829–1913* (New York, 1957). Some source material illustrating the lines of influence may be found in *State Prisons and the Penitentiary System Vindicated . . . by an Officer of the Massachusetts State Prison at Charlestown* (Charlestown, Mass., 1821), 41–42, 51; see too the 1830 report of a New Jersey investigatory committee reprinted in Harry E. Barnes, *A History of the Penal, Reformatory and Correctional Institutions of the State of New Jersey* (Trenton, 1918), 402–419. A good summary of attitudes and events is found in the New York Society for the Prevention of Pauperism, *Report of the Penitentiary System,* of 1822. Here, as with the spread of other institutions, the South, while not untouched by the movement, certainly did not participate in it to the extent that other sections did. The ideology and social realities promoting the program had less appeal and relevance to the South, given its particular problems and conditions. Indeed, one indication of the differentiation of the South from the rest of the nation is the pace of institutionalization. In the 1820's the differences were not so great by this measurement; in the 1850's, they were.

2. Many of these visitors published full accounts which, where valuable, are cited below. For a less well-known visitor, who helped to change the penal system of Hungary, see Alfred Reich, *The Contribution of Sandor Boloni Farkas. . . .* (unpublished doctoral dissertation, Columbia University, 1970).

3. The literature below provides ample sources for discussing the two systems. Probably the best introduction to the debate, and the rival plans, remains Beaumont and Tocqueville, *On the Penitentiary System.* Almost all of what follows below focuses on the state institutions, for they were most affected by the changes in penitentiary design. The ideas filtered down to the county and city level, but, given intricacy and expense, they were rarely acted upon. See Orlando Lewis, *The Development of American Prisons,* ch. 22. For the condition of the county jails, and the state of thinking, see *Report on Gaols and Houses of Correction in the Commonwealth of Massachusetts* (Boston, 1834), carried out by John Lincoln and Louis Dwight; *Report of the Secretary of the [Pennsylvania] Commonwealth, Relative to County Prisons* (Harrisburg, Pa. 1839).

4. Samuel Gridley Howe, *Prison Discipline,* 40–41; see too Beaumont and Tocqueville, *On the Penitentiary System,* 55.

5. Gershom Powers, *A Brief Account of Auburn,* 34; Stephan Allen, Samuel Hopkins, and George Tibbitts, "Report from the Committee Appointed to Visit the State Prison," *Journal of the Assembly of the State of New-York,* January 15, 1825, Doc. 14, p. 5.

6. B.P.D.S., *Fourth Annual Report,* 54–55. For a rare criticism, made by a onetime inmate of a penitentiary, see John Reynolds, *Recollections of Windsor Prison* (Boston, 1834), 209: "The science of

architecture," he declared, "has been exhausted in experiments to construct a reformatory prison, as if the form of a cell could regenerate a vicious heart into virtue."

7. Franklin Bache, *Observations and Reflections on the Penitentiary System* (Philadelphia, 1829) , 5.

8. Beaumont and Tocqueville, *On the Penitentiary System,* 80. Francis Bowen, "Review of Francis Gray's *Prison Discipline in America,*" *North American Review,* 66 (1848), 152; B.P.D.S., *Fourth Annual Report,* 55–61. On the prison visits of Tocqueville and Beaumont, see J. P. Mayer, ed., *Alexis de Tocqueville: Journey to America* (New Haven, Conn., 1959) and George W. Pierson, *Tocqueville and Beaumont in America* (New York, 1938) . Of interest too is Seymour Drescher, *Tocqueville and Beaumont on Social Reform* (New York, 1968) .

9. James B. Finley, *Memorials of Prison Life* (Cincinnati, Ohio, 1851) , 41–42.

10. Samuel Gridley Howe, *Prison Discipline,* 88–89; Edward Livingston, *Introductory Report to the Code of Prison Discipline . . .* (Philadelphia, 1827) , 51. See too Inspectors of the Eastern State Penitentiary, *First and Second Annual Report,* 9–10, 19. Almost every report contained a defense of solitary.

11. George W. Smith, *A Defense of the System of Solitary Confinement of Prisoners* (Philadelphia, 1833) , 71, 75. See too Roberts Vaux, *Letter on the Penitentiary System of Pennsylvania* (Philadelphia, 1827) , 10.

12. *Ibid.,* 24, for Smith arguing that labor would produce "relief and pleasure." See too Edward Livingston, *Code of Prison Discipline,* 52–54; Anon., "Prison Discipline: The Auburn and Pennsylvania Systems Compared," *New York Review,* 1840, 15.

13. Frederick Packard, *An Inquiry into the Alleged Tendency of the Separation of Convicts . . . to Produce Disease and Degeneration* (Philadelphia, 1849) , 42; and his *A Vindication of the Separate System of Prison Discipline* (Philadelphia, 1839) , 32. See too Edward Livingston, *Code of Prison Discipline,* 19, and Samuel Gridley Howe, *Prison Discipline,* 54–55.

14. Samuel Gridley Howe, *Prison Discipline,* 25, 28–29, 38–39, 48; Richard Vaux, *The Convict, His Punishment; What It Should Be; And How Applied* (Philadelphia, 1884) , 31. See also Edward Everett, "Review of the Tocqueville-Beaumont Report on American Penitentiary Systems," *North American Review,* 37 (1833) , 133; Thomas McElwee, *A Concise History of the Eastern Penitentiary of Pennsylvania* (Philadelphia, 1835) , 15; George Smith, *A Defense of Solitary Confinement,* 63.

15. Dorothea Dix, *Remarks on Prisons,* 77; Howe, *Prison Discipline,* 31. Edward Livingston, *Letter . . . on the Advantages of the Pennsylvania System of Prison Discipline* (Philadelphia, 1828) , 8–12, as well as *Code of Prison Discipline,* 13, 19.

16. Anon., *Thoughts on Prison Discipline* (Boston, 1839), 13; this work was issued by a supporter of the B.P.D.S. See also Francis Wayland, "Prison Discipline," *North American Review*, 49 (1839), 31–38; Beaumont and Tocqueville, *On the Penitentiary System*, 199.

17. Francis Wayland, "Prison Discipline," 38; Francis C. Gray, *Prison Discipline in America* (Boston, 1847), 181–182. B.P.D.S., *Second Annual Report* (Boston, 1827), 66; almost every report of the society defended the Auburn system. For the response of the Pennsylvania school, see, in addition to the above, *Report of the Committee Appointed to Visit and Inquire into the Condition and Circumstances of the Eastern Penitentiary* (Harrisburg, Pa., 1837), 4; and, Franklin Bache, *Observations of the Penitentiary System*, 9.

18. Anon., *Thoughts on Prison Discipline* (Boston, 1839), 11; Matthew Carey, *Thoughts on Penitentiaries and Prison Discipline* (Philadelphia, 1831), 35. See too Francis Wayland, "Prison Discipline," 32, 39–40. European legislators also made this calculation, at least when first comparing the two systems; later, as in the case of the French, they went over to the Pennsylvania camp. See Seymour Drescher, *Dilemmas of Democracy: Tocqueville and Modernization* (Pittsburgh, Pa., 1968), 136.

19. "Annual Report of Auburn Prison," *N.Y. Senate Docs.*, 1835, I, no. 13, p. 3.

20. On early prison history in Europe, see Max Grünhut, *Penal Reform, A Comparative Study* (Oxford, 1948). Americans certainly knew of Bentham's plans and were familiar with the English structures, as witness Haviland in Pennsylvania. But borrowing was not the heart of the story; they had to work out for themselves the administration and organization of the penitentiary, and they did so in novel ways. See N.Y.P.A., *Second Annual Report* (New York, 1846), 15.

21. Negley Teeters, *The Cradle of the Penitentiary: The Walnut Street Jail at Philadelphia, 1773–1835* (Philadelphia, 1935), describes the structure and operation of this institution; for its influence on New York, see W. David Lewis, *From Newgate to Dannemora*, 29–30. For New Jersey, see Harry E. Barnes, *Penal Institutions of New Jersey*, 60.

22. Board of Visitors, *An Account of the Massachusetts State Prison* (Charlestown, Mass., 1806), 4; *Report of the Committee Appointed by the Legislature of Connecticut, to Inspect the Condition of New-Gate Prison* (Hartford, 1825), 4–18.

23. For the chaotic conditions in the first prisons, see Harry E. Barnes, *Penal Institutions of New Jersey*, 402–419, and Negley Teeters, *The Cradle of the Penitentiary*, 105–106. See also Orlando Lewis, *The Development of American Prisons*, 48, 58, 71–73, which includes a description of the uniforms; Thomas Eddy, *An Account of the State Prison*, 39; *Rules and Regulations for the Government of the Massachusetts State Prison* (Boston, 1823), esp. p. 39; *The Acts of Assembly . . . and the Rules and Regulations Respecting the Peni-*

tentiary of Maryland (Baltimore, 1819) , 24–25. There was to be an element of shame in the donning of uniforms, but no sense of discipline or order.

24. Caleb Lownes, *An Account of the Alteration and Present State of the Penal Law of Pennsylvania* (Philadelphia, 1793) , 81–88; Robert Turnbull, *A Visit to the Philadelphia Prison,* 53–56; Negley Teeters, *The Cradle of the Penitentiary,* 41. For Massachusetts, see Board of Visitors, *The Massachusetts State Prison* (1806) , 13; Samuel Sewall and Nathan Dane, *A Communication . . . for the Regulation of the [Massachusetts] State Prison* (Boston, 1805) , 10–11. See also Thomas Eddy, *An Account of the State Prison,* 14, 19; Harry E. Barnes, *Penal Institutions of New Jersey,* 66, 395; and W. David Lewis, *From Newgate to Dannemora,* 32, 46.

25. Thomas Eddy, *An Account of the State Prison,* 35, 53, 56–58; Caleb Lownes, *The Penal Law of Pennsylvania,* 92–96, and his *Description and Historical Sketch of the Massachusetts State Prison* (Charlestown, Mass., 1816) , 10–13.

26. In addition to the above, see Harry E. Barnes, *Penal Institutions of New Jersey,* 62–63, 414–416; New Jersey, *Revised Statutes,* 1821, code of 1798, p. 272. See also the 1819 compilation of *Rules and Regulations Respecting the Penitentiary of Maryland,* 24–25, and Board of Directors, *Rules and Regulations for the Government of the Massachusetts State Prison* (Boston, 1811) , 12, 19. The New York treadmill experiment is recounted in James Hardie, *The History of the Tread-Mill* (New York, 1824) , 16, 21–22, 181.

27. John Bristed, *The Resources of the United States of America* (New York, 1818) , 436, as quoted in W. David Lewis, *From Newgate to Dannemora,* 62. See also Matthew Carey, *Thoughts on Penitentiaries,* 76; and note 12, ch. 3, above. Compare *Minutes of the Philadelphia Society for Alleviating the Miseries of Public Prisons,* entries of February 9, 1819; November 8, 1820, manuscript record at the Pennsylvania Prison Society.

28. R. Sullivan, *et al., Report of [Massachusetts] Committee, "To Inquire into the Mode of Governing the Penitentiary of Pennsylvania"* (Boston, 1817) , 2; Philadelphia Society for Alleviating the Miseries of Public Prisons, *Penal Code of Pennsylvania,* 5. The New York Society for the Prevention of Pauperism, *Report on the Penitentiary System,* 96. See also *The Committee to Inspect the Condition of New-Gate,* 12.

29. Inspectors of the Eastern State Penitentiary, *Twenty-First Annual Report* (Philadelphia, 1850) , 27, *Fourth Annual Report* (Philadelphia, 1833) , 9–10; Anon., "Prison Discipline," 9. Also, Negley Teeters and John Shearer, *The Prison at Philadelphia,* 169.

30. Gershom Powers, *A Brief Account of Auburn,* 1–2, 16; Inspectors of the State Prisons of New York, *Eighth Annual Report* (Albany, 1856) , 339, where Chaplain John Luckey recounts his early service

at Sing-Sing. The warden's quote is found in *Letter of Gershom Powers, Esq. . . . in relation to Auburn State Prison* (Albany, 1829) , 14.

31. N.Y.P.A., *Fifth Annual Report* (Albany, 1850) , 186–187, surveys the prevailing practices of many penitentiaries on this matter. See too "Annual Report of Mt. Pleasant Prison," *N.Y. Senate Docs.*, 1842, II, no. 39, pp. 25–26; Inspectors of the State Prisons of New York, *First Annual Report* (New York, 1848) , 144–145, 253, 348. For confiscations, see "Annual Report of Mt. Pleasant Prison," *N.Y. Senate Docs.*, 1844, I, no. 20, pp. 21–22.

32. Harry E. Barnes, *Penal Institutions of New Jersey*, 408.

33. James Blaine, *Report of the System of Disbursements, Labor, and Discipline in the Maine State Prison* (Augusta, Me., 1859) , 36. And see, *Laws of the Commonwealth for the Government of the Massachusetts State Prison* (Charlestown, Mass., 1830) , 24.

34. B.P.D.S., *Eleventh Annual Report* (Boston, 1836) , 80; Matthew Carey, *Thoughts on Penitentiaries*, 41–42, 46–47. The medical analogy is made by Samuel Gridley Howe, *Prison Discipline,* 79; see also Franklin Bache, *Observations of the Penitentiary System,* 39, and the 1823 *Rules for the Government of the Massachusetts State Prison*, 8–10.

35. Beaumont and Tocqueville, *On the Penitentiary System,* 57. See also the defenses of the Pennsylvania system cited above.

36. *Ibid.,* 65. Samuel Gridley Howe also raises this image, *Prison Discipline,* 22–23, describing a "stillness . . . that of death." The construction is detailed in W. David Lewis, *From Newgate to Dannemora,* ch. 6.

37. "Annual Report of Auburn Prison," *N.Y. Senate Docs.*, 1835, I, no. 13, p. 3. See also "Report of the Standing Committee on State Prisons," *N.Y. Senate and Assembly Docs.*, 1830, IV, no. 407, p. 1.

38. Orlando Lewis, *The Development of American Prisons*, chs. 7–8, 14–15. Moses Kimball, "Report on Prisons," *Massachusetts Senate Docs.*, January 15, 1855, no. 38, pp. 21–22; *Report of the Committee . . . on the Connecticut State Prison* (New Haven, Conn., 1842) , 47. Accusations and defenses were a regular part of the Connecticut prison system; see, for example, *Report of the Committee . . . on the Connecticut State Prison* (Hartford, 1833) , and the rejoinder, *Minutes of the Testimony Taken Before . . . [the] Committee . . . on the Connecticut State Prison* (Hartford, 1834) .

39. *Annual Report of the Ohio Penitentiary for 1847*, 142, and *Annual Report . . . for 1852*, 25–28; quotation is on p. 25.

40. *Reports of the Illinois Penitentiary for 1855–1856* (Alton, Ill., 1856) , 46; see too *Reports . . . for 1859–1860* (Springfield, Ill., 1861) , 3–4, 12.

41. Board of Inspectors of Iowa Penitentiary, *Reports for the Two Years ending October 1, 1859* (Des Moines, Ia., 1859) , 10–11.

42. The quotations and the punishment methods appear in an excellent summary of Sing-Sing practices, "A Detailed Statement on the Government, Discipline, etc., of the New-York State Prison at Mount-Pleasant," appended to the "Annual Report of Mt. Pleasant Prison," *N.Y. Senate Docs.*, 1834, II, no. 92; see pp. 38, 41–42 for quotations. For the split between those intent on reform and on discipline, see W. David Lewis, *From Newgate to Dannemora*, 83–87, 101–107. But I argue below that the differences between the groups ought not to be exaggerated.

43. "Annual Report of Auburn Prison," *N.Y. Assembly Docs.*, 1840, I, no. 18, pp. 13–14; see too Inspectors of the State Prisons of New York, *Eighth Annual Report* (New York, 1856), 322–323.

44. *Report of the Joint Committee of the Legislature of Pennsylvania, Relative to the Eastern State Penitentiary at Philadelphia* (Harrisburg, Pa., 1835), 41; see also Thomas McElwee, *Concise History of the Eastern Penitentiary*, 19–20. For the Ohio prison, see *Annual Report of the Ohio Penitentiary for 1852*, 25. Examples could be endlessly added. See N.Y.P.A., *Fifth Annual Report*, 166–167, for a survey of several penitentiaries; and the observations of Beaumont and Tocqueville, *On the Penitentiary System*, 74, 77. Also, *Report of the Committee . . . on the Connecticut State Prison* (1842), 47. As the French visitors put it, the prisons were a "complete despotism."

45. "Annual Report of Mt. Pleasant Prison," *N.Y. Senate Docs.*, 1832, I, no. 14, p. 6; John Reynolds, *Recollections of Windsor Prison*, 206.

46. Beaumont and Tocqueville, *On the Penitentiary System*, 90. See also *Letter of Gershom Powers*, 22–23, Francis Lieber, in his translator's preface to *On the Penitentiary System*, 184–187, and N.Y.P.A., *Fifth Annual Report*, 144–167. There were limits, as the dismissal of Lynds made clear; but that the system on the whole was despotic there can be no doubt. See also J. P. Mayer, ed., *Alexis de Tocqueville: Journey to America*, 204: "The system at Sing-Sing," claimed Tocqueville, "seems in some sense like the steamships which the Americans use so much. Nothing is more comfortable, quick, and, in a word, perfect in the ordinary run of things. But if some bit of apparatus gets out of order, the boat, the passengers and the cargo fly into the air."

47. Francis Gray, *Prison Discipline in America*, 70–72. See too Samuel Gridley Howe, *Prison Discipline*, 26; B.P.D.S., *Fourth Annual Report*, 60–61. Also, George Smith, *A Defense of Solitary Confinement*, 24.

48. Orlando Lewis, *The Development of American Prisons*, brings together the data on costs and returns. See 173, 181, for Auburn and Wethersfield; Ohio also showed a profit, 259, 263. By no means, however, was this true for all penitentiaries. For the New York

returns, see Inspectors of the State Prisons of New York, *Sixth Annual Report* (New York, 1853), 25.

49. Despite Lewis's insistence that the prison innovation can be mostly explained in terms of its profitability, the data he gathers shows how much juggling went into the returns. See *The Development of American Prisons*, 201–202, for New Jersey's attempts, and 208–209 for Maryland. A convenient table of the costs of construction in on page 239 — and the sums make eminently clear how much greater the investment was than the returns.

50. The verdict of an excellent survey of prisons, to be discussed further in ch. 10 below, is that the profit and loss issue cannot be easily resolved. E. C. Wines and Theodore W. Dwight, *Report on the Prisons and Reformatories of the United States and Canada* (Albany, 1867), 266. "The matter," they concluded, "is present in the annual reports, in a manner so complex, confused and obscure, that we find it, in the majority of cases, quite impossible to arrive at clear and satisfactory results." The verdict is even more true for the earlier period. There is a mass of detail, as even a glance at any annual report would reveal, but the general conclusions are hardly persuasive.

51. W. D. Lewis, *From Newgate to Dannemora*, ch. 8; Orlando Lewis, *The Development of American Prisons*, 133–146. See also, for the New York story, Walter Hugins, *Jacksonian Democracy and the Working Class* (Stanford, 1960), 155–161; "Annual Report of Auburn Prison," *N.Y. Assembly Docs.*, 1842, II, no. 31, p. 14, and "Annual Report of Mt. Pleasant Prison," *N.Y. Senate Docs.*, 1846, I, no. 16, pp. 31–32. A good discussion of the issue is in William Leggett, "The State Prison Monopoly," *Political Writings of William Leggett* (Boston, 1840), 63–64, 83, 263–271. The problems were also found in Tennessee: Jesse C. Crowe, "The Origin and Development of Tennessee's Prison Problem," *Tennessee Historical Quarterly*, 15 (1956), 111–135.

52. "Government, Discipline of the New-York State Prison," (1834), 18. See too Lieber's translator's preface to *On the Penitentiary*, 14, and *Letter of Gershom Powers*, 16.

53. Gershom Powers, *A Brief Account of Auburn*, 4. The lockstep was found in practically every penitentiary. For one example, see *Rules and Regulations for the Government of the Maryland Penitentiary* (Baltimore, 1853), 15.

54. Samuel Gridley Howe, *Prison Discipline*, 55, was a rare exception to the rule. "People generally admire," he unhappily concluded, "the strict discipline, the military precision of the maneuvers, and the instantaneous obedience to every order, which are seen in some congregate prisons." For another description, see B.P.D.S., *First Annual Report* (Boston, 1826), 57–58.

55. Beaumont and Tocqueville, *On the Penitentiary*, 62, 65; for the Sing-Sing routine, see the 1834 description, "Government, Discipline

of the New-York State Prison." For a similar pattern in Ohio, see J. H. Matthews, *Historical Reminiscences on the Ohio Penitentiary, from its Erection in 1835 to the Present Time* (Columbus, Ohio, 1884), 16–25, 36, 39.

56. "Government, Discipline of the New-York State Prison" (1834), 16. Beaumont and Tocqueville also noted the military career line, *On the Penitentiary,* 62, citing Lynds in New York, Austin in Massachusetts, and Moses Pilsbury in Connecticut. Many of the careers of the prison leaders are obscure; of the several I examined, no clear pattern emerged. Unlike medical superintendents, there was no prior training or experience. Some came up through the ranks, others entered from the law, on the basis of political influence; still others left a small mercantile business, ostensibly equipped to manage the prison industries.

57. The design and appearance of the institutions are in the annual reports and the secondary literature cited above. See also George Smith, *A Defense of Solitary Confinement,* 21.

CHAPTER FIVE

1. For European ideas in their American context, see Norman Dain, *Concepts of Insanity in the United States, 1789–1865* (New Brunswick, N.J., 1964). Dain's major interest is with medical thought and development; I have emphasized the social basis of medical superintendents' thinking. This material is also covered, but much less satisfactorily than by Dain, in Ruth B. Caplan, *Psychiatry and the Community in Nineteenth-Century America* (New York, 1969). The title promises more than the book delivers. For the European story, the most stimulating starting point is Michel Foucault, *Madness and Civilization: A History of Insanity in the Age of Reason* (New York, 1965); for the English experience, see Kathleen Jones, *Lunacy, Law, and Conscience, 1744–1845* (London, 1955).

2. Isaac Ray, *A Treatise on the Medical Jurisprudence of Insanity* (Boston, 1853, 3rd ed.), 69, 129–130. The volume first appeared in 1838. For similar views see the remarks of Samuel Woodward, superintendent, Worcester State Lunatic Hospital, *Seventh Annual Report* (Boston, 1840), 65–66; see too Connecticut Retreat for the Insane, *Eighteenth Annual Report* (Hartford, 1842), 14.

3. New York State Lunatic Asylum at Utica, "Annual Report," *N.Y. Assembly Docs.,* 1845, I, no. 29, p. 24, table VIII; Tennessee Hospital for the Insane, *Fifth Biennial Report* (Nashville, Tenn., 1861), 22, table VII; Connecticut Retreat, *Thirty-Seventh Annual Report* (Hartford, Conn., 1861), 19, table IX. Almost every institutional report contained a similar chart in these years.

4. Worcester Lunatic Hospital, *Seventh Annual Report,* 76.

5. Edward Jarvis, *Causes of Insanity: An Address delivered before the Norfolk, Massachusetts, District Medical Society* (Boston, 1851), 17; Butler Hospital for the Insane, *Annual Report for 1854* (Providence, R.I., 1855), 13. See too Norman Dain, *Concepts of Insanity,* ch. 4.

6. Pliny Earle, *An Address on Psychologic Medicine* (Utica, N.Y., 1867), 18; Dorothea Dix, *Memorial Soliciting a State Hospital for the Insane, submitted to the Legislature of Pennsylvania* (Harrisburg, Pa., 1845), 5. This theme has been widely discussed in American literature; see, R. W. B. Lewis, *The American Adam* (Chicago, 1955), and Leo Marx, *The Machine in the Garden* (New York, 1964).

7. Pliny Earle, *A Visit to Thirteen Asylums for the Insane in Europe* (Philadelphia, 1841), 124; he cited the travels of Humboldt. Dorothea Dix, "Memorial Praying a Grant of Land for the Relief and Support of the Indigent Curable and Incurable Insane in the United States," 30th Congress. 1st sess., 1848, *Senate Miscellaneous Doc.,* no. 150, p. 2. See, too, Amariah Brigham, *Remarks on the Influence of Mental Cultivation and Mental Excitement upon Health* (Boston, 1833), 91.

8. Worcester Lunatic Hospital, *Sixth Annual Report* (Boston, 1839), 10; B.P.D.S., *Twelfth Annual Report* (Boston, 1837), 95; Butler Hospital, *Annual Report for 1854,* 26. The Dix estimate was in the petition to Congress, "Memorial Praying for a Grant of Land," 1–2; for Howe, see "Insanity in Massachusetts," *North American Review,* 56 (1843), 6.

9. See Samuel Tuke's introduction to Maximilian Jacobi, *On the Construction and Management of Hospitals for the Insane* (London, 1841), lxiii. Henry Maudsley, *The Pathology of the Mind* (New York, 1880; 1st ed., London, 1867), 127–129, 133, 170–171.

10. Wilhelm Griesinger, *Mental Pathology and Therapeutics* (London, 1867; 1st ed., 1845), 138–139, 157. See too James C. Pritchard, *A Treatise on Insanity and Other Disorders Affecting the Mind* (Philadelphia, 1837; 1st ed., London, 1835), 251. This literature is discussed in George Rosen, "Social Stress and Mental Disease from the Eighteenth Century to the Present," *Milbank Memorial Fund Quarterly,* 37 (1959), 5–32; Mark D. Altschule, *Roots of Modern Psychiatry: Essays in the History of Psychiatry* (New York, 1957), ch. 7.

11. W. A. F. Browne, *What Asylums Were, Are, and Ought To Be* (Edinburgh, 1837), 52–53, 62–63; the foreign spokesmen were far more circumspect than their American counterparts.

12. Butler Hospital, *Annual Report for 1853* (Providence, R.I., 1854), 12.

13. Edward Jarvis, *Causes of Insanity,* 14–17, as well as his *Address*

Delivered at the Laying of the Corner Stone of the Insane Hospital at Northampton (Northampton, Mass., 1856) , 7–8.

14. Butler Hospital, *Annual Report for 1853,* 22–23.
15. William Sweetser, *Mental Hygiene* (New York, 1850) , 358.
16. Edward Jarvis, *On the Supposed Increase of Insanity* (pamphlet reprinted from the *American Journal of Insanity,* Utica, 1852) , 34; see too his *Causes of Insanity,* 16. Woodward's remarks appeared in Worcester Lunatic Hospital, *Tenth Annual Report* (Boston, 1843) , 62. The 1857 panic was analyzed in N.Y. Lunatic Asylum, "Annual Report," *N.Y. Senate Docs.,* 1859, I, no. 41, p. 21.
17. B.P.D.S., *Twelfth Annual Report,* 95.
18. Butler Hospital, *Annual Report for 1853,* 28–29; Isaac Ray, *Mental Hygiene* (Boston, 1863) , 250–256. See too Amariah Brigham, *Mental Cultivation and Mental Excitement,* 78–79.
19. Edward Jarvis, *Address at Northampton,* 11–12, and *On the Supposed Increase of Insanity,* 31.
20. Butler Hospital, *Annual Report for 1853,* 23–24; Isaac Ray, *Mental Hygiene,* 257.
21. Samuel Woodward discussed this issue in his reports; see Worcester Lunatic Hospital, *Sixth Annual Report,* 49; *Tenth Annual Report,* 40–41; *Eleventh Annual Report* (Boston, 1844) , 52. See too for a denunciation of the Millerite movement, N.Y. Lunatic Asylum, "Annual Report," 1859, 21–22.
22. Amariah Brigham, *Mental Cultivation and Mental Excitement,* 50, 82–83; Worcester Lunatic Hospital, *Tenth Annual Report,* 63.
23. Butler Hospital, *Annual Report for 1859* (Providence, R.I., 1860) , 20–21, and *Annual Report for 1853,* 25.
24. Edward Jarvis, "Tendency of Misdirected Education and the Unbalanced Mind to Produce Insanity," *Barnard's Journal of Education* (1858) , 605; *On the Supposed Increase of Insanity,* 32–33. See too his *Address at Northampton,* 9.
25. Edward Jarvis, "Causes of Mental Disease," *North American Review,* 89 (1859) , 325–326. See too William Sweetser, *Mental Hygiene,* 79; Amariah Brigham, *Mental Cultivation and Mental Excitement,* 14–15, 46–47, 50.
26. Butler Hospital, *Annual Report for 1852* (Providence, R.I., 1853) , 18–21; Isaac Ray, *Mental Hygiene,* 259–261. Cf. Norman Dain, *Concepts of Insanity,* 95–96.
27. The quotations from this volume are found on pp. 134–135. See too, pp. 24–33, 69–71, 138, 250.
28. Connecticut Retreat, *Thirty-Ninth Annual Report* (Hartford, 1863) , 27. Kentucky Asylum, *Annual Report for 1846* (Frankfort, 1847) , 20, and its *Report for the Years 1854–1855* (Frankfort, 1856) , 35.
29. Edward Jarvis, *On the Supposed Increase of Insanity,* 34, and his *Increase of Human Life* (n.p., 1872) , 228.
30. Worcester Lunatic Asylum, *Tenth Annual Report,* 61. The presence of many agricultural workers in the asylums was puzzling and

somewhat disconcerting to the medical superintendents; for their efforts to explain this, see Worcester Lunatic Asylum, *Fifth Annual Report* (Boston, 1838), 45–46, *Sixth Annual Report,* 46, *Eighth Annual Report* (Boston, 1841), 64–65. See too Tennessee Hospital for the Insane, *Third Biennial Report* (Nashville, Tenn., 1857), 41–42.

31. From the careers of fifteen medical superintendents it is clear that most of them attended a medical school, rather than serving some form of apprenticeship; many of them worked their way up the asylum ladder, beginning as a physician, later becoming superintendent. It was not uncommon for chiefs to cross over from one institution to another. A few practiced medicine and took an interest in politics, first serving on an investigatory committee for a state legislature, later getting a legislative appointment to head an asylum. The career lines of this group, as compared with wardens and almshouse heads, was established and certain.

32. Worcester Lunatic Asylum, *Eighth Annual Report,* 70; see too, *Sixth Annual Report,* 50, and *Seventh Annual Report,* 72–75. For similar discussions, see Edward Jarvis, *On the Comparative Liability of Males and Females to Insanity* (Utica, N.Y., 1850), 20–21; Pliny Earle, *Visit to Thirteen Asylums,* 109; Connecticut Retreat, *Eighteenth Annual Report,* 16–17; Butler Hospital, *Report for 1854,* 27. See too Norman Dain, *Concepts of Insanity,* 108–113.

33. Herbert Goldhamer and A. W. Marshall, *Psychosis and Civilization* (New York, 1953).

34. Edward Jarvis, *Address at Northampton,* 12, and *On the Supposed Increase of Insanity,* 21; Dorothea Dix, *Memorial to the Legislature of Pennsylvania,* 5; Samuel Gridley Howe, "Insanity in Massachusetts," 5.

CHAPTER SIX

1. For asylums' dates of origin, see John M. Grimes, *Institutional Care of Mental Patients in the United States* (Chicago, 1934), 123–125. Brief histories of the nineteenth-century asylums can be found in Henry M. Hurd, *The Institutional Care of the Insane in the United States and Canada* (Baltimore, 1916, 4 vols.). A useful survey also is Albert Deutsch, *The Mentally Ill in America: A History of their Care and Treatment* (New York, 1937).

2. A convenient summary of the optimistic statements is in Pliny Earle, *The Curability of Insanity* (Philadelphia, 1887). The quotations are from pp. 23, 27–29; see too, 38–39, 209, table VI. Earle helped to puncture the myth, but he too had once been guilty of perpetuating it: *Visit to Thirteen Asylums,* 130–131. Almost every memorial of Dorothea Dix repeated these declarations.

3. Pliny Earle, *Curability of Insanity*, was the most important statement; see especially pp. 9, 41–42. Some officials did admit to their techniques: Pennsylvania Hospital, *Fifth Annual Report* (Philadelphia, 1846), 25. For the defensiveness of most superintendents, see Worcester Lunatic Hospital, *First Annual Report* (Boston, 1833), 3, 22–23.

4. Dorothea Dix, *Memorial to the Legislature of Pennsylvania*, 3; quotation is condensed from the original. For other examples of her appeal, see *Memorial Soliciting an Appropriation for the State Hospital for the Insane at Lexington [Kentucky]*, (Frankfort, Ky., 1846), 10–11; *Memorial Praying a Grant of Land*, 25–27; *Memorial Soliciting a State Hospital for the Insane submitted to the Legislature of New Jersey* (Trenton, N.J., 1845), 36–37.

5. *Report of Commissioners to Superintend the Erection of a Lunatic Hospital at Worcester* (Boston, 1832), 19–20; *Report of the Committee on the Insane Poor in Connecticut* (New Haven, Conn., 1838), 3–4. See too Philadelphia Citizens Committee on an Asylum for the Insane Poor, *An Appeal to the People of Pennsylvania* (Philadelphia, 1838), 9; Pliny Earle, *Insanity and Insane Asylums* (Louisville, 1841), 34–39; "Investigation of the Bloomingdale Asylum," *N.Y. Assembly Docs.*, 1831, I, no. 263, pp. 30–31.

6. For an introduction to the literature on moral treatment, see Norman Dain, *Concepts of Insanity*, chs. 1, 5; see, also, J. Sanbourne Bockoven, "Moral Treatment in American Psychiatry," *Journal of Nervous and Mental Disease*, 124 (1956), 183–194, 299–309.

7. *Report of the Insane Poor in Connecticut*, 4–5.

8. (Philadelphia, 1880, 2nd ed.). The volume first appeared in 1847. The entire first part was given over to physical details, the second to administrative details. In this same spirit, see Pennsylvania Hospital, *Second Annual Report* (Philadelphia, 1843), 31–32; Ohio Lunatic Asylum, *Thirteenth Annual Report* (Columbus, Ohio, 1852), 60–61.

9. *History of the Association of Medical Superintendents of American Institutions for the Insane*, John Curwen, compiler (n.p., 1875), 4–7, 24–26, 28–30.

10. Pliny Earle, *Institutions for the Insane in Prussia, Austria, and Germany* (Utica, N.Y., 1853), *passim*, and pp. 107–122, 150–151. Earle traveled in 1849. His trip was not an uncommon one; the regularity with which he and his colleagues went to Europe for investigatory purposes ought to warn intellectual historians about taking the notions of a corrupt old world too literally.

11. Sir James Clark, *A Memoir of John Conolly* (London, 1869), 149. Just as Europeans were more cautious about linking civilization with insanity, so they were wary about a cult of institutionalization; see John Conolly, *An Inquiry Concerning the Indications of Insanity* (London, 1830; reprinted, London, 1964).

12. "Report of the Commissioners to Build a Lunatic Asylum," *N.Y. Senate Docs.*, 1839, I, no. 2, pp. 1–2; N.Y. Lunatic Asylum, "Annual Report," *N.Y. Senate Docs.*, 1842, I, no. 20, pp. 1–2, Appendix A, 47 ff. (Hereafter, "Description of Asylums in the U.S."). This survey of hospital practices is an invaluable compendium of information about the pre–Civil War asylums.

13. Isaac Ray, *Mental Hygiene*, 316; Butler Hospital, *Annual Report for 1856* (Providence, R.I., 1857), 19.

14. Edward Jarvis, *Address at Northampton*, 21–23, 25; Pennsylvania Hospital, *Second Annual Report*, 22–23; Philadelphia Citizens Committee, *An Appeal to the People*, 10–11; Ohio Lunatic Asylum, *Thirteenth Annual Report*, 17, 21; B.P.D.S., *Thirteenth Annual Report* (Boston, 1838), 200; and *Fifteenth Annual Report* (Boston, 1840), 420–421.

15. Thomas Kirkbride, *On the Construction of Hospitals for the Insane*, 36–38; *History of the Association of Medical Superintendents*, 24. Isaac Ray, *Mental Hygiene*, 24; Butler Hospital, *Annual Report for 1856*, 24.

16. Butler Hospital, *Annual Report for 1850* (Providence, R.I., 1851), 23; *Annual Report for 1856*, 19; and *Annual Report for 1855*, 13–14, 18. See also Edward Jarvis, *Visit to Thirteen Asylums*, 136, and his *Address at Northampton*, 26; Philadelphia Citizens Committee, *An Appeal to the People*, 10–11; Connecticut Retreat, *Thirty-Ninth Annual Report*, 27.

17. On location of asylums, see N.Y. Lunatic Asylum, "Description of Asylums in the U.S.," 47–49, 55–56. For the Philadelphia story, Pennsylvania Hospital, *First Annual Report* (Philadelphia, 1842), 17, and *Second Annual Report*, 6; cf. New Hampshire Asylum for the Insane, *Annual Report for 1843* (Concord, N.H., 1843), 20.

18. Pennsylvania Hospital, *Second Annual Report*, 27–28. See also Connecticut Retreat, *Twenty-Eighth Annual Report* (Hartford, 1852), 30, and *Thirty-First Annual Report* (Hartford, 1855), 21.

19. N.Y. Lunatic Asylum, "Annual Report," 1842, 29–30, 32, and "Annual Report," *N.Y. Assembly Docs.*, 1843, III, no. 50, pp. 52–53, 55.

20. Ohio Lunatic Asylum, *Second Annual Report* (Columbus, Ohio, 1840), 40–42.

21. N.Y. Lunatic Asylum, "Description of Asylums in the U.S.," 66, 132; New Hampshire Asylum, *Annual Report for 1843*, 19; N.Y. Lunatic Asylum, "Annual Report," *N.Y. Senate Docs.*, 1847, I, no. 30, pp. 18–19. See also Connecticut Retreat, *Twenty-Eighth Annual Report*, 29. On Pennsylvania Hospital and premature removals, see *Fourth Annual Report* (Philadelphia, 1845), 8–9.

22. Edward Jarvis, *The Law of Insanity and Hospitals for the Insane in Massachusetts* (pamphlet reprinted from the *Law Reporter*, Boston, 1859), 16–17. The best survey of commitment practices is N.Y. Lunatic Asylum, "Description of Asylums in the

U.S.," 63, 81–82, 93, 123, 149. The New York incident is recounted in the N.Y. Lunatic Asylum, "Annual Report," 1843, 56–59.

23. Francis Bowen, "The Jurisprudence of Insanity," *North American Review*, 60 (1845), 1–37. Most legal discussions of insanity centered on the issue of criminal responsibility, not on procedures for protecting the insane.

24. N.Y. Lunatic Asylum, "Descriptions of Asylums in the U.S.," 185, letter of Dr. James Macdonald, in response to the trustees' request for a plan of organization (italics added).

25. *Ibid.*, 63, 220–221 (italics added).

26. Pennsylvania Hospital, *First Annual Report*, 23–24.

27. Worcester Lunatic Hospital, *Seventh Annual Report*, 86–87; there too, bell-ringing accompanied every shift. N.Y. Lunatic Asylum, "Annual Report," 1842, 30–31. An excellent study of the origins and routine of the Worcester institution is Gerald N. Grob, *The State and the Mentally Ill: A History of the Worcester State Hospital in Massachusetts, 1830–1920* (Chapel Hill, N.C., 1966). See chs. 2–3 for its daily functioning.

28. Pennsylvania Hospital, *First Annual Report*, 27–29. See also its *Seventh Annual Report* (Philadelphia, 1848), 32–33.

29. Worcester Lunatic Hospital, *Seventh Annual Report*, 86–87; quotation is on p. 94; N.Y. Lunatic Asylum, "Annual Report," 1843, 46–49.

30. Pennsylvania Hospital, *First Annual Report*, 13–14, 22, 26; *Second Annual Report*, 41–44; *Fourth Annual Report*, 33–34.

31. "Comptroller's Investigation of Several Institutions of New York State," *N.Y. Assembly Docs.*, 1840, IV, no. 214, p. 90; Governors of the N.Y. Hospital, "Annual Report," *N.Y. Assembly Docs.*, 1842, V, 8–9. See too William L. Russell, *The New York Hospital: A History of the Psychiatric Service, 1771–1936* (New York, 1945), chs. 13–16.

32. N.Y. Lunatic Asylum, "Description of Asylums in the U.S.," 87–90.

33. N.Y. Lunatic Asylum, "Annual Report," 1842, 5–6, 21–23, 27; "Annual Report," 1843, 51–52.

34. *Ibid.*, "Annual Report," 1843, 51–52, 63; "Annual Report," *N.Y. Senate Docs.*, 1851, I, no. 42, pp. 43–45.

35. Worcester Lunatic Hospital, *Third Annual Report* (Boston, 1836), 9, 29–30; *Fourth Annual Report* (Boston, 1837), 21; *Fifth Annual Report*, 10–11; *Sixth Annual Report*, 81. The Horace Mann quotation is from the *Ninth Annual Report* (Boston, 1842), 8.

36. *Ibid.*, *Thirteenth Annual Report* (Boston, 1846), 6–7; *Fourteenth Annual Report* (Boston, 1847), 6–8. For discharge policies, see *Fifth Annual Report*, 6–7. For details, see Gerald N. Grob, *The State and the Mentally Ill*, chs. 3–4.

37. Kentucky Asylum, *Annual Report for 1845* (Frankfort, Ky., 1846), 27 ff.; Indiana State Central Hospital for the Insane, *First Annual*

Report (Indianapolis, Ind., 1849), 43; N.Y. Lunatic Asylum, "Description of Asylums in the U.S.," 126.

38. N.Y. Lunatic Asylum, "Annual Report," 1851, 44; Worcester Lunatic Hospital, *Ninth Annual Report*, 69; Governors of the New York Hospital, "Annual Report," 1842, 7.

39. N.Y. Lunatic Asylum, "Annual Report," 1843, 55–56; Indiana State Central Hospital for the Insane, *First Annual Report*, 36–37; Pennsylvania Hospital, *First Annual Report*, 12. For Kirkbride's instructions, see Pennsylvania Hospital, *Fourth Annual Report*, 35.

40. See the 1832 *Report of Commissioners to Superintend the Erection of a Lunatic Hospital at Worcester*, 1–2.

41. For designs see N.Y. Lunatic Asylum, "Description of Asylums in the U.S.," 72 (McLean), 122–123, 128–129 (Virginia), 165 (Pennsylvania), 169–170 (Bloomingdale). For Utica, see N.Y. Lunatic Asylum, "Annual Report," 1843, 39–41; for Connecticut Retreat, *Forty-Fifth and Forty-Sixth Annual Reports* (Hartford, 1869–1870), 21. The first annual reports of an asylum invariably contained a picture or a verbal description of the structure. See too Thomas Kirkbride, *On the Construction of Hospitals for the Insane, passim.*

42. N.Y. Lunatic Asylum, "Description of Asylums in the U.S.," 126. In a letter to the New York trustees, Philip Barbiza, chief of the Virginia institution, displayed all the ambivalence one might expect on this issue. For example: "The law of kindness should be the order of the house; nevertheless, discipline and restraint are absolutely necessary."

CHAPTER SEVEN

1. For citations to the Yates and Quincy reports, see ch. 2, note 1; Board of Guardians of the Poor of the City and Districts of Philadelphia, *Report of the Committee to Visit the Cities of Baltimore, New York, Providence, Boston, and Salem* (Philadelphia, 1827). The New York Society for the Prevention of Pauperism (hereafter, N.Y.S.P.P.), issued annual reports for this period.

2. Yates report, 393. Compare J. R. Poynter, *Society and Pauperism*, xiii, and ch. 4. Americans were closest on outlook, probably without knowing it, to Jeremy Bentham. Also, no economic crises here set off the debate.

3. Yates report, 47; New York Almshouse Commissioner, *Annual Report for 1847* (New York, 1848), 6. See too Anon., *Miscellaneous Remarks on the Poor of Boston* (Boston, 1814), 4.

4. N.Y.S.P.P., *Second Annual Report* (New York, 1819), Appendix, 6.

5. N.Y.S.P.P., *Fourth Annual Report* (New York, 1821), 4–5; and its *Fifth Annual Report* (New York, 1822), 14–15; Theodore Sedgwick, *Public and Private Economy, Part First* (New York, 1836), 95.

6. Yates report, 79–81; the costs were probably even higher, for the returns did not include all towns.

7. Quincy report, 13, and *passim;* Philadelphia Board of Guardians, *Report of the [1827] Committee,* 4–7, 21.

8. Stanley Lebergott, *Manpower in Economic Growth: The American Record Since 1800* (New York, 1964), 188.

9. N.Y.S.P.P., *Second Annual Report,* Appendix, 66.

10. Yates report, 6, 20; Quincy report, 31. The western county was Oneida, Yates report, 47.

11. Philadelphia Board of Guardians, *Report of the [1827] Committee,* 26; N.Y.S.P.P., *Fifth Annual Report,* 33.

12. New York Association for Improving the Condition of the Poor, *Thirteenth Annual Report* (New York, 1856), 36–37. (Hereafter, A.I.C.P.) See also its *Eleventh Annual Report* (New York, 1854), 59. For its early history, see Roy Lubove, "The New York Association for Improving the Condition of the Poor: The Formative Years," *New York Historical Society Quarterly,* 43 (1959), 307–328.

13. Yates report, 37; Quincy report, 9.

14. A.I.C.P., *Twelfth Annual Report* (New York, 1855), 19, and its *Eleventh Annual Report,* 58; New York Almshouse Commissioner, *Annual Report for 1848* (New York, 1849), 86–87. See too Thomas R. Hazard, *Report on the Poor and Insane in Rhode-Island* (Providence, R.I., 1851), 10–11.

15. A.I.C.P., *Fourteenth Annual Report* (New York, 1857), 16.

16. Quincy report, 4; Yates report, 392. A.I.C.P., *Twelfth Annual Report,* 18–19; see too Bernard J. Klebaner, "Poverty and its Relief in American Thought, 1815–1861," *Social Service Review,* 38 (1964), 382–383.

17. New York Select Committee, "Report of Charitable Institutions supported by the State, and all City and County Poor and Work Houses and Jails," *N.Y. Senate Docs.,* I, no. 8, 1857, p. 7.

18. Quincy report, 9; Yates report, 393.

19. N.Y.S.P.P., *Fifth Annual Report,* 15; Philadelphia Board of Guardians, *Report of the [1827] Committee,* 25.

20. Yates report, 3, 392; Philadelphia Board of Guardians, *Report of the [1827] Committee,* 24.

21. Yates report, 392; Quincy report, 6. See also N.Y.S.P.P., *Fifth Annual Report,* 31; John T. Sargent, *An Address on Pauperism* (New York, 1846), 9–13. Cf., Bernard J. Klebaner, "Poverty and its Relief in American Thought," 391–392.

22. Leah H. Feder, *Unemployment Relief in Periods of Depression* (New York, 1936), ch. 2, for the response to the 1857 crisis. A.I.C.P., *Eleventh Annual Report,* 18, *Twelfth Annual Report,* 17.

23. *Ibid., Thirteenth Annual Report,* 13, and *Eleventh Annual Report,* 21, 31.

24. *Ibid., Fourteenth Annual Report,* 16–17; Bernard J. Klebaner, "Poverty and its Relief in American Thought," 384–389.

25. Yates report, 57–58; Quincy report, 23.
26. Yates report, 395; Quincy report, 5. The most articulate spokesman in opposition to these views was Matthew Carey, the printer and pamphleteer. See, *Essays on Public Charities of Philadelphia* (Philadelphia, 1830), *Letters on the Condition of the Poor* (Philadelphia, 1835), and *A Plea for the Poor* (Philadelphia, 1836).
27. Cincinnati Orphan Asylum, *Annual Report for 1848* (Cincinnati, Ohio, 1848), 3.
28. Thomas Smyth, *Oration Delivered on the Forty-Eighth Anniversary of the Orphan House in Charleston, S.C.* (Charleston, S.C., 1837), 6; *Minutes of the Union Society; Being an Abstract of Existing Records, 1750–1858* (Savannah, Ga., 1860), quoting an 1835 sermon by W. Preston, 129. See too Jewish Foster Home Society, *Constitution and By Laws* (Philadelphia, 1855), 3; its *First Annual Report* (Philadelphia, 1856), 4, and *Fifth Annual Report* (Philadelphia, 1860), 5.
29. Boston Asylum for Boys, *A Statement of the Present Depression Conditions of the Funds . . .* (Boston, 1831), 6–7.
30. New York Juvenile Asylum, *Fourth Annual Report* (New York, 1856), 35–37; and *Eighth Annual Report* (New York, 1860), 17, quoting an earlier statement of aims.
31. Walter Channing, *An Address on the Prevention of Pauperism* (Boston, 1843), 18–19.
32. *Ibid.,* 20–21.
33. *Ibid.,* 24, 35–36.
34. *Ibid.,* 22.
35. *Ibid.,* 62, 23.
36. *Ibid.,* 39.
37. For a contemporary's appreciation of Tuckerman's career, see Samuel Lothrop, *Address to the Benevolent Fraternity of Churches in Boston* (Boston, 1856); for a later one, Daniel McColgan, *Joseph Tuckerman, Pioneer in American Social Work* (Washington, D.C., 1940). For the New York counterpart, see *Mr. Arnold's Second Semi-Annual Report of his Services as Minister At Large in New-York* (New York, 1834).
38. Joseph Tuckerman, *On the Elevation of the Poor* (E. E. Hale, ed., Boston, 1874), 62; the reports were given 1826–1833.
39. *Ibid.,* 69, 77, 81.
40. *Ibid.,* 168–169, 103, 105, 177.
41. *Ibid.,* 115, 111, 131.
42. *Ibid.,* 103.
43. *Ibid.,* 105. For a dramatic comparison of the shift in the content of sermons, see Abiel Holmes, *A Discourse Delivered at the Opening of the New Almshouse in Cambridge* (Cambridge, Mass., 1818), very reminiscent of the eighteenth century; and Charles Burroughs, *A Discourse delivered in the Chapel of the New Almshouse, in Portsmouth, New Hampshire* (Portsmouth, N.H., 1835), for the new

style. See also John S. Stone, *Considerations on the Care of the Poor in Large Cities* (Boston, 1838); Andrew Peabody, *"Who is My Neighbor:" A Sermon* (Newburyport, Mass., 1841), 11–13.

44. Commissioners of the [Massachusetts] Pauper Laws, *Report of 1833* (Boston, 1835), 37–43.

CHAPTER EIGHT

1. Commissioners of the [Massachusetts] Pauper Laws, *Report of 1833*, surveyed a majority of towns, reporting on methods of relief, and dates of origin of the almshouse; the Quincy report also contained a survey. The first thorough count appeared in 1837, Secretary of the Commonwealth, *Abstract of Returns of the Overseers of the Poor in Massachusetts, 1833–1855* (Boston, 1855). The structures numbered 163 in 1837. See "Abstract of 1833," and "Abstract of 1840," for expenditures and investments.

2. Massachusetts Board of State Charities, *First Annual Report* (Boston, 1865), 384–385, table 81. The figures were: 6,948 persons relieved in state almshouses; 3,487 in county ones; 969 persons received full-time support out of the almshouse; 14,574 received temporary outdoor relief. Among urban counties, Worcester had 50 almshouses, Middlesex, 43, Essex, 25; among the rural, Berkshire, 2, Hampshire, 6.

3. Yates report, *passim;* David M. Schneider, *Public Welfare in New York State,* 242. For acreage and numbers, see Secretary of State of New York, "Annual Report Relative to Statistics on the Poor," *N.Y. Senate Docs.,* 1853, I, no. 72, pp. 52–54.

4. *Ibid.,* 48–49; New York Select Committee, *Report of Charitable Institutions* [1857], 27–95. Blanche D. Coll, *Perspectives in Public Welfare* (Washington, D.C., 1969), chs. 2–3, is a broad account.

5. Thomas R. Hazard, *Poor and Insane in Rhode Island,* 9–10, 64–65.

6. Philadelphia Board of Guardians, *Report of the [1827] Committee, passim;* Bernard J. Klebaner, "The Home Relief Controversy in Philadelphia, 1782–1861," *Pennsylvania Magazine of History and Biography,* 78 (1954), 413–423. Philadelphia in 1879 again abolished outdoor relief. See too Charles Lawrence, *History of the Philadelphia Almshouses and Hospitals* (n.p., 1905).

7. Aileen E. Kennedy, *The Ohio Poor Law and Its Administration* (Chicago, 1934), ch. 3; Isabel Campbell Bruce, *The Michigan Poor Law* (Chicago, 1936), 18, 23–27. See too John L. Gillin, *History of Poor Relief Legislation in Iowa* (Iowa City, Iowa, 1914), 43–46.

8. James Brown, *The History of Public Assistance in Chicago, 1833 to 1893* (Chicago, 1941), 38–43.

9. Fern Boan, *A History of Poor Relief Legislation and Administration*

in Missouri (Chicago, 1941), 74–75; Dorothea Dix, *A Review of the Present Condition of the State Penitentiary of Kentucky with Brief Notices and Remarks upon the Jails and Poor-Houses* (Frankfort, Ky., 1846), 17–18, 29, 31, 33.

10. Part II of the Yates report has a convenient summary of settlement laws in many of the states; see too David M. Schneider, *Public Welfare in New York State*, 239–240; Edward Warren Capen, *Poor Law of Connecticut*, 97–115, 172–181; for his summary judgment, p. 169; Sophonisba P. Breckinridge, *The Illinois Poor Law and Its Administration* (Chicago, 1939), 18–25.

11. Margaret Creech, *Three Centuries of Poor Law Administration*, ch. 7; quotation is from p. 156.

12. Alice Shaffer and Mary Wysor Keefer, *The Indiana Poor Law* (Chicago, 1936), 20, 31; Aileen E. Kennedy, *The Ohio Poor Law*, 16–18, 25–27; Fern Boan, *Poor Relief in Missouri*, 23.

13. Yates report, 393; Quincy report, 7–9, 16.

14. Yates report, 395; see also the remarks of Walter Channing and Joseph Tuckerman, below, notes 18, 19.

15. Quincy report, 18, 30, 17, 25, 18, 23.

16. Yates report, 393; see also 75, 395–396. Edward Livingston, *Introductory Report to the Code of Prison Discipline*, 25.

17. Charles Burroughs, *A Discourse Delivered in the Chapel of the New Alms-House*, 87, 90–91.

18. Walter Channing, *The Prevention of Pauperism*, 62.

19. Joseph Tuckerman, *On the Elevation of the Poor*, 174–175, 182.

20. New York Almshouse Commissioner, *Annual Report for 1847*, 4–7; Governors of the [New York] Almshouse, *Fourth Annual Report* (New York, 1853), 157–158.

21. Governors of the [New York] Almshouse, *First Annual Report* (New York, 1850), 180–181, and *Fourth Annual Report*, 157–158, and *Sixth Annual Report* (New York, 1855), 166, 209.

22. *Ibid., Sixth Annual Report*, 197; *Second Annual Report* (New York, 1851), 203–211; see too, *Third Annual Report* (New York, 1852), 9.

23. See, in the Massachusetts Historical Society, manuscript volume, *Charlestown Monthly Meetings:* "Report of the Committee on Rules and Regulations for the Government of the House," December 25, 1847, especially rules II, IV, VI, IX. Cf., *Rules and Regulations for the Internal Government of the [Philadelphia] Almshouse and House of Employment* (Philadelphia, 1822), 4–12. See too Artemas Simonds, *Report on Almshouses and Pauperism* (Boston, 1835), *passim;* Simonds described many of the eastern urban institutions, but not in very discriminating fashion.

24. Thomas R. Hazard, *Poor and Insane in Rhode Island*, 69, 71, 72.

25. *Ibid.*, 70, 71.

26. Biographical information on almshouse superintendents is in very

short supply, a reflection of their lack of prominence. But from all accounts, they were untrained and barely middle-class in status. See Michigan Board of State Commissioners, *Report of the Charitable, Penal, Pauper and Reformatory Institutions for 1873* (Lansing, Mich., 1873), 67; and their *Second Biennial Report* (Lansing, Mich., 1875), 46.

27. Quincy report, 9, 21; Yates report, 395–396: "It will relieve the poor," Yates concluded, "with greater humanity, and emphatically with more economy." See there too, 62–63. Cf. James Brown, *Public Assistance in Chicago*, 39, quoting newspaper reports.

28. Quincy report, 30, 16, 23–24.

29. Yates report, 62, 26–27; also, 16, 18.

30. Commissioners of the [Massachusetts] Pauper Laws, *Report of 1833*, 44–45.

31. *Ibid.*, 46–47, 51–52, 55–56, 67–68, 71–73, 75.

32. *Ibid.*, 56, 70, 72, on labor; 59, 60, 69, on solitary; 42, on the lack of a model institution.

33. New York Almshouse Commissioner, *Annual Report for 1846* (New York, 1847), 373–374, 389. Governors of the [New York] Almshouse, *First Annual Report*, 24. Commissioners of [New York] Public Charities and Correction, *First Annual Report* (New York, 1861), 3.

34. Governors of the [New York] Almshouse, *First Annual Report*, 11, 180–181.

35. *Ibid.*, 23–24; see too, *Second Annual Report*, 9–10. Commissioners of [New York] Public Charities and Correction, *First Annual Report*, 3.

36. Governors of the [New York] Almshouse, *First Annual Report*, 18–20, 181; *Second Annual Report*, 10.

37. New York Select Committee, *Report of Charitable Institutions*, 2–3, 6.

38. *Ibid.*, 7, 33, 70.

39. *Ibid.*, 29, 30, 37–38, 33–34, 61–62, 84–85.

40. Secretary of State of New York, "Annual Report Relative to Statistics on the Poor," 99, 108, 100, 104–106; the letters first appeared in the *Columbia Republican* in 1853.

41. Bernard J. Klebaner, "Employment of Paupers in Philadelphia's Almshouse before 1861," *Pennsylvania History*, 24 (1957), 144–147. It is true that the medical facilities of the Philadelphia almshouse were well used for training students. Given the standards of the time, it is not altogether clear if the patients profited from this arrangement. More to the point, the hospital was just one part of the original almshouse reform design.

42. James Brown, *Public Assistance in Chicago*, 20, 32.

43. Dorothea Dix, *Memorial Soliciting a State Hospital for the [New Jersey] Insane*, 19–20; and *Review of the State Penitentiary of Kentucky*, 35.

44. Dorothea Dix, *Memorial Soliciting a State Hospital for the [New Jersey] Insane,* 5–6, 8, 9.

45. Dorothea Dix, *Review of the State Penitentiary of Kentucky,* 17, 20, 15.

46. Dorothea Dix, *Memorial Soliciting a State Hospital for the Protection and Cure of the Insane, submitted to the General Assembly of North Carolina* (Raleigh, N.C., 1848), 15, 17, 22.

47. Thomas R. Hazard, *Poor and Insane in Rhode Island,* 25, 10, 50.

48. Secretary of State of New York, "Annual Report relative to Statistics on the Poor," 117, 123–124. Cf., S. H. Elliot, *A Look at Home, or Life in the Poor Houses of New England* (New York, 1860, 2nd ed.), 224–225, 234.

CHAPTER NINE

1. Homer Folks, *The Care of Destitute, Neglected, and Delinquent Children* (Albany, N.Y., 1900), 30–36.

2. *Ibid.,* 35–36, for Folks's "List of Children's Charities." For New York's public and private children's institutions, see the 1857 New York Select Committee, *Report of Charitable Institutions,* 97–111. See too the survey of Henry Thurston, *The Dependent Child* (New York, 1930).

3. The Boston Asylum and Farm School admitted the poor, the vagrant, and those from homes that were, to the trustees, morally deficient; the New York Juvenile Asylum took in vagrants but not criminals. The Philadelphia Orphan Asylum accepted only very young children: boys below six, girls below eight; the Baltimore Home for Friendless Children admitted the poor as well as the orphaned.

4. Managers and Superintendents of Houses of Refuge and Schools of Reform, *Proceedings of the First Convention* (New York, 1857). They collected a wide range of information about the institutions, from admissions to disciplinary habits. Table A, 85–89, puts much of the data in summary form. See too Philadelphia House of Refuge, *Seventh Annual Report* (Philadelphia, 1835), 3, 23–24, and *The Design and Advantages of the House of Refuge* (Philadelphia, 1850), 11, 28–29.

5. Philadelphia Orphan Society, *Sixteenth Annual Report* (Philadelphia, 1831), 3–4; Boston Children's Friend Society, *Eighteenth Annual Report* (Boston, 1851), 5.

6. New Hampshire State Reform School, *Report for 1852* (Concord, N.H., 1852), 9; Philadelphia House of Refuge, *Fourteenth Annual Report* (Philadelphia, 1842), 3, and its *Second Annual Report* (Philadelphia, 1830), 5. See too New York House of Refuge, *Thirtieth Annual Report,* 55.

7. In Boston, the Temporary Home for the Destitute, as well as the Children's Mission, followed this course; so did the Children's Aid Society, founded by Charles Loring Brace in 1852, which soon became a model for other organizations.

8. Philadelphia House of Refuge, *Fifth Annual Report* (Philadelphia, 1833), 4, italics added. House of Refuge Managers, *Proceedings of the First Convention,* 49; see there too, 29, 125.

9. Boston Asylum and Farm School, *Report for 1845* (Boston, 1845), 14; see also, *Report for 1839* (Boston, 1839), 11.

10. Managers of the Philadelphia House of Refuge, *An Address to their Fellow Citizens of Philadelphia* (Philadelphia, 1826), 6–7; Boston Children's Friend Society, *Fifth Annual Report* (Boston, 1839), 7; New York House of Refuge, *Second Annual Report* (New York, 1827), 80.

11. Orphan House of Charleston, S.C., *Proceedings of the Sixty-Sixth Anniversary* (Charleston, S.C., 1855), 50.

12. Boston Asylum and Farm School, *Report for 1845,* 6, 15; *Report for 1849* (Boston, 1849), 12. Cf., *Report for 1842* (Boston, 1842), 7.

13. New York Juvenile Asylum, *Fourth Annual Report,* 25.

14. New York House of Refuge, *Second Annual Report,* 78, 103, 92, 83. See too, *First Annual Report* (New York, 1826), 57, and *Third Annual Report* (New York, 1828), 57.

15. Managers of the Philadelphia House of Refuge, *An Address to their Fellow Citizens,* 6, 10–11.

16. House of Refuge Managers, *Proceedings of the First Convention,* 48–49.

17. For a survey of some of this literature, see Anne L. Kuhn, *The Mother's Role in Childhood Education: New England Concepts, 1830–1860* (New Haven, Conn., 1947); and Robert Sunley, "Early Nineteenth-Century American Literature on Child Rearing," *Childhood in Contemporary Cultures,* Margaret Mead and Martha Wolfenstein, eds. (Chicago, 1955), 150–167.

18. Artemas Muzzey, *The Fireside: An Aid to Parents* (Boston, 1854), 38, 296; Herman Humphrey, *Domestic Education* (Amherst, Mass., 1840), 22, 16, 17, 21; Nicholas M. Kirwan, *The Happy Home* (New York, 1858), v. See too Ann E. Porter, *Uncle Jerry's Letters to Young Mothers* (Boston, 1854), 78–79; L. H. Sigourney, *Letters to Mothers* (New York, 1846, 6th ed.), 14.

19. Erastus Hopkins, *The Family a Religious Institution* (Troy, N.Y., 1840), x–xi; Nicholas Kirwan, *The Happy Home,* 21–22, 63–64; Herman Humphrey, *Domestic Education,* 22; Artemas Muzzey, *The Fireside,* 59.

20. Artemas Muzzey, *The Fireside,* 82–83; Ann E. Porter, *Uncle Jerry's Letters,* 49. See too Herman Humphrey, *Domestic Education,* 28, 36–37; Jason Whitman, *Lecture on Home Preparation for School* (Boston, 1846), 16, 30.

21. Catherine E. Beecher, *A Treatise on Domestic Economy for the*

Use of Young Ladies at Home and at School (Boston, 1842), 224, 227; Jacob Abbott, *The Rollo Code of Morals* (Boston, 1841), 42.

22. L. H. Sigourney, *Letters to Mothers*, 48, 115–117; William A. Alcott, *The Young Mother* (Boston, 1836, 2nd ed.), 193.

23. Anon., *Letters on the Moral and Religious Duties of Parents, by a Clergyman* (Boston, 1844), 42, 78–79, 87, 92; John Abbott, *The Mother at Home* (New York, 1833), 21, 25–26.

24. Lydia M. Child, *The Mother's Book* (New York, 1844, 6th. ed.), 49–50; John Abbott, *The Mother at Home*, 13, 11.

25. John Hall, *On the Education of Children* (New York, 1835), 41–45, 95–96; quotation is on p. 45; Nicholas Kirwan, *The Happy Home*, 48; Theodore Dwight, Jr., *The Father's Book* (Boston, 1834), 111–117.

26. Erastus Hopkins, *The Family a Religious Institution*, 90, 103–106; Ann E. Porter, *Uncle Jerry's Letters*, 50, 46. See too Mrs. Louisa Tuthill, *The Nursery Book* (New York, 1849), 95.

27. See, for example, Boston Female Asylum, *An Account of the Rise, Progress and Present State* (Boston, 1803), 10.

28. Philadelphia Orphan Society, *Constitution and By Laws* (Philadelphia, 1815), 9; District of Columbia Orphan Asylum, Act of Incorporation, reprinted in *Fourteenth Annual Report* (Washington, D.C., 1830), 7.

29. New York House of Refuge, *Fifth Annual Report* (New York, 1830), 187; House of Refuge Managers, *Proceedings of the First Convention*, 60–65. For the exceptions, see Boston Children's Friend Society, *Act of Incorporation, Constitution, Government, and By Laws* (Boston, 1834), 5, 19; and, Temporary Home for the Destitute, *Fifth Annual Report* (Boston, 1851), 5.

30. New York Juvenile Asylum, *Eighth Annual Report*, 29–30; Baltimore Home of the Friendless, *First Annual Report* (Baltimore, 1854), 8; Boston Children's Friend Society, *Act of Incorporation*, 6–7.

31. New York House of Refuge, *Seventh Annual Report* (New York, 1832), 286; Philadelphia House of Refuge, *Seventh Annual Report*, 34–35, and *Fourth Annual Report* (Philadelphia, 1832), 26–27.

32. Philadelphia House of Refuge, *Twentieth Annual Report* (Philadelphia, 1848), 9; Boston Asylum and Farm School, *Report for 1849*, 12; New York Juvenile Asylum, *Fourth Annual Report*, 19–20.

33. New York House of Refuge, *Fifth Annual Report*, 189, 209–210; and manuscript volume, at Syracuse University Library, *Minutes of the Managers of the Indenture Committee*, 1827. See too Philadelphia House of Refuge, *Second Annual Report*, 6–7, *Fourth Annual Report*, 3–12, 23. For general observations, House of Refuge Managers, *Proceedings of the First Convention*, 63. Most notable was the absence of a concern with aftercare in the institution reports.

34. New York House of Refuge, *Seventh Annual Report*, 253–255.
35. New York House of Refuge, *Tenth Annual Report* (New York, 1835), 5–6; *Twenty-First Annual Report* (New York, 1846), 13; and *Thirtieth Annual Report*, 81–85.
36. Philadelphia House of Refuge, *First Annual Report* (Philadelphia, 1829), 8 ff.; *Fourth Annual Report*, 26–27; for the quotation, *Sixth Annual Report* (Philadelphia, 1834), 19–20. The counting procedure was first mentioned in the *Tenth Annual Report* (Philadelphia, 1838).
37. J. F. Richmond, "The House of Reformation," *New England Magazine*, 3 (1832), 382–390.
38. House of Refuge Managers, *Proceedings of the First Convention*, 85, table A; 95–96.
39. *History of the Orphan Asylum in Philadelphia* (Philadelphia, 1832), 33–34, 40–44; Orphan House of Charleston, S.C., *Proceedings of the Sixty-Sixth Anniversary Convention*, 46–47, 61–62. Lydia M. Child, *Letters from New York* (New York, 1845), 210.
40. *Minutes of the [Savannah] Union Society*, 166; Baltimore Home of the Friendless, *First Annual Report*, 7; District of Columbia Orphan Asylum, *Fourteenth Annual Report*, 3–7. *History of the Orphan Asylum in Philadelphia*, 54–55.
41. Baltimore Home of the Friendless, *First Annual Report*, 9; Governors of the [New York] Almshouse, *Sixth Annual Report* (New York, 1854), 87. Lydia M. Child, *Letters from New York*, 210; New York Juvenile Asylum, *First Annual Report* (New York, 1853), 20. See too Orphan House of Charleston, S.C., *Proceedings of the Sixty-Sixth Anniversary Convention*, 13.
42. Lydia M. Child, *Letters from New York*, 209. See also Mary Howland, *The Infant School Manual* (Worcester, Mass., 1830), 21, 28–29; New York Juvenile Asylum, *First Annual Report*, 20.
43. Philadelphia House of Refuge, *Sixth Annual Report*, 20; House of Refuge Managers, *Proceedings of the First Convention*, 92, 128–129.
44. Providence Reform School, *First Annual Report* (Providence, R.I., 1851), 21; New York House of Refuge, *Seventh Annual Report*, 255–256.
45. House of Refuge Managers, *Proceedings of the First Convention*, 90–93.
46. *Ibid.*, 46, 126–127, 139. See too New York Juvenile Asylum, *Eighth Annual Report*, 76–77.
47. Edited from the manuscript entries of case histories of 1825, in order of citation: case 5, January 17; case 8, March 5, 8, 10; case 9, April 25; case 10, March 30; case 11, January 9, 11, 13, 15; case 12, April 12; case 15, March 20; case 26, March 28; case 14, February 24. For the similarities to the Philadelphia refuge see Negley Teeters, "The Early Days of the Philadelphia House of Refuge," *Pennsylvania History*, 27 (1960), 175–177, 183–185.

48. From the manuscript volume, *Daily Journal of the New York House of Refuge*, I, 1825, condensed from the notes of March. For the jury of inmates, see entry of March 30.
49. Robert S. Pickett, *House of Refuge: Origins of Juvenile Reform in New York State, 1815–1857* (Syracuse, N.Y., 1969), 144–145.
50. *Ibid.*, 148, 160–161.
51. Baltimore Home of the Friendless, *First Annual Report*, 9; New York Juvenile Asylum, *Second Annual Report* (New York, 1854), 7.
52. Remarks of F. S. W. Gleason, at House of Refuge Managers, *Proceedings of the First Convention*, 135.

CHAPTER TEN

1. Quotations are on pp. 62 and 286.
2. George Underwood, *et al.*, "Report of the Committee Appointed to Examine the Several State Prisons," *N.Y. Assembly Docs.*, 1852, no. 20, p. 14. N.Y. State Prison Commission, *Investigations of the State Prisons and Report Thereon* (New York, 1876), 2–6, 8, 353–361.
3. "Report from the Association Relative to Prison Reform," *American Social Science Association Journal*, 7 (1874), 364–365; see also Negley Teeters and John Shearer, *The Prison at Philadelphia*, 218–219 and the entry in the *Minutes of the Proceedings of the Committee on the Eastern Penitentiary*, May 31, 1854, manuscript record at the Pennsylvania Prison Society. For New York conditions see A. Webster, Jr., "A Visit to Our State Prisons," *Appleton's Journal*, 2 (1874), 229–230. Also, New Jersey Prison Discipline Committee, *Report of the Commissioners to Examine the Various Systems of Prison Discipline* (Trenton, N.J., 1869), 4–5, and Franklin B. Sanborn, "The Progress in Our Prisons," *Old and New*, 2 (1870), 242.
4. E. C. Wines and Theodore Dwight, *Report on the Prisons*, 175–177. "Communication, then, we must believe," they wrote, "takes place among convicts continually, and, in most prisons, to a very great extent." On the decline of other restrictions, see there, 213–222, and N.Y.P.A., *Fifth Annual Report* (Albany, 1850), 186–187.
5. Franklin B. Sanborn, "The Progress in Our Prisons," 242, and his "American Prisons," *North American Review*, 103 (1866), table on p. 398. Of 25 prisons that Sanborn examined, only six had a profit, and even there it was meager (402–403). See too N.Y.P.A., *Nineteenth Annual Report* (Albany, 1864), 353.
6. *Ibid.*, 108–117, for the N.Y.P.A. survey of conditions in Sing-Sing. See also New Jersey Prison Discipline Committee, "Report of Prison Discipline," 7. For general statements, A. Webster, Jr., "A

Visit to Our State Prisons," 230, and Franklin B. Sanborn, "American Prisons," 403. On Charlestown, see "Report from the [American Social Science] Association relative to Prison Reform," 365–369; Gideon Haynes, *Pictures from Prison Life: An Historical Sketch of the Massachusetts State Prison* (Boston, 1869). Gresham M. Sykes, *The Society of Captives* (Princeton, 1958) provides not only an excellent description of a present-day prison but a theoretical framework for understanding why discipline would be so fitful.

7. E. C. Wines and Theodore Dwight, *Report on Prisons*, 178–179, 181. The same fears reappeared in the 1852 New York Underwood Committee "Report of Several State Prisons," 55.

8. Wines and Dwight, *Report on Prisons,* 110; similar sentiments were expressed in the "Report from the [American Social Science] Association Relative to Prison Reform," 370–372.

9. Underwood Committee, "Report of Several State Prisons," 40–41, 55; Warren Spalding, "Some Methods of Preventing Crime," *Seventh Annual National Conference of Charities and Correction* (Boston, 1880), 60. (Hereafter, N.C.C.C.) For other statements revealing a new sensitivity to the cruelty of the prison systems, see Zebulon Brockway, *et al.,* "Report of the Standing Committee on Crimes and Penalties," *Tenth Annual N.C.C.C.* (Madison, Wisc., 1883), 165–166; Henry Hoyt, "The Evolution of Prisons," *Twelfth Annual N.C.C.C.* (Boston, 1885), 294–297.

10. For an introduction to these programs, see Franklin B. Sanborn, "The Present State of the Prison Discipline Question," *North American Review,* 102 (1866), 210–225. See also Wines and Dwight, *Report on Prisons,* 72–76; N.Y.P.A., *Nineteenth Annual Report,* 14–15, 20–21, 46–47; A. Woodbury, "Prison Reform," *Old and New,* 3 (1871), 759 ff. For later developments, Zebulon Brockway, *et al.,* "Report on Crimes and Penalties," 168, is important, and so is Roeliff Brinkerhoff, "Post-Penitentiary Treatment of Criminals," *Tenth Annual N.C.C.C.,* 218–228, and "Prison Reform," *Thirteenth Annual N.C.C.C.* (Boston, 1886), 91–97.

11. Franklin B. Sanborn, "American Prisons," 384–385.

12. See, for example, the reports of New York wardens Levi Lewis and William Beardsley in the 1850's, which are almost exclusively concerned with financial matters. The chaplain's reports added whatever comments there were on other concerns.

13. Critics in the post-1850 period were very distressed with the baneful effects of the contract labor system; for a summary of their position, see Wines and Dwight, *Report on Prisons,* 252–262.

14. See the discussion of biographical sketches of prison inmates in ch. 3, above; cases such as those of convicts no. 342 and 358 make this point clearly.

15. *Report of the Connecticut State Penitentiary for 1840* (New Haven,

1840) , 25, Table 1, and its *Report . . . for 1839* (New Haven, 1839) , 12.

16. "Annual Report of Auburn Prison," *N.Y. Assembly Docs.,* 1838, III, no. 86, tables of B. C. Smith, chaplain (n.p.) ; and "Annual Report of Auburn Prison," *N.Y. Assembly Docs.,* 1840, I, no. 18, pp. 13–15.

17. *Annual Report of the Ohio Penitentiary for 1839* (Columbus, Ohio, 1840) , 12–24. All the inmates are listed by name, place of birth, age, occupation, crime, sentence. On literacy, see *Annual Report of the Ohio Penitentiary for 1848* (Columbus, Ohio, 1849) , 18. The Virginia statistics, along with those for other states as well, are found in the N.Y.P.A., *Fifth Annual Report* (Albany, 1850) , 56–57. These figures are not to be taken too precisely. But the bulk of the returns point in the same direction.

18. Massachusetts Board of State Charities, *Special Report on Prisons and Prison Discipline* (Boston, 1865) , 96–97, Table XII.

19. Compiled from the *Annual Report of the Ohio Penitentiary for 1839,* 12–24; *Biennial Report of the Illinois State Penitentiary, 1857–1858* (Springfield, Ill., 1859) , 50–73. The latter, too, has a list of names, place of birth, age, crime, and sentence. See also Wines and Dwight, *Report on Prisons,* 273; Board of Inspectors of the Massachusetts State Prison, *Annual Report for 1859* (Boston, 1859) , 28–31. Compare, also, prisoners admitted with those remaining, in Inspectors of the State Prisons of New York, *Tenth Annual Report* (Albany, 1858) , 46–47, 156–157.

20. E. C. Wines, "The Sources of Crime," *American Presbyterian Review,* 1 (1863) , 572; once again the phrase, "seminary of vice," began to reappear in descriptions of penitentiaries.

21. The earlier discussion, especially the work cited above in note 10, includes the most important writings of the penologists of this period. The quotation from Wines and Dwight, *Report on Prisons,* is on p. 115. For the popularity of the suggestions, see New Jersey Prison Discipline Committee, *Report of Various Systems of Prison Discipline,* 43–45; Henry Hoyt, "The Evolution of Prisons," 296–297. The program was becoming the focus of attention, and did make gains. But its victory was still a long way off. For the later period, see "Report of the Committee on Penal and Reformatory Systems, *Eighteenth Annual N.C.C.C.* (Boston, 1891) , 210–213.

22. N.Y.P.A., *Ninth Annual Report* (Albany, 1854) , 61, for such a complaint.

23. Inspectors of the State Prisons of New York, *Sixth Annual Report* (Albany, 1853) , 117–118, for the Sing-Sing figures. For the others, see the survey in the N.Y.P.A., *Fifth Annual Report* (New York, 1850) , 80–81. On the Pennsylvania data, consult Inspectors of the Eastern State Penitentiary, *Nineteenth Annual Report* (Philadelphia, 1848) , 30, and *Twentieth Annual Report* (Philadelphia, 1849) , 14, and *Twenty-First Annual Report* (Philadelphia, 1850) ,

8. See also Wines and Dwight, *Report on Prisons,* 250; A. Woodbury, "Prison Reform," 758, for an estimate that 82 percent of 1,000 convicts in 1870 were laborers or servants. Woodbury also calculated that 44 percent were illiterate.

24. "Annual Report of Auburn Prison," *N.Y. Assembly Docs.,* 1838, III, no. 86, tables of B. C. Smith, chaplain (n.p.) ; see too, N.Y.P.A., *Eighteenth Annual Report* (New York, 1863) , 111.

25. Inspectors of the Eastern State Penitentiary, *Fifteenth Annual Report* (Philadelphia, 1844), 21; *Annual Report of the Ohio Penitentiary for 1839,* 12–24.

26. N.Y.P.A., *Fifth Annual Report,* 57; Inspectors of the State Prisons of New York, *Second Annual Report* (Albany, 1850) , 133, 265, 337, and *Eleventh Annual Report* (Albany, 1859) , 91, 149, 158. On Charlestown, see Board of Inspectors of the Massachusetts State Prison, *Annual Report for 1859,* 32–33.

27. Inspectors of the Eastern State Penitentiary, *Twenty-Fourth Annual Report* (Philadelphia, 1853) , 17, and *Thirty-First Annual Report* (Philadelphia, 1860) , 36. The Illinois material is in the *Biennial Report of the Illinois State Penitentiary, 1857–1858,* 50–73. A. Woodbury, "Prison Reform," estimated that slightly more than half of the convicts in 1870 were foreign-born and that of the remainder, another half were second generation. Wines and Dwight, *Report on Prisons,* calculated that between one-third to one-half of the convicts were foreign-born.

28. For figures on construction and the concern with classification, see House of Refuge Managers, *Proceedings of the First Convention,* 16–26, 85.

29. New York House of Refuge, *Thirty-Third Annual Report* (New York, 1858) , 6–7; Michael Katz, *The Irony of Early School Reform* (Cambridge, Mass., 1968) , 197–199.

30. New York Juvenile Asylum, *Eighth Annual Report,* 12; Massachusetts Board of State Charities, *First Annual Report,* 179. Michael Katz, *Irony of Early School Reform,* 199.

31. Illinois Board of State Commissioners, *Report of Charitable, Penal, Pauper, and Reformatory Institutions for 1873* (Springfield, Ill., 1873) , 34–35. House of Refuge Managers, *Proceedings of the First Convention,* 31.

32. Charles Loring Brace, *The Dangerous Classes of New York, and Twenty Years' Work Among Them* (New York, 1872) , 76–77, 224–225, 236, 398. For a survey of his life and work, see Miriam Z. Langsam, *Children West: A History of the Placing-Out System of the New York Children's Aid Society, 1853–1890* (Madison, Wisc., 1964) .

33. See the minutes of the discussion of E. P. Putnam, "The Work of Auxiliary Visitors," *Eighth N.C.C.C.,* 298–305; Hastings Hart, "Placing Out Children in the West," *Eleventh N.C.C.C.* (Boston, 1884) , 143–149. See too the discussion of Charles Loring Brace,

"The Best Method of Founding Children's Charities in Towns and Villages," *Seventh N.C.C.C.*, 238–241. For the Massachusetts position, see its Board of State Charities, *Second Annual Report* (Boston, 1866) , lxiv.

34. House of Refuge Managers, *Proceedings of the First Convention*, 16; Wines and Dwight, *Report on Prisons*, 363; Massachusetts Board of State Charities, *Second Annual Report*, lxiv–lxxii.

35. New Hampshire House of Reformation, *Fourth Annual Report* (Concord, N.H., 1860) , 13, tables 5, 6; 15–16, tables 9, 10.

36. *Ibid.*, 7.

37. Philadelphia House of Refuge, *Second Annual Report*, 28–29; *Report of the Committee Appointed to Inquire into the Management of the [Philadelphia] House of Refuge* (Harrisburg, Pa., 1838) , 4–5. New Hampshire House of Reformation, *Fourth Annual Report*, 15, table 10; Michael Katz, *Irony of Early School Reform*, 175.

38. New York House of Refuge, *Twenty-Seventh Annual Report* (New York, 1847) , 17; Robert Pickett, *House of Refuge*, 184. For statistics of other institutions, see H. H. Hart, "Comparative Statistics of Reformatories for Children," *Twelfth N.C.C.C.* (Boston, 1885) , 397.

39. New York House of Refuge, *Sixth Annual Report* (New York, 1831) , 224; 60 of the 144 inmates were native. In its *Twenty-Fifth Annual Report*, 69 of the 247 inmates were native; 134 of them were Irish immigrants (p. 32) . See too Robert Pickett, *House of Refuge*, 190.

40. Philadelphia House of Refuge, *Twenty-Seventh Annual Report* (Philadelphia, 1855) ; 81 were American-born, 102 native to Ireland, and another 60 miscellaneous, mostly foreigners. Michael Katz, *Irony of Early School Reform*, 176; Cincinnati House of Refuge, *First Annual Report* (Cincinnati, Ohio, 1852) , 29–30; there were 87 American-born, 47 from Germany, 41 Irish, the rest miscellaneous.

41. Wines and Dwight, *Report on Prisons*, 354.

42. Managers of the Philadelphia House of Refuge, *An Address to their Fellow Citizens*, 7–9; *First Annual Report*, 9 ff.; *Twenty-Third Annual Report* (Philadelphia, 1851) , 8. House of Refuge Managers, *Proceedings of the First Convention*, 86; H. H. Hart, "Comparative Statistics of Reformatories, "396. Wines and Dwight brought together descriptions, admissions data, schedules, and commitment procedures from many of the houses of refuge; see *Report on Prisons*, Appendix, IV, 399–457.

43. New York House of Refuge, *Twenty-Seventh Annual Report*, 3–4. For release patterns, see its *Fifth Annual Report*, 209–211, *Seventh Annual Report*, 247–249, *Tenth Annual Report*, 4–5, *Twentieth Annual Report*, 25, *Twenty-Fifth Annual Report*, 33, *Twenty-Eighth Annual Report*, 6.

CHAPTER ELEVEN

1. Worcester Lunatic Hospital, *Twenty-Second Annual Report* (Boston, 1855), 8–9; *Twenty-Seventh Annual Report* (Boston, 1859), 31; James Leiby, *Charity and Correction in New Jersey*, 57–59; see, too, J. Sanbourne Bockoven, "Moral Treatment in American Psychiatry," 177. By 1872, the situation was so prevalent that the Association of Medical Superintendents noted: "The custom of admitting a greater number of patients than the buildings can properly accommodate . . . is now becoming . . . common in hospitals for the insane in nearly every section of the country." *History of the Association of Medical Superintendents*, 88.

2. "Annual Meeting of the Association of Medical Superintendents," *American Journal of Insanity*, 19 (1862–63), 57–70. Massachusetts Board of State Charities, *Fourth Annual Report*, 1867, xl, quoted in Gerald Grob, *The State and the Mentally Ill*, 193. Professor Grob, who is writing a multivolume history of mental hospitals in the United States, kindly lent me an article summarizing some of his views, "Mental Illness, Indigency and Welfare: The Mental Hospital in Nineteenth-Century America." He quotes there, p. 18, John Bucknell, *Notes on Asylums for the Insane in America* (London, 1876), with similar observations. See too Ruth Caplan, *Psychiatry and the Community in Nineteenth-Century America*, 162–163.

3. New Hampshire Asylum, *Report of 1854* (Concord, N.H., 1854), 15; J. Sanbourne Bockoven, "Moral Treatment," 177–183, traces out the implications of overcrowding in detail. See too William A. Hammond, *A Treatise on Insanity in Its Medical Relations* (New York, 1883), 726–727; and the remarks of Edward Mann, *Second N.C.C.C.* (Boston, 1875), 62.

4. E. C. Seguin, *Lunacy Reform: Historical Considerations* (New York, 1879), Part I, 4 ff.; Franklin B. Sanborn, "Presidential Address," *Sixth N.C.C.C.* (Boston, 1879), 12–13. See too William Hammond, "A Treatise on Insanity," 725–726; Worcester Lunatic Hospital, *Twenty-Second Annual Report*, 25. On the Bloomingdale investigation, *American Journal of Insanity*, 29 (1872–73), 594–595.

5. Pliny Earle, *Curability of Insanity*, 8–9. The article of 1876 became a book in 1887. Recently, J. Sanbourne Bockoven has disputed Earle's figures for the Worcester asylum, showing that he in fact underestimated the percentage of cures: "Moral Treatment in American Psychiatry," 292–298. Still, the figures that Bockoven presents are considerably lower than the claims of the 1830's and 1840's; and he makes no attempt to question just what "recovery" meant in the original records.

6. Pliny Earle, *Curability of Insanity,* 58, 61. See also his "A Glance at Insanity and the Management of the Insane in the United States," *Sixth N.C.C.C.,* 53, and Franklin B. Sanborn, *Memoirs of Pliny Earle* (Boston, 1898), xiv–xv.

7. Edward Jarvis, *Proper Provision for the Insane* (Boston, 1872, reprinted from the 1872 report of the Massachusetts Board of State Charities), 9–15; Franklin B. Sanborn, "Presidential Address," *Eighth N.C.C.C.* (Boston, 1881), 5–6. For other comments, see J. Sanbourne Bockoven, "Moral Treatment in American Psychiatry," 295–298.

8. William A. Hammond, *The Non-Asylum Treatment of the Insane* (New York, 1879), 2, 13–14.

9. William A. Hammond, *A Treatise on Insanity,* 718–719, 721; and *The Non-Asylum Treatment of the Insane,* 12, 17. See there too, 7–8, 14–15, for further declarations on asylum confinement as "lifelong imprisonment." See also E. C. Seguin, *Lunacy Reform* (New York, 1880), Part I, 131–134; Part II, 4–7; Part IV ("The Right of the Insane to Liberty,"), 5–6. Significant was the organization of the National Association for the Protection of the Insane and the Prevention of Insanity. See their *Papers and Proceedings* (New York, 1882), esp. pp. 12–16. The rallying cry was antiinstitutionalism.

10. "Reports of American Asylums," *American Journal of Insanity* 20 (1863–64), 20; William Hammond, *A Treatise on Insanity,* 723. A convenient summary of these arguments is in Ruth Caplan, *Psychiatry and the Community in Nineteenth-Century America,* Part II.

11. Isaac Ray, "Statistics of Insanity in Massachusetts," *North American Review,* 82 (1856), 90–91. See also below, notes 36 and 37.

12. The predominance of the chronic was well recognized in the post-1850 period. The National Association for the Protection of the Insane complained that "in the course pursued with reference to the insane, this matter of cure has been too often lost sight of." (*Papers and Proceedings,* 12). And individuals noted how "as soon as such institutions are opened . . . they are filled up with a class of cases, three-fourths of which are chronic" (Edward Mann, *Second N.C.C.C.,* 62).

13. *Report of Commissioners to Superintend the Erection of a Lunatic Hospital at Worcester,* 11–13; Gerald Grob, *The State and the Mentally Ill,* 84–87.

14. Worcester Lunatic Hospital, *First Annual Report,* 24; N.Y. Lunatic Asylum, "Description of Asylums in the U.S.," 81–82.

15. Worcester Lunatic Hospital, *First Annual Report,* 5, 21–22.

16. The institution's records carefully distinguished between recent cases — less than one year — and chronic cases — over one year. For the record of the 1840's, see Worcester Lunatic Hospital, *Eighth Annual Report,* 33; *Ninth Annual Report,* 33; *Eleventh Annual*

Report, 31; *Fourteenth Annual Report,* 41; *Fifteenth Annual Report,* 32; *Seventeenth Annual Report,* 35. For 1857–1859, *Twenty-Fifth Annual Report,* 17; *Twenty-Sixth Annual Report,* 19; *Twenty-Seventh Annual Report,* 11. The results were:

YEAR	ADMISSION OF RECENT CASES	ADMISSION OF CHRONIC CASES
1840	75	87
1841	84	79
1843	129	91
1846	156	137
1847	159	72
1849	163	99
1857	161	110
1858	120	144
1859	119	81

17. "Laws of the Commonwealth of Massachusetts relating to the State Lunatic Hospital," appendix to Worcester Lunatic Hospital, *Nineteenth Annual Report.* On the foreign-born, see Commission on Lunacy, *Report on Insanity and Idiocy in Massachusetts* (Boston, 1855), 65–68, 112; Worcester Lunatic Hospital, *Nineteenth Annual Report,* 8.
18. Worcester Lunatic Hospital, *Ninth Annual Report,* 39, 55; *Twenty-Fifth Annual Report,* 23.
19. Worcester Lunatic Hospital, *Fifth Annual Report,* 6; *Seventeenth Annual Report,* 4; *Eighteenth Annual Report,* 3. The experience of the state institution at Northampton was no different; in the Civil War era, superintendent Earle estimated that of 334 patients not one in ten was curable: "Reports of American Asylums," *American Journal of Insanity,* 21 (1864–1865), 557.
20. New Hampshire Asylum for the Insane, *Report for 1847* (Concord, N.H., 1847), 14; *Report for 1849,* 14–31. Of the eleven patients resident since the opening day, six had case histories of over ten years when admitted; of inmates with more than four years' stay, only sixteen percent had been recent cases upon admission.
21. *Ibid., Report for 1844,* 11.
22. *Ibid., Report for 1846,* 16–17.
23. *Ibid., Report for 1848,* 14; *Report for 1854,* 14.
24. See the John Galt Papers, Williamsburg, Virginia, items entitled "1840, Memo," and "Conclusions from Facts: 1845."
25. Eastern Lunatic Asylum, *Annual Report for 1843* (Williamsburg, Va., 1843), 7; *Annual Report for 1850,* 11; *Annual Report for 1860* (n.p.). The patient population grew from 135 in 1843 to 373

in 1860. See too New York Lunatic Asylum, "Description of Asylums in the U.S.," 51; Western Lunatic Asylum, *Annual Report for 1858–61* (Staunton, Va., 1863), table VII.

26. Kentucky Eastern Lunatic Asylum, *Annual Report for 1845* (Frankfort, Ky., 1846), 16; *Annual Report for 1846,* 16; *Annual Report* for 1848, 14.

27. *Ibid., Annual Report for 1845,* 24.

28. *Ibid., Reports for 1852–1853,* 19; *Reports for 1854–1855,* 15, 17. Cf., Butler Hospital for the Insane, *Annual Report for 1859,* 7; *Annual Report for 1860,* 11.

29. William L. Russell, *The New York Hospital,* 125–134, 150–151; the quotation is on pp. 152–153.

30. *Ibid.,* 200, 250–252, 288; Governors of the New York Hospital, "Annual Report," *N.Y. Assembly Docs.,* 1848, VI, no. 194, p. 7. The Dix report was never published, but submitted as a memorandum to the trustees. Russell, 516–518, reprinted it.

31. Hartford Retreat, *Sixteenth Annual Report* (Hartford, 1840), 16; *Nineteenth Annual Report,* 16–21, has a census of all the patients.

32. *Ibid., Nineteenth Annual Report,* 5, For the changes in patients, see *Thirty-Seventh Annual Report* (Hartford, 1861), 18, table VI. The data covers patients 1844–53, 1854–59, 1859–60, 1860–61. See too, *Forty-Second Annual Report,* 5, 20.

33. *Ibid., Forty-Third Annual Report,* 29; *Forty-Fourth and Forty-Fifth Reports* (Hartford, 1870), 21. For the fate of the Connecticut public institution, see "Review of Asylum Reports," *American Journal of Insanity,* 29 (1872–1873), 94–95; of the 262 patients in the asylum, 242 were chronic.

34. Pennsylvania Hospital, *First Annual Report,* 20; *Fourth Annual Report,* 11; *Eighth Annual Report,* 42.

35. *Ibid., First Annual Report,* 41; *Third Annual Report,* 16; *Fourth Annual Report,* 11, 16; *Fifth Annual Report,* 23. For the later figures, see *Eleventh Annual Report,* 13; *Twelfth Annual Report,* 13; *Thirteenth Annual Report,* 13; *Nineteenth Annual Report,* 45; *Twentieth Annual Report,* 19.

36. For the pro-separation side, see T. S. Clouston, *Review of Dr. Kirkbride's Work on Construction, etc., of Insane Hospitals* (Syracuse, N.Y., 1881), 6–7. He, like many others in this period, had little patience for Kirkbride's arguments. See too Henry Lord, "Hospitals and Asylums for the Insane," *Fifth N.C.C.C.* (Boston, 1879), 94; Nathan Allan, "Report on Insanity," *First N.C.C.C.,* 43–44; Standing Committee on Insanity, "Report," *Seventh N.C.C.C.,* 92–95.

37. Nathan Allan, "Insanity in Its Relations to the Medical Profession and Lunatic Hospitals," National Association for the Protection of the Insane, *Papers and Proceedings,* 8 ff.; for the 1866 policy, see *History of the Association of Medical Superintendents,* 61. Charles H. Nichols, "On the Best Mode of Providing for the

Subjects of Chronic Insanity," *Transactions of the International Medical Congress* (Philadelphia, 1876), 21–23. See too Ruth Caplan, *Psychiatry and the Community in Nineteenth-Century America,* 111–113.

38. Worcester Lunatic Hospital, *Eighteenth Annual Report,* 41; *Twenty-Second Annual Report,* 72; Commission of Lunacy, *Report on Insanity,* 65–68, 112. See too, "Reports of American Asylums," *American Journal of Insanity,* 20 (1864), 480–481.

39. New York Lunatic Asylum, "Annual Report," *N.Y. Senate Docs.,* 1853, I, no. 27, p. 13. The Utica hospital also treated fewer of the chronic; see "Annual Report," *N.Y. Senate Docs.,* 1852, I, no. 46, p. 14, and "Annual Report," *N.Y. Assembly Docs.,* III, no. 76, pp. 14–15. For the other figures, see Gerald Grob, "Mental Illness, Indigency, and Welfare," 17, 32.

40. New Hampshire Asylum, *Report for 1861,* 7. Worcester Lunatic Hospital, *Nineteenth Annual Report,* 39, 48; Commission on Lunacy, *Report on Insanity,* 18, 45, 52. Thomas R. Hazard, *Report on the Poor and Insane in Rhode Island,* 67.

41. Ohio Lunatic Asylum, *Thirteenth Annual Report;* Kentucky Eastern Lunatic Asylum, *Annual Report for 1845,* 24–25, 27; *Annual Report for 1846,* 20, and *Report for 1854–1855,* 37–39. Tennessee Hospital for the Insane, *Third Biennial Report,* 40–41.

42. Pliny Earle, "Confinement of the Insane," originally published in the *American Law Review,* reprinted in Earle, *Contributions to Mental Pathology,* 168–179. For the new concern, see L. C. Davis, "A Modern Lettre de Cachet," *Atlantic Monthly,* 21 (1868), 588 ff., and there, 22 (1868), 227 ff., "A 'Modern Lettre de Cachet' Reviewed."

43. Worcester Lunatic Hotspital, *Fifteenth Annual Report,* 33, and *Twenty-Second Annual Report,* 8; see, too, Commission on Lunacy, *Report on Insanity,* 61–63, 149–150, in favor of separate institutions for foreigners. See also Gerald Grob, *The State and the Mentally Ill,* 136–142, 203.

44. Isaac Ray, *Mental Hygiene,* 174; and his "Statistics on Insanity in Massachusetts," 92–94. See too, *History of the Association of Medical Superintendents,* 19; and Ruth Caplan, *Psychiatry and the Community in Nineteenth-Century America,* 149–151.

45. Massachusetts Board of State Charities, *First Annual Report,* 334–335; Pennsylvania Board of Commissioners of Public Charities, *Second Annual Report* (Harrisburg, Pa., 1872), xxxi; and General Agent and Secretary of the Pennsylvania Board of Public Charities, *Second Annual Report,* 15–22; quotation is on p. 22.

46. Michigan Board of State Commissioners, *Report of the Charitable Institutions for 1873,* 66–67, 75; and *Second Biennial Report,* 44.

47. Illinois Board of State Commissioners of Public Charities, *First Biennial Report* (Springfield, Ill., 1871), 192–194.

48. Franklin B. Sanborn, "Indoor and Outdoor Relief," *Seventeenth N.C.C.C.* (Boston, 1890), 80; Lowell's response was there, "The Economic and Moral Effects of Public Outdoor Relief," 82. The tone at these sessions did not change dramatically between 1877 and 1890; cf., Lowell's "Considerations upon a Better System of Public Charities and Correction for Cities," *Eighth N.C.C.C.,* 179.

49. Pennsylvania Board of Commissioners of Public Charities, *Second Annual Report,* 98–99; outdoor relief made up only $156,000 of disbursements of $948,000; in Philadelphia, $87,000 went to outdoor relief, $287,000 to indoor. Results elsewhere were less one-sided. For Providence, see Thomas R. Hazard, *Poor and Insane in Rhode Island,* 29; the almshouse proper received $6,846 of funds, outdoor relief, $7,740; but the municipality also spent $4,693 on the insane poor, and $1,226 on the sick poor. For Massachusetts, see Board of State Charities, *First Annual Report,* 354, and *Fifth Annual Report* (Boston, 1869), 402–405. In New York State, the following figures emerge from the reports of the secretary of state:

YEAR	INDOOR RELIEF	OUTDOOR RELIEF
1845	$359,000	$217,220
1850	437,713	296,904
1855	899,694	480,264
1860	839,556	524,948

Frederick Wines, *Report on the Defective, Dependent, and Delinquent Classes of the Population of the United States* (Washington, D.C., 1888), 254–255; he reports that there were 66,203 paupers in almshouses, and only 21,595 poor receiving outdoor relief. But this difference is undoubtedly exaggerated.

50. Seth Low, "Outdoor Relief in the United States," *Eighth N.C.C.C.,* 147–153; see too his "The Problem of Pauperism in the Cities of Brooklyn and New York," *Sixth N.C.C.C.,* 202–203. For other debates on the issue of outdoor versus indoor relief, see "Report on Outdoor Relief," *Fourth N.C.C.C.,* 48–59; "Public Outdoor Relief," *Eighteenth N.C.C.C.* (Boston, 1891), 28–49, 314–315.

51. *Report of the Special Committee on Outdoor Alms of the Town of Hartford* (Hartford, Conn., 1891), xv.

52. Commissioners of Alien Passengers and Foreign Paupers, *Report for 1857* (Boston, 1857), 21, and *Report for 1858* (Boston, 1858), 18–19; Massachusetts Board of State Charities, *First Annual Report,* 308. Although the colonial almshouse also held outsiders, it did so only temporarily, until they could be moved on. The almshouse of the 1850's, however, was a permanent form of relief for a sizable group fixed in the population, not just for the exceptional case.

53. Thomas R. Hazard, *Poor and Insane in Rhode Island*, 25–28; New York Select Committee, *Report of Charitable Institutions*, 204–205, table A; 212, table C; and "Paupers and Crime," *DeBow's Review*, 19 (1855), 283. Pennsylvania Board of Commissioners of Public Charities, *Second Annual Report*, 100–101.

54. Michigan County Superintendents of the Poor, *Abstract of Annual Reports for 1871* (Lansing, Mich., 1872), 19, table A; Illinois Board of State Commissioners of Public Charities, *First Biennial Report*, 178–179; James Brown, *Public Assistance in Chicago*, 28. Frederick Wines, *Report of Defective, Dependent, and Delinquent Classes*, 454–455.

55. Massachusetts Board of State Charities, *First Annual Report*, 260, quoting an 1858 investigation.

56. New York Select Committee, *Report of Charitable Institutions*, 204–207, table A, and pp. 33, 70; the total inmate population was 4,956. New York State Board of Charities, *Fifteenth Annual Report* (Albany, N.Y., 1882), 306. See too Charles Lawrence, *History of the Philadelphia Almshouses*, 167–174, 200.

57. Michigan Board of State Commissioners, *Report of Charitable Institutions for 1873*, 68; C. S. Watkins, "Poorhouses and Jails in the North-Western States," *Sixth N.C.C.C.*, 98–99. See too, *Eleventh N.C.C.C.* (Boston, 1884), appendix, 418–419.

58. Again, it was Massachusetts officials who most clearly expressed this sentiment: Commissioners of Alien Passengers and Foreign Paupers, *Report for 1859* (Boston, 1859), 10–11.

59. New York Select Committee, *Report of Charitable Institutions*, 199–203. See too Committee on the Jail and House of Industry, Correction and Reformation, *Report to Boston City Council* (Boston, 1834), 1–13. The house of correction there was an adjunct to the jail, housing the intemperate, the petty larcenist, and the vagrant picked up by the police. Cf., "Report of House of Industry and Reformation," *Boston Common Council, 1847 Doc.*, no. 22, 8–14; investigators complained that the house of correction was indistinguishable from the almshouse, for almost all its residents were sick and helpless. For a survey demonstrating how general these conditions were, see, Board of Directors for Boston Public Institutions, *Report of Committee on the Subject of Their Visit to Penal and Reformatory Institutions* (Boston, 1875), 6–11.

60. See the first reports of such organizations as the Boston Provident Association, or the New York A.I.C.P. See too Robert Bremner, *From the Depths: The Discovery of Poverty in the United States* (New York, 1956), for late-nineteenth-century and Progressive-era developments.

Index

David J. Rothman is Bernard Schoenberg Professor of Social Medicine and Professor of History at Columbia University, and director of its Center for the Study of Society and Medicine. He has explored the history and policy of confinement in *Conscience and Convenience: The Asylum and Its Alternatives in Progressive America* (1980) and *The Willowbrook Wars* (1984, with Sheila M. Rothman). His most recent work addresses social and ethical issues in the history of medicine.

His awards include the Albert J. Beveridge Award from the American Historical Association for *The Discovery of the Asylum*. He has served as Falkner Fellow at the University of Sydney Hospital, as Samuel Paley Lecturer at Hebrew University, as Distinguished Lecturer at the Kyoto American Studies Seminar, and as Fulbright Professor to India. He has received an honorary Doctor of Law degree from the John Jay School of Criminal Justice.

David Rothman has also been active in the field of civil liberties and serves as chairman of the board of directors of the Mental Health Law Project.